C0-ASP-045

THE WORKS OF

Sir John Suckling

The Plays

A HUNTING SCENE

Inigo Jones's Drawing, possibly for the Court Production of *Aglaura*, Christmas 1637/38

THE WORKS OF

Sir John Suckling

The Plays

EDITED BY L. A. BEAURLINE

OXFORD
AT THE CLARENDON PRESS
1971

Oxford University Press, Ely House, London W. 1

GLASGOW NEW YORK TORONTO MELBOURNE WELLINGTON
CAPE TOWN SALISBURY IBADAN NAIROBI DAR ES SALAAM LUSAKA ADDIS ABABA
BOMBAY CALCUTTA MADRAS KARACHI LAHORE DACCA
KUALA LUMPUR SINGAPORE HONG KONG TOKYO

PRINTED IN GREAT BRITAIN
AT THE UNIVERSITY PRESS, OXFORD
BY VIVIAN RIDLER
PRINTER TO THE UNIVERSITY

CONTENTS

FOREWORD

THE purpose of this edition is primarily to establish the texts of three plays and a fragment of a play that Suckling wrote. Although none of them is a good play by our standards, parts of them are interesting and deserve attention, as well as an accurate text. They were highly thought of in their day and for some years in the Restoration they held the stage, but they have never been edited reliably. Previous editors have never consulted the first editions of two of the plays nor the manuscript of one, and they seem to have based their texts on the second, third, and sixth editions of *Fragmenta Aurea*.

The Commentary has been kept to a minimum, presenting facts for understanding the texts, and it does not pretend to be a critical analysis. In the headnotes to each play there are summaries of what we know concerning date, sources, transmission of the text, and stage history; but when G. E. Bentley has given the information fully in his *Jacobean and Caroline Stage*, I have not repeated it. When I have new facts, I discuss them in the context of Bentley's remarks. Under the heading 'Sources', I make additional observations about the way Suckling shaped this material, and its importance in the history of the drama.

Much is usually made of Suckling's interest in Shakespeare, suggested by the anecdote in Rowe's *Life* of Shakespeare, in his edition of the *Works of Mr. William Shakespear* (1709):

> In a Conversation between Sir *John Suckling*, Sir *William D'Avenant*, *Endymion Porter*, Mr. *Hales* of *Eaton*, and *Ben Johnson*; Sir *John Suckling*, who was a profess'd Admirer of *Shakespear*, had undertaken his Defence against *Ben Johnson* with some warmth; Mr. *Hales*, who had sat still for some time hearing *Ben* frequently reproaching him with the want of Learning, and Ignorance of the Antients, told him at last, *That if Mr.* Shakespear *had not read the Antients, he had likewise not stollen any thing from 'em*; (a Fault the other made no Conscience of) *and that if he would produce any one Topick finely treated by any of them, he would undertake to shew something upon the same Subject at least as well written by* Shakespear.[1]

The rediscovery of the great Van Dyck portrait, now in the Frick Collection, further supports this view, since Suckling chose to be painted reading a folio edition of Shakespeare, open at *Hamlet*. (See the frontispiece to Vol. i of this edition and the discussion of Suckling's

[1] A different version of this story, in which Suckling plays a less prominent role, appears in *Miscellaneous Letters and Essays on Several Subjects*, ed. Charles Gildon (1694), pp. 85–6.

portraits.) Therefore I felt obliged to examine all the alleged parallels between the two writers and to search other writers for the same expressions. I found that at least half the supposed borrowings were commonplace. Tilley's *Dictionary of the Proverbs in England* proved invaluable in this work, and I believe that if we ever have a concordance to Beaumont and Fletcher's plays, we will find that Suckling depended upon them almost as much as he did upon Shakespeare. Nevertheless the debt to Shakespeare is still written large in the dialogue of these plays, as anyone can see. But Suckling's interest in proverbs deserves a second place of importance. His wit seems to lie in the elegant variation on commonplaces; thus, instead of saying the ordinary 'Common as a barber's chair', he says 'She's as common too, as a Barber's glasse'. In the same way, his well-known lyric 'Out upon it, I have lov'd Three whole days together' is a variation on 'After three days one tires of a woman, a guest, and the weather.' The third important influence on his plays remains, as we have long known, his own poems, which he raided continually to supply fresh dialogue for the plays. His impulse was lyric and consequently he wrote a peculiar kind of dramatic line, varying between three, four, and five feet, usually ended by the completion of a short grammatical unit and signalled by a mark of punctuation. This habit made it easy for him to adapt lines from his poems, as my notes record. He could write blank verse when he wanted to, but frequently, in the less formal and more conversational passages, he chose three- and four-foot lines. The effect is similar to that of the old fourteeners.

Since this prosy kind of verse puzzled the early printers as much as it has the editors, many speeches of genuine prose were set as verse, and much verse was mislined. Nevertheless a comparison of the lining in independent witnesses for two of the plays shows that there was a consistent principle working in Suckling's mind.

Suckling was one of the originators of the *à la mode* style—Alexander Pope's term in *The Art of Sinking in Poetry*—of seventeenth-century poetry and drama, a style which 'is fine by being new', since it draws its images from 'the present Customs and best Fashions of our Metropolis'. It was urbane wit, such as Dryden later cultivated and perfected. In the commentary, therefore, I have been careful to identify as many of the contemporary allusions as I could, and to explain the gentlemen's activities that are such a large part of Suckling's imagery: references to bowls, card games, dice games, sword fighting, hunting, hawking, tavern life, court life, plays, contemporary poetry,

French romances, politics, and military life. The evidence of these images verifies Dryden's observation that Suckling was one of the first to write in the language of gentlemen. Unfortunately, I found no references to cribbage, a game that Aubrey said was invented by Suckling, but I think the allusions to Suckling in Richard Brome's *Court Beggar* are sufficient to allow us to associate him with the game, if not as its inventor. (See the headnote to *Brennoralt* in the present commentary.)

If Suckling's main attractions were to Shakespeare and urbanity, his great literary aversion was Ben Jonson, as the commentary tries to show. From the poet laureat in *The Sad One* to the drunken poet in *The Goblins*, from the parody of 'Have you seen but a bright lily grow' to the boasting old dramatist in 'A Sessions of the Poets', Suckling relentlessly lampooned Jonson. And his attitude is understandable, for Suckling was a studied amateur and admirer of romance, who suspected the professional poet and craftsman. Jonson's court masks bored him and he rejected similar classical paraphernalia from his writings. Suckling was friendly with Davenant and presumably with Inigo Jones, Jonson's arch-enemy, and Suckling was a luminary of the court that undervalued Jonson's works. From Jonson's point of view, no doubt, Suckling was the embodiment of everything he disliked—an incarnation of Peniboy Junior, a prodigal, a vaunter, and a fast talker and flashy dresser, Sir Amorous La Foole of the Caroline age. This antagonism lends credibility to the story of a debate between Suckling and Jonson about the value of Shakespeare.

I owe the greatest obligation to the late Professor R. C. Bald, under whose wise and gentle guidance this edition began. In the early stages of work, I was aided by a Fulbright Scholarship, a grant from the American Philosophical Society, and by the Research Council of the Richmond Area. Mr. John Crow answered numerous inquiries about proverbs and obscure passages. Mr. John Freehafer helped me a great deal with the Restoration prompt books of *Aglaura* and *Brennoralt*. Fredson Bowers, who has instructed and advised me in innumerable other ways, generously discussed with me the textual problems and apparatus. Without his encouragement, I would scarcely have come to the end of this task. Finally, my wife showed a continued interest in all phases of the investigation, checking references and comparing editions.

L. A. B.

Charlottesville, Va.

THE TREATMENT OF THE TEXT

SINCE this is an old spelling, critical edition, the copy-text in every case has been that early witness that stands closest to the author's manuscript. The first edition provided this for *The Sad One*, *Aglaura*, and *The Goblins*; but the second edition of *Brennoralt*, included in *Fragmenta Aurea*, 1646, proves to be more authoritative, because it goes back more directly to Suckling's fair copy than does the corrupt first quarto, nor does the first quarto seem to have influenced the text of the second edition in any way. Details of spelling, punctuation, and the like (the accidentals) are faithful to the copy-texts, except where small changes have been made, and these are noted in the apparatus.

Substantive emendations (changes in wording) sometimes have been made by reference to other independent early witnesses: contemporary manuscripts and independent printed editions. These variant texts have been useful because they contain many readings that are clearly not printers' errors or scribes' happy guesses; their new readings are sometimes derived from a separate tradition. In R. B. McKerrow's terminology, they are 'substantive' texts, even though their accidentals may not represent Suckling's habits as well as the copy-texts do. The Royal manuscript of *Aglaura* is an entirely 'collateral' text, as are most of the manuscripts of the songs. The corrected texts of *The Goblins* and *Brennoralt* in *Fragmenta*, 1648, are collateral with respect to their new substantives but derivative with respect to their accidentals, for *Fragmenta*, 1648, is basically a reprint of the 1646 edition, but someone seems to have carefully compared the texts with independent manuscripts and made a number of alterations. Following Sir Walter W. Greg's 'Rationale of Copy-Text',[1] I have, therefore, sometimes imported readings from other substantive texts into the copy-text. Occasionally even the bad quarto of *Brennoralt* supplies a plausible emendation, and occasionally I have made conjectural emendations, when I thought that all the substantive texts were in error. But since the likelihood of common or divergent errors in collateral texts is very small, I have had less reason to find many such errors. Further discussion of problems peculiar to each play may be found in the commentary.

In addition, certain alterations in accidentals have been made

[1] *Studies in Bibliography*, iii (1950–1), 19–36.

silently. Modern style is used for s, u, v, i, j, and ligatures; broken type, turned letters, and wrong founts, have been silently corrected, except when the change influences the sense, in which case it has been recorded in the apparatus. Spacing of lines, words, and elisions have been normalized. Roman type has been used as the basic fount, and I have followed the seventeenth-century convention of using italics for proper names in the dialogue, regardless of variation in the original. I have expanded speech prefixes, with a normalized spelling, and designated disguised persons by their real names in speech prefixes and stage directions. Faulty punctuation at the end of a complete speech has been raised to a period. Half lines are indented in the usual fashion. Act and scene divisions, indicated in the margin, conform to the originals except where noted, but in order to save space I have taken out the heading for each act and scene and noted the style of the divisions at the beginning of each play. Abbreviations in stage directions and dialogue have been silently expanded, but otherwise any additions to the stage directions have been placed in brackets. Stage directions such as *Aside* and *Whisper* have normally been moved from the right margin to the beginning of the speech or that part of the speech so delivered. Punctuation of stage directions has been normalized. In stage directions, dramatis personae, dedicatory epistles, addresses to the reader, prologues, and epilogues, I have silently changed the typography, use of capitals, italics, parentheses, brackets, and ornamental letters. Throughout the text display capitals have been reduced to normal size. When in the copy-text a dash separates dialogue from stage directions, without suggesting any break in speech or shift of address, the dash has been silently removed. Although Suckling probably used dashes in such a way, with stage directions they were often strictly conventional and without importance.

APPARATUS

THE notes at the foot of each page record departures from the copy-text in the wording or in more significant punctuation. When two early editions appear to have descended independently from the author's manuscript, their substantive variants have also been noted. Thus for *The Sad One* only one text is of any authority, so no other seventeenth-century text has been regularly cited. But *Aglaura* survives in a printed text and a manuscript of independent and almost equal authority; therefore, although the printed edition of 1638 is the copy-text, rejected variants from the manuscript are noted. *The Goblins*, printed in *Fragmenta Aurea*, 1646, is the primary authority, but it was carefully corrected in the 1648 edition by reference to another manuscript; therefore word variants from 1648 are noted for this play. *Brennoralt*, printed in *Fragmenta Aurea*, 1646, provides the copy-text, but substantive variants from the independently derived quarto of 1642(?) are recorded. When an emendation appeared in some editions before this one, I have noted only the place where it was first proposed.

A second list of departures from copy, relegated to the end of each play, records changes in lineation, trivial punctuation, spelling, and capitalization. It is assumed that the average reader will seldom wish to look at these minutiae, but an occasional scholar may wish to see how a certain passage stood in the copy-text, down to the small details.

The textual notes are similar to those of *The Dramatic Works in the Beaumont and Fletcher Canon*, set forth by the general editor, Fredson Bowers (Cambridge, 1966), I. xvii–xxiv, except for a special system of referring to deletions and insertions in manuscripts. I have adopted the abbreviations (*c*) and (*u*), normally used to designate the differences between uncorrected and corrected states of press correction, to apply to uncorrected and corrected readings in manuscripts as well. Thus, a note

mee] *Ag*, *R*(*c*); *om.* R(*u*)

means that the copy-text reads *mee*, manuscript *R* omitted the word in its first state, and in its second state the manuscript has the word inserted. The note

dare not] *Ag*, *R*(*c*); must *R*(*u*)

means that the copy-text reads *dare not*, *R* first read *must*, but it was deleted and *dare not* written in.

Another difference between this apparatus and the Beaumont and Fletcher edition is the absence of a historical collation. I have collated editions of Suckling's plays, dated 1646, 1648, 1658–9, the pirated '1658', 1672, and the works 1694–6, along with Collier's edition of *The Goblins*, Hazlitt's editions of 1874 and 1892, and Thompson's edition of 1910; but it was thought that a full record of their variants would swell the apparatus unnecessarily. Suckling's plays are not as important as that, and previous editions were not carefully prepared. Therefore I have cited these editions only when I have adopted one of their emendations or when their emendations seem to have some special value, as many of those do in *The Goblins*, 1648.

When songs from the plays have been found with variant texts in seventeenth-century books and manuscripts, I have recorded the readings from independent witnesses only. In other words, since the copies of copies of manuscript poems and the reprints of poetical miscellanies are of no authority, their errors have not been included in the notes. Almost all the surviving miscellanies, song-books, and manuscripts in public hands have been examined, however, as well as some private collections. I have been reasonably thorough in my search in the British Museum, the Bodleian Library, the National Library of Scotland, the Sackville (Knole) manuscripts, the Folger Library, the New York Public Library, the Huntington Library, the Newberry Library, the major university libraries in the United States, and the Rosenbach and Osborn collections. The extensive lists of variants for 'Why so pale and wan' and 'No, no, fair heretic' from *Aglaura* may be found in the apparatus of the poems in volume i of the present edition. Although Mr. Clayton and I both worked on these songs, we did not find it necessary to duplicate the collations.

THE COLLECTED EDITIONS

SINCE the early collected editions form a somewhat confusing sequence, a summary of their contents may help readers of this volume. More detailed accounts are in the introduction to the volume of the non-dramatic works, in Greg's *Bibliography* (iii. 1130–6), and in W. A. Jackson's catalogue of *The Carl H. Pforzheimer Library* (1940), p. 1034–7. Bibliographical matters of special concern to the individual plays are discussed in the commentary.

FA46—Fragmenta Aurea, 1646

Under this general title, in 356 octavo pages, Humphrey Moseley gathered the works for which Suckling was best known. Following the general title-page and an address to the readers, the first section, *Poems, &c.*, contains the non-dramatic works: poems, letters, and prose tracts (sigs. A1–H4). The second, third, and fourth sections, like the first, are separate bibliographical units with title-pages, separate sets of signatures, and separate pagination. *Aglaura*, printed by Thomas Warren, is the second edition of the play (sigs. ²A1–D8ᵛ). It was set from the 1638 folio edition, and apparently Thomas Walkley, who had entered it in the Stationers' Register 18 April 1638, still retained some rights in the copy, for its title-page exists in two states. The first state has the imprint: 'Printed by T. W. for Humprey [*sic*] Moseley.' In the later state the imprint says 'Printed for Tho. Walkley . . . sold by Humphrey Moseley.' *The Goblins* (sigs. ³A1–D8ᵛ), printed in Susan Islip's shop, is the authoritative first edition, and Moseley owned the rights, having entered it in the Stationers' Register on 24 July 1646. *Brennoralt* (sigs. ⁴A1–D4ᵛ), also from Susan Islip's shop, is the second edition of that play, but it is textually independent of the first, a quarto printed in 1642 for Francis Eglesfield (entered 5 April 1642). Moseley secured rights from Eglesfield and Henry Twiford on 1 August 1646. (Twiford's interest in the copy is not otherwise known.)

FA48—Fragmenta Aurea, 1648

The second edition of *Fragmenta* is a page-for-page reprint of the first, with the same contents. On 22 February 1648 Moseley finally secured the rights to *Aglaura*, and he dropped Walkley's name from the title-page. Some of the poems, *Brennoralt*, and especially *The Goblins* seem to have been compared with other witnesses, and numerous corrections and a few additions made. Thomas Warren printed the non-dramatic works, apparently William Wilson did *Aglaura*, and Edward Griffin *The Goblins* and *Brennoralt*.

FA58—Fragmenta Aurea, 1658

The third edition 'with some New Additionals' included *The Last Remains of Sir John Suckling*, dated 1659, and it gave Restoration readers a more complete canon. But since the two parts are bibliographically independent and were sometimes sold separately, they can be treated separately. The texts from *Fragmenta* reprinted by Thomas Newcombe are the same as in 1646, and none of the corrections are carried over from 1648.

LR—The Last Remains of Sir John Suckling, 1659

This slim octavo, printed by Thomas Newcombe, was gathered by Humphrey Moseley from Suckling's sister, Lady Southcot, and from 'the several Cabinets of his Noble and faithful Friends', according to the stationer's dedication and address to the reader. It consists of forty-three poems, twelve letters, and the fragment of *The Sad One* (sigs. E1–G8). Most of these that are authentic, including the unfinished play, are apparently Suckling's early compositions, hitherto unpublished. The British Museum copy (E1768) was received by George Tomason in June 1659, but Moseley did not enter the book in the Stationers' Register until a year later, 29 June 1660. Such a delay, although unusual, was not unheard of, as Greg notes (*The Library*, 4th ser. vii. 380).

FA'58'—Fragmenta Aurea, *c.* 1661–2

An edition known to Greg from only a fragment in the Bodleian Library is found in a complete copy, dated 1658, in the Harvard Library (EC/su 185/646fc). It is easily distinguished from the authentic edition of 1658 by the different ornaments throughout and by the wording on the general title-page. Moseley's edition says, above the imprint, 'Printed by his own Copies.' This edition says 'Printed by his own Copy.' It was probably the work of T. Johnson, who made similar piracies for Francis Kirkman. The large ornament of dogs licking a man's face (sig. S6) is found in Kirkman's piracy of Beaumont and Fletcher's *The Elder Brother*, '1637' (Greg 515c), and of Kirkman's *The Wits*, printed for Henry Marsh, 1662. The ornamental 'B' (sig. O5) recurs in *The Elder Brother*, '1637', and in the pirated *King and No King*, 1661. (See 'Notes on Early Editions of *Fragmenta Aurea*', *Studies in Bibliography*, xxiii (1970).)

FA72—Fragmenta Aurea, 1672

A fraudulent reprint of *Fragmenta Aurea*, part from 1648 and part from 1658, along with *The Last Remains*, from 1659, probably printed in 1672, with a general title-page dated 1648. Some copies have a cancel title-page dated 1676. (See *The Library*, 5th ser., i. 85.)

Works 94—The Works of Sir John Suckling, 1694–6

The first attempt to rearrange the canon, integrating the contents of *The Last Remains* with *Fragmenta*; hence we find the poems, letters, the account of religion, and plays grouped together. The title-pages of the plays are dated 1694 and the general title 1696.

Subsequent reprints of the works appeared in 1709, 1719, 1766 (Dublin), and 1770. The first serious attempt at an edition is that of the Revd. Alfred Suckling, the Norfolk historian and descendant of the poet, entitled *Selections from the Works of Sir John Suckling*, 1836. It contains all except a few bawdy poems; the text of the plays has been bowdlerized, but the editor's sixty-two-page memoir contributed much new information. W. C. Hazlitt's two-volume edition of *The Poems, Plays and Other Remains of Sir John Suckling*, 1874, was a great advance over all previous texts, because he returned to some of the seventeenth-century witnesses. Hazlitt, unfortunately depended too much on the 1658–9 editions, and he did not know of the corrections in *Fragmenta Aurea*, 1648, nor did he examine the folio text of *Aglaura* or the quarto of *Brennoralt*. Hazlitt's revised edition of 1892 added a few items of the non-dramatic works but nothing to the plays. *The Works of Sir John Suckling in Prose and Verse*, edited by A. Hamilton Thompson, 1910, offers little significant improvement of Hazlitt's text. Some variants and glosses appear in Thompson's notes.

ABBREVIATIONS

Bentley	G. E. Bentley, *The Jacobean and Caroline Stage*, 1941–68.
Greg	W. W. Greg, *A Bibliography of the English Printed Drama to the Restoration*, 1939–59.
Hazlitt	*The Poems, Plays and Other Remains of Sir John Suckling*, edited by W. C. Hazlitt, 1874.
Jonson	*Ben Jonson*, edited by C. H. Herford and Percy and Evelyn Simpson, 1925–52.
Shakespeare	*The Works of Shakespeare*, edited by J. Dover Wilson *et al.*, 1921–66.
Thompson	*The Works of Sir John Suckling in Prose and Verse*, edited by A. Hamilton Thompson, 1910.
Tilley	M. P. Tilley, *A Dictionary of the Proverbs in England in the Sixteenth and Seventeenth Centuries*, 1950.

(*c*)	the corrected state of an edition or manuscript.
cw	catchword
om.	omitted
S.D.	stage direction
S.P.	speech prefix
(*u*)	the uncorrected state of an edition or manuscript.
Σ	all other copies besides those specified
~ ‸	the tilde represents the same word(s) repeated, and the inferior caret calls attention to the absence of punctuation.
15.1	The first line of a stage direction following line 15
0.1	The first line of a stage direction preceding line 1 at the beginning of a scene.

THE SAD ONE.

A TRAGEDY.

BY

Sr *JOHN SUCKLING.*

LONDON:
Printed for *Humphrey Moſeley* at the Prince's Arms in St. *Pauls* Churchyard. 1659.

The Title-page of the First Edition, in *The Last Remains of Sir John Suckling. Folger Shakespeare Library copy.*

TEXTS CONSULTED

LR	*The Last Remains of Sir John Suckling*, 1659, the copy-text.
Poems	'Hast thou seen the Doun ith' air', the song in IV. iv, variant text in the section of poems in *The Last Remains*, 1659.
MB	'Come, come away, to the Tavern I say', IV. v, another version in the song book, *A Musical Banquet*, 1651.
Folg.409	'Come, come away, to the Tavern I say', IV. v, another version of the song in Folger Library manuscript V.a.409.

The Sad One was reprinted in the pirated edition of *Fragmenta Aurea*, dated 1672, the works of 1694–6, 1709, 1719, 1766, 1770, 1836, Hazlitt's editions of 1874, and 1892, and Thompson's edition of 1910. Textual problems concerning this play are discussed in the commentary.

TO THE READER

I HOPE I shall not need to crave your pardon for publishing this Dramatick Piece of Sir *John Suckling*, (Imperfect I cannot say, but rather unfinish'd) there being a kind of Perfection even in the most deficient Fragments of this incomparable Author. To evince that this Copy was a faithful Transcript from his own handwriting, I have said enough in my former Epistle, and I thought it much better to send it into the world in the same state I found it, without the least addition, then procure it supplied by any other Pen; which had been not less preposterous then the finishing of *Venus* Picture, so skilfully begun by *Apelles*, by some other hand. Nor are we without a sufficient President in Works of this nature, and relating to an Author who confessedly is reputed the Glory of the English Stage (whereby you'll know I mean *Ben: Johnson*) and in a Play also of somewhat a resembling name, *The Sad Shepherd*, extant in his Third Volume; which though it wants two entire Acts, was nevertheless judg'd a Piece of too much worth to be laid aside, by the Learned and Honorable Sir *Kenelme Digby*, who published that Volume. We have also in Print (written by the same hand) the very Beginning only (for it amounts not to one full Scene) of a Tragedy call'd *Mortimer*. So that we find the same fate to have hapned in the Works of two of the most celebrated and happy Wits of this Nation. Now, as it is to have been wish'd that this Tragedy had come whole and compleat to publick View, so is it some happiness that there is so much of it preserved; It being true of our Author, what Dr *Donne* said of a famous Artist of his time,

——A hand or eye
By Hilliard *drawn, is worth a History*
By a worse Painter made.——

I shall add no more, but only say (with some just confidence) that I could not have answer'd my self or the world, if I had suppressed this Tragedy; and therefore may hope for some favor by its publication.

Farewell.

H. M.

THE ARGUMENT INTRODUCING TO THE FOLLOWING SCENES

SICILY had been a long time tormented with civil wars, and the Crown was still in dispute, till *Aldebrand* geting the upper hand in a set Battel, establish'd himself in the throne, and gave a period to all those troubles in shew only; for the old Factions were set on foot again shortly after, and the House of the *Florettíes* and the *Cleonaxes* strove now as much who should be most powerful with the King, as before who should make him. In conclusion, the favor of *Aldebrand* inclining to the *Cleonaxes*, and by degrees resting wholly upon them, the *Florettíes* took Arms, but in a set Field lost all; The Father and the Son being both taken prisoners, the one was banish'd, the other condemned suddenly to lose his head.

Thus far the Author drew the curtain; the rest of the Plot is wrapt up in the following Scenes.

THE ACTORS

ALDEBRAND, *King of* Sicily
CLEONAX SENIOR, *Treasurer*
CLEONAX JUNIOR, *His Son* [= Lorenzo]
BELLAMINO, *Favorite of Pleasure, and Cousin to* Cleonax
CLARIMONT, *An old Lord*
CLARIMONT JUNIOR, *His Son*
FIDELIO, *Friend to* Clarimont
FLORELIO, *A Lord married to* Francelia
FLORELIO JUNIOR, *His Brother*
LORENZO, *An ambitious Courtier*
PARMENIO, *His supposed Creature*
DROLLIO } *Two Courtiers*
LEPIDO }
DOCO DISCOPIO, *One that pretends to be a great Statesman*
Signior MULTECARNI, *The Poet*
PETRUCHIO, *Servant to* Florelio
Ambassador from Spain
Actors, Keeper, [*attendants,* SILEO]

AMASIA, *Queen to* Aldebrand
FRANCELIA, *Daughter to* Clarimont

The Scene, SICILY

18 *Keeper*] follows line 20 *LR*

The Sad One

Enter old CLARIMONT *in Prison, in his Night-gown,* [I. i]
his Servant following him.

OLD CLARIMONT. Condemn'd unheard! Just heavens, it cannot be:
Why, Tyranny it self could do no more;
The pale ghosts of *Tiberius* and *Nero*
Would blush to see an act so foul and horrid,
So full of black ingratitude as this.
'Twas I that set the Crown upon his head,
And bid him live King of his Enemies,
When he durst hardly hope it:
And does he thus requite me! Now I see,
Who by the Compass of his Merit sails,
May guide his Fraught of Hopes in seasons fair
And calm; but when storms come,
All his good deeds, with his good days, must perish:
Oh my unhappy Stars!——— *Beats his breast.*
SERVANT. My Lord, let not a fruitless passion
Make you to die less Man then you have lived.
OLD CLARIMONT. Who art thou?
SERVANT. I was lately one, my Lord,
Of the vast Crowd that waited on your fortunes,
But am now become the whole Train,
The rest have left you.
OLD CLARIMONT. Prethee do thou leave me too. *Servant exit.*
The clap o'th'Vulgar, and loud popular applause,
Are not the Eccho of our Acts, but Fortunes.
Great men but Dials are, which when the Sun
Is gone, or hides his face, are hardly lookt upon.
But yesterday I was Times Minister;
On me the whole Court gaz'd, as at

I. i. 0.1 Act. I. Scæn. I. *The style of each act and scene heading, except where noted LR*
1 S.P. OLD CLARIMONT] *om. LR*
17 S.P. OLD CLARIMONT] *Clar. LR, as are the rest of his prefixes in the scene*

Some Comet set in *Cassiopeia's* chair:
Who but old *Clarimont* could with Nodds create,
And with a speaking Eye, command bare heads and knees?
But now——— *Beats his breast again.*
Greatness is but the shadow of the beams
Of Princes favors, nourisht in extreams;
First taught to creep, and feed on hopes, to live
Upon the glance, and humbly to observe
Each Under-Minion, till its own desire
Work it self neer enough to set it self on fire. *Studies a little.*
Fain would I make my Audit up with Heaven,
For 'tis a large one; but the small vain hopes
Which yet I have of life and of revenge,
Smother these thoughts within me
Faster then they are born.

Enter FIDELIO *disguised like a Friar.*

———A Ghostly Father!
My minutes are but few, I see by this.
Sir, you are welcom:
I was but now considering how to die,
And, trust me, I do find it something hard,
I shall extreamly need some such good help
As yours, to do it well.

FIDELIO. Faith, my Lord, Divines do hold,
The way to die well, is to live well first. *Discovers himself.*

OLD CLARIMONT. *Fidelio!*

FIDELIO. Not too loud, there's danger in't:
The King has promised life, but none as yet
Must know't; the Enemies are too potent,
And must be softned by degrees.

OLD CLARIMONT. Why then I see, he hath not quite forgot
Past services.

FIDELIO. ———Not too much of that:
This is not gratitude; or if it be, it does
As thankfulness in great ones use to do,
It looks asquint and seems to turn to favors,
But regards new ends.

OLD CLARIMONT. Prethee unriddle.

FIDELIO. Why to be short, it is your daughters beauty,
Not your merit.

OLD CLARIMONT. My fears prompt me too quick;
She's not turn'd whore, is she?
FIDELIO. No, but her honesty is so strait beset,
That if she be not victualled well within
And have some sudden succors,
She will I fear ere long surrender.
OLD CLARIMONT. O *Fidelio*, when Kings do tempt,
Th'had need be Angels that endure the shock,
Not women———
FIDELIO. 'Tis true, my Lord,
Yet let not incertain fears create new griefs:
Doubt is of all the sharpest passion,
And often turns distempers to diseases:
Collect your self, and be assur'd my zeal
Shall watch abroad; and when I may reveal
My self your servant, I'll not do't in breath,
But with the adventure of my life or death.
OLD CLARIMONT. Oh you are noble, Sir, I know't,
And mean to hope the best, Farewell.

Exeunt.

Enter LORENZO *and his Father with servants, whispering together and frowning, pass over the Stage, Exeunt.* [I. ii]

Enter LORENZO *solus, as going to Prison.*

LORENZO. Arm'd with the love of soveraignty and revenge,
Ile ravish Fortune and all Engines trie
That heaven or hell have yet discovered,
But I will scale my end, and plant desire
As high as any thought durst ere aspire:
The dotage of the King shall not secure thee, poor old man;
Clarimont, I come; this night our quarrel ends,
Nothing but death could ever make us friends.

Knocks at the Prison-door.

Enter the Keeper.

Where's old *Clarimont*?
KEEPER. In's bed, my Lord.

I. ii. 0.1] *no scene division LR* 1 S.P. LORENZO] *om. LR*

LORENZO. In's grave, thou wouldst have said.
KEEPER. Must he then die to night?
LORENZO. The King will have it so,
He fears the people love him, and to save
His life may prove tumultuous.
KEEPER. Poor Gentleman! how quick is Fate come on him!
———How sudden is all woe!
Bad days have wings, the good on crutches go.
My Lord, wilt please you walk into that private chamber?
The Executioner shall strait be here.

LORENZO *goes forth, murders him within, enters again.*

LORENZO. You must be sure to keep it secret now:
Perchance the King, to try your honesty,
And blind his daughters eyes, will send to ask
Of's welfare.
KEEPER. Oh my Lord!
LORENZO. Nay I know you understand, Farewell.

Turns back again.

One thing I had forgot: If any ask
What groan that was, say 'tis an usual thing
Against great mens death to hear a noise
At midnight———
So, now Royal Letcher set you safe,
'Tis you death must secure my life:
I'le on, Danger is but a bug-word,
My Barque shall through,
Did mountains of black horrors me surround,
———When Fortunes hang in doubt,
Bravely to dare, is bravely to get out.

[*From hence to the beginning of the Second Act,*
the written Copy was deficient.]

LORENZO, PARMENIO *attending.* [II. i]

LORENZO. All leave the chamber; if any come,
I'm busie. *Parmenio*, be nigher, nigher yet:
What dar'st thou do to make thy Master King,
Thy self a Favorite?

36. 1–2 *From…deficient.*] *Errata LR*
II. i. 1 S.P. LORENZO] *om. LR*

PARMENIO. 'Tis something blunt, my Lord, *Studies.*
Why, I dare do——That which I dare not speak.
LORENZO. By all my hopes, spoke like the man I want!
'Twould be lost time to use much circumstance
To thee: shall we this night dispatch the King?
PARMENIO. This minute, were he my Father;
He's not the first, nor shall he be the last.
LORENZO. Soul of my soul! My better Angel sure
Foresaw my wants, and sent thee hither.
Parmenio, there's none but he
Stands 'twixt a Crown and me:
The Cloud that interpos'd betwixt my Hopes before,
Is like a Vapor faln, and seen no more.
The house of *Claremont* is lost,
The King has sent one Son to banishment,
And I have sent the Father.
PARMENIO. How Sir!——You have not murdered him! *Starts.*
LORENZO. Why?
PARMENIO. Nothing my Lord, onely I'm sorry
I had no hand in't.
(*Aside*) S'death, hath the villain killed him?
LORENZO. Oh thou art jealous,
Thy hand comes well enough; this night
I have determined that soon, ere
The Royal Bloods atilt, you shall to horse,
'Tis easie to out-ride——
PARMENIO. Imagination it self, my Lord.
LORENZO. For then report will say thou kildst him.
No matter——
PARMENIO. Oh none at all my Lord.
LORENZO. When I am King,
I can restore at ease.
PARMENIO. True my Lord.
What if your Excellence cast out when I'm gone,
That *Claremonts* yongest son did this, and took
His flight upon't. His discontent's known well enough
To make of a Suspition a most received Truth;
Besides, wheresoev'r I go, I'll swear 'twas he.
LORENZO. By *Jove* most rare, when I am King I shall
Be poorer then I am, by giving thee

Thy due: Away, let's lose no time in words,
We're both resolv'd to put this cause to swords:
I'le to the King; thou to prepare for night,
Four hours hence wait me in the gallery.

Exeunt.

Enter CLARIMONT *solus.* [II. ii

CLARIMONT. Break heart and burst! My Father murdered,
And in the midst of all his hopes of life!
Methinks I see millions of Furies stand
Ready to catch my Rages sacrifice:
O for a man that could invent more plagues
Then hell could hold———
I have conceiv'd of wrong, and am grown great
Already: O sweet Revenge! I humbly thee intreat,
Be my Griefs midwife; let the mother die,
So thou bringst forth her long'd for progenie.
Methinks I feel the Villain grow within me,
And spread through all my veins:
How I could murder now, poison, or stab!
My head is full of mischief, sulphur and flaming pitch
Shall be but mercy to those deaths I'le give.

Exit.

Enter the KING, FIDELIO. [II. ii

FIDELIO [*aside*]. Though it be not safe for Subjects
To prie into the secrets of their Prince,
Much less to question about them,
Yet the implicite faith of blind obedience,
Poison'd with pleasing oft———And't like
Your Majesty, why do you court this Lady thus?
KING. Why dost thou ask?
FIDELIO. I know 'tis insolence to make reply,
Yet hear me as the eccho of the Court, great Sir,
They call your last giv'n mercy and those favors
But fairer ends to Lust.
KING. Thy zeal hath got thy pardon: *Stares upon him.*
No more, he that does offer to give direction
To his Prince, is full of pride, not of discretion. *Exit.*

II. ii. 1 S.P. CLARIMONT] *om. LR*   II. iii. 5 And't] *Fid.* And't *LR*

FIDELIO. So, to give Kings good advice,
May shew, I see, men faithful, but not wise:
I'm honest yet, and I do fare the worse for't,
Oh the Court!———
There humors reign, and merits only serve
To mock with idle hopes those best deserve.
Exit.

Enter FRANCELIA, BELLAMINO. [II. iv]

FRANCELIA. Sir, leave your complement;
Methinks the sweetest speech is that that's meant.
BELLAMINO. Wrong not my Love, best Creature, so, to think
My words are not the true ambassadors
Of my heart; by thy fair self I swear,
Nature has been too partial
In robbing heaven and earth to give you all.
FRANCELIA. Their weaknesses you mean, and I confess my Lord———
BELLAMINO. Their richest graces, sweetest,
Oh do not rack me thus:
I love, can you give love again?
FRANCELIA. Yes, any love that you dare ask,
Or I dare give, my Lord.
BELLAMINO. Oh but, fair Lady, Love must have no bounds,
It pines in prison.
FRANCELIA. Oh but, my Lord, hot Loves, if not contained,
Like fiery meteors, promise no good to others,
And are themselves consum'd.
Enter the KING *and Lords attend.*
BELLAMINO. O leave me not in doubts distracting trance.
KING. How, my boy, what, courting!
BELLAMINO. No, Sir.
KING. What was he doing then, *Francelia*?
FRANCELIA. So please your Grace, he was ith' midst
Of all your praises, when your Highness entred.
BELLAMINO (*aside*). Hum———
There's yet some hope then.
KING. Oh you are glad we are come then!
That discourse was tedious.

II. iv. 7 In] n *LR*

FRANCELIA. No, my Lord, I should have been well pleased
To have heard him longer.
KING. You are grown a Courtier, Fair one!
Sileo, are the Coaches ready?
SILEO. Yes and't please your Majesty.
KING. Come, we'll abroad then,
This day invites us forth; where's our Queen?

Exeunt.

Enter CLARIMONT, FIDELIO, *Young* FLORELIO. [II.

CLARIMONT.——Then with a pause fill'd up with sighs,
Ask him how strong his Guards are; but above all,
Be sure t'apply inflaming Corrosives,
Scrue up his anger to the height,
And make his fears be double:
Officious friends and mediation
May else prove remedies.
FIDELIO. Enough; If we do fail to act
Our parts to th' life in's tragedy,
May all those horrors that do threaten him
Fall upon us, Farewell.

Exeunt [FIDELIO *and* FLORELIO].

CLARIMONT. So, my revenge flies high:
The Vilain first shall kill his Father,
And while his hands are hot ith' blood,
This sword shall pierce him.
———Murdered he shall sink quick to hell,
I will not give him leave t'unload himself
Of one poor single sin of thought:
But lest he should wake out
Of's great security, and shun his fate,
I will rock him on———
Mischiefs are like the Cockatrices eye,
If they see first, they kill; if seen, they dye.

Exit.

Enter KING, *young* FLORELIO, FIDELIO. [III.

KING. And must the Vilain kill me too?
Y. FLORELIO. This very night.

III. i. 2 S.P. Y. FLORELIO] *Flor. LR, as are the rest of his prefixes in this scene*

KING. Why 'tis not possible, what would he have had more?
He had my heart, and might have had
All but the name of King: Oh, heaven had tyed
So strict a friendship, we could not part with't;
I durst have thought that I had merited
Fidelity from him.
FIDELIO. O my Lord, let ne'r so many drops
Sweet as the morning-dew fall on the sea,
The brinish water turns them all to salt:
Where there's an ocean of ingratitude,
Favors must needs be lost.
KING. Thou speak'st but truth; who does to merit trust,
But writes an obligation in the dust.
Your councels now my faithful life preserve,
Is there a way for pardon?
FIDELIO. Faith Sir, it would pollute mercy to use it here;
The fact's so foul, it calls it self for death.
KING. And it shall have it:
Traitor's enough; but when Ungrateful comes,
It stops the mouth of pity: Go take our guards
And apprehend him straight.
Y. FLORELIO. Soft great Sir,
'Twere fit your Justice should consider
What way is made, if you shall apprehend him,
For Treason unborn, and which he only did intend:
Foolish report which never was ith' right,
May clear his guiltiness, and censure Majesty.
If youl'd permit him to approach the Chamber,
(Yet who'ld advise Treason should come so near?)
You would take him in the act,
And leave no place for foul suspition:
Then if your Grace sent for his father,
And kept him with pretence of business by you,
Till he became the witness of the attempt,
Envy it self could have no cause to bark.
KING. Thou art my Oracle; I cannot tell
Whether my debt be greater to thy faith,
Or to thy councel: Go and watch abroad,
And let these cares wait upon fate and me.
The Captain of the Guard 'twere fit you sounded,

He may do mischief: *Florelio*, you
Shal to his father, the rest is mine to manage.

Exeunt [FLORELIO *and* FIDELIO].

These men are honest, and must be rewarded,
They do deserve it; 'tis most rare to find
A Greatness that enjoys true friends:
For commonly it makes us fear'd and hated;
The one doth breed offence, th'other leaves naked.
Let the impartial eye but look upon
All we call ours, and then again behold
The many hungry eyes of expectation
That wait upon our bounty, and it shall find
That we have scarce enough to keep mens hopes up,
We are rich if we can purchase friends:
Thrones, though they advance their glory ne'r so high,
Are but the seats of fear and misery.

Exit.

Enter PARMENIO, LORENZO. [III.

PARMENIO. In deep security, my Lord,
The Lady's at one window courted;
The King with *Florelio* and the Favorite
Contriving of a Masque, which he must never see.
LORENZO. Good! which he must never see.
Oh thou dost hug my Fates:
How I am ravisht to think upon
Ensuing joys!———
Parmenio, he's dead already.
PARMENIO. Six hours ago, my Lord, you cannot think
How much ado I had to keep my self
From saying, And't shall please your Majesty,
Ith' open presence to you:
Methinks one while I see your Highness sit
Like *Jupiter* in state,
With all the petty gods about you;
And then again in a more tempting shape
Then was the shower of gold,
Lie in some *Danae's* lap
More wanton then *Europa's* Bull;
Another time with some great train,

As if you went to battel;
Rockt in a douny coach, go take the air,
And have the thronging City
Crowded into a handfull,
Looking alow to bless your eyes,
And striving who shall cry loudest,
God bless your Majesty!

LORENZO. And all the while thou, like my *Ganimede*,
Shalt taste *Ambrosia* with me, while the petty gods
Burst with repining at thy happiness:
Thou shalt dispose of all, create, displace,
Be call'd my Boy, revel and mask, what not?
Oh, for one half year I will not speak unto the people,
Take you that office, keep that part for yours.
Oh how I long for night!
Thou canst not name the pleasure
Could make the time not tedious.
Away unto thy watch, and when the King's abed,
Be here.

PARMENIO. I shall, my Lord,
And't please your Majesty, I shall.

Exeunt.

Enter the Queen AMASIA, BELLAMINO *her Favorite*, DROLLIO, *Attendants.* [III. iii]

BELLAMINO. What is the matter, Madam, that the Court
Is in such clouds to night? The King
Feigns mirth and freeness, but withall
Flashes of fury make escapes.

QUEEN. 'Tis strange, my Lord, you should not know.

BELLAMINO. Faith Madam, I know nothing.

QUEEN. Troth nor I, but I suspect:
The clock no sooner struck, but all the Statesmen
Started, as if they had been to run a race,
And the King told me 'twere fit I took my rest:
There's something in't; but these designs of State
We women know no more then our own fate.
To turn our talk, Faith my Lord, where lies
That Beauty that so captivates you all?

III. ii. 22 battel;] ~, *LR* 26 alow] along *LR*

She has a graceful garb, 'tis true.
BELLAMINO. Who, Madam, *Francelia*?
Oh she has a dainty foot,
And daintier hand, an eye round as a globe
And black as jet, so full of majesty and life,
That when it most denies, it most invites.
QUEEN. These parts she has indeed, but is here all?
BELLAMINO. All! heaven forbid:
Her hair's so preciously fair and soft,
That were she faln into some river and
In danger, one would make a conscience
To save her life, for fear of spoiling it.
Her lips are gently swelled like unto
Some blushing cherry, that hath newly tasted
The dew from heaven; and her cheeks——
QUEEN. Hold, hold my Lord, all this is Poetry,
A Painter could not flatter more:
To my eye now she is so slender,
She's scarce, I think, a span about ith' middle.
BELLAMINO. Oh, Madam, you must think wise Nature
Of such rich mould as she was framed
Would make as little waste as could be.
QUEEN. So, so,
What think you of the upper part o'th' nose then;
Does it not look as if it did give way
The eyes should shortly have an interview?
BELLAMINO. You're too severe a Critick, Madam;
So good a wit as yours could make,
Where there were any, all blest perfections.
After all, next to your Highness, I'm resolved to think
She is chiefest Beauty.
QUEEN. Not next to me, my Lord, now I am sure you flatter,
But 'tis too late to chide you for it,
Goodnight.
Exeunt.

Enter the KING *going to bed*, CLEONAX, *Lords*, *Attendants*. [III.

KING. God night to all. (*Whisper.*) Lord *Cleonax*, a word in private;
Take away the lights and shut the door. *Exeunt.*

III. iii. 39 it did] did it *Hazlitt*   43 Where there were] Were there not *Hazlitt*

Enter PARMENIO *and* LORENZO.

LORENZO. Is the King gone to bed?
PARMENIO. An hour ago, my Lord.
LORENZO. What if he should not be asleep yet?
PARMENIO. No matter; ere his tongue can speak, our swords
Shall kill: What though he call us Traitors?
'Twill be his last, and may be pardoned.
Come Sir, bravely on!
———Fear's worse then death,
You're Lord of all, or not of your own breath.
LORENZO. Nay if I fear, may I not live.
Follow———

The KING *calls out Treason! Old* CLEONAX *rising to go out at the door to call for help, is met by his son, who took him for the* KING *and kill'd him*: LORENZO *is presently of set purpose run through by* PARMENIO.

Enter the KING *in his Night-gown, Lords,* [CLARIMONT, Y. FLORELIO,] *Attendants.*

KING. Trust me, most sad and strange!
A flood of grief beats at my eyes for vent:
Poor *Cleonax*, I'm truly sorry for thee.
LORDS. So are we all.
KING. This accident commands our pity,
But what is done, is done:
Let it not be as yet divulged;
Remove the corps, and let it be the care
Of thee, *Florelio*, to see his burial
Honorable and private.———
Good thanks to all the rest,
Clarimont, stay you with me. *Exeunt* [*others*].
The Traitor's dead by *Parmenio*; but you must know,
There's one yet lives within me; I love, *Clarimont*.
CLARIMONT. That passion of all others, Sir, heaven easiliest pardons;
He lives not sure, that loves not.
KING. I, but my Love's not pure,
'Tis great, not good, *Clarimont*,
I love—*Francelia*.

III. iv. 12.5 *LR begins a new scene here, scene v.*

CLARIMONT. Take heed of unchaste fires, great Sir,
They mischief Sir; Forget her, faith forget her:
Such fits as these are ever cur'd like Agues,
Best when they are most starved:
If you shall give them their desired fuel,
They'l not be quencht with ease, and it is ever seen
(Heaven keep my Soveraign!)
The house they're bred in, feels them first and ever.

KING. *Clarimont*, thou wert ne'r in Love;
Thou art Philosophical, and wouldst have Reason
Guide where it was never yet Companion:
Thou shewst thy want of Love,
But helpst not mine: Councel is now too late,
It's like Smiths water flung upon the coals
Which more inflames, here———
Thou twice hast sav'd my life, if thou now speed'st;
Go to *Francelia*, and present
This Jewel to her, and withall my Love, *Gives him a Jewel.*
Do't with thy best of language and respect:
Fair means at first we'll use,
But foul shall come, if she the fair refuse:
Good night, and good success.

CLARIMONT. Obedience is the best of what I am,
Your will's my Law, Sir. *Exit* [KING].

CLARIMONT *solus.*

———Why then it must be:
Was there no woman in the Court
To feed thy lust with, but my sister,
And none to be the Bawd but I?
Couldst thou not think of any other way
To express thy greatness, but by doing me wrong?
My fathers angry ghost, I see,
Is not full appeased yet: *Studies.*
Why should I make, of murther thus begun,
A massacre?———
He did my father right in his revenge;
I, but he wrong'd him first; and yet who knows
But it was justice to attempt by force?

34 Such] Since *cw LR* 55 S.D. *Exit*] *at line 53 LR*

The removal of great Favorites, though enemies to th' State,
Is not so warrantable—I'm in a maze:
Something I'll do, but what I cannot tell,
I fear the worst, Lust never ended well.

Exit.

Enter FRANCELIA *and* BELLAMINO. [IV. i]

FRANCELIA. Fie, leave this importunity, my Lord,
I shall yield else, by this kiss I shall.
BELLAMINO. By this, and this, and this, thou shalt:
Heavens, what a breath is here!
Thy father fed on musk and amber
When he begot thee, sure; the wanton air
Chaf'd by the hot scents of Arabick spices
Is nothing nigh so sweet; the *Ambrosia*
The Gods themselves were drunk with,
Dwells on thy lips.

Enter FLORELIO *senior* [*concealed*].

FRANCELIA. Come, come, you flatter, 'tis on yours, my Lord.
BELLAMINO. On mine! alas, Nature gave us the prickles,
You the roses, but meant that they should grow together.

Kisses again.

FRANCELIA. So, so, what if the King or *Florelio* saw ye?
BELLAMINO. What if they did? I can fear nothing now
But surfeits: Come, we lose time, my Fairest,
Do we not? this is the minute——— *Kisses her again.*
FLORELIO SR. By heaven this is not fair, Madam.
FRANCELIA. Wonder strikes me dumb. *Exit.*
FLORELIO SR. How does she kiss, Favorite?
BELLAMINO. Who, my Lord?
FLORELIO SR. My wife, my Lord: draw, draw, or by all my hopes,
My rage will make me turn a murderer.
BELLAMINO. Not so easily——— *They fight.*
FLORELIO SR. Hold, let's breathe: Why should I do him right,
Who has done me such wrong? or die for her
That will not live for me——— *Puts up.*
Go enjoy her——— *Offers to go out.*

IV. i. 18 S.P. FLORELIO SR] *Flor. LR, as are the rest of his prefixes in this scene*

BELLAMINO. Soft——— *Pulls him back.*
You have stolne a secret here
That you must give again, or take my life—draw.
FLORELIO SR. Prethee disturb me not.
BELLAMINO. No, unless you promise never to disclose
What you have here discover'd,
This must be the passage. *Stands betwixt the door and him.*
FLORELIO SR. Hum! I will be mute, credit me,
I will not speak one word. *Offers to go out again.*
BELLAMINO. Nay— *Pulls him back.*
You must swear it too.
FLORELIO SR. If I must, I must.—By heaven
And by my honor—How tame a thing
A Cuckold is! *Exit.*
BELLAMINO. S'death, why did I let him go?
We can no more subsist together
Then fire and water———
———One of us two must die;
And charity tells me, better he then I.
But how? it is not for my honor
To kill him basely— *Studies.*
Nor is it for hers to kill him otherwise;
The whole Court will ghess the quarrel,
If it be a Duel— *Studies again.*
It is decreed; No matter which way, so he fall:
Mine, in respect of hers, are no respects at all.
Exit.

Enter DOCODISAPIO, DROLLIO. [IV. i

DOCODISAPIO. Abused, grossly abused! a base affront, believe it *Drollio.*

DROLLIO. Why, what's the matter, Signior?

DOCODISAPIO. Why, do you hear nothing?

DROLLIO. No, why what should it be?

DOCODISAPIO. *Pisaro* is the man.

DROLLIO. Fie, fie, it cannot be; the State could not commit so great an oversight, neglect a man of merit for *Pisaro*, fie, fie!

DOCODISAPIO. Want of judgment, *Drollio*; an unlearned Council, I ever told you so, never more heads, nor never less wit, believe't.

DROLLIO. Say you so, Seignior, that's hard: what say you to *Dinao*?

DOCODISAPIO. Alas an ordinary Brain, talks and talks it's true, but speaks more then he is, believe't, betwixt you and I a meer pratler. There's *Falorio* too; why, he cannot read his own hand; *Vasquez* cannot speak sence without two days premeditation, *Sillio*, *Vechio*, *Caronnio*, all Stones in their Head———

DROLLIO. If I should tell these Lords now, Seignior, what you say, it might cost an Eare or so.

DOCODISAPIO. I, why there's another abuse i'th' State, a man shall have his ears cut off for speaking a truth. A sick Government, *Drollio*, and a weak one believe't; it never thrived since *Spain* and we grew so great. There's a mystery in that too, *Drollio*. I will know all, before they have any more of my money.

DROLLIO. Peace Seignior, the King. *Exeunt.*

Enter the KING, QUEEN, *Lords, an Ambassador from* Spain, *who has his Audience; after which the* KING *goes out talking with* FIDELIO, *the rest follow. Then enters the two Brothers, the* FLORELLIES, *the elder speaks earnestly.*

FLORELIO SR. I prethee leave me, by all that's good, thou canst not know it, why shouldst thou thus in vain torment thy self and me. *They whisper.*

FLORELIO JR. Well, I ghess, and 'tis enough. *Exit.*

The elder FLORELIO *goes out at another door.*

Enter CLARIMONT, FRANCELIA. [IV. iii]

FRANCELIA. Think not, good Sir, your elegant inforcements
Can seduce my weaker innocence; its a resolution grounded,
And sooner shall the fixed Orbs be lifted off their hinges,
Then I be mov'd to any act
That bears the name of foul:
You know the way you came, Sir.

CLARIMONT. Is this all the respect the King shall have?
No, you would do well to clothe this harsh denial
In better language.

FRANCELIA. You may please to say,
I owe my life unto my Soveraign,
And should be proud to pay it in

IV. ii. 18 Eare or so] *Eareorso LR* IV. iii. 2 weaker] weak *Hazlitt*

At any warning, were it nere so short:
But for my Chastity, it doth so much concern another,
I can by no means part with it:
So fare you well Sir. *Exit.*

CLARIMONT. By heaven a Saint, no woman;
Sure she was born o'th vertues of her Mother,
Not of her Vices; the whole sexe
May come to be thought well of for her sake.
I long to meet *Florelio*; my joy is not compleat
Till I have cured his jealousies as well as mine.
Exit.

Enter FLORELIO [SR.], *and a Boy.* [IV.

FLORELIO SR. There was a time when Snakes and Adders had no being,
When the poor Infant-world had no worse reptiles
Then were the Melon and the Strawberry:
Those were the golden times of Innocence,
There were no Kings then, nor no lustful Peers,
No smooth-fac'd Favorites, nor no Cuckolds sure.
Oh!—how happy is that man, whose humbler thoughts
Kept him from Court, who never yet was taught
The glorious way unto damnation;
Who never did aspire
Further then the cool shades of quiet rest,
How have the heavens his lower wishes blest!
Sleep makes his labors sweet, and innocence
Does his mean fortunes truly recompence:
He feels no hot Loves, nor no Palsie-fears,
No fits of filthy Lusts, or of pale Jealousies:
He wants, it's true, our clothes, our masks, our diet,
And wants our cares, our fears, and our disquiets.
But this is all but raving,
And does distemper more; I'le sleep:
Lies all along on the ground.
Boy, sing the Song I gave you.

IV. iii. 18 Vices] *Hazlitt*; Nieces *LR*
IV. iv. 0.1 *no scene division LR*
1 S.P. FLORELIO SR.] *Flor. LR as are the rest of his prefixes in this scene*

A Song to a Lute.

Hast thou seen the Doun ith' air
when wanton blasts have tost it;
Or the Ship on the Sea,
when ruder winds have crost it?
Hast thou markt the Crocodiles weeping,
or the Foxes sleeping?
Or hast view'd the Peacock in his pride,
or the Dove by his Bride,
when he courts for his leachery?
Oh so fickle, oh so vain, oh so false, so false is she!

FLORELIO SR. Good Boy, leave me! *Boy exit.*

Enter CLARIMONT.

CLARIMONT. How now *Florellio*, Melancholy?
FLORELIO SR. No, I was studying, prethee resolve me
Whether it be better to maintain
A strong implicit faith,
That can by no means be opprest;
Or falling to the bottom at the first,
Arm'd with disdain and with contempts, to scorn the worst?
CLARIMONT. This is a subtile one; but why studying about this?
FLORELIO SR. Faith, I would find a good receipt for the head-ach,
That's all.———
CLARIMONT. Hum, I know now whereabouts you are;
No more on't, I'm come to clear those doubts,
Your wife is chaste, chaste as the Turtle-dove.
FLORELIO SR. Ha, ha, ha!
CLARIMONT. Ha, why do you laugh? I know she is, tis not
So many hours, since I tempted her with all my eloquence,
And for the King, yet found her cold as ice.
FLORELIO SR. Ha, ha, ha!
CLARIMONT. You do not well to tempt a Friend,
You do forget she is my sister.
FLORELIO SR. I would I nere had known you had one.
CLARIMONT. You'll give a reason now for this.
FLORELIO SR. None.

22–31] *Variant text: Poems of* Last Remains 1659 22 *ith'*] *in the* Poems
25 *winds*] Poems; *waves LR* 32 S.P. FLORELIO SR.] *om. LR*

CLARIMONT. By all that's good, since our dear father left us,
We are become his scorn; look you Sir, *Draws.*
I dare maintain it.

FLORELIO SR. But I dare not; put up, put up, young man,
When thou hast known a woman, thou wilt be tamer. *Exit.*

CLARIMONT. Ha! what should this mean?
I know he's valiant, wise, discreet: and what of that?
Passion, when it hath got the bit, doth oft-times throw the Rider:
———Yet why should I be peremptory?
She may, for ought I know, be yet unchaste
With some unworthy Groom. *Studies.*
What if I stole into some corner, and heard her at Confession?
'Twould not be amiss———
For souls, at such a time, like ships in tempests
Throw out all they have. And now I think on't,
Her trial shall be quick: Friend I'll do thee right,
Come on't what will, she dies if she be light.

Exit.

Enter Signior MULTECARNI *the Poet, and two of the Actors.* [IV.

MULTECARNI. Well, if there be no remedy, one must act two parts; *Rosselio* shall be the Fool and the Lord, and *Tisso* the Citizen and the Cuckold.

1. ACTOR. That cannot be, Signior, you know, one still comes in, when the other goes out.

MULTECARNI. By *Jove* 'tis true; let me see, we'll contrive it, the Lord and the Usurer, the Citizen and the Polititian; and sure they never are together. But who shall act the Honest Lawyer? 'Tis a hard part, that.

2. ACTOR. And a tedious one, it's admired you would put it in, Squire; and 'tis against your own rules, to represent any thing on the Stage, that cannot be.

MULTECARNI. Why, dost think 'tis impossible for a Lawyer to be honest?

1. ACTOR. As 'tis for a Lord Treasurer to be poor, or for a King not to be cozened. There's little *Robin*, in debt within these three years, grown fat and full by the trade: and then there's *Borachio*, an unknown man, got it all by speaking loud and bawling: believe it, Signior, they have no more conscience then an Inn-keeper.———

IV. V. 0.1 *headed* Act. 4. Scæn. 4. *LR*

MULTECARNI. I grant you all this; An old Cook, and a good, will please all palates: There's that for the young Tapers of the Law; then there's a bawdy Jest or two extraordinary for the Ladies; and when it comes to be acted in private, I'll have a jerk at the State for the Country-Gentlemen: If it does not take, my masters, it lies not upon me, I have provided well; and if the stomack of the times be naught, the fault's not in the meat or in the Cook. Come, let's find out *Lepido* and dine at the Mermaid——Come let us have one Rowse, my *Joves*, in *Aristippus*, we shall conceive the better afterwards.

ACTORS. Agreed, agreed——

Come, come away, to the Tavern I say,
For now at home is Washing-day:
Leave your prittle-prattle, let's have a Pottle,
We are not so wise as Aristotle.

Exeunt singing.

Enter CLARIMONT, FLORELIO [SR]. [IV. vi]

CLARIMONT. By heaven she's false, false as the tears of Crocodiles,
Or what is yet more feign'd: I do confess,
Your pardon, *Florelio*, come pray your pardon,
Perchance I may deserve it.

FLORELIO SR. You have it, so has she;
Would heaven would do it as easily as I.

CLARIMONT. Heaven cannot do so foul an act,
She has—oh, she has done too much!
And should not I see justice done,
The gods would punish me. Brother, clear up,
The world shall not be one day elder
Ere I see thy injuries revenged:
This night the King will revel
And be gamesom; he will change beds with thee,
Deny him not, and leave the rest to me.

IV. V. 30 S.P. ACTORS] *Act. LR* 31–4 *Revised text in A Musicall Banquet*, 1651; *MS Folg.409* 31 *Come, come*] *Come, lets Folg.409* 32 *is*] *'tis MB. Folg.409* 33 *let's have*] *and fill us MB, Folg.409* 34 *two additional lines MB, Folg.409*:
Drawer come away, let's make it holy day,
Anon, anon, anon, sir, what is't you say?
34. 1 *Exeunt singing.*] *follows line 30* LR
IV. vi. 0.1 *headed* Act. 4. Scæn. 5. *LR* 5 S.P. FLORELIO SR.] *Flor. LR, as are the rest of his prefixes in this scene*

FLORELIO SR. Thy youth I see doth put thee on too fast,
Thou hast too much of passion, gentle brother:
Thinkst thou the death of a poor lustful King
Or Peer can give me ease?
No, for if it could, my hand durst go as far that way
As thine———
Had she been chaste, there had no tempters bin,
Or if there had, I had not thought it sin.
Draw not thy sword at all, I do beseech thee,
'Twill not deserve one drop of Noble blood;
Forget it, do, for my sake.———

CLARIMONT. May heaven forget me then!
Where is the courage of thy house become?
When didst thou cease to be thy self?
Shall two brave Families be wrong'd,
Most basely wrong'd———
And shall we tamely like Philosophers
Dispute it with our reasons?
First may I live the scorn of all the world,
Then die forgotten.—No, no:
Were there as many Actors in thy wrong,
As does the vast Stage of the world now bear,
Not one should scape my rage, I and my ghost
Would persecute them all.
By all our ties of Love, of Brother, Friend,
By what thou holdst most dear, I do conjure thee
To leave this work to me;
And if ere thou canst think
That I present thee not a full revenge,
Then take it out on me.

FLORELIO SR. Thy zeal hath overcome me,
What wouldst thou have me do?

CLARIMONT. Nothing but this; Obey the King in all
He shall desire, and let your servants be at my dispose
This night; one of your faithfull'st Confidents
Send hither presently.

FLORELIO SR. Well I shall; but what you'l do, heaven knows,
I know not, nor will I:———
It is enough that I, against my will,

33 with our *Hazlitt*; without *LR*

Am made a passive instrument of ill.
Farewell. *Exit.*

CLARIMONT. So, there is but this,
The wanton King this night thinks to embrace
My sister; his bed shall prove his grave,
His own Favorite shall make it so:
I have perswaded him she yields,
And this night doth expect him:
He, to make sure oth' Husband,
By my advice, as if he did intend
Some jest, means to change lodgings
With wrong'd *Florelio*; the Favorite———

Enter PETRUCHIO.

Oh *Petruchio*, welcom! You have other clothes,
These I should borrow for a little while;
In Masquing times Disguises are in fashion:
I have a pretty plot in hand, and if it take,
'Twill be some Crowns in thy way.

PETRUCHIO. I shall pray hard it may, Sir,
My Clothes howsoever are at your service.

CLARIMONT. And I at yours, *Petruchio*;
But you must be dumb
And secret now.

PETRUCHIO. . As any Statue, Sir.

CLARIMONT. Come then, let's about it

Exeunt.

Enter LEPIDO, DROLLIO. [v. i]

DROLLIO. A rare Masque no doubt, who contriv'd it?

LEPIDO. Marry he that says 'tis good, howsoere he has made it, Signior *Multecarni*.

DROLLIO. Who, the Poet Laureat?

LEPIDO. The same.

DROLLIO. Oh then 'twere blasphemy to speak against it: What, are we full of *Cupids*? Do we sail upon the vast, and resail, and fetch the Masque from the clouds?

LEPIDO. Away Critick, thou never understoodst him.

DROLLIO. Troth I confess it; but my comfort is, others are troubled

65 *Florelio;*] ~, *LR* 67 should] would *Hazlitt*

with the same disease, 'tis epidemical, *Lepido*, take't on my word, and so let's in, and see how things go forward.

Exeunt.

Enter FRANCELIA *sola weeping.* [V.

FRANCELIA. Swell on my griefs, and O ye gentler tears
Drop still, and never cease to fall
Till you become a boundless Ocean;
Then drown the source that sent you out, and hide
Francelia from her husbands sight,
Her wronged husbands:
Oh could my *Florelio* but see
How all hot flames within me are gone forth,
Sure he would love again:
Yet sure he would not: Heavens! how just you are,
And oh how wicked I am!
My heart beats thick as if my end were nigh,
And would it were! a better time death
Cannot take; an Absolution I have had,
And have confest my unchaste Love
Unto my ghostly Father; my peace is made above,
But here below———What mak'st thou here *Petruchio*?

Enter CLARIMONT *like to* PETRUCHIO.

CLARIMONT [*aside*]. She weeps, the whore repents perchance:
Madam, it is my Masters pleasure that this night
You keep your chamber.
FRANCELIA. Thy voice and countenance are not the same,
They tell me that thy Master is displeas'd.
CLARIMONT. Madam, it may be so; but that to me
Is as unknown as is the new-found world,
I am his servant and obey commands.
FRANCELIA. And so am I, I prethee tell him so,
I will not stir. *Exit.*
CLARIMONT. How cunning is the Devil in a Womans shape!
He had almost again perswaded me
To have become her brother.

v. ii. 1 S.P. FRANCELIA.] *om. LR* 11 I am] am I *Hazlitt*

Enter Servant.

SERVANT. *Petruchio,* the Favorite is lighted at the door,
And asks to see my Lady.
CLARIMONT. My Lady is retired, where is he?
[*aside.*] This to my hearts desire falls out.

Enter BELLAMINO *the Favorite.*

BELLAMINO. Where's *Francelia*?
CLARIMONT. My Lord, she is not well,
And craves your Lordships pardon.
BELLAMINO. What, sick upon a Masque-night,
And when the King sends for her!
Come, come, that must not be;
Which way is she? CLARIMONT *steps to him and whispers.*
BELLAMINO. By heaven——— *He starts.*
CLARIMONT. By heaven, nor will she ever see you more, if he———
BELLAMINO. I understand you, I am *Bellamino*;
If ere he see the morning,
I had decreed it, nor should he have surviv'd
Three days, had he been nere so silent:
This night's his last, *Petruchio,*
This arm shall make it so,
I will not trust my brother with the act.
CLARIMONT. Nobly resolv'd; but how, or where, my Lord?
BELLAMINO. No matter where; rather then fail,
I'll make the Presence-chamber be
The place of execution.
CLARIMONT. Still nobly, but my Lord———
BELLAMINO. But again, *Petruchio.*
CLARIMONT. ———And again, my Lord, why
Think you that *Petruchio,* when he is
Entrusted in a business, will not see
It rightly done, and for his Ladies honor?
You'll kill him, and in publick, then forsooth
When you're ith' saddle, all the Court shall cry
Francelia was weary of her husband:
No, no, my Lady loves you well,
But loves her honor too; and there are ways, I hope,
To keep the one, and yet not lose the other:

Do not I know my Lady lies alone,
And will feign herself sick this night,
And all on purpose too? am not I to let you
Into her chamber, and to give out, the fact once done,
That he killed himself.———

[*The rest of the Tragedy was also wanting in the Manuscript.*]

FINIS

70.1 *The...Manuscript.*] *Errata LR*

EMENDATIONS OF ACCIDENTALS

This is a record of the editor's departures from copy, in lining of verse, minor punctuation, and other details not listed among textual notes at the foot of the page.

To The Reader

4 Author] *Author*
14 *Sad Shepherd*] *SAD SHEPHERD*
15 Acts] *Acts*
19 Scene] *Scene*
19 *Mortimer*] *MORTIMER*
24 Author] *Author*
24 Dr] D^{r}
26 Hilliard] HILLIARD

I. i

28 *Cassiopeia's*] *Cassopeia's*
71 incertain] *LR* (*u*); uncertain *LR* (*c*) *state 2*

II. i

5 *LR lines* Why...do— | That...speak.
17 *Claremont*] *LR* (*u*); *Clarimont LR* (*c*)
35 *Claremonts*] *LR* (*u*); *Clarimonts LR* (*c*) *state 1*
36 discontent's‸] *LR* (*c*) *state 1*; ~, *LR* (*u*)
41 let's lose] *LR* (*c*) *state 2*; let' slose *LR* (*u*)

II. ii

8 intreat,] ~‸

II. iii

10 mercy‸] ~,

II. v

2 are;] ~‸

III. i

5 *LR lines* All...King: | Oh...tyed
14 *LR lines* Thou...truth; | Who...trust,

III. iv

26 me;] ~,

IV. i

11 *LR lines* Come...flatter, | 'Tis...Lord.

IV. ii

1–27 *LR lines as verse*
25 good,] ~‸

IV. v

1–30 *LR lines as verse*

IV. vi

5–6 *One line in LR*
65 Favourite‸—] ~. —
67 while;] ~,

V. i

1–12 *LR lines as verse*

V. ii

17 *LR lines* But... here | *Petruchio?*

J Brackley.

AGLAURA.

LONDON,
Printed by *Iohn Haviland* for *Thomas Walkley*, and are
to be ſold at his ſhop at the Signe of the Flying
Horſe betweene York-houſe
and Britaines Burſe. 1638.

The Title-page of the Folio Edition, with the signature of J. Brackley, the son of the Earl of Bridgewater, who acted in Milton's *Comus*. *Huntington Library copy.*

TEXTS CONSULTED

Ag	*Aglaura*, folio, 1638, the copy text.
Ag-t	The tragic version of Act V in the folio, 1638.
Ag-c	The tragi-comic version of Act V in the folio, 1638.
Bodl[2]	Manuscript corrections and additions in the Bodleian Library copy 2 (Selden copy) of the folio, 1638.
R	British Museum, Royal MS. 18 C xxv, a scribal copy of the tragic version, *c.* 1637. See pp. 256–9 of the commentary for a discussion of the relations between this manuscript and the folio.
H	British Museum, Harleian MS. 3889, a transcription of the first prologue, personae, and text, to I. ii. 16.
	For 'Why so pale and wan' (IV. ii)[1]
EP9	Bodleian MS. Eng. Poet. e. 97.
W3	Bodleian copy of Playford's *Select Musicall Ayres and Dialogues*, 1653 (shelf-mark Wood 397), with a manuscript of the song and music, anonymous.
Eg9	British Museum, Egerton MS. 923.
A47	British Museum, Additional MS. 47111.
Dx4	New York Public Library, Drexel MS. 4041, music by William Lawes.
F308	Folger Library MS. V.a.308.
F24	Folger Library MS. V.a.124.
O2	James M. Osborn Collection, Yale University, MS. Chest II no. 21.
Poems	The song as found in the section of poems in *Fragmenta*, 1646.
AC	*The Academy of Complements*, 1646.
LS	*Latine Songs*, by Henry Bold, 1685, English text and Latin translation.
Wind-D	*Windsor Drollery*, 1671.
	For 'No, no fair heretic' (IV. iv)[1]
HL	Henry Lawes's MS. of his and his brother's music, owned by Miss Naomi D. Church, formerly British Museum loan 25.
Dx4	New York Public Library, Drexel MS. 4041, with music by Henry Lawes.
Dx42	New York Public Library, Drexel MS. 4257, with music.
Poems	The song as found in the section of poems in *Fragmenta*, 1646.
SMA	*Select Musical Ayres and Dialogues*, 1652, with music.

Aglaura was reprinted in the collected editions of *Fragmenta*, 1646, 1648, 1658, '1658', 1672, the works of 1694–6, 1709, 1719, 1766, 1770, 1836, Hazlitt's editions of 1874 and 1892, and Thompson's edition of 1910. See 'The Collected Editions' for further details.

[1] Variants are recorded in volume i of this edition.

PROLOGUE

I'VE thought upon't; and cannot tell which way
Ought I can say now, should advance the Play.
For Playes are either good or bad; the good
(If they doe beg) beg to be understood.
And in good faith, that has as bold a sound,
As if a beggar should aske twentie pound.
———Men have it not about them:
Then (Gentlemen) if rightly understood,
The bad doe need lesse Prologue than the good:
For if it chance the Plot be lame, or blinde,
Ill cloath'd, deform'd throughout, it needs must finde
Compassion,—It is a beggar without Art:—
But it fals out in penny-worths of Wit.
As in all bargaines else, Men ever get
All they can in; will have London measure,
A handfull over in their verie pleasure.
And now yee have't; hee could not well deny'ee,
And I dare sweare hee's scarce a saver by'ee.

Prologue. 2 should] can *R*, *H* 5 has] hath *H* 13 Wit.] *R*; ~‸ *H*; ~, *Ag*
14 else,] *R*; ~. *Ag* 17 deny'ee] deny't *H* 18 by'ee] *R*; by't *H*; by yee *Ag*

PROLOGUE TO THE COURT

THOSE common passions, hopes, and feares, that still
The Poets first and then the Prologues fill,
In this our age, hee that writ this, by mee,
Protests against as modest foolerie.
Hee thinks it an odd thing to be in paine,
For nothing else, but to be well againe.
Who writes to feare is so; had he not writ,
You nere had been the Judges of his wit;
And when hee had, did hee but then intend
To please himselfe, hee sure might have his end
Without th'expence of hope, and that hee had
That made this Play, although the Play be bad.
Then Gentlemen be thriftie, save your doomes
For the next man, or the next Play that comes;
For smiles are nothing, where men doe not care,
And frownes as little, where they need not feare.

To the King.

This (Sir) to them, but unto Majestie
All hee has said before, hee does denie.
Yet not to Majestie: that were to bring
His feares to be, but for the Queene and King,
Not for your selves; and that hee dares not say:
Y'are his Soveraignes another way:
Your soules are Princes, and yee have as good
A title that way, as yee have by blood
To governe, and here your powers more great
And absolute, than in the royall Seat.
There men dispute, and but by Law obey,
Here is no Law at all, but what yee say.

Prologue to the Court. 1–28] *om. H* 0.1 TO] FOR *R* 6 but] then *R* 11 Without th'] With the *a caret after* with *R* 16 And] as *R* 16.1 *To the King.*] *R*; *Ag centres this* S.D. *as if another prologue follows.* 17 Majestie‸] *R*; ~. *Ag* 23 yee] *R*; you *Ag*

[DRAMATIS PERSONAE]

KING, Lustfull and cruell, in love with *Aglaura*
THERSAMES, Prince, in love with *Aglaura*
ORBELLA, Queene, at first Mistresse to *Ziriff*: in love with *Ariaspes*
ARIASPES, Ambitious, Brother to the King
ZIRIFF, Otherwayes ZORANNES disguised, Captaine of the Guard, in love with *Orbella*, brother to *Aglaura*, a blunt brave
JOLAS, A Lord of the Councell, seeming friend to the Prince, but a Traytour, in love with *Semanthe*
AGLAURA, In love with the Prince, but nam'd Mistresse to the King
ORSAMES, A young Lord antiplatonique; friend to the Prince
PHILAN, The same
SEMANTHE, In love with *Ziriff*; platonique
ORITHIE, In love with *Thersames*
PASITHAS, A faithfull servant, blunt
JOLINA, *Aglaura's* waiting-woman
[ANDRAGES, A doctor.]
Courtiers, Huntsmen, Priest, Guard, [*Expresse, Serving-men*]

Scena PERSIA

Dramatis Personae. 1 Lustfull and cruell] *R, H; om. Ag* 4 Ambitious] *R, H; om. Ag* 5 ZORANNES] Sorannez *R, Ag*; Zorames *H* 6 a blunt brave] *R, H; om. Ag* 14 blunt] *R, H; om. Ag* 15 JOLINA] JOLINAS *Ag, R, H* 17 *Priest, Guard*] *A Priest, A Guard R, H*

Aglaura

Enter JOLAS, JOLINA [I. i]

JOLAS. Married? and in *Diana's* Grove!
JOLINA. So was th'appointment, or my Sense deceiv'd me.
JOLAS. Married!
Now by those Powers that tye those prettie knots,
'Tis verie fine, good faith 'tis wondrous fine.
JOLINA. What is, Brother?
JOLAS. Why to marrie, Sister—
T'injoy 'twixt lawfull and unlawfull thus
A happinesse, steale as 'twere ones owne;
Diana's Grove, sayest thou?——— *Scratcheth his head.*
JOLINA. That's the place; the hunt once up, and all
Ingag'd in the pursuite, they meane to leave
The company, and steale unto those thickets,
Where there's a Priest attends them.
JOLAS. And will they lye together, think'st thou?
JOLINA. Is there distinction of sex thinke you?
Or flesh and bloud?
JOLAS. True; but the King, Sister!
JOLINA. But love, Brother!
JOLAS. Thou sayest well; 'tis fine, 'tis wondrous fine:
Diana's grove———
JOLINA. Yes, *Diana's* grove,
But brother if you should speake of this now,———
JOLAS. Why thou know'st a drowning man holds not
A thing so fast:

Enter SEMANTHE, *she sees* JOLAS, *and goes in agen.*

Semanthe! she shuns me too.
JOLINA. The wound festred sure!
The hurt the boy gave her, when first shee look'd
Abroad into the world, is not yet cur'd.
JOLAS. What hurt?

0.1] *Headed* Actus I. Scena I. *Other acts headed in the same style in Ag* 6 Why‸] *R*; ~? *Ag* 11 pursuite] *R*, *H*; sport *Ag* 21 drowning] drown'd *H*

JOLINA. Why, know you not?
Shee was in love long since with young *Zorannes*,
(*Aglaura's* brother,) and the now Queenes betroth'd.
JOLAS. Some such slight Tale I've heard.
JOLINA. Slight?
She yet does weepe, when she but heares him nam'd,
And tels the prettiest and the saddest stories
Of all those civill wars, and those Amours,
That, trust me, both my Lady and my selfe
Turne weping Statues still.
JOLAS. Pish, 'tis not that.
'Tis *Ziriff*, and his fresh glories here have robb'd
Me of her. Since he thus appear'd in Court,
My love has languish'd worse than Plants in drought.
But time's a good Physician: come, lets in:
The King and Queene by this time are come forth.
Exeunt.

Enter SERVING-MEN *to Zorannes.* [I. i

1. SERVANT. Yonder's a crowd without, as if some strange sight were to be seene to day here.

2. SERVANT. Two or three of them with Carbonadoes afore in stead of faces mistooke the doore for a breach, and at the opening of it, are striving still which should enter first.

3. SERVANT. (*Knocks.*) Is my Lord busie?

Enter ZORANNES *as in his Studie* [*disguised as* ZIRIFF].

1. SERVANT. My Lord, there are some Souldiers without———
ZORANNES. Well, I will dispatch them presently.
2. SERVANT. Th'Embassadours from the Cadusians too———
ZORANNES. Shew them the Gallerie.
3. SERVANT. One from the King———
ZORANNES. Againe? I come, I come. *Exeunt Serving men.*

ZORANNES *solus.*

Greatnesse, thou vainer shadow of the Princes beames,
Begot by meere reflection, nourish'd in extreames;
First taught to creepe, and live upon the glance,

29 I've] I have *R, H* 29 Slight] *om. R, H* 30 does] doth *H*
I. ii. 3 of them] *R, H*; *om. Ag* 6.1 S.D. ZORANNES] ZIRIFF *is his prefix throughout the tragic version of Ag*, ZORANNES *in some revised sections of tragi-comic version of Act V.*
8 will dispatch] wilbe for *R, H* 9 Cadusians] Sadusians *H*

Poorely to fare, till thine owne proper strength
Bring thee to surfet of thy selfe at last.
How dull a Pageant would this States-play seeme
To mee now, were not my love and my revenge
Mixt with it?———
Three tedious Winters have I waited here,
Like patient Chymists blowing still the coales,
And still expecting, when the blessed houre
Would come, should make me master of
The Court *Elixar*, Power, for that turnes all:
'Tis in projection now; downe, sorrow, downe,
And swell my heart no more, and thou wrong'd ghost
Of my dead father, to thy bed agen,
And sleepe securely———
It cannot now be long, for sure *Fate* must,
As't has beene cruell, so, a while be just.

Exit.

Enter KING, [ARIASPES, THERSAMES,] *and Lords, the Lords intreating for Prisoners.* [I. iii]

KING. I say they shall not live; our mercie
Would turne sinne, should we but use it er'e:
Pittie, and Love, the bosses onely be
Of government, merely for shew and ornament.
Feare is the bit that mans proud will restraines,
And makes its vice its vertue———See it done.

Enter to them Queene [ORBELLA], AGLAURA, *Ladies; the* KING *addresses himselfe to* AGLAURA.

So early, and so curious in your dresse, (faire Mistresse?)
These prettie ambushes and traps for hearts
Set with such care to day, looke like designe:
Speake, Lady, is't a massacre resolv'd?
Is conquering one by one growne tedious sport?
Or is the number of the taken such,
That for your safetie you must kill out-right?

AGLAURA. Did none doe greater mischiefe (Sir) than I,
Heav'n would not much be troubled with sad storie,

16 *H ends its transcription here.*
I. iii. 0.1 KING] *The* KING *R* 2 er'e] here *R* 9 designe] designes *R* 14 doe] noe *R*

Nor would the quarrell man has to the Starres
Be kept alive so strongly.
KING. When hee does leav't
Woman must take it up, and justly too;
For robbing of the sex and giving all to you.
AGLAURA. Their weaknesses you meane, and I confesse, Sir.
KING. The greatest subjects of their power and glorie.
Such gentle rape thou act'st upon my soule,
And with such pleasing violence dost force it still,
That when it should resist, it tamely yeilds,
Making a kinde of haste to be undone,
As if the way to victorie were losse,
And conquest came by overthrow.

Enter an Expresse delivering a Packet upon his knee.
The KING *reads.*

ORBELLA. Prettie! *The Queene looking upon a flower in one of the Ladies heads.*
Is it the child of nature, or of some faire hand?
LADY. 'Tis as the beautie Madam of some faces,
Arts issue onely.
KING. *Thersames*,
This concernes you most.
[*To the Expresse.*] Brought you her picture?
EXPRESSE. Something made up for her in haste I have. *Presents the Picture. Exit.*
KING. If she does owe no part of this faire dower
Unto the Painter, she is rich enough.
AGLAURA. A kinde of merrie sadnesse in this face
Becomes it much.
KING. There is indeed, *Aglaura*,
A prettie sullennesse drest up in smiles,
That sayes this beautie can both kill, and save.
How like you her *Thersames*?
THERSAMES. As well as any man can doe a house
By seeing of the portall; here's but a face,
And faces (Sir) are things I have not studied;

20 Sir] *om. R* 21] *R assigns the line to Aglaura* 21 and] *R*; or *Ag* 23 pleasing] pleasant *R* 27.1 S.D. *delivering a*] *deliverie*: *A R* 29 of some] some *R* 34 S.D. *Exit.*] *R*; *om. Ag* 36 the] her *R*

I have my dutie, and may boldly sweare,
What you like best will ever please me most.

KING. Spoke like *Thersames*, and my sonne.
Come! the day holds faire,
Let all the Hunts-men meet us in the vale;
We will uncouple there. *Exeunt.*

ARIASPES: *solus stayes behinde.*

ARIASPES. How odd a thing a croud is unto me!
Sure nature intended I should be alone;
Had not that old doting man-mid-wife *Time*
Slept, when he should have brought me forth, I had
Beene so too——— *Studies and scratches his head.*
To be borne neere, and onely neere a crowne———

Enter JOLAS.

JOLAS. How now my Lord? What? walking o'th' tops of Pyramids? whispering your selfe away like a deny'd lover? Come! to horse, to horse, and I will shew you streight a sight shall please you more than kinde lookes from her you dote upon after a falling out.

ARIASPES. Prithee what is't?

JOLAS. Ile tell you as I goe.

Exeunt.

Enter Hunts-men hollowing and whooping. [I. iv]

HUNTS-MEN. Which way? which way? [*Exeunt.*]

Enter THERSAMES, AGLAURA *muffled.*

THERSAMES. This is the grove, 'tis somewhere here within.

Exeunt.

Enter dogging of them, ARIASPES, JOLAS.

JOLAS. Gently! Gently! [*Exeunt.*]

Enter ORSAMES, PHILAN, *a Huntsman, two Courtiers.*

HUNTSMAN. No hurt, my Lord, I hope.

ORSAMES. None, none. Thou wouldst have warranted it to another, if I had broke my neck: what? do'st thinke my horse and I shew tricks? that which way soever he throwes me, like a Tumblers

49 us] *Ag*, *R(c)*; mee *R(u)* 54 he] she *R* 59 shall] will *R*
I. iv. 2.2 JOLAS] *and* JOLAS *R* 3.1 *two*] *and two R*

boy I must fall safe? was there a bed of roses there? would I were an Eunuch if I had not as lief h'a falne in the state, as where I did; the ground was as hard, as if it had been pav'd with Platonicke Ladies hearts, and this unconscionable fellow askes whether I have no hurt; where's my horse?

1. COURTIER. Making love to the next mare I thinke.

2. COURTIER. Not the next I assure you; hee's gallop't away, as if all the spurs i'th' field were in his sides.

ORSAMES. Why there's it: the jade's in the fashion too. Now h'as done me an injurie, he will not come neere me. Well when I hunt next, may it be upon a starv'd cow, without a saddle too. And may I fall into a saw-pit, and not be taken up, but with suspition of having beene private, with mine owne beast there. Now I better consider on't too, Gentlemen, 'tis but the same thing we doe at Court; here's everie man striving who shall be formost, and hotly pursuing of what he seldome overtakes, or if he does, it's no great matter.

PHILAN. He that's best hors'd (that is best friended) gets in soonest, and then all hee has to doe is to laugh at those that are behind. Shall we help you my Lord?———

ORSAMES. Prithee doe—stay! To be in view, is to be in favour, is it not?

PHILAN. Right, and he that has a strong faction against him, hunts upon a cold sent, and may in time come to a losse.

ORSAMES. Here's one rides two miles about, while another leapes a ditch and is in before him.

PHILAN. Where note the indirect way's the nearest.

ORSAMES. Good againe———

PHILAN. And here's another puts on, and fals into a quagmire, (that is) followes the Court till he has spent all (for your Court quagmire is want of money); there a man is sure to stick, and then not one helps him out, if they doe not laugh at him.

1. COURTIER. What thinke you of him, that hunts after my rate and never sees the Deere?

2. COURTIER. Why hee is like some young fellow, that followes the Court, and never sees the King.

ORSAMES. To spurre a horse till he is tir'd, is———

PHILAN. To importune a friend till he be wearie of you.

I. iv. 9 an] *R*; *om. Ag* 14 the] to the *R* 23 it's] 'tis *R* 24 (that is best friended)] (that is) best friended *R* 25 hee] that hee *R* 32 before] afore *R* 33 way's] way is *R* 39 rate] rates *R* 41 hee is] hee's *R*

ORSAMES. Not amisse, for then upon the first occasion y'are throwne off, as I was now.

PHILAN. This is nothing to the catching of your horse *Orsames.*

ORSAMES. Thou say'st true, I thinke he is no transmigrated Philosopher, and therefore not likely to be taken with moralls. Gentlemen—your help, the next fall I hope will bee yours, and then 'twill bee my turne. *Exeunt.*

Enter againe married, THERSAMES, AGLAURA, *Priest.*

THERSAMES. Feare not my Deare, if when Loves diet
Was bare lookes and those stolne too,
He yet did thrive! what then
Will he doe now? when everie night will be
A feast, and everie day fresh revelrie.

AGLAURA. Will he not surfet, when he once shall come
To grosser fare (my Lord) and so grow sicke,
And Love once sicke, how quickly will it dye?

THERSAMES. Ours cannot; 'tis as immortall as the things
That elemented it, which were our soules:
Nor can they ere impaire in health, for what
These holy rites doe warrant us to doe,
More than our bodies would for quenching thirst.
Come let's to horse, we shall be mist, for we
Are envies marke, and Court eyes carrie farre.
Your prayers and silence Sir:——— *To the Priest.*
Exeunt.

Enter ARIASPES, JOLAS [*from hiding*].

ARIASPES. If it succeed? I weare thee here my *Jolas*———

JOLAS. If it succeed? will night succeed the day?
Or houres one to another? is not his lust
The Idoll of his soule? and was not she
The Idoll of his lust? as safely he might
Have stolne the Diadem from off his head,
And he would lesse have mist it.
You now, my Lord, must raise his jealousie,
Teach it to looke through the false opticke feare,

45 Not amisse,] *R*; *om. Ag* 50 fall] *R*; *om. Ag* 68 my] *om. R* 69 the] to *R*

And make it see all double: Tell him the Prince
Would not have thus presum'd, but that he does
Intend worse yet; and that his crowne and life
Will be the next attempt.

ARIASPES. Right, and I will urge
How dangerous 'tis unto the present state,
To have the creatures, and the followers
Of the next Prince (whom all now strive to please)
Too neere about him.

JOLAS. What if the male-contents
That use to come unto him were discovered?

ARIASPES. By no meanes; for 'twere in vaine to give
Him discontent (which too must needs be done)
If they within him gave't not nourishment.

JOLAS. Well, Ile away first, for the print's too big
If we be seene together. *Exit.*

ARIASPES. I have so fraught this Barke with hope, that it
Dares venture now in any storme, or weather;
And if hee sinke or splits, all's one to me.
Ambition seemes all things, and yet is none,
But in disguise stalkes to opinion
And fooles it into faith, for everie thing:
'Tis not with the ascending to a Throne,
As 'tis with staires, and steps, that are the same;
For to a Crowne, each humor's a degree;
And as men change, and differ, so must wee.
The name of vertue doth the people please,
Not for their love to vertue, but their ease,
And Parrat Rumour I that tale have taught.
By making love I hold the womans grace;
'Tis the Court double key, and entrance gets
To all the little plots; the fierie spirits
My love to Armes hath drawne into my faction;
All, but the minion of the Time, is mine,
And he shall be, or shall not be at all.
He that beholds a wing in pieces torne,
And knowes not that to heav'n it once did beare
The high-flowne and selfe-less'ning bird, will think

98 the] *R*; th' *Ag* 103 ease,] ~‸ *R* 104 taught.] ~‸ *R* 108 hath] have *R*
113 and] *om. R*

And call them idle Subjects of the winde:
When he that has the skill to imp and binde
These in right places, will this truth discover;
That borrowed Instruments doe oft convey
The Soule to her propos'd Intents, and where
Our Stars deny, Art may supply.

Exit.

Enter SEMANTHE, ORITHIE, ORSAMES, PHILAN. [I. v]

SEMANTHE. Thinke you it is not then
The little jealousies (my Lord) and feares,
Joy mixt with doubt, and doubt reviv'd with hope
That crownes all love with pleasure? These are lost
When once wee come to full fruition;
Like waking in the morning when all night
Our fancie has beene fed with rare delight.
ORSAMES. I grant you, Madam, that the feares, and joyes,
Hopes, and desires, mixt with despaires, and doubts,
Doe make the sport in love; that they are
The verie dogs by which we hunt the hare;
But as the dogs would stop, and streight give o're
Were it not for the little thing before,
So would our passions; both alike must be
Flesh't in the chase.
ORITHIE. Will you then place the happinesse, but there,
Where the dull plow-man and the plow-mans horse
Can finde it out? Shall soules refin'd, not know
How to preserve alive a noble flame,
But let it die, burne out to appetite?
SEMANTHE. Love's a Chamelion, and would live on aire;
Physick for agues, starving is his food.
ORSAMES. Why? there's it now! a greater Epicure
Lives not on earth; my Lord and I have beene
In's privie kitchin, seene his bills of Fare.
SEMANTHE. And how, and how my Lord?
ORSAMES. A mightie Prince,

116 this] *R*; thus *Ag*
I. v. 0.1 PHILAN] *and* PHILAN *R* 4 pleasure? These] pleasure, which *R* 6 waking] wakening *R* 7 rare] *R*; true '*Against Fruition*' *in Poems FA46*; some new strange *Ag* 12] *R has* S.D.: sings 13 not] *om. R* 17 the dull] a dull *R* 21 on] by *R*; that lives on meer ayre '*Against Fruition*' *FA46*

And full of curiositie—Harts newly slaine
Serv'd up intire, and stucke with little Arrowes
In stead of Cloves———
PHILAN. Sometimes a cheeke plumpt up
With broth, with creame and clarret mingled
For sauce, and round about the dish
Pomegranate kernells, strew'd on leaves of Lillies.
ORSAMES. Then will he have black eies, for those of late
He feeds on much, and for varietie
The gray———
PHILAN. You forget his cover'd dishes
Of *Je-ne-scays-quas* and Marmalade of lips,
Perfum'd by breath sweet as the beanes first blossomes.
SEMANTHE. Rare!
And what's the drinke to all these meats, my Lord?
ORSAMES. Nothing but pearle dissolv'd, teares still fresh fetch'd
From Lovers eyes, which if they come to be
Warme in the carriage, are streight cool'd with sighs.
SEMANTHE. And all this rich proportion, perchance
We would allow him.
ORSAMES. True! but therefore this his common diet
Onely serves
When his chiefe Cookes, *Liking* and *Opportunitie*,
Are out o'th'way; for when hee feasts indeed,
'Tis there, where the wise people of the world
Did place the vertues, i'th' middle—Madam.
ORITHIE. My Lord,
There is so little hope we should convert you;
And if we should, so little got by it,
That wee'll not lose so much upon't as sleepe.
Your Lordships servants———
ORSAMES. Nay Ladies
Wee'll wait upon you to your chambers.
PHILAN. Prithee
Lets spare the complement, we shall doe no good.
ORSAMES. By this hand Ile try;
They keepe me fasting, and I must be praying.

Exeunt.

36 *Je-ne-scays-quas* and] Jene-strayes, and *Ag*; Jene-scays and quas (quas *deleted*) *R* 39 these meats] *R*; this meat *Ag* 42 cool'd] cold *R* 45 this] *R*; this is but *Ag* 45 diet‸] *R*; ~; *Ag* 50 i'th'] in the *R*

[*Discover*] AGLAURA *undressing of her selfe*, JOLINA. [I. vi]

AGLAURA. Undresse mee:—Is it not late, *Jolina*?
It was the longest day, this———

Enter THERSAMES.

THERSAMES. Softly, as Death it selfe comes on,
When it does steale away the sicke mans breath,
And standers by perceive it not,
Have I trod the way unto these lodgings.
How wisely doe those Powers
That give us happinesse, order it?
Sending us still feares to bound our joyes,
Which else would over-flow and lose themselves:
See where shee sits,
Like Day retir'd into another world.
Deare mine! where all the beautie man admires
In scattered pieces, does united lye.
Where sense does feast, and yet where sweet desire
Lives in its longing, like a misers eye,
That never knew, nor saw sacietie:
Tell me, by what approaches must I come
To take in what remaines of my felicitie?
AGLAURA. Needs there any new ones, where the breach
Is made already? you are entred here—
Long since (Sir) here, and I have giv'n up all.
THERSAMES. All but the Fort, and in such wars, as these,
Till that be yeilded up, there is no peace,
Nor triumph to be made; come! undoe, undoe,
And from these envious clouds slide quicke
Into Loves proper Sphere, thy bed:
The wearie traveller, whom the busie Sunne
Hath vex't all day, and scortch'd almost to tinder,
Nere long'd for night, as I have long'd for this.
What rude hand is that? *One knocks hastily.*
Goe *Jolina*, see,
But let none enter——— JOLINA *goes to the Doore.*
JOLINA. 'Tis *Ziriff*, Sir.

I. vi. 0.1 AGLAURA] *Enter* AGLAURA *R* 1–12 *om. R* 14 scattered] scattering *R*
29 Hath] Has *R* 31 that] this *R*

THERSAMES. —Oh—
Something of weight hath falne out it seemes,
Which in his zeale he could not keepe till morning.
But one short minute, Deare, into that chamber.———

Enter ZORANNES.

How now? thou start'st as if thy sinnes had met thee,
Or thy Fathers ghost; what newes man?
ZORANNES. Such as
Will send the blood of hastie messengers
Unto the heart, and make it call
All that is man about you into councell;
Where is the Princesse, Sir?
THERSAMES. Why? what of her?
ZORANNES. The King must have her———
THERSAMES. How?
ZORANNES. The King must have her (Sir).
THERSAMES. Though feare of worse makes ill still relish better,
And this looke handsome in our friendship, *Ziriff*,
Yet so severe a preparation
There needed not; come, come! what ist?

ZORANNES *leads him to the doore, and shewes him a Guard.*

A Guard! *Thersames*, thou art lost; betray'd
By faithlesse and ungratefull man,
Out of a happinesse:———

He steps betweene the doore and him, and drawes.

The verie thought of that,
Will lend my anger so much noble justice,
That wert thou master of as much fresh life,
As th'ast beene of villany, it should not serve,
Nor stocke thee out to glorie, or repent
The least of it.
ZORANNES. Put up: put up! Such unbecoming anger
I have not seene you weare before.
What? draw upon your friend, *Discovers himselfe.*
Doe you beleeve me right now?———
THERSAMES. I scarce beleeve mine eyes:—*Zorannes.*

33 hath] is *R* 38 messengers] *R*; messages *Ag* 41 Where is] *R*; Where's *Ag*
49.1 *He*] *om. R* 53 th'ast] thou hast *R*

ZORANNES. The same, but how preserv'd, or why thus long
Disguis'd to you, a freer houre must speake:
That y'are betrai'd is certaine, but by whom,
Unlesse the Priest himselfe, I cannot ghesse.
More than the marriage, though he knowes not of:
If you now send her on these early summons
Before the sparks are growne into a flame,
You doe redeeme th'offence, or make it lesse;
And (on my life) yet his intents are faire,
And he will but besiege, not force affection.
So you gaine time; if you refuse, there's but
One way; you know his power and passion.
THERSAMES. Into how strange a labyrinth am I
Now falne! what shall I doe *Zorannes*?
ZORANNES. Doe (Sir) as Sea-men, that have lost their light
And way: strike saile, and lye quiet a while.
Your forces in the Province are not yet
In readinesse, nor is our friend *Zephines*
Arriv'd at Delphos; nothing is ripe, besides———
THERSAMES. Good heav'ns, did I but dreame that she was mine?
Upon imagination did I climbe
Up to this height? let mee then wake and dye,
Some courteous hand snatch mee from what's to come,
And ere my wrongs have being, give them end.
ZORANNES. How poore, and how unlike the Prince is this?
This trifle woman does unman us all;
Robs us so much, it makes us things of pittie.
Is this a time to loose our anger in?
And vainly breathe it out? when all wee have
Will hardly fill the saile of Resolution,
And make us beare up high enough for action.
THERSAMES. I have done (Sir) pray chide no more;
The slave whom tedious custome has enur'd
And taught to thinke of miserie as of food,
Counting it but a necessarie of life,
And so digesting it, shall not so much as once
Be nam'd to patience, when I am spoken of:
Marke mee; for I will now undoe my selfe
As willingly, as virgins give up all

67 are] or *R* 93 has] hath *R*

First nights to them they love:——— *Offers to goe out.*

ZORANNES. Stay, Sir, 'twere fit *Aglaura* yet were kept
In ignorance: I will dismisse the Guard,
And be my selfe againe. *Exit.*

THERSAMES. In how much worse estate am I in now,
Than if I nere had knowne her; privation
Is a miserie as much above bare wretchednesse,
As that is short of happinesse:
So when the Sunne does not appeare,
'Tis darker 'cause it once was here.

Enter ZORANNES *speakes to* ORSAMES *and others halfe entred.*

ZORANNES. Nay, Gentlemen:
There needs no force, where there is no resistance:
Ile satisfie the King my selfe.

THERSAMES. ———Oh 'tis well y'are come;
There was within me fresh Rebellion,
And reason was almost unking'd agen.
But you shall have her Sir——— *Goes out to fetch* AGLAURA.

ZORANNES. What doubtfull combats in this noble youth
Passion and reason have!———

Enter THERSAMES *leading* AGLAURA.

THERSAMES. Here Sir——— *Gives her, goes out.*

AGLAURA. What meanes the Prince, my Lord?

ZORANNES. Madam,
His wiser feare has taught him to disguise
His love, and make it looke a little rude at parting.
Affaires that doe concerne, all that you hope from
Happinesse, this night force him away:
And lest you should have tempted him to stay,
(Which hee did doubt you would and would prevaile)
He left you thus: he does desire by mee
You would this night lodge in the little towre,
Which is in my command; the reasons why
Himselfe will shortly tell you.

AGLAURA. 'Tis strange, but I am all Obedience. *Exeunt.*

100 nights] nighte *R* 109 it] hee 110 Nay, Gentlemen] *om. R* 118.1 S.D. *leading*] *leading in R* 120 him] *om. R*

Enter THERSAMES, JOLAS *a Lord of the Counsell.* [II. i]

JOLAS. I told him so, Sir, urg'd 'twas no common knot, that to the tying of it two powerfull Princes, Vertue and Love were joyn'd, and that a greater than these two was now ingaged in it, Religion; but 'twould not doe.
The corke of passion boy'd up all reason so
That what was said, swam but o'th' top of th'eare,
Nere reach't the heart.

THERSAMES. Is there no way for Kings to shew their power,
But in their Subjects wrongs? no subject neither
But his owne sonne?

JOLAS. Right Sir:
No quarrie for his lust to gorge on, but
On what you fairely had flowne at, and taken:
Well—wert not the King, or wert indeed
Not you, that have such hopes, and such a crowne
To venter, and yet—'tis but a woman.

THERSAMES. How? that *but* againe, and thou art more injurious
Than hee, and woul't provoke me sooner.

JOLAS. Why Sir?
There are no altars yet addrest unto her,
Nor sacrifice; if I have made her lesse
Than what she is, it was my love to you:
For in my thoughts, and here within, I hold her
The noblest peece Nature ere lent our eyes,
And of the which, all women else, are but
Weake counterfeits, made up by her journey-men:
But was this fit to tell you?
I know you value but too high all that,
And in a losse we should not make things more;
'Tis miseries happinesse, that wee can make
It lesse by art, throw a forgetfulnesse
Upon our ills, yet who can doe it here?
When everie voyce, must needs, and everie face,
By shewing what she was not, shew what she was.

THERSAMES. Ile instantly unto him——— *Drawes.*

II. i. 1 I] *Ag*, *R*(*c*); we *R*(*u*) 6 o'th'] to'th' *R* 8 way] ways *R* 9 subject] subjects *R* 16 *but*] but *Ag*; *om.* *R* 16 art] *R*; arr *Ag* 17 woul't] would *R* 23 the which,] thee, which *R* 29 throw] through *R*

JOLAS. Stay Sir:
Though't be the utmost of my Fortunes hope
To have an equall share of ill with you:
Yet I could wish we sold this trifle life,
At a farre dearer rate, than we are like to doe,
Since 'tis a King's the Merchant.
THERSAMES. Ha! King, I! 'tis indeed,
And there's no Art can cancell that high bond.
JOLAS (*to himselfe*). ———Hee cooles againe.———
True Sir, and yet mee thinks to know a reason—
For passive nature nere had glorious end,
And he that States preventions ever learn'd,
Knowes, 'tis one motion to strike and to defend.

Enter Serving-man.

SERVING-MAN. Some of the Lords without, and from the King,
They say, wait you.
THERSAMES. What subtle State tricke now?
But one turne here, and I am back my Lord. *Exit.*
JOLAS. This will not doe; his resolution's like
A skilfull horse-man, and reason is the stirrop,
Which though a sudden shock may make it loose,
Yet does it meet it handsomely agen.
Stay, 'tmust be some sudden feare of wrong
To her, that may draw on a sudden act
From him, and ruine from the King; for such
A spirit will not like common ones
Be rais'd by everie spell, 'tis in loves circle
Onely 'twill appeare.

Enter THERSAMES.

THERSAMES. I cannot beare the burthen of my wrongs
One minute longer.
JOLAS. Why! what's the matter Sir?
THERSAMES. They doe pretend the safetie of the State
Now, nothing but my marriage with *Cadusia*
Can secure th'adjoyning countrey to it;
Confinement during life for me, if I refuse,

39 I] Yea *R* 45.1 S.D. *Serving-man*] *Serving-men R* 47 State] States *R* 48.1] S.D. *Jolas solus. R* 49 doe] *om. R* 63 to it] too't *R*

Diana's Nunnerie for her—And at that Nunn'rie, *Jolas*,
Allegiance in mee like the string of a watch
Wound up too high, and forc'd above the nicke,
Ran backe, and in a moment was unravell'd all.

JOLAS. Now by the love I beare to Justice, that Nunn'rie
Was too severe; when vertuous love's a crime
What man can hope to scape a punishment,
Or who's indeed so wretched to desire it?

THERSAMES. Right!

JOLAS. What answer made you, Sir?

THERSAMES. None,
They gave me till to morrow, and ere that be,
Or they or I must know our destinie:
Come friend let's in, there is no sleeping now;
For time is short, and we have much to doe.

Exeunt.

Enter ORSAMES, PHILAN, [*two*] *Courtiers.* [II. ii]

ORSAMES. Judge you, Gentlemen, if I be not as unfortunate as a gamester thinks himselfe upon the losse of the last stake; this is the first she I ever swore too heartifye, and (by those eyes) I thinke I had continued unperjur'd a whole moneth, (and that's faire you'll say.)

1. COURTIER. Verie faire———

ORSAMES. Had she not run mad betwixt.———

2. COURTIER. How? mad? who? *Semanthe*?

ORSAMES. Yea, yea, mad, aske *Philan* else.
People that want cleere intervalls talke not
So wildly: Ile tell you Gallants; 'tis now,
Since first I found my selfe a little hot,
And quivering 'bout the heart, some ten dayes since,
(A tedious Ague) Sirs; (but what of that?)
The gratious glance, and little whisper past,
Approches made from th'hand unto the lip,
I came to visit her, and (as you know we use)
Breathing a sigh or two by way of prologue,
Told her, that in Loves Physicke 'twas a rule,
Where the disease had birth to seeke a cure;
I had no sooner nam'd love to her,

72 who's] whoe *R* 77 we] me *R*
II. ii. 3 too heartifye] *R*; to heartily *FA46*; to heartily] *Ag*

But she began to talke of Flames, and Flames,
Neither devouring, nor devour'd, of Aire,
And of Camelions———

1. COURTIER. Oh the *Platoniques.*

2. COURTIER. Those of the new religion in love! your Lordship's merrie, troth how doe you like the humor on't?

ORSAMES. As thou would'st like red haire, or leannesse in thy Mistresse, scurvily; 'tdoes worse with handsomnesse, than strong desire would doe with impotence; a meere tricke to inhance the price of kisses———

PHILAN. Sure these silly women, when they feed our expectation so high, doe but like ignorant Conjurers, that raise a Spirit which handsomly they cannot lay againe.

ORSAMES. True, 'tis like some that nourish up young Lions till they grow so great, they are affraid of them theirselves, they dare not grant at last, for feare they should not satisfie.

PHILAN. Who's for the Towne? I must take up againe.

ORSAMES. This villanous Love's as chargeable as the Philosophers Stone, and thy Mistresse as hard to compasse too!

PHILAN. The Platonique is ever so; they are as tedious before they come to the point, as an old man fall'n into the Stories of his youth———

2. COURTIER. Or a widow into the praises of her first husband.

ORSAMES. Well, if she hold out but one moneth longer, if I doe not quite forget, I ere beleaguer'd there, and remove the siege to another place, may all the curses beguil'd virgins lose upon their perjur'd Lovers fall upon mee.

PHILAN. And thou woult deserve 'em all.

ORSAMES. For what?

PHILAN. For being in the company of those that tooke away the Prince's Mistresse from him.

ORSAMES. Peace, that will be redeem'd——— I put but on this wildnesse to disguise my selfe; there are brave things in hand, hearke i'thy eare:——— (*Whisper.*)

1. COURTIER. Some severe plot upon a maiden-head. These two young Lords make love, as Embroyderers worke against a Maske, night and day; They thinke importunitie a neerer way than merit,

24 Those] These *R* 30 Sure] Methinks *R* 34 them theirselves] *R*; themselves *Ag* 38 thy] this *R* 47 woult] wilt *R* 51 but] *om. R*

and take women as Schoole-boyes catch Squirrells, hunt 'em up and downe till they are wearie, and fall downe before 'em.

ORSAMES. Who loves the Prince failes not———

PHILAN. And I am one: my injuries are great as thine, and doe perswade as strongly.

ORSAMES. I had command to bring thee; faile not and in thine owne disguise.

PHILAN. Why in disguise?

ORSAMES. It is the Princes policie and love; for if wee should miscarrie, some one taken might betray the rest; unknowne to one another, each man is safe, in his owne valour.

2. COURTIER. And what Mercers wife are you to cheapen now in stead of his silks?

ORSAMES. Troth; 'tis not so well; 'tis but a Cozen of thine——— come *Philan* let's along.

Exeunt.

Enter Queene [ORBELLA] *alone.* [II. iii]

ORBELLA. What is it thus within whispering remorse,
And calls Love Tyrant? all powers but his,
Their rigour and our feare have made divine!
But everie Creature holds of him by sense,
The sweetest Tenure; yea! but my husbands brother:
And what of that? doe harmlesse birds or beasts
Aske leave of curious Heraldrie at all?
Does not the wombe of one faire spring,
Bring unto the earth many sweet rivers,
That wantonly doe one another chace,
And in one bed, kisse, mingle, and embrace?
Man (Natures heire) is not by her will ti'de,
To shun all creatures are alli'd unto him,
For then hee should shun all; since death and life
Doubly allies all them that live by breath:
The Aire that does impart to all lifes brood,
Refreshing, is so neere to it selfe, and to us all,
That all in all is individuall:
But, how am I sure one and the same desire
Warmes *Ariaspes*: for Art can keepe alive
A beddred love.

62 thine] thy *R* 66 might] may *R* 66 rest;] ~‸ *Ag*; ~. *R*
II. iii. 14 since] for *R*

Enter ARIASPES.

ARIASPES. Alone, (Madam) and overcast with thought?
Uncloud—uncloud—for if wee may beleeve
The smiles of Fortune, love shall no longer pine
In prison thus, nor undelivered travell
With throes of feare, and of desire about it.
The Prince, (like to a valiant beast in nets)
Striving to force a freedome suddenly,
Has made himselfe at length, the surer prey:
The King stands only now betwixt, and is
Just like a single tree, that hinders all the prospect:
'Tis but the cutting downe of him, and wee———

ORBELLA. Why wouldst thou thus imbarque into strange seas,
And trouble Fate, for what wee have already?
Thou art to mee what thou now seek'st, a Kingdome;
And were thy love as great as thy ambition,
I should be so to thee.

ARIASPES. Thinke you, you are not Madam?
As well and justly may you doubt the truths,
Tortur'd, or dying men doe leave behinde them:
But then my fortune turnes my miserie,
When my addition shall but make you lesse;

ARIASPES. By this—and this—loves break-fast: *Kisses her.*
By his feasts too yet to come,
By all the beautie in this face,
Divinitie too great to be prophan'd———
ORBELLA. O doe not sweare by that;
Cankers may eat that flow'r upon the stalke,
(For sicknesse and mischance, are great devourers)
And when there is not in these cheeks and lips,
Left red enough to blush at perjurie,
When you shall make it, what shall I doe then?
ARIASPES. Our soules by that time (Madam)
Will by long custome so acquainted be,
They will not need that duller truch-man Flesh,
But freely, and without those poorer helps,
Converse and mingle; meane time wee'll teach
Our loves to speake, not thus to live by signes,
And action is his native language, Madam,

Enter ZORANNES *unseene.*

This box but open'd to the Sense will doe't.
ORBELLA. I undertake I know not what.
ARIASPES. Thine owne safetie (Dearest).
Let it be this night, if thou do'st *Whisper and kisse.*
Love thy selfe or mee.
ORBELLA. That's verie sudden.
ARIASPES. Not if wee be so, and we must needs be wise,
For when their Sunne sets, ours begins to rise. *Exeunt.*

ZORANNES *solus.*

ZORANNES. Then all my feares are true, and shee is false;
False as a falling Star, or Glow-wormes fire:
This Devill Beautie is compounded strangely,
It is a subtill point, and hard to know,
Whether't has in't more active tempting,
Or more passive tempted; so soone it forces,
And so soone it yeelds———
Good Gods! shee seiz'd my heart, as if from you
Sh'ad had Commission to have us'd mee so;
And all mankinde besides—and see,

60 this] his *R* 77.1 *unseene*] *om. R* 77 Thine] Thy *R* 78 do'st‸] *R*; ~; *Ag* 80 needs] *R*; now *Ag* 81 ours] our *R*

If the just Ocean makes more haste to pay
To needy rivers, what it borrow'd first,
Then shee to give, where shee nere tooke;
Mee thinks I feele anger, Revenges harbenger
Chalking up all within, and thrusting out
Of doores, the tame and softer passions;———
It must be so:
To love is noble frailtie, but poore sin
When wee fall once to Love, unlov'd agen.
Exit.

Enter KING, ARIASPES, JOLAS. [II.

ARIASPES. 'Twere fit your Justice did consider, (Sir)
What way it tooke; if you should apprehend
The Prince for Treason (which hee never did)
And which, unacted, is unborne
(At least will be beleev'd so); lookers on,
And the loud talking croud, will thinke it all
But water colours laid on for a time,
And which wip'd off, each common eye would see,
Strange ends, through stranger wayes.
KING. Think'st thou I will compound with Treason then?
And make one feare anothers Advocate?
JOLAS. Vertue forbid Sir, but if you would permit
Them to approch the roome (yet who would advise
Treason should come so neare?) there would be then
No place left for excuse.
KING. How strong are they?
JOLAS. Weake, considering the enterprize;
They are but few in number, and those few too,
Having nothing but their resolutions
Considerable about them. A Troope indeed
Design'd to suffer what they come to execute.
KING. Who are they are thus wearie of their lives?
JOLAS. Their names I cannot give you.
For those hee sent for, hee did still receive
At a back doore, and so dismist them too.
But I doe thinke *Ziriff* is one.———

93 it] is *R* 94 where shee nere tooke] *Ag corrupt*; were she neer too't *R*; where she nere justly tooke *is probably correct in meaning* 95 Mee] My *R*

II. iv. 12 forbid] forbids *R* 17 those] these *R* 18 Having] Have *R* 20 what] that *R*

KING. Take heed! I shall suspect thy hate to others,
Not thy love to mee, begot this service;
This Treason thou thy selfe do'st say has but
An houres age, and I can give accompt
Of him, beyond that time.———Brother,
In the little Tower where now *Aglaura's* prisoner,
You shall finde him; bring him along,
Hee yet doth stand untainted in my thoughts,
And to preserve him so, hee shall not stirre
Out of my eyes command till this great cloud
Be over.

JOLAS. Sir, 'twas the Prince who first———

KING. I know all that! urge it no more! I love
The man; and 'tis with paine, wee doe suspect,
Where wee doe not dislike: th'art sure hee will
Have some, and that they will come to night?

JOLAS. As sure as night will come it selfe.

KING. Get all our Guards in readinesse;
We will our selfe disperse them afterwards;
And both be sure to weare your thoughts within:
Ile act the rest.

Exeunt.

Enter PHILAN, ORSAMES, *Courtiers.* [II. v]

2. COURTIER. Well.—If there be not some great storme towards, nere trust mee; Whisper (Court Thunder) is in everie corner, and there has beene to day about the Towne a murmuring and buzzing, such as men use to make, when they doe feare to vent their feares.

1. COURTIER. True, and all the States-men hang downe their heads, like full ear'd corne; two of them where I sup't, ask't what time of night it was, and when 'twas told them, started, as if they had beene to run a race.

2. COURTIER. The King too (if you marke him,) doth faigne mirth and jollitie, but through them both, flashes of discontent, and anger make escapes.

ORSAMES. Gentlemen! 'tis pittie heav'n design'd you not to make the Almanacks. You ghesse so shrewdly by the ill aspects, or neere

27 thy] *om. R* 28 do'st] does *R* 33 doth] does *R* 36 'twas...first] that 'twas the Prince at first *R* 42 our] your
II. v. 6 them] them were *R* 7 it was] *om. R* 7 they had] tha'd *R* 11 make] *Ag*, *R*(*c*); makes *R*(*u*)

conjunctions of the great ones, at what's to come still; that without all doubt the Countrey had beene govern'd wholly by you, and plow'd and reap'd accordingly; for mee, I understand this mysterie as little as the new Love, and as I take it too, 'tis much about the Time that everie thing but Owles, and Lovers take their rest; Goodnight.———*Philan*—away. *Exeunt.*

1. COURTIER. 'Tis early yet; let's goe on the Queens side and foole a little; I love to warme my selfe before I goe to bed, it does beget handsome and sprightly thoughts, and makes our dreames halfe solid pleasures.

2. COURTIER. Agreed: agreed.

Exeunt.

Enter Prince [THERSAMES]: *Conspiratours*: [ORSAMES, PHILAN, *and Courtiers.*]

THERSAMES. Couldst thou not finde out *Ziriff*?
1. COURTIER. Not speake with him my Lord;
Yet I sent in by severall men.
ORSAMES. I wonder *Jolas* meets us not here too.
THERSAMES. 'Tis strange, but let's on now how ere;
When Fortunes, honour, life, and all's in doubt,
Bravely to dare, is bravely to get out.

Excursions: [*Enter*] *The Guard upon them.*

THERSAMES. Betrai'd! Betrai'd!
ORSAMES. Shift for your selfe Sir, and let us alone,
Wee will secure your way, and make our owne. *Exeunt.*

Enter the KING, *in his night gowne, and Lords.*

KING. Follow Lords, and see quick execution done,
Leave not a man alive.
Who treads on fire, and does not put it out,
Disperses feare in many sparks of doubt. *Exeunt.*

Enter Conspirators, and the Guard upon them.

ORSAMES. Stand friends, an equall partie——— *Fight.*
PHILAN. Brave *Orsames*, 'tis pleasure to dye neere thee.
ORSAMES. Talke not of dying *Philan*, we will live,
And serve the noble Prince agen.

15 you] us *R* 19 Goodnight. ——] ~, ‸ *Ag*; ~‸ ‸ *R* 19 S.D. *Exeunt.*] *Exit. Ag*; *om. R* 23 pleasures] pleasure *R* 24 Agreed: agreed] Agreed *R* III. i. 0.1 *Conspirators*] *and Conspirators R* 1 out] then *R*(*c*); them *R*(*u*) 2 Not] Noe nor *R* 10.1 S.D. *in his night gowne*] *R deleted*; *om. Ag* 15 *Fight*] *They fight R*

Three of the Conspirators fall, and three of the Kings side: ORSAMES *and* PHILAN *kill the rest.*

We are alone;
Off then with thy disguise, and throw it in the bushes;
Quick, quick; before the torrent comes upon us:
Wee shall be streight good Subjects, and I despaire not
Of reward for this nights service: so.———

They throw off their disguises.

Wee two now kill'd our friends! 'tis hard,
But 'tmust be so.

Enter ARIASPES, JOLAS, *two Courtiers, part of the Guard.*

ARIASPES. Follow! Follow!
ORSAMES. Yes; so you may, now y'are not likely to overtake.
JOLAS. *Orsames*, and *Philan*, how came you hither?
ORSAMES. The neerest way it seemes; you follow'd (thank you)
As if 'thad beene through quicksets.
JOLAS. 'Sdeath have they all escap'd?
ORSAMES. Not all, two of them wee made sure;
But they cost deare, looke here else.
ARIASPES. Is the Prince there?
PHILAN. They are both Princes I thinke,
They fought like Princes I am sure.

JOLAS *puls off the vizors.*

JOLAS. *Stephines*, and *Odiris*—we trifle. Which way tooke the rest?
ORSAMES. Sunke I thinke, two of them are certainly here abouts.
ARIASPES. Upon my life they swam the river; some streight to horse, and follow ore the bridge;———you and I my Lord, will search this place a little better.
ORSAMES. Your Highnesse will I hope remember, who were the men were in———
ARIASPES. Oh! feare not, your Mistresse shall know y'are valiant.
ORSAMES. *Philan*! if thou lov'st mee, let's kill them upon the place.
PHILAN. Fie: thou now art wild indeed; thou taught'st mee to be wise first, and I will now keepe thee so.—Follow, follow.

Exeunt.

22.1 S.D.] *placed at line 19 in Ag* 24.1 *two*] *with two R* 36 Sunke Earth-didapers—Philan, and I| Were watching when they would rise. *R* (*first version*); Sunke I thinke | Two of 'em I am certaine are hereabouts. *R* (*revised version*); Two of them are certainly here abouts. *Ag* 46 Follow, follow] *placed after* indeed *in line 45 R*

Enter AGLAURA *with a Lute.*

The PRINCE *comes and knocks within.*

THERSAMES. Madam!
AGLAURA. What wretch is this that thus usurps
Upon the priviledge of Ghosts, and walks
At mid-night?
THERSAMES. *Aglaura.*
AGLAURA. Betray mee not
My willing sense too soone, yet if that voyce
Be false———
THERSAMES. Open faire Saint, and let mee in.
AGLAURA. It is the Prince—as willingly as those
That cannot sleepe doe light; welcome (Sir,) *Opens.*
Welcome above.——— *Spies his sword drawne.*
Blesse mee,
What meanes this unsheath'd minister of death?
If, Sir, on mee quick Justice be to passe,
Why this? absence alas, or such strange lookes
As you now bring with you would kill as soone.
THERSAMES. Softly! for I, like a hard hunted Deere,
Have only hearded here; and though the crie
Reach not our eares, yet am I follow'd close:
O my heart! since I saw thee,
Time has beene strangely Active, and begot
A Monstrous issue of unheard of Storie:
Sit; thou shalt have it all! nay, sigh not.
Such blasts will hinder all the passage;
Do'st thou remember, how wee parted last?
AGLAURA. Can I forget it Sir?
THERSAMES. That word of parting was ill plac'd, I sweare,
It may be ominous; but do'st thou know
Into whose hands I gave thee?
AGLAURA. Yes into *Ziriffs* Sir.
THERSAMES. That *Ziriff* was thy brother, brave *Zorannes*
Preserv'd by miracle in that sad day
Thy father fell, and since thus in disguise,
Waiting his just revenge.

III. ii. 0.1 S.D. *with a*] *Ag*, *R*(*c*); playing on her *R*(*u*) 0.2 S.D. *within*] *om. R* 8 S.D. *sword drawne*] *Ag*, *R*(*c*); *naked Sword R*(*u*) 12 as] a *R*

AGLAURA. You doe amaze me, Sir.
THERSAMES. And must doe more, when I tell all the Storie.
  The King, the jealous King, knew of the marriage,
  And when thou thought'st thy selfe safe
  By my direction, thou wert his Prisoner;
  Unlesse I would renounce all right,
  And cease to love thee, (O strange, and fond request!)
  Immur'd thou must have beene in some sad place,
  And lockt for ever, from *Thersames* sight,
  For ever—and that unable to indure,
  This night I did attempt his life.
AGLAURA. Was it well done Sir?
THERSAMES. O no! extremely Ill!
  For to attempt and not to act was poore:
  Here the dead-doing Law, (like ill-paid Souldiers)
  Leaves the side 'twas on, to joyne with power.
  Royall villany now will looke so like to Justice
  That the times to come and curious posteritie
  Will finde no difference:
  Weep'st thou *Aglaura*? come, to bed my Love!
  And wee will there mock Tyrannie, and Fate,
  Those softer houres of pleasure, and delight,
  That like so many single pearles, should have
  Adorn'd our thread of life, wee will at once,
  By Loves mysterious power, and this nights help
  Contract to one, and make but one rich draught
  Of all.
AGLAURA. What meane you Sir?
THERSAMES. To make my selfe incapable of miserie,
  By taking strong preservative of happinesse:
  I would this night injoy thee.
AGLAURA. Doe: Sir, doe what you will with mee,
  For I am too much yours, to deny the right
  How ever claim'd—but———
THERSAMES. But what *Aglaura*?
AGLAURA. Gather not roses in a wet and frowning houre;
  They'll lose their sweets then, trust mee they will Sir.
  What pleasure can Love take to play his game out,

32 of the] of'th *R* 33 safe] *R*; *om.* *Ag* 39–40 indure, This night‸] ~‸ ~, *Ag*
50 pleasure] *Ag*, *R*(*c*); Terrour *R*(*u*) 62 frowning] *R*; frowing *Ag*

When death must keepe the Stakes——— *A noise without.*
Harke Sir———
Grave bringers, and last minutes are at hand;
Hide, hide your selfe, for Loves sake hide your selfe.
THERSAMES. As soone the Sunne may hide himselfe, as I.
The Prince of *Persia* hide himselfe?———
AGLAURA. O talke not Sir; the Sunne does hide himselfe
When night and blacknesse comes———
THERSAMES. Never sweet Ignorance,
He shines in th'other world then; and so shall I,
If I set here in glorie:
Opens the doore, enter ZORANNES.
Enter
Yee hastie seekers of life. *Zorannes.*———
AGLAURA. My brother!
If all the joy within mee come not out,
To give a welcome to so deare an object,
Excuse it Sir; sorrow locks up all doores.
ZORANNES. If there be such a Toy about you, Sister,
Keep't for your selfe, or lend it to the Prince;
There is a dearth of that Commoditie,
And you have made it Sir. Now?
What is the next mad thing you meane to doe?
Will you stay here? when all the Court's beset
Like to a wood at a great hunt, and busie mischiefe hastes
To be in view, and have you in her power.
THERSAMES. To mee all this———
For great griefe's deafe as well as it is dumbe,
And drives no trade at all with Counsell: (Sir)
Why doe you not Tutor one that has the Plague,
And see if hee will feare an after ague fit?
Such is all mischiefe now to mee; there is
None left is worth a thought, death is the worst
I know, and that compar'd to shame, does looke
More lovely now than a chaste Mistresse, set
By common woman—and I must court it Sir!
ZORANNES. No wonder if that heav'n forsake us,
When wee leave our selves: what is there done
Should feed such high despaire? were you but safe———

73 th'] the *R* 74 set] sitt *R* 75 Yee] You *R*

AGLAURA. Deare (Sir) be rul'd,
If love, be love, and magick too,
(As sure it is where it is true;)
Wee then shall meet in absence, and in spight
Of all divorce, freely enjoy together,
What niggard Fate thus peevishly denies.
THERSAMES. Yea: but if pleasures be themselves but dreames,
What then are the dreams of these to men?
That monster, Expectation, will devoure
All that is within our hope or power,
And ere wee once can come to shew, how rich
Wee are, wee shall be poore,
Shall wee not *Zorannez*?
ZORANNES. I understand not this;
In times of envious penurie (such as these are)
To keepe but love alive is faire, wee should
Not thinke of feasting him: come (Sir)
Here in these lodgings is a little doore,
That leads unto another; that againe,
Unto a vault, that has his passage under
The little river, opening into the wood;
From thence 'tis but some few minutes easie journey
Unto a Servants house of mine (who for his faith
And honestie, hereafter must
Looke big in Storie); there you are safe however;
And when this Storme has met a little calme,
What wild desire dares whisper to it selfe,
You may enjoy, and at the worst may steale.
THERSAMES. What shall become of thee *Aglaura* then?
Shall I leave thee their rages sacrifice?
And like dull Sea-men threatned with a storme,
Throw all I have away, to save my selfe.
AGLAURA. Can I be safe when you are not? my Lord!
Knowes love in us divided happinesse?
Am I the safer for your being here?
Can you give that you have not for your selfe?
My innocence is my best guard, and that your stay

106 Yea] *om. R* 121 some few minutes easie journey] *R second corr.*; some few minutes easie businesse *Ag*, *R first corr.*; a short howers easie businesse *R(u)* 131 I have away] *R*; away, I have *Ag*

Betraying it unto suspition, takes away.
If you did love mee?———
THERSAMES. Growes that in question? then 'tis time to part:———
Kisses her.
When wee shall meet againe Heav'n onely knowes,
And when wee shall I know we shall be old:
Love does not calculate the common way,
Minutes are houres there, and the houres are dayes,
Each day's a yeare, and everie yeare an age;
What will this come to thinke you?
ZORANNES. Would this were all the ill,
For these are prettie little harmlesse nothings;
Times horse runs full as fast, hard borne and curb'd,
As in his full carreere, loose-rain'd and spurr'd:
Come, come, let's away.
THERSAMES. Happinesse, such as men lost in miserie
Would wrong in naming, 'tis so much above them.
All that I want of it, all you deserve,
Heav'n send you in my absence.
AGLAURA. And miserie, such as wittie malice would
Lay out in curses, on the thing it hates,
Heav'n send mee in the stead, if when y'are gone
I welcome it, but for your sake alone. *Exeunt.*
Leads him out, and enters up out of the vault.
ZORANNES. Stir not from hence, Sir, till you heare from me,
So goodnight deere Prince.
THERSAMES. Goodnight deere friend.
ZORANNES. When wee meet next all this will but advance———
Joy never feasts so high,
As when the first course is of miserie.
Exeunt.

Enter three or foure Courtiers.

1. COURTIER. By this light—a brave Prince, hee made no more of the Guard, than they would of a Taylor on a Maske night, that has refus'd trusting before.

2. COURTIER. Hee's as Active as he is valiant too; did'st mark him how hee stood like all the points o'th' Compasse, and as good Pictures, had his eyes, towards everie man?

139.1 S.D. *Kisses her.*] *om. R* 163 of] *om. R* IV. i. 1–2 of the] oth' *R* 4 he is] *om. R*

3. COURTIER. And his sword too, all th'other side walk up and downe the Court now, as if they had lost their way, and stare, like Grey-hounds, when the Hare has taken the furze.

1. COURTIER. Right, and have more troubles about 'em than a Serving-man that has forgot his message when hee's come upon the place.———

2. COURTIER. Yonder's the King within, chafing, and swearing like an old Falconer upon the first flight of a young Hawke, when some Clowne has taken away the quarrie from her; and all the Lords stand round about him, as if hee were to be baited, with much more feare, and at much more distance,———

3. COURTIER. Than a Countrey Gentlewoman sees the Lions the first time: looke: hee's broke loose.———

Enter KING *and Lords.*

KING. Finde him; or by *Osiris* selfe, you all are Traitours;
And equally shall pay to Justice; a single man,
And guiltie too, breake through you all!

Enter ZORANNES.

ZORANNES [*aside*]. Confidence!
(Thou paint of women, and the States-mans wisdome,
Valour for Cowards, and of the guilties Innocence,)
Assist mee now.———
Sir, send these Starers off:
I have some businesse will deserve your privacie.
KING. Leave us.
JOLAS. How the villaine swells upon us? *Exeunt.*
ZORANNES. Not to punish thought, or keepe
It long upon the wrack of doubt, know Sir,
That by corruption of the waiting woman,
The common key of Secrets, I have found
The truth at last, and have discover'd all:
The Prince your Sonne was by *Aglaura's* meanes,
Convey'd last night unto the Cypresse Grove,
Through a close vault that opens in the lodgings:
Hee does intend to joyne with *Carimania*,
But ere hee goes, resolves to finish all

7 side] side now *R* 8 now] *om. R* 10 troubles] trouble *R* 10 'em] them *R* 18 S.P. 3. COURTIER] *R*; *om. Ag* 28 JOLAS. How the villaine swells upon us?] *om. R*

The rites of Love, and this night meanes to steale
What is behinde.
KING. How good is Heav'n unto mee!
That when it gave mee Traitours for my Subjects,
Would lend mee such a Servant!
ZORANNES. How just (Sir) rather,
That would bestow this Fortune on the poore.
And where your bountie had made debt so infinite
That it grew desperate, their hope to pay it——
KING. Enough of that, thou do'st but gently chide
Mee for a fault, that I will mend; for I
Have beene too poore, and low in my rewards
Unto thy vertue; but to our businesse;
The question is, whether wee shall rely
Upon our Guards agen?
ZORANNES. By no meanes Sir:
Hope on his future fortunes, or their Love
Unto his person, has so sicklied ore
Their resolutions, that wee must not trust them.
Besides, it were but needlesse here;
Hee passes through the vault alone, and I
My selfe durst undertake that businesse,
If that were all, but there is something else,
This accident doth prompt my zeale to serve you in.
I know you love *Aglaura* (Sir) with passion,
And would enjoy her; I know besides
Shee loves him so, that whosoere shall bring
The tidings of his death, must carrie back
The newes of hers, so that your Justice (Sir)
Must rob your hope: but there is yet a way——
KING. Here! take my heart; for I have hitherto
Too vainly spent the treasure of my love;
Ile have it coyn'd streight into friendship all,
And make a present to thee.
ZORANNES. Sir,
If any part of this rich happinesse,
(Fortune prepares now for you) shall owe it selfe
Unto my weake endevours, I have enough.
Aglaura without doubt this night expects

58 else] more *R* 69 Sir] *R*; *om. Ag*

The Prince, and why you should not then supply
His place by stealth, and in disguise———
KING. I apprehend thee *Ziriff*, but there's difficultie———
ZORANNES. Who trades in Love must be an adventurer, (Sir)
But here is scarce enough to make the pleasure dearer:
I know the Cave; your Brother and my selfe
With *Jolas*, (for those w'are sure doe hate him,)
With some few chosen more betimes will wait
The Princes passing through the vault; if hee
Comes first, hee's dead; and if it be your selfe,
Wee will conduct you to the chamber doore,
And stand 'twixt you and danger afterwards.
KING. I have conceiv'd of Joy, and am growne great:
Till I have safe deliverance, time's a cripple
And goes on crutches.———As for thee my *Ziriff*,
I doe here entertaine a friendship with thee,
Shall drowne the memorie of all patternes past;
Wee will oblige by turnes; and that so thick,
And fast, that curious studiers of it,
Shall not once dare to cast it up, or say
By way of ghesse, whether thou or I
Remaine the debtors, when wee come to die.

Exeunt.

Enter SEMANTHE, ORITHIE, PHILAN, ORSAMES, *Lords and Ladies.* [IV. ii]

ORITHIE. Is the Queene ready to come out?

PHILAN. Not yet sure, the Kings brother is but newly entred.

SEMANTHE. Come my Lord, the Song then.

ORITHIE. I! The Song.

ORSAMES. A vengeance take this love, it spoyles a voyce worse than the losing of a maiden-head. I have got such a cold with rising and walking in my shirt a nights, that a Bittorne whooping in a reed is better musike.

ORITHIE. This modestie becomes you as ill, my Lord, as wooing would us women; pray, put's not to't.

ORSAMES. Nay Ladies, you shall finde mee, as free, as the Musicians

84 With] *Ag*, *R*(*c*); And *R*(*u*) 81 betimes] by times *R*
IV. ii. 1 ORITHIE] SEMAN *R* 4 I!] *R*; *om. Ag* 11 as the] at the *R*

of the woods themselves; what I have, you shall not need to call for, nor shall it cost you any thing.

SONG.

Why so pale and wan fond Lover?
Prithee why so pale?
Will, when looking well can't move her,
Looking ill prevaile?
Prithee why so pale?

Why so dull and mute young Sinner?
Prithee why so mute?
Will, when speaking well can't win her,
Saying nothing doo't?
Prithee why so mute?

Quit, quit, for shame, this will not move,
This cannot take her;
If of her selfe shee will not Love,
Nothing can make her,
The Devill take her.

ORITHIE. I should have ghest it had been the issue of your braine, if I had not beene told so.

ORSAMES. A little foolish counsell (Madam) I gave a friend of mine foure or five yeares agoe, when he was falling into a Consumption.

Enter Queene [ORBELLA].

ORBELLA. Which of all you have seene the faire prisoner
Since shee was confinde?
SEMANTHE. I have Madam.
ORBELLA. And how behaves shee now her selfe?
SEMANTHE. As one
That had intrench'd so deepe in Innocence,
She fear'd no enemies, beares all quietly,
And smiles at Fortune, whil'st shee frownes on her.
ORBELLA. So gallant! I wonder where the beautie lies,
Sir, that thus inflames the royall bloud?

12 I] *Ag*, *R*(*c*); you *R*(*u*) 14–28 *SONG*] *See the 'Texts Consulted' for MSS and books containing variants of this song. The full collation of variants may be found in the notes on the text in volume one of this edition.* 30 so] ont *R* 32 yeares] yeare *R* 40 Sir] *R*; *om. Ag*

ORSAMES. Faces, Madam, are like bookes, those that
Doe study them know best, and to say truth,
'Tis still much as it pleases the Courteous Reader.
ORBELLA. These Lovers sure are like Astronomers,
That when the vulgar eye discovers, but
A Skie above, studded with some few Stars,
Finde out besides strange fishes, birds, and beasts.
SEMANTHE. As men in sicknesse scortch'd into a raving
Doe see the Devill, in all shapes and formes,
When standers by wondring, aske where, and when;
So they in Love, for all's but feaver there,
And madnesse too.
ORBELLA. That's too severe *Semanthe*;
But wee will have your reasons in the parke;
Are the doores open through the Gardens?
LORD. The King has newly led the way.

Exeunt.

Enter ARIASPES: ZORANNES, *with a warrant sealed.* [IV. iii]

ARIASPES. Thou art a Tyrant, *Ziriff*: I shall die
With joy.
ZORANNES. I must confesse my Lord; had but
The Princes ills prov'd sleight, and not thus dangerous,
Hee should have ow'd to mee, at least I would
Have laid a claime unto his safetie; and
Like Physicians, that doe challenge right
In Natures cures, look'd for reward and thanks;
But since 'twas otherwise, I thought it best
To save my selfe, and then to save the State.
ARIASPES. 'Twas wisely done.
ZORANNES. Safely I'me sure, my Lord! You know 'tis not
Our custome, where the Kings dislike, once swells to hate,
There to ingage our selves; Court friendship
Is a Cable, that in stormes is ever cut,
And I made bold with it; here is the warrant seal'd
And for the execution of it, if you thinke
Wee are not strong enough, wee may have
Jolas, for him the King did name.

41 S.P. ORSAMES] ORITHIE *Ag*, *R* IV. iii. 4 mee, at least‸] ~‸ ~, *R*
14 ever] never *R* 16 the] th *R*

ARIASPES. And him I would have named.
ZORANNES. But is hee not too much the Prince's (Sir?)
ARIASPES. Hee is as lights in Scenes at Masques,
What glorious shew so ere hee makes without,
I that set him there, know why, and how;

Enter JOLAS.

But here hee is.———
Come *Jolas*; and since the Heav'ns decreed,
The man whom thou should'st envie, should be such,
That all men else must doo't; be not asham'd
Thou once wert guiltie of it;
But blesse them, that they give thee now a meanes,
To make a friendship with him, and vouchsafe
To finde thee out a way to love, where well
Thou could'st not hate.
JOLAS. What meanes my Lord?
ARIASPES. Here, here hee stands that has preserv'd us all!
That sacrifis'd unto a publique good,
(The dearest private good wee mortalls have)
Friendship: gave into our armes the Prince,
When nothing but the sword (perchance a ruine)
Was left to doe it.
JOLAS. How could I chide my love,
And my ambition now, that thrust mee upon
Such a quarrell? here I do vow———
ZORANNES. Hold, doe not vow my Lord; let it deserve it first;
And yet (if Heav'n blesse honest mens intents)
'Tis not impossible. My Lord, you will
Be pleas'd to informe him in particulars,
I must be gone.———
The King I feare already has beene left
Too long alone.
ARIASPES. Stay—the houre and place.
ZORANNES. Eleven, under the Tarras walke.
ARIASPES. I will not faile you there.
ZORANNES. (*Goes out, returnes back againe.*) I had forgot:———
'Tmay be, the small remainder of those lost men

37 perchance] perhaps *R* 49 ARIASPES. I...there. ZORANNES. I...forgot:—] *R(c)*; I...forgot.— *R(u)*; I...there. I...forgot:— *Ag*, *one continuous speech by Zorannes 48–53*

That were of the Conspiracie, will come along with him:
'Twere best to have some chosen of the Guard
Within our call———

ARIASPES. Honest, and carefull *Ziriff*: *Exit* ZORANNES.

JOLAS *stands musing*.

How now Planet strooke?———

JOLAS. This *Ziriff* will grow great with all the world.

ARIASPES. Shallow man!
Short sightedder than Travellers in mists,
Or women that outlive themselves; do'st thou
Not see, that whil'st hee does prepare a Tombe
With one hand for his friend, hee digs a Grave
With th'other for himselfe?

JOLAS. How so?

ARIASPES. Do'st thinke hee shall not feele the weight of this,
As well as poore *Thersames*?

JOLAS. Shall wee then kill him too at the same instant?

ARIASPES. And say, the Prince made an unluckie thrust.

JOLAS. Right.

ARIASPES. Dull, dull, hee must not dye so uselesly.
As when wee wipe of filth from any place,
Wee throw away the thing that made it cleane,
So this once done, hee's gone.
Thou know'st the People love the Prince; to their rage
Something the State must offer up; who fitter
Than thy rivall and my enemy?

JOLAS. Rare! our witnesse will be taken.

ARIASPES. Pish! let mee alone.
The Giants that made mountaines ladders,
And thought to take great *Jove* by force, were fooles:
Not hill on hill, but plot on plot, does make
Us sit above, and laugh at all below us.

Exeunt.

Enter AGLAURA, *and a Singing Boy*. [IV. iv]

BOY. Madam, 'twill make you melancholly,
Ile sing the *Prince's* Song, that's sad enough.

AGLAURA. What you will Sir.

73 my] mine *R*

SONG.

No, no, faire Heretique, it needs must bee
But an ill Love in mee,
And worse for thee.
For were it in my Power,
To love thee now this hower,
More than I did the last;
'Twould then so fall,
I might not love at all;
Love that can flow, and can admit increase,
Admits as well an Ebb, and may grow lesse.

2.

True Love is still the same; the torrid Zones,
And those more frigid ones,
It must not know:
For Love growne cold or hot,
Is Lust, or Friendship, not
The thing wee have;
For that's a flame would die,
Held downe, or up to high:
Then thinke I love more than I can expresse,
And would love more, could I but love thee lesse.

AGLAURA. Leave mee! for to a Soule, so out of Tune
As mine is now, nothing is harmony:
When once the maine-spring, *Hope*, is falne into
Disorder; no wonder, if the lesser wheeles,
Desire, and *Joy*, stand still; my thoughts like Bees
When they have lost their King, wander
Confusedly up and downe, and settle no where.

Enter ORITHIE.

Orithie, flie! flie the roome,
As thou would'st shun the habitations
Which Spirits haunt, or where thy nearer friends
Walk after death; here is not only Love,

IV. iv. 4–23 *SONG*] *See the 'Texts Consulted' for a list of manuscripts and books containing variants of this song. A full collation of variants may be found in the notes to the text in volume one of this edition. Here is given only the one substantive departure from copy.* 10 *'Twould*] *R, HL, Dx4, FA48 the play*; *It would Dx42*; *I would Ag, FA46 the poems*

But Loves plague too—mis-fortune; and so high,
That it is sure infectious!

ORITHIE. Madam,
So much more miserable am I this way than you,
That should I pitie you, I should forget my selfe:
My sufferings are such, that with lesse patience
You may endure your owne, than give mine Audience.
There is that difference, that you may make
Yours none at all, but by considering mine!

AGLAURA. O speake them quickly then! the marriage day
To passionate Lovers never was more welcome,
Than any kinde of ease would be to mee now.

ORITHIE. Could they be spoke, they were not then so great.
I love, and dare not say I love; dare not hope,
What I desire; yet still too must desire———
And like a starving man brought to a feast,
And made say grace, to what he nere shall taste,
Be thankfull after all, and kisse the hand,
That made the wound thus deepe.

AGLAURA. 'Tis hard indeed,
But with what unjust scales, thou took'st the weight
Of our mis-fortunes, be thine owne Judge now.
Thou mourn'st for losse of that thou never hadst,
Or if thou hadst a losse, it never was
Of a *Thersames*———
Would'st thou not thinke a Merchant mad, *Orithie*?
If thou shouldst see him weepe, and teare his haire,
Because hee brought not both the Indies home?
And wouldst not thinke his sorrowes verie just,
If having fraught his ship with some rich Treasure,
Hee sunke i'th' verie Port? This is our case.

ORITHIE. And doe you thinke there is such odds in it?
Would Heaven we women could as easily change
Our fortunes as ('tis said) wee can our minds.
I cannot (Madam) thinke them miserable,
That have the Princes Love.

AGLAURA. Hee is the man then———
Blush not *Orithie*; 'tis a sinne to blush

47 dare not hope] I dare not hope *R* 48 must] much *R* 60 Because] For that *R* 66 as ('tis said)] (as 'tis said) *R* 69 sinne] shame *R*

For loving him, though none at all to love him.
I can admit of rivalship without
A jealousie—nay shall be glad of it:
Wee two will sit, and thinke, and thinke, and sigh,
And sigh, and talke of love—and of *Thersames*.
Thou shalt be praising of his wit, while I
Admire he governes it so well:
Like this thing said thus, th'other thing thus done,
And in good language him for these adore,
While I want words to doo't, yet doe it more.
Thus will wee doe, till death it selfe shall us
Divide, and then whose fate 'tshall be to die
First of the two, by legacie shall all
Her love bequeath, and give her stock to her
That shall survive; for no one stock can serve,
To love *Thersames* so as hee'll deserve.

Enter KING, ZORANNES.

KING. What have wee here impossibilitie?
A constant night, and yet within the roome
That, that can make the day before the Sunne?
Silent *Aglaura* too?
AGLAURA. I know not what to say:
Is't to your pitie, or your scorne, I owe
The favour of this visit (Sir?) for such
My fortune is, it doth deserve them both.
KING. And such thy beautie is, that it makes good
All Fortunes; sorrow lookes lovely here;
And there's no man, that would not entertaine
His griefes as friends, were hee but sure they'd shew
No worse upon him—but I forget my selfe,
I came to chide.
AGLAURA. If I have sinn'd so high,
That yet my punishment reach not my crimes,
Doe Sir; I should be loth to die in debt
To Justice, how ill soere I paid
The scores of Love.———

76 Admire] *Ag*, *R*(*c*); Admirer *R*(*u*) 77 th'other] tother *R* 85.1 S.D. KING] *Ag*, *R*(*c*); KING. LORDS. *R*(*u*) 86 impossibilitie] impossibilities *R* 100 reach] *R*; equalls *Ag* 100 crimes] *R*; crime *Ag*

KING. And those indeed thou hast but paid indifferently
To mee; I did deserve at least faire death,
Not to be murthered thus in private:
That was too cruell, Mistresse.
And I doe know thou do'st repent, and wilt
Yet make mee satisfaction.

AGLAURA. What satisfaction Sir?
I am no monster, never had two hearts;
One is by holy vowes anothers now,
And could I give it you, you would not tak't,
For 'tis alike impossible for mee,
To love againe, or you love Perjurie.
O Sir! consider, what a flame love is.
If by rude meanes you thinke to force a light,
That of it selfe it would not freely give,
You blow it out, and leave your selfe i'th' darke.
The Prince once gone, you may as well perswade
The light to stay behinde, when the Sun posts
To th'other world, as mee; alas! wee two,
Have mingled soules more than two meeting brooks;
And whosoever is design'd to be
The murtherer of my Lord, (as sure there is,
Has anger'd heav'n so farre, that 'tas decreed
Him to encrease his punishment that way)
Would hee but search the heart, when hee has done,
Hee there would finde *Aglaura* murther'd too.

KING. Thou hast orecome mee, mov'd so handsomely
For pitie, that I will dis-inherit
The elder brother, and from this houre be
Thy Convert, not thy Lover.———
Ziriff, dispatch away———
And hee that brings newes of the Prince's welfare,
Looke that hee have the same reward, wee had
Decreed to him, brought tidings of his death.
'Tmust be a busie and bold hand, that would
Unlinke a chaine the Gods themselves have made:
Peace to thy Thoughts: *Aglaura*. *Exit.*

108 wilt] wouldst *R* 113 tak't] *R*; take it *Ag* 115 or] R; as *Ag*
136 had] have *R* 140 to] *om. R*

ZORANNES *steps back and speakes.*

ZORANNES. What ere he sayes beleeve him not *Aglaura*:
For lust and rage ride high within him now:
Hee knowes *Thersames* made th'escape from hence,
And does conceale it only for his ends:
For by the favour of mistake and night,
Hee hopes t'enjoy thee in the Prince's roome;
I shall be mist—else I would tell thee more;
But thou mayest ghesse, for our condition
Admits no middle wayes; either wee must
Send them to Graves, or lie ourselves in dust. *Exit.*

AGLAURA *stands still and studies.*

AGLAURA. Ha!
'Tis a strange Act thought puts me now upon;
Yet sure my brother meant the selfe same thing,
And my *Thersames* would have done't for mee:
To take his life, that seekes to take away
The life of Life, (honour) from mee, and from
The world, the life of honour, *Thersames*,
Must needs be something sure of kin to Justice.
If I doe faile, th'attempt howere was brave,
And I shall have at worst a handsome grave.

Exit.

Enter JOLAS, SEMANTHE.

SEMANTHE *steps back*, JOLAS *stayes her.*

JOLAS. What? are we growne, *Semanthe*, night, and day?
Must one still vanish when the other comes?
Of all that Love did ever yet bring forth
(And 't has beene fruitfull too,) this is the strangest
Issue.———
SEMANTHE. What my Lord?
JOLAS. Hate, *Semanthe*.
SEMANTHE. You doe mistake; if I doe shun you, 'tis,
As bashfull Debtors shun their Creditors,
I cannot pay you in the selfe same coyne,
And am asham'd to offer any other.

160 worst] worse *R*
IV. v. 3 Love did ever] *R*; ever Love did *Ag*

JOLAS. It is ill done, *Semanthe*, to plead bankrupt,
When with such ease you may be out of debt;
In loves dominions, native commoditie
Is currant payment, change is all the Trade,
And heart for heart, the richest merchandize.
SEMANTHE. 'Twould here be meane my Lord, since mine would prove
In your hands but a Counterfeit, and yours
In mine worth nothing; Sympathy not greatnesse,
Makes those Jewells rise in value.
JOLAS. Sympathy! O teach but yours to love then,
And two so rich no mortall ever knew.
SEMANTHE. That heart would Love but ill that must be taught;
Such fires as these still kindle of themselves.
JOLAS. In such a cold, and frozen place, as is
Thy breast? how should they kindle of themselves
Semanthe?
SEMANTHE. Aske how the Flint can carrie fire within?
'Tis the least miracle that Love can doe.
JOLAS. Thou art thy selfe the greatest miracle,
For thou art faire to all perfection,
And yet do'st want the greatest part of beautie,
Kindnesse; thy crueltie (next to thy selfe,)
Above all things on earth takes up my wonder.
SEMANTHE. Call not that crueltie, which is our fate;
Beleeve me *Jolas*, the honest Swaine
That from the brow of some steepe cliffe far off,
Beholds a ship labouring in vaine against
The boysterous and unruly Elements, ne're had
Lesse power, or more desire to help than I;
At everie sigh, I die, and everie looke,
Does move; and any passion you will have
But Love, I have in store: I will be angrie,
Quarrell with destinie, and with my selfe
That 'tis no better; be melancholy;
And (though mine owne disasters well might plead
To be in chiefe,) yours only shall have place;
Ile pitie, and (if that's too low) Ile grieve,
As for my sinnes, I cannot give you ease;

20 knew] sawe *R* 24 of]*Ag*, *R*(*c*); by *R*(*u*) 26 Aske‸] *R*; ~? *Ag*

All this Ile doe, and this I hope will prove
'Tis greater Torment not to love, than Love. *Exit.*

JOLAS. So perishing Sailours pray to stormes,
And so they roare agen. So men
With death about them, looke on Physitians that
Have given them o're, and so they turne away:
Two fixed Stars that keepe a constant distance,
And by lawes made within themselves must know
No motion excentrick, may meet as soone as wee:
The anger that the foolish Sea does shew,
When it does brave it out, and rore against
A stubborne rock that still denies it passage,
Is not so vaine and fruitlesse, as my prayers.
Yee mightie Powers of Love and Fate, where is
Your Justice here? It is thy part (fond Boy)
When thou do'st finde one wounded heart, to make
The other so, but if thy Tyranny
Be such, that thou wilt leave one breast to hate,
If wee must live, and this survive,
How much more cruell's Fate?

Exit.

Enter ZORANNES, ARIASPES, JOLAS

JOLAS. A Glorious night! [v
ARIASPES. Pray Heav'n it prove so.
Are wee not there yet?
ZORANNES. 'Tis about this hollow. *Enter the Cave.*
ARIASPES. How now! what region are we got into?
Th'inheritance of night;
Have wee not mistaken a turning *Ziriff*,
And stept into the confines of some melancholy
Devills Territorie?

48 Ile] *R*; I *Ag* 51 roare] heare *Ag*, *R* 52 that] *om. R* 55 within] *FA48*; with *Ag*, *R* 59 stubborne] sullen *R* 66 this] thus '*The Invocation*' *in Poems FA46*
v (t). i. 6–10] *Ag-c*; *Ag-t reads*:
Are wee not mistaken a turning *Ziriff*,
And stept into some melancholy Devils Territorie?
Sure 'tis a part of the first *Chaos*,
That would endure no change.
R reads: the aires as blacke
As if twere made of Sinners Consciences
Resolvd to Attoms, sure tis the Gallerie
Of some melancholLie Spiritt.

JOLAS. Sure 'tis a part of the first *Chaos*,
That would not suffer any change.
ZORANNES. No matter Sir, 'tis as proper for our purpose,
As the Lobbie for the waiting womans:
Stay you here, Ile move a little backward,
And so wee shall be sure to put him past
Retreat, you know the word if't be the Prince.

Goes to the mouth of the Cave.

Enter KING.

Here Sir, follow mee, all's quiet yet.———
KING. Is hee not come then?
ZORANNES. No.
KING. Where's *Ariaspes*?
ZORANNES. Waiting within.
JOLAS. I doe not like this waiting, nor this fellowes leaving of us.
ARIASPES. This place does put odd thoughts into thee, then thou art in thine owne nature too, as jealous as Love, or Honor: weare thy sword in readiness, and thinke how neere wee are a crowne.

Hee [ZORANNES] *leads him* [the KING] *on, steps behinde him, gives the false word, they kill the* KING.

ZORANNES. Revenge!
So let's drag him to the light, and search his pockets;
There may be papers there that will discover
The rest of the Conspiratours.
Jolas, your hand——— *Draw him out.*
JOLAS. Whom have wee here? the King!
ZORANNES. Yes, and *Zorrannes* too, Illo! hoe!———

Enter PASITHAS *and others.*

Unarme them.
D'ee stare?
This for my Fathers injuries and mine:

Points to the KINGS *dead body.*

Halfe Love, halfe Duties Sacrifice.
This—for the noble Prince, an offering to friendship.

Runs at JOLAS.

17 Is hee] *Ag-c*, *R*; Hee is *Ag-t* 21–4 *R sets these lines to the right of lines 16–24, with an asterisk for insertion between Zorannes' words* within *: Revenge! 21 of] *Ag-c*; *om. Ag-t*, *R* 22 does] doth *R* 22 then] then then *R* 23 Love] *Ag-c*, *R*; either Love *Ag-t* 23 weare] *Ag-c*, *R*; Come weare *Ag-t* 24.1–2] S.D. *placed after line 20 Ag-c* 29 wee] *om. R.* 30.1 S.D.] *om. R* 33.1 *Points*] *Point R* 34 Sacrifice.] ~, *Ag*, *R*

JOLAS. Basely! and tamely——— *Dies.*
ARIASPES. What hast thou done?
ZORANNES. Nothing—kill'd a Traytour,
So—away with them, and leave us;
Pasithas be onely you in call.
ARIASPES. What do'st thou pawse?
Hast thou remorse already murtherer?
ZORANNES. No foole: 'tis but a difference I put
Betwixt the crimes: *Orbella* is our quarrell;
And I have thought it fit, that love should have
A nobler way of Justice, than Revenge
Or Treason; follow mee out of the wood,
And thou shalt be Master of this againe:
And then, best arme and title take it. *They goe out and enter agen.*
There——— *Gives him his sword.*
ARIASPES. Extremely good! Nature tooke paines I sweare,
The villaine and the brave are mingled handsomly.
ZORANNES. 'Twas Fate that tooke it, when it decreed
Wee two should meet, nor shall they mingle now.
Wee are but brought together strait to part.——— *Fight, Pawse.*
ARIASPES. Some Devill sure has borrowed this shape.
My sword ne're stay'd thus long to finde an entrance.
ZORANNES. To guiltie men, all that appeares is Devill,
Come Trifler, come.——— *Fight againe,* ARIASPES *falls.*
ARIASPES. Whither, whither, thou fleeting Coward life?
Bubble of Time, Natures shame, stay; a little, stay!
Till I have look'd my selfe into revenge,
And star'd this Traytour to a carcasse first.
———It will not be:——— *Falls.*
The Crowne, the Crowne too,
Now is lost—for ever lost—oh!—
Ambition's but an *Ignis fatuus,* I see
Misleading fond mortalitie,
That hurries us about, and sets us downe
Just—where—wee—first—begun——— *Dies.*
ZORANNES. What a great spreading mightie thing this was,

36 Basely...*Dies*] *om. R* 39 leave] *R*; leaves *Ag* 45 have thought] *Ag-c*; doe hold *Ag-t, R* 49 *They goe out*] *Exeunt R* 53 when it] *om. R* 55 but] *Ag-c, R*; *om. Ag-t* 55 S.D. *Fight*] *om. R* 55 *Pawse*] *Ag places at line 56* 58 appeares] appeare *Ag-c* 59 *Fight againe*] *They fight R* 61 little, stay] a while *R* 68 mortalitie] moralitie *R* 70 begun] began *R* 71 this was] was this *R*

And what a nothing now? how soone poore man
Vanishes into his noone-tide shadow?
But hopes o're fed have seldome better done:——— *Hollowes.*

Enter PASITHAS.

Take up this lump of vanitie, and honour,
And carrie it the back way to my lodging;
There may be use of States-men, when th'are dead:
So.—for the Cittadell now, for in such times
As these, when the unruly multitude
Is up in swarmes, and no man knowes which way
They'll take, 'tis good to have retreat. *Exeunt.*

Enter THERSAMES.

THERSAMES. The Dog-star's got up high, it should be late:
And sure by this time everie waking eare,
And watchfull eye is charm'd; and yet mee thought
A noyse of weapons strucke my eare just now.
'Twas but my Fancie sure, and were it more,
I would not tread one step, that did not lead
To my *Aglaura*, stood all his Guard betwixt,
With lightning in their hands;
Danger! thou Dwarfe drest up in Giants clothes,
Thou shew'st farre off, still greater than thou art:
Goe, terrifie the simple, and the guiltie, such
As with false Opticks, still doe looke upon thee:
But fright not Lovers, wee dare looke on thee
In thy worst shapes, and meet thee in them too.
Stay—These trees I made my marke, 'tis hereabouts,
———Love guide mee but right this night,
And Lovers shall restore thee back againe
Those eyes the Poets tooke so boldly from thee. *Exit.*

[*Enter*] AGLAURA *with a torch in one hand, and a dagger in the other.*

AGLAURA. How ill this does become this hand, much worse
This suits with this, one of the two should goe.
The shee within mee sayes, it must be this———
Honour sayes this—and honour is *Thersames* friend.

76 it] 't *R* 77 use] need *R* 91 Thou] *R*; That *Ag* 95 shapes] *Ag-c*; shape *Ag-t*, *R* 100 much] *Ag-c*, *R*; how much *Ag-t*

What is that shee then? is it not a thing
That sets a Price, not upon mee, but on
Life in my name, leading mee into doubt,
Which when 'tas done, it cannot light mee out?
For feare does drive to Fate, or Fate if wee
Doe flie, oretakes, and holds us, till or death,
Or infamie, or both doe cease us.——— *Puts out the light.*
Ha!—would 'twere in agen.
Antiques and strange mishapes,
Such as the Porter to my Soule, mine Eye,
Was ne're acquainted with, Fancie lets in,
Like a disrouted multitude, by some strange accident
Piec'd together; feare now afresh comes on,
And charges Love to home.
—Hee comes—hee comes——— *A little noyse below.*
Woman,
If thou would'st be the Subject of mans wonder,
Not his scorne hereafter, now shew thy selfe.

Enter Prince [THERSAMES] *rising from the vault, shee stabs him two or three times, hee falls, shee goes back to her chamber.*

Sudden and fortunate.
My better Angell sure did both infuse
A strength, and did direct it.

ZORANNES [*within*]. *Aglaura!*

Enter ZORANNES.

AGLAURA. Brother———

ZORANNES. The same.
So slow to let in such a long'd for Guest?
Must Joy stand knocking Sister, come, prepare, prepare.———
The King of *Persia's* comming to you strait!
The King!—marke that.

AGLAURA. I thought how poore the Joyes you brought with you,
Were in respect of those that were with mee:
Joyes are our hopes stript of their feares,
And such are mine; for know, deare Brother,

104 is it] *Ag-c*; it is *Ag-t*, *R* 107 out?] *Ag-c*; ~. *Ag-t*; ~‸ *R* 110 doe] *Ag-c*; doth *Ag-t*, *R* 113 Eye] Eyes *R* 115 disrouted] *Ag-c*; discontented *R*; distracted *Ag-t* 118 S.D.] *Ag-c*; *om. R*, *Ag-t* 120.2 S.D. *shee*] R; *shees Ag* 124.1 S.D. Enter ZORANNES] *placed at 123 Ag*, *R*

The King is come already, and is gone———marke that.

ZORANNES. Is this instinct, or riddle? what King? how gone?

AGLAURA. The Cave will tell you more———

[He] goes out, enters hastily againe.

ZORANNES. Some sad mistake—thou hast undone us all.
The Prince! the Prince! cold as the bed of earth
Hee lies upon, as senselesse too; death hangs
Upon his lips, like an untimely frost,
Upon an early Cherrie; the noble Guest,
His Soule, tooke it so ill that you should use
His old Acquaintance so, that neither pray'rs,
Nor teares, can e're perswade him back againe.———

AGLAURA *swounes: rubs her.*

Hold, hold! wee cannot sure part thus!
Sister! *Aglaura*! *Thersames* is not dead,
It is the Prince that calls———

AGLAURA. The Prince, where?———
Tell mee, or I will strait goe back againe,
Into those groves of Gessemine, thou took'st mee from,
And finde him out, or lose my selfe for ever.

ZORANNES. For ever.—I, there's it!
For in those groves thou talk'st of,
There are so many by-wayes, and odd turnings,
Leading unto such wild and dismall places,
That should wee goe without a guide, or stir
Before Heav'n calls, 'tis strongly to be feared
Wee there should wander up and downe for ever,
And be benighted to eternitie!———

AGLAURA. Benighted to eternitie?—What's that?

ZORANNES. Why 'tis to be benighted to eternitie;
To sit i'th'darke, and doe I know not what;
Unriddle at our owne sad cost and charge,
The doubts the learned here doe onely move———

AGLAURA. What place have murtherers brother there? for sure
The murtherer of the Prince must have
A punishment that Heaven is yet to make.———

ZORANNES. How is religion fool'd betwixt our loves,
And feares? poore Girle, for ought that thou hast done,

163 at] up *R* 163 cost] costs *R*

Thy Chaplets may be faire and flourishing,
As his in the *Elysium*.
AGLAURA. Doe you thinke so Sir?
ZORANNES. Yes, I doe thinke so.
AGLAURA. The juster Judges of our Actions,
Would they have beene severe upon our weaknesses,
Would (sure) have made us stronger.———
ZORANNES. Fie! those teares
A Bride upon the marriage day as properly
Might shed as thou; here widowes doo't
And marrie next day after:
To such a funerall as this, there should be
Nothing common———
Wee'll mourne him so, that those that are alive
Shall thinke themselves more buried far than hee;
And wish to have his grave, to finde his Obsequies:
But stay—the Body. *Brings up the bodie, shee swounes and dies.*
Agen! Sister—*Aglaura*—O speake once more,
Once more looke out faire Soule.—Shee's gone.—
Irrevocably gone.—And winging now the Aire,
Like a glad bird broken from some cage:
Poore Bankrupt heart, when 'thad not wherewithall
To pay to sad disaster all that was
Its due, it broke—would mine would doe so too.
My soule is now within mee
Like a well metled Hauke, on a blinde Faulk'ners fist;
Mee thinks I feele it baiting to be gone:
And yet I have a little foolish businesse here
On earth I will dispatch. *Exit.*

Enter PASITHAS, *with the body of* ARIASPES. [

PASITHAS. Let mee bee like my burthen here, if I had not as lieve kill two of the Bloud-royall for him, as carrie one of them; These Gentlemen of high actions are three times as heavie after death, as your private retir'd ones; looke if hee be not reduc'd to the state of a Courtier of the second forme now? and cannot stand upon his

172 Sir] *R*; *om. Ag* 173 AGLAURA. The] *R*; The *Ag* 175 ZORANNES. Fie] *R*; Fie *Ag* 176 Bride upon] Bridegroome on *R* 194 Mee] My *R* 196 earth‸] *R*; ~; *Ag*
v (t). ii. 0.1 S.D. PASITHAS] *servant to* Sorannez *R* 2 two] *Ag*, *R*(*c*); one *R*(*u*)

owne legs, nor doe any thing without help, Hum.—And what's become of the great Prince, in prison as they call it now, the toy within us, that makes us all talke, and laugh, and fight, I! why there's it; well, let him be what hee will, and where hee will, Ile make bold with the old Tenement here. Come Sir—come along.

Exit.

Enter ZORANNES. [v (t). iii]

ZORANNES. All fast too, here—They sleepe to night
I'their winding sheets I thinke, there's such
A generall quiet. Oh! here's light I warrant you:
For lust does take as little rest, as care, or age.———
Courting her glasse, I sweare; fie! that's a flatterer Madam,
In mee you shall see trulier what you are. *Knocks.*

Enter the Queene [ORBELLA].

ORBELLA. What make you up at this strange houre my Lord?
ZORANNES. My businesse is my boldnesse warrant (Madam),
And I could well afford t'have beene without it
Now, had Heav'n so pleas'd.
ORBELLA. 'Tis a sad Prologue;
What followes in the name of vertue?
ZORANNES. The King.
ORBELLA. I: what of him? is well is hee not?
ZORANNES. Yes.—If to be free from the great load
Wee sweat and labour under, here on earth
Be to be well, hee is.
ORBELLA. Why hee's not dead, is hee?
ZORANNES. Yes Madam, slaine—and the Prince too.
ORBELLA. How? where?
ZORANNES. I know not, but dead they are.
ORBELLA. Dead!
ZORANNES. Yes Madam.
ORBELLA. Didst see them dead?
ZORANNES. As I see you alive.
ORBELLA. Dead!

6 what's] what is *R* 8 all] *R*; *om. Ag* 8 I] yea *R* 9 there's] there is *R* v (t). iii. 1 All] *R*, *Ag-c*; All's *Ag-t* 3 you] *R*, *Ag-c*; *om. Ag-t* 6.1 S.D. *Enter the* QUEENE.] *om. R* 12 I] yea *R* 13–14 If...earth] If't be on's journey to the other world *Ag-c* 17 slaine] dead *Ag-c* 17 and...too] *om. Ag-c* 19] I doe not know particulars *Ag-c* 22 them] him *Ag-c* 23] Madam I know him as certainly dead, As I know you too must die heareafter *Ag-c*

Zorannes. Yes, dead.
Orbella. Well, wee must all die;
The Sisters spin no cables for us mortalls;
Th'are threds; and Time, and chance———
Trust mee I could weep now,
But watrie distillations doe but ill on graves,
They make the lodging colder. *Shee knocks.*
Zorannes. What would you Madam?
Orbella. Why my friends, my Lord;
I would consult, and know what's to be done.
Zorannes. Madam 'tis not so safe to raise the Court;
Things thus unsetled, if you please to have———
Orbella. Where's *Ariaspes*?
Zorannes. In's dead sleepe by this time sure.
Orbella. I know hee is not! find him instantly.
Zorannes. I'm gone.——— *Turnes back againe.*
But Madam, why make you choyce of him, from whom
If the succession meet disturbance, all
Must come of danger?
Orbella. My Lord, I am not yet so wise, as to be jealous;
Pray dispute no further.
Zorannes. Pardon mee Madam, if before I goe
I must unlock a secret unto you;
Such a one as while the King did breathe
Durst know no aire: *Zorannes* lives.
Orbella. Ha!
Zorannes. And in the hope of such a day as this
Has lingred out a life, snatching, to feed
His almost famish'd eyes,
Sights now and then of you, in a disguise.
Orbella. Strange! this night is big with miracle!
Zorannes. If you did love him, as they say you did,
And doe so still; 'tis now within your power!
Orbella. I would it were my Lord, but I am now
No private woman; if I did love him once
(As 'tis so long agoe, I have forgot)
My youth and ignorance may well excuse't.

26 Well] *om. Ag-c* 26 all die] die all *R* 28 threds] *Ag-c*, *R*; thred *Ag-t* 31 *Shee*] *om. R* 32 Lord] Lords *R* 33 consult, and know‸] *R*; ~‸ ~, *Ag* 36 sure] *Ag-c*; I'm sure *Ag-t*, *R* 45 unto] to *Ag-t* 48 the] *om. R* 57 As] *Ag-c*; And *Ag-t*, *R*

ZORANNES. Excuse it?
ORBELLA. Yes, excuse it Sir.
ZORANNES. Though I confesse I lov'd his father much,
And pitie him, yet having offer'd it
Unto your thoughts, I have discharg'd a trust;
And zeale shall stray no further.
Your pardon Madam. *Exit.*
Queene studies.

ORBELLA. May be 'tis but a plot to keep off *Ariaspes*
Greatnesse, which hee must feare, because hee knowes
Hee hates him: for these great States-men,
That when time has made bold with King and Subject,
Throwing downe all fence that stood betwixt their power
And others right, are on a change,
Like wanton Salmons comming in with flouds,
That leap o're wyres and nets, and make their way
To be at the returne to everie one a prey.

Enter ZORANNES, *and* PASITHAS *throwing downe the dead body of* ARIASPES. [*Exit* PASITHAS.]

ORBELLA. Ha! murthered too! treason—treason———
ZORANNES. But such another word, and halfe so loud,
And th'art———
ORBELLA. Why? thou wilt not murther mee too?
Wilt thou villaine?
ZORANNES. I doe not know my temper———
Discovers himselfe.

Looke here vaine thing, and see thy sins full blowne:
There's scarce a part in all this face, thou hast
Not beene forsworne by, and Heav'n forgive thee for't!
For thee I lost a Father, Countrey, friends,
My selfe almost, for I lay buried long;
And when there was no use thy love could pay
Too great, thou mad'st the principle away:
Had I but staid, and not began revenge
Till thou had'st made an end of changing,
I had had the Kingdome to have kill'd:
As wantons entring a Garden, take the first

59 Sir] *om. R* 64 but] *Ag-c, R*; *om. Ag-t* 67 has] was *R* 67 King] *R*; the King *Ag* 76 Wilt] Wouldst *R* 80 a] *Ag*, *R*(*c*); my *R*(*u*) 81 buried] busied *R*

Faire flower they meet, and treasure't in their laps,
Then seeing more, doe make fresh choyce agen,
Throwing in one and one, till at length
The first poore flower o're-charg'd, with too much weight
Withers, and dies: so hast thou dealt with mee,
And having kill'd mee first, I will kill———

ORBELLA. Hold—hold—
Not for my sake, but *Orbella's* (Sir); a bare
And single death is such a wrong to Justice,
I must needs except against it.
Finde out a way to make mee long a dying;
For death's no punishment, it is the sense,
The paines and feares afore that makes a death:
To thinke what I had had, had I had you,
What I have lost in losing of my selfe,
Are deaths farre worse than any you can give
Yet kill mee quickly, for if I have time,
I shall so wash this soule of mine with teares,
Make it so fine, that you would be afresh
In love with it, and so perchance I should
Againe come to deceive you.

Shee rises up weeping, and hanging downe her head.

ZORANNES. So rises day, blushing at nights deformitie:
And so the prettie flowers blubber'd with dew,
And over-washt with raine, hang downe their heads;
I must not looke upon her. *Goes towards him.*

ORBELLA. Were but the Lillies in this face as fresh
As are the roses; had I but innocence
Joyn'd to these blushes, I should then be bold,
For when they went a begging they were ne're deni'de;
'Tis but a parting kisse Sir———

ZORANNES. I dare not grant it.———

ORBELLA. Your hand Sir then, for that's a part I shall
Love after death (if after death wee love)
'Cause it did right the wrong'd *Zorannes*, here———

Steps to him, and open the box of poyson, ZORANNES *falls.*

Sleepe, sleepe for ever, and forgotten too,

88 treasure't] treasur'de *R* 111 over-washt] *Ag-c*, *R*; ever-washt *Ag-t* 113 S.P. ORBELLA] AGLAURA *R* 115 these] *Ag-c*; their *Ag-t*, *R* 116 a] *Ag-c*; on *Ag-t*, *R* 117 dare not] *Ag*, *R*(*c*); must *R*(*u*) 120.1 S.D. *open*] *opens R*

All but thy ills, which may succeeding time
Remember, as the Sea-man does his marks,
To know what to avoyd; may at thy name
All good men start, and bad too; may it prove
Infection to the Aire, that people dying of it
May helpe to curse thee for mee.———

Turnes to the body of ARIASPES.

Could I but call thee back as eas'ly now;
But that's a Subject for our teares, not hopes!
There is no piecing Tulips to their stalks,
When they are once divorc'd by a rude hand;
All wee can doe is to preserve in water
A little life, and give by courteous Art
What scanted Nature wants Commission for,
That thou shalt have: for to thy memorie
Such Tribute of moyst sorrow I will pay,
And that so purifi'd by love, that on thy grave
Nothing shall grow but Violets and Primroses,
Of which too, some shall be of the mysterious
Number, so that Lovers shall come thither
Not as to a Tombe, but to an Oracle.

Shee knocks, and raises the Court.

Enter: Ladies [ORITHIE *and* SEMANTHE] *and Courtiers, as out of their beds.*

ORBELLA. Come! Come! help mee to weep my selfe away,
And melt into a grave, for life is but
Repentance nurse, and will conspire with memorie,
To make my houres my tortures.
ORITHIE. What Scene of sorrow's this? both dead!
ORBELLA. Dead? I! and 'tis but halfe death's triumphs this:
The King and Prince lye somewhere,
Just such emptie truncks as these.
ORITHIE. The Prince?
Then in griefes burthen I must beare a part.
SEMANTHE. The noble *Ariaspes*—valiant *Ziriff* too. *Weeps.*
ORBELLA. Weep'st thou for him, fond Prodigall? do'st know
On whom thou spend'st thy teares? this is the man
To whom wee owe our ills; the false *Zorannes*

122 time] times *R* 123 marks] mark *R* 134 wants] *Ag*, *R*(*c*); makes *R*(*u*)
147 I] yea *R* 147 triumphs] triumph *R*

Disguis'd, not lost; but kept alive, by some
Incensed Power, to punish *Persia* thus:

Enter PASITHAS, *surveyes the bodies, findes his Master.*

Hee would have kill'd mee too, but Heav'n was just,
And furnisht mee with meanes, to make him pay
This score of villanie, ere hee could doe more.

PASITHAS. Were you his murth'rer then?

PASITHAS *runs at her, kills her, and flies.*

ORITHIE. Ah mee! the Queene.———*Rub her till shee come to her selfe.*

SEMANTHE. How doe you Madam?

ORBELLA. Well,—but I was better, and shall——— *Dies.*

SEMANTHE. Oh! shee is gone for ever.

Enter Lords in their night gownes, ORSAMES.

ORSAMES. What have wee here? a Church-yard? nothing
But silence, and grave?

ORITHIE. Oh! here has been (my Lords)
The blackest night the *Persian* world e're knew:
The King and Prince are not themselves exempt
From this arrest; but pale and cold, as these,
Have measured out their lengths.

LORD. Impossible! which way?

SEMANTHE. Of that wee are as ignorant as you:
For while the Queene was telling of the Storie,
An unknowne villaine here has hurt her so,
That like a sickly Taper, shee but made
One flash, and so expir'd.

Enter [PHILAN] *tearing in* PASITHAS.

PHILAN. Here hee is, but no confession.

ORSAMES. Torture must force him then:
Though 'twill indeed, but weakly satisfie
To know now they are dead, how they did die.

PHILAN. Come take the bodies up, and let us all
Goe drowne our selves in teares; this massacre
Has left so torne a state, that 'twill be policie
As well as debt, to weep till wee are blinde,
For who would see the miseries behinde?

[*Exeunt*]

156.1 *bodies*] *body R* 157 have] 'a *R* 162 S.D. *Dies*] *om. R* 163.1 S.D. ORSAMES] ORSAMES, PHILAN *Ag*; *om. R* 164 S.P. ORSAMES] *Ag*; LORD *R* 172 has] as *R* 176 S.P. ORSAMES] OR. *Ag*; *Ori. FA48*; LORDS *R*

EPILOGUE.

OUR Play is done, and yours doth now begin:
What different Fancies, people now are in?
How strange, and odd a mingle it would make,
If e're they rise; 'twere possible to take
All votes.———
But as when an authentique Watch is showne,
Each man windes up, and rectifies his owne,
So in our verie Judgements; first there sits
A grave Grand Jurie on it of Towne-wits;
And they give up their verdict; then agin
The other Jurie of the Court comes in
(And that's of life and death) for each man sees
That oft condemnes what th'other Jurie frees:
Some three dayes hence, the Ladies of the Towne
Will come to have a Judgement of their owne:
And after them, their servants; then the Citie,
For that is modest, and is still last wittie.
'Twill be a weeke at least yet e're they have
Resolv'd to let it live, or give't a grave:
Such difficultie, there is to unite
Opinion, or bring it to be right.

EPILOGUE FOR THE COURT.

SIR:

THAT th'abusing of your eare's a crime,
Above th'excuse any six lines in Rhime
Can make, the Poet knowes: I am but sent
T'intreat hee may not be a President,
For hee does thinke that in this place there bee
Many have done't as much and more than hee;
But here's, hee sayes, the difference of the Fates,
Hee begs a Pardon after't, they Estates.

FINIS.

Epilogue (*t*). 10 verdict] verdicts *R* 12 sees‸] ~; *Thompson*
Epilogue for the Court (*t*). 9 *R ends here, lacking the comic version of Act V.*

Aglaura

[The Tragi-Comic Version]

PROLOGUE.

FORE Jove, a mightie Sessions: and I feare,
Though kind last Sizes, 'twill be now severe;
For it is thought, and by judicious men,
Aglaura 'scap't onely by dying then:
But 'twould be vaine for mee now to indeare,
Or speake unto my Lords, the Judges here;
They hold their places by condemning still,
And cannot shew at once mercie and skill;
For wit's so cruell unto wit, that they
Are thought to want, that find not want i'th' play.
But Ladies you, who never lik'd a plot,
But where the Servant had his Mistresse got,
And whom to see a Lover dye it grieves,
Although 'tis in worse language that he lives,
Will like't w'are confident, since here will bee,
That your Sex ever lik'd, varietie.

PROLOGUE TO THE COURT.

TIS strange perchance (you'll thinke) that shee that di'de
At Christmas, should at Easter be a Bride:
But 'tis a privilege the Poets have,
To take the long-since dead out of the grave:
Nor is this all, old *Heroës* asleepe
'Twixt marble coverlets, and six foot deepe
In earth, they boldly wake, and make them doe
All they did living here—sometimes more too,
They give fresh life, reverse and alter Fate,
And yet more bold, Almightie-like create:
And out of nothing onely to defie
Reason, and Reasons friend, Philosophie.

Prologue to the Court (*c*). 11 defie] *Ag*(*u*); deifie *Ag*(*c*) 12 Philosophie.] ~, *Ag*

Fame, honour, valour, all that's great, or good,
Or is at least 'mongst us, so understood,
They give, heav'ns theirs, no handsome woman dies,
But if they please, is strait some star i'th' skies———
But oh———
How those poore men of Meetre doe
Flatter themselves with that, that is not true,
And 'cause they can trim up a little prose,
And spoile it handsomly, vainly suppose
Th'are Omnipotent, can doe all those things
That can be done onely by Gods and Kings.
[*To the King.*]
Of this wild guilt, hee faine would bee thought free,
That writ this Play, and therefore (Sir) by mee,
Hee humbly begs, you would be pleas'd to know,
Aglaura's but repriev'd this night, and though
Shee now appeares upon a Poets call,
Shee's not to live, unlesse you say shee shall.

Enter ZORANNES, PASITHAS, *and Guard: hee places 'em: and Exit* [ZORANNES]. [v (c). i]

A State set out.

Enter ZORANNES, JOLAS, ARIASPES.

JOLAS. A Glorious night!
ARIASPES. Pray Heav'n it prove so.
Are wee not there yet?
ZORANNES. 'Tis about this hollow. *They enter the Cave.*
ARIASPES. How now! what region are wee got into?
The inheritance of night;
Have wee not mistaken a turning *Ziriff*,
And stept into the confines of some melancholy
Devills Territorie?
JOLAS. Sure 'tis a part of the first *Chaos*,
That would not suffer any change.
ZORANNES. No matter Sir, 'tis as proper for our purpose,
As the Lobbie for the waiting womans:

v (c). i. 0.2 S.D. ZORANNES] ZIRIFF *in speech prefixes and stage directions in most of this act;* ZORANNES *in* v (c). i. 29–54, iii. 32–140 6–10 *See note on* v (t). i. 6–10

Stay you here, I'le move a little backward,
And so wee shall be sure to put him past
Retreat, you know the word if't be the Prince.

ZORANNES goes to the Doore.

Enter KING.

Here Sir, follow mee, all's quiet yet.

KING. Is hee not come then?

ZORANNES. No.

KING. Where's *Ariaspes*?

ZORANNES. Waiting within.

JOLAS. I doe not like this waiting, nor this fellowes leaving of us.

ARIASPES. This place does put odd thoughts into thee, then thou art in thine owne nature too as jealous, as Love, or Honour; weare thy sword in readinesse, and thinke how neere wee are a Crowne.

ZORANNES. Revenge!——— *Guard seiseth on 'em.*

KING. Ha! what's this?

ZORANNES. Bring them forth.——— *Brings them forth.*

ARIASPES. The King.

ZORANNES. Yes, and the Princes friend———

Discovers himselfe.

D'you know this face?

KING. *Zorannes.*

ZORANNES. The verie same,
The wrong'd *Zorannes*,—King—D'you stare,———
Away with them where I appointed.

KING. Traytours, let mee goe;
Villaine, thou dar'st not doe this———

ZORANNES. Poore Counterfeit,
How faine thou now would'st act a King, and art not:
Stay you,——— *To ARIASPES.*
Unhand him,——— *Whispers [to the Guard.]*
Leave us now. *Exeunt [Guard and prisoners.]*

Manet ARIASPES, ZORANNES.

ARIASPES. What does this meane?
Sure hee does intend the Crowne to mee.

ZORANNES. Wee are alone, follow mee out of the wood,

15 if't *Ag-t*; if it *Ag-c* 16 Here] *Ag-t*; ZIR. Here *Ag-c* 17 Is hee] Hee is *Ag-t* 21 of] *om. Ag-t* 23 weare] Come weare *Ag-t* 26 S.D.] *placed after line 20 Ag*

And thou shalt be Master of this againe,
And then best arme and title take it.

ARIASPES. Thy offer is so noble, in gratitude
I cannot but propound gentler conditions:
Wee will divide the Empire.

ZORANNES. Now by my fathers soule,
I doe almost repent my first intents,
And now could kill thee scurvily, for thinking
If I had a minde to rule, I would not rule
Alone; let not thy easie faith (lost man)
Foole thee into so dull an heresie;
Orbella is our quarrell, and I have thought it fit,
That love should have a nobler way of Justice,
Than Revenge, or Treason.
If thou dar'st dye handsomly, follow mee. *Exeunt.*

And enter both agen.

ZORANNES. There,——— *Gives him his sword.*

ARIASPES. Extremely good; Nature tooke paines I sweare,
The villaine and the brave are mingled handsomely.———

ZORANNES. 'Twas Fate that tooke it, when it decreed
Wee two should meet, nor shall they mingle now,
Wee are but brought together strait to part.———
Fight [*Pawse.*]

ARIASPES. Some Devill sure has borrowed this shape,
My sword ne're staid thus long to finde an entrance.

ZORANNES. To guiltie men, all that appeares is Devill;
Come trifler, come.——— *Fight.*

ARIASPES. Dog, thou hast it.

ZORANNES. Why then it seemes my star's as great as his,
I smile at thee. ARIASPES *pants, and runs at him to catch his sword.*
Thou now would'st have me kill thee,
And 'tis a courtesie I cannot afford thee;
I have bethought my selfe, there will be use
Of thee,———*Pasithas*—to the rest with him. *Exit.*
Enter PASITHAS, *and two of the Guard.* *Exeunt.*

Enter THERSAMES.

THERSAMES. The Dog-star's got up high, it should be late:
And sure by this time every waking eare,

50 have thought] doe hold *Ag-t* 59 but] *om. Ag-t* 62 appeares] *Ag-t*; appeare *Ag-c*

And watchfull eye is charm'd; and yet mee thought
A noyse of weapons struck my eare just now.
'Twas but my Fancie sure, and were it more,
I would not tread one step, that did not lead
To my *Aglaura*, stood all his Guard betwixt,
With lightning in their hands.
Danger, thou Dwarfe drest up in Giants clothes,
Thou shew'st far off still greater than thou art;
Goe, terrifie the simple, and the guiltie, such
As with false Opticks still doe looke upon thee:
But fright not Lovers, wee dare looke on thee
In thy worst shapes, and meet thee in them too.———
Stay—these trees I made my marke, 'tis hereabouts,
———Love guide mee but right this night,
And Lovers shall restore thee back againe
Those eyes the Poets tooke so boldly from thee. *Exit.*

A Taper, Table out.

Enter AGLAURA, *with a Torch in one hand, a Dagger in the other.*

AGLAURA. How ill this does become this hand? much worse
This suits with this, one of the two should goe:
The shee within mee sayes, it must be this,———
Honour sayes this—and honour is *Thersames* friend.
What is that shee then? Is it not a thing
That sets a price, not upon mee, but on
Life in my name, leading mee into doubt,
Which when 'thas done, it cannot light mee out?
For feare does drive to Fate, or Fate if wee
Doe flie, ore-takes, and holds us, till or death,
Or infamie, or both doe seise us. *Puts out the light.*
Ha!—would 'twere in agen. Antiques and strange mishapes,
Such as the Porter to my Soule, mine Eye,
Was ne're acquainted with, fancie lets in,
Like a disrouted multitude, by some strange accident
Piec'd together; feare now afresh comes on,
And charges Love to home.
———Hee comes—hee comes.——— *A little noyse below.*

79 Thou] *R*; That *Ag* 83 shapes] shape *Ag-t* 88 much] how much *Ag-c* 92 Is it] It is *Ag-t* 95 out?] ~. *Ag-t* 98 doe] doth *Ag-t* 102 disrouted] distracted *Ag-t* 105 S.D.] *om. Ag-t*

Woman,
If thou would'st be the Subject of mans wonder,
Not his scorne hereafter,—now shew thy selfe.

Enter THERSAMES *from the vault, she stabs him as he riseth.*

THERSAMES. Unkindly done———
AGLAURA. The Princes voyce, defend it Goodnesse!
THERSAMES. What art thou that thus poorely
Hast destroy'd a life?
AGLAURA. Oh sad mistake, 'tis hee!
THERSAMES. Hast thou no voyce?
AGLAURA. I would I had not, nor a being neither.
THERSAMES. *Aglaura*, it cannot be!
AGLAURA. Oh still beleeve so, Sir,
For 'twas not I indeed, but fatall Love.
THERSAMES. Loves wounds us'd to be gentler than these were;
The paines they give us have some pleasure
In them, and that these have not. Oh doe
Not say 'twas you, for that does wound agen.

Enter ZORANNES *with a taper.*

ZORANNES. Guard mee my better Angell,
Doe I wake? my eyes (since I was man)
Ne're met with any object gave them so much trouble;
I dare not aske neither to be satisfied,
Shee lookes so guiltily———
AGLAURA. Why doe you stare and wonder at a thing
That you your selfe have made thus miserable?
ZORANNES. Good gods, and I o'the partie too.
AGLAURA. Did you not tell mee that the King this night
Meant to attempt my honour, that our condition
Would not admit of middle wayes, and that wee must
Send them to graves, or lye our selves in dust?
ZORANNES. Unfortunate mistake! ZORANNES *knocks.*
I never did intend our safetie by thy hands:

Enter PASITHAS.

Pasithas, goe instantly and fetch *Andrages*
From his bed; how is it with you Sir?

119.1] S.D. *one line earlier in Ag Bodl*[2]; THERSAMES *continues speaking in Ag* 120 S.P. ZORANNES] ZIR. *MS. correction in Ag*

THERSAMES. As with the besieg'd: my soule is so beset
It does not know, whether't had best to make
A desperate sally out by this port or not!
AGLAURA. Sure I shall turne statue here.
THERSAMES. If thou do'st love mee, weepe not *Aglaura*:
All those are drops of bloud, and flow from mee.
[*Offers to kill herself*, ZORANNES *stays her hand*.]
ZORANNES. Now all the gods defend this way of expiation:
Think'st thou thy crime, *Aglaura* would be lesse,
By adding to it? or canst thou hope
To satisfie those powers, whom great sins
Doe displease, by doing greater?
AGLAURA. Discourteous courteise!
I had no other meanes left mee than this,
To let *Thersames* know I would doe nothing
To him, I would not doe unto my selfe,
And that thou takest away.
THERSAMES. Friend, bring mee a little nearer;
I finde a kinde of willingnesse to stay,
And finde that willingnesse something obey'd.
My bloud now it perswades it selfe you did
Not call in earnest, makes not such haste———
AGLAURA. Oh my dearest Lord,
This kindnesse is so full of crueltie,
Puts such an uglinesse on what I have done,
That when I looke upon it, needs must fright
Mee from my selfe, and which is more insufferable,
I feare from you.
THERSAMES. Why should that fright thee, which most comforts mee?
I glorie in it, and shall smile i'th' grave,
To thinke our love was such, that nothing
But it selfe could e're destroy it.
AGLAURA. Destroy it? can it have ever end?
Will you not be thus courteous then in the other world?
Shall wee not be together there as here?
THERSAMES. I cannot tell whether I may or not.
AGLAURA. Not tell?

142.1 S.D.] *MS. addition in Ag Bodl*[2] *badly cropped. What survives is:* ⟨offers to⟩ kill | ⟨herself, Zir⟩ if | ⟨stays her⟩ hand

THERSAMES. No:
The Gods thought mee unworthy of thee here,
And when thou art more pure,
Why should I not more doubt it?
AGLAURA. Because if I shall be more pure,
I shall be then more fit for you.
Our Priests assure us an *Elysium*,
And can that be *Elysium* where true Lovers
Must not meet? Those Powers that made our loves,
Did they intend them mortall,
Would sure have made them of a courser stuffe,
Would they not my Lord?
THERSAMES. Prethee speake still;
This musique gives my soule such pleasing businesse,
Takes it so wholly up, it findes not leasure to
Attend unto the summons death does make;
Yet they are loud and peremptorie now,
And I can onely——— *Faints.*
AGLAURA. Some pitying Power
Inspire mee with a way to follow him:
Heart wilt thou not breake yet of thy selfe?
ZORANNES. My griefes besot mee:
His soule will saile out with this purple tide,
And I shall here be found staring after't
Like a man that's come too short o'th ship,
And's left behinde upon the land.

Enter ANDRAGES.

Oh welcome, welcome, here lyes, *Andrages*,
Alas too great a triall for thy art.
ANDRAGES. There's life in him: from whence these wounds?
ZORANNES. Oh 'tis no time for storie.
ANDRAGES. 'Tis not mortall my Lord, bow him gently,
And help mee to infuse this into him;
The soule is but asleepe, and not gone forth.
THERSAMES. Oh—oh:———
ZORANNES. Hearke, the Prince does live.
THERSAMES. What e're thou art hast given mee now a life,

190 yet of thy] *Works 94*; it of thy *Ag* 195 S.D.] *Shee swounes Ag*; *MS. deletion in Bodl*[2] *copy of Ag*

And with it all my cares and miseries,
Expect not a reward, no not a thanks.
If thou would'st merit from mee,
(Yet wh'would be guiltie of so lost an action)
Restore mee to my quietnesse agen,
For life and that are most incompatible.

ZORANNES. Still in despaires:
I did not thinke till now 'twas in the power
Of Fortune to have robb'd *Thersames* of himselfe,
For pitie, Sir, and reason, live;
If you will die, die not *Aglaura's* murther'd,
That's not so handsome: at least die not
Her murthered, and her murtherer too;
For that will surely follow. Looke up, Sir;
This violence of Fortune cannot last ever:
Who knowes but all these clouds are shadowes,
To set off your fairer dayes; if it growes blacker,
And the stormes doe rise, this harbour's alwayes open.

THERSAMES. What say'st thou, *Aglaura*?

AGLAURA. What sayes *Andrages*?

ANDRAGES. Madam,
Would Heaven his mind would admit as easie cure,
As his body will. 'Twas onely want of bloud,
And two houres rest restores him to himselfe.

ZORANNES. And by that time it may be Heaven will give
Our miseries some ease: come Sir, repose
Upon a bed, there's time enough to day.

THERSAMES. Well, I will still obey, though I must feare
It will be with mee, but as 'tis with tortured men,
Whom States preserve onely to wrack agen.

Exeunt.
Take off table.

Enter ZORANNES *with a taper.*

ZORANNES. All fast too, here—They sleepe to night
I'their winding sheets I thinke, there's such
A generall quiet. Oh! here's light I warrant you:
For lust does take as little rest, as care, or age.

214 reason,] *FA46*; ~‸ *Ag*
v (c). ii. 1 All] All's *Ag-t* 3 you] *om. Ag-t*

Courting her glasse, I sweare; fie! that's a flatterer Madam,
In mee you shall see trulier what you are. *He knocks.*

Enter Queene [ORBELLA].

ORBELLA. What make you up at this strange houre my Lord?
ZORANNES. My businesse is my boldnesse warrant (Madam),
And I could well afford t'have beene without it
Now, had Heav'n so pleas'd.
ORBELLA. 'Tis a sad Prologue;
What followes in the name of vertue?
ZORANNES. The King———
ORBELLA. I: what of him? is well is hee not?
ZORANNES. Yes,—If to be on's journey to the other world
Be to be well, hee is.
ORBELLA. Why hee's not dead, is hee?
ZORANNES. Yes, Madam, dead.
ORBELLA. How? where?
ZORANNES. I doe not know particulars.
ORBELLA. Dead!
ZORANNES. Yes (Madam).
ORBELLA. Art sure hee's dead?
ZORANNES. Madam I know him as certainly dead,
As I know you too must die hereafter.
ORBELLA. Dead!
ZORANNES. Yes, dead.
ORBELLA. Well, wee must all die,
The Sisters spin no cables for us mortalls;
Th'are threds; and Time, and chance———
Trust mee I could weep now,
But watrie distillations doe but ill on graves,
They make the lodging colder. *Shee knocks.*
ZORANNES. What would you Madam?
ORBELLA. Why my friends, my Lord;
I would consult and know, what's to be done.
ZORANNES. (Madam) 'tis not so safe to raise the Court,
Things thus unsetled, if you please to have———
ORBELLA. Where's *Ariaspes*?

13 If...world] If to be free from the great load wee sweat and labour under, here on earth *Ag-t* 16 dead] slaine—and the Prince too *Ag-t* 18 I...particulars] I know not but dead they are *Ag-t* 21 Art...dead] Didst see them dead? *Ag-t* 22–3 As I see you alive. *Ag-t* 26 Well, wee] *Ag-t*; Wee *Ag-c* 28 threds] thred *Ag-t*

ZORANNES. In's dead sleepe by this time sure.
ORBELLA. I know hee is not! find him instantly.
ZORANNES. I'm gone.——— *Turnes back againe.*
But (Madam) why make you choyce of him, from whom
If the succession meet disturbance, all
Must come of danger?
ORBELLA. My Lord, I am not yet so wise, as to be jealous;
Pray dispute no further.
ZORANNES. Pardon mee (Madam) if before I goe
I must unlock a secret unto you;
Such a one as while the King did breathe
Durst know no aire: *Zorannes* lives.
ORBELLA. Ha!
ZORANNES. And in the hope of such a day as this
Has lingred out a life, snatching, to feed
His almost famish'd eyes,
Sights now and then of you, in a disguise.
ORBELLA. Strange! this night is big with miracle!
ZORANNES. If you did love him, as they say you did,
And doe so still; 'tis now within your power!
ORBELLA. I would it were, my Lord, but I am now
No private woman; if I did love him once,
(As 'tis so long agoe, I have forgot)
My youth and ignorance may well excuse't.
ZORANNES. Excuse it?
ORBELLA. Yes, excuse it Sir.
ZORANNES. Though I confesse I lov'd his father much,
And pitie him, yet having offer'd it
Unto your thoughts, I have discharg'd a trust;
And zeale shall stray no further.
(Your pardon Madam.) *Exit.*
ORBELLA. May be 'tis but a plot to keep off *Ariaspes*
Greatnesse, which hee must feare, because hee knowes
Hee hates him: for these great States-men,
That when time has made bold with King and Subject,
Throwing downe all fence that stood betwixt their power
And others right, are on a change,
Like wanton Salmons comming in with flouds,

36 sure] I'm sure *Ag-t* 45 unto] *Ag-t*; to *Ag-c* 67 King] *R the tragic version*; the King *Ag* (*both tragic and tragi-comic versions*)

That leap o're wyres and nets, and make their way
To be at the returne to everie one a prey.

Enter ZORANNES.

ZORANNES. Looke here vaine thing, and see thy sins full blowne:
There's scarce a part in all this face, thou hast
Not beene forsworne by, and Heav'n forgive thee for't!
For thee I lost a Father, Countrey, friends,
My selfe almost, for I lay buried long;
And when there was no use thy love could pay
Too great, thou mad'st the principle away:
As wantons entring a Garden, take the first
Faire flower they meet, and treasure't in their laps,
Then seeing more, doe make fresh choyce agen,
Throwing in one and one, till at the length
The first poore flower o're-charg'd, with too much weight
Withers, and dies: so hast thou dealt with mee,
And having kill'd mee first, I will kill———

ORBELLA. Hold—hold—
Not for my sake, but *Orbella's* (Sir); a bare
And single death is such a wrong to Justice,
I must needs except against it.
Finde out a way to make mee long a dying;
For death's no punishment, it is the sense,
The paines and feares afore that makes a death:
To thinke what I had had, had I had you,
What I have lost in losing of my selfe,
Are deaths farre worse than any you can give:
Yet kill mee quickly, for if I have time,
I shall so wash this soule of mine with teares,
Make it so fine, that you would be afresh
In love with it, and so perchance I should
Againe come to deceive you. *Shee rises up weeping, and hanging downe her head.*

ZORANNES. So rises day, blushing at nights deformitie:
And so the prettie flowers blubber'd with dew,
And over-washt with raine, hang downe their heads;
I must not looke upon her. *Queene goes towards him.*

ORBELLA. Were but the Lillies in this face as fresh

79 S.D. *Prompt Ag-c* 104 over-washt] ever-washt *Ag-t*

As are the roses; had I but innocence
Joyn'd to these blushes, I should then be bold,
For when they went a begging they were ne're deni'de;
'Tis but a parting kisse Sir———

ZORANNES. I dare not grant it.———

Enter PASITHAS *and two Guard.*

Pasithas—away with her.

[*Exeunt.*]

A bed put out: THERSAMES *and* AGLAURA *on it,* ANDRAGES *by.* [v

THERSAMES. Shee wake't mee with a sigh,
And yet shee sleepes her selfe, sweet Innocence,
Can it be sinne to love this shape,
And if it be not, why am I persecuted thus?———
Shee sighs agen, sleepe that drownes all cares,
Cannot I see charme loves? blest pillowes,
Through whose finenesse does appeare
The violets, lillies, and the roses
You are stuft withall, to whose softnesse
I owe the sweet of this repose,
Permit mee to leave with you this,——— *Kisses them, shee wakes.*
See if I have not wake't her; sure I
Was borne, *Aglaura*, to destroy thy quiet.

AGLAURA. Mine, my Lord;
Call you this drowsinesse a quiet then?
Beleeve mee, Sir, 'twas an intruder I much
Struggled with, and have to thanke a dreame,
Not you, that it thus left mee.

THERSAMES. A dreame! what dreame, my Love?

AGLAURA. I dream't (Sir) it was day,
And the feare you should be found here.

Enter ZORANNES.

ZORANNES. Awake; how is it with you, Sir?

THERSAMES. Well, extremely well, so well, that had I now
No better a remembrancer than paine,
I should forget I e're was hurt,

108 these] their *Ag-t* 109 a] on *Ag-t*

Thanks to Heaven, and good *Andrages.*
ZORANNES. And more than thanks I hope wee yet shall live
To pay him. How old's the night?
ANDRAGES. Far-spent I feare, my Lord.
ZORANNES. I have a cause that should be heard
Yet ere day breake, and I must needs entreat
You Sir to be the Judge in't.
THERSAMES. What cause, *Zorannes*?
ZORANNES. When you have promis'd———
THERSAMES. 'Twere hard I should denie thee any thing.
Exit ZORANNES.
Know'st thou, *Andrages*, what hee meanes?
ANDRAGES. Nor cannot ghesse, Sir; *Draw in the bed.*
I read a trouble in his face, when first
Hee left you, but understood it not.

Enter ZORANNES, KING, ARIASPES, JOLAS, *Queene* [ORBELLA], *and two or three Guard.*

ZORANNES. Have I not pitcht my nets like a good Huntsman?
Looke, Sir, the noblest of the Herd are here.
THERSAMES. I am astonished.
ZORANNES. This place is yours.——— *Helps him up* [*on the State*].
THERSAMES. What would'st thou have mee doe?
ZORANNES. Remember, Sir, your promise,
I could doe all I have to doe, alone;
But Justice is not Justice unlesse't be justly done:
Here then I will begin, for here began my wrongs.
This woman (Sir) was wondrous faire, and wondrous kinde,———
I, faire and kinde, for so the storie runs,
She gave me looke for looke, and glance for glance,
And every sigh like *Eccho's* was return'd;
Wee sent up vow by vow, promise on promise,
So thick and strangely multiplyed,
That sure we gave the heavenly Registers
Their businesse, and other mortalls oaths
Then went for nothing; wee felt each others paines,
Each others joyes, thought the same thoughts,
And spoke the verie same;
Wee were the same, and I have much adoe

v (c). iii. 55 thoughts] thought *Ag*

To thinke shee could be ill, and I not
Be so too, and after this, all this (Sir),
Shee was false, lov'd him, and him,
And had I not begun revenge,
Till shee had made an end of changing,
I had had the Kingdome to have kill'd.
What does this deserve?

THERSAMES. A punishment hee best can make
That suffered the wrong.

ZORANNES. I thanke you, Sir;
For him I will not trouble you; [*Points to* ARIASPES.]
His life is mine, I won it fairly,
And his is yours, hee lost it fouly to you—— [*Points to* JOLAS.]
To him, Sir, now: [*Points to* KING.]
A man so wicked that he knew no good,
But so as't made his sins the greater for't.
Those ills, which singly acted bred despaire
In others, he acted daily, and ne're thought upon them.
The grievance each particular has against him
I will not meddle with; it were to give him
A long life, to give them hearing,
Ile onely speake my owne.
First then, the hopes of all my youth,
And a reward which Heaven had settled on mee,
(If holy contracts can doe any thing)
Hee ravisht from mee, kill'd my father,
Aglaura's father, Sir, would have whor'd my sister,
And murther'd my friend, this is all:
And now your sentence, Sir.

THERSAMES. We have no punishment can reach these crimes:
Therefore 'tis justest sure to send him where
Th'are wittier to punish than we are here:
And cause repentance oft stops that proceeding,
A sudden death is sure the greatest punishment.

ZORANNES. I humbly thanke you, Sir.

KING. What a strange glasse th'have shew'd me now my selfe in;
Our sins like to our shadowes,
When our day is in its glorie scarce appear'd,
Towards our evening how great and monstrous they are.

ZORANNES. Is this all you have to say?——— *Drawes.*
THERSAMES. Hold: —now goe you up.
ZORANNES. What meane you, Sir?
THERSAMES. Nay, I denyed not you,———
[ZORANNES *mounts the state.*]

That all thy accusations are just,
I must acknowledge,
And to these crimes, I have but this t'oppose,
Hee is my Father, and thy Soveraigne.———
'Tis wickednesse (deare Friend) wee goe about
To punish, and when w'have murther'd him,
What difference is there 'twixt him and
Our selves, but that hee first was wicked?———
Thou now would'st kill him 'cause he kill'd thy Father,
And when th'hast kill'd, have not I the selfe same quarrell?
ZORANNES. Why Sir, you know you would your selfe have done it.
THERSAMES. True: and therefore 'tis I beg his life;
There was no way for mee to have redeem'd
Th'intent, but by a reall saving of it.
If hee did ravish from thee thy *Orbella*,
Remember that that wicked issue had
A noble parent, Love,—Remember
How he lov'd *Zorannes* when he was *Ziriff*,———
Ther's something due to that.———
If you must needs have bloud for your revenge,
Take it here—despise it not *Zorannes*: ZORANNES *turnes away.*
The gods themselves, whose greatnesse
Makes the greatnesse of our sins,
And heightens 'em above what wee can doe
Unto each other, accept of sacrifice
For what wee doe 'gainst them;
Why should not you, and 'tis much thriftier too:
You cannot let out life there, but my honour
Goes, and all the life you can take here,
Posteritie will give mee back agen;
See, *Aglaura* weepes:
That would have beene ill Rhetorique in mee,

112 S.D. *Be ready Courtiers, and Guard, with their swords drawne, at the brests of the Prisoners. Ag, deleted from Bodl*[2] *of Ag* 156 penitence;] ~, *Ag*

But where it is, it cannot but perswade.
ZORANNES. Th'have thaw'd the ice about my heart;
I know not what to doe.
KING. Come downe, come downe, I will be King agen;
There's none so fit to be the Judge of this
As I; the life you shew'd such zeale to save,
I here could willingly returne you back;
But that's the common price of all revenge.

Enter Guard, ORSAMES, PHILAN, *Courtiers*, ORITHIE, SEMANTHE.

JOLAS, ARIASPES. Ha, ha, ha: how they looke now?
ZORANNES. Death: What's this?
THERSAMES. Betray'd agen;
All th'ease our Fortune gives our miseries is hope,
And that still proving false, growes part of it.
KING. From whence this Guard?
ARIASPES. Why Sir,
I did corrupt, while we were his prisoners,
One of his owne to raise the Court; shallow
Soules, that thought wee could not countermine;
Come Sir, y'are in good posture to dispatch them.
KING. Lay hold upon his instrument: Fond man,
Do'st thinke I am in love with villany?
All the service they can doe mee here
Is but to let these see the right I doe
Them now is unconstrain'd, then thus I doe proceed.
Upon the place *Zorannes* lost his life,
I vow to build a tomb, and on that tomb
I vow to pay three whole yeares penitence;
If in that time I finde that heaven and you
Can pardon, I shall finde agen the way
To live amongst you.
THERSAMES. Sir, be not so cruell to your selfe; this is an age.
KING. 'Tis now irrevocable; thy Fathers lands
I give thee back agen, and his commands,
And with them leave to weare the Tyara,
That man there has abus'd.——— [*Points to* ARIASPES.]
To you *Orbella*,
Who it seemes are foule as well as I,
I doe prescribe the selfe same physick I

Doe take my selfe: but in another place,
And for a longer time, *Diana's* Nunnerie.
ORBELLA. Above my hopes.
KING [*To* ARIASPES]. For you, who still have beene
The ready instrument of all my cruelties,
And there have cancell'd all the bonds of brother,
Poyntes to ORBELLA.
Perpetuall banishment: nor, should
This line expire, shall thy right have a place.
ARIASPES. Hell and Furies. *Exit.*
KING [*to* JOLAS]. Thy crimes deserve no lesse, yet 'cause thou wert
Heavens instrument to save my life,
Thou onely hast that time of banishment,
I have of penitence.———
JOLAS. May it be plague and famine here till I returne. [*Exit.*]
[KING] *comes downe.* ZORANNES *offers to kiss his hand.*
KING. No: thou shalt not yet forgive mee.
Aglaura, thus I freely part with thee,
And part with all fond flames and warme desires;
I cannot feare new agues in my bloud: *Joynes there hands.*
Since I have overcome the charmes
Thy beautie had, no other ever can
Have so much power. *Thersames*, thou look'st pale;
Is't want of rest?
THERSAMES. No Sir; but that's a storie for your eare———
They whisper.
ORSAMES. A strange and happie change.
ORITHIE. All joyes wait on you ever.
AGLAURA. *Orithie*,
How for thy sake now could I wish
Love were no Mathematick point,
But would admit division, that *Thersames* might,
Though at my charge, pay thee the debt hee owes thee.
ORITHIE. Madam, I loved the Prince, not my selfe;
Since his vertues have their full rewards,
I have my full desires.

170.1 S.D.] *MS. addition in Bodl*² *of Ag* 178.1 S.D.] *MS. correction in Bodl*²; *Ag placed S.D. at line* 177: *Comes downe.* Ziriff *offers to kisse the Kings hand.* 179 S.P. KING] *MS. correction in Bodl*²; *Ag assigns* 179 *to* JOLAS *and* 180–6 *to* KING 182 S.D.] *MS. addition to Bodl*² *of Ag*

KING. What miracles of preservation have wee had?
How wisely have the stars prepar'd you for felicitie?
Nothing endeares a good more than the contemplation
Of the difficultie wee had to attaine to it:
But see, Nights Empire's out,
And a more glorious auspitiously does begin;
Let us goe serve the gods, and then prepare
For jollitie; this day Ile borrow from my vowes,
Nor shall it have a common celebration,
Since 'tmust be,
A high record to all posteritie.

Exeunt omnes.

EPILOGUE.

Playes are like Feasts, and everie Act should bee
Another Course, and still varietie:
But in good faith provision of wit
Is growne of late so difficult to get,
That doe wee what wee can, w'are not able,
Without cold meats to furnish out the Table.
Who knowes but it was needlesse too? may bee
'Twas here, as in the Coach-mans trade, and hee
That turnes in the least compasse, shewes most Art:
How e're, the Poet hopes (Sir) for his part,
You'll like not those so much, who shew their skill
In entertainment, as who shew their will.

FINIS.

EMENDATIONS OF ACCIDENTALS

This is a record of the changes that the editor has made in minor punctuation, lining of verse, capitalization, word separation, and the use of italics. After the bracket appears the original reading in the copy text, *Aglaura*, 1638. Occasionally the emendation is taken from an early edition, but no attempt has been made to record the alterations of accidentals through all derivative editions. When *Aglaura*, 1638, has lined prose as verse that fact has been noted, but the exact division not recorded, for the sake of economy. I have silently capitalized the first word in each line of verse, whereas *Ag* is normally uncapitalized; and dashes between the last word in a speech and a stage direction have often been silently removed.

Prologue

3 either good‸] ~,
3 the good‸] ~,

Prologue to the Court

2 fill,] ~‸

I. i

6 marrie,] ~‸
13 Where ‸] ~,
18] *Ag lines* Thou...well; | 'Tis...fine:
21–2] *Ag lines as prose*
24–5] *Ag lines* The...first | Shee...cur'd.
26 not?] *R*; ~‸ *Ag*
28 betroth'd.] ~?
29–30] *Ag lines* Some...heard. | Slight... nam'd,
35–6] *Ag lines* 'Tis...here | Have...her. | Since...Court,

I. ii

18 Pageant‸] ~,
19 now,] ~;
29 securely—] *R*; ~; *Ag*

I. iii

23 still,] ~;
33 most. Brought] most, brought
43 portall;] ~,
47 sonne. Come] sonne, come
49 vale;] ~,
52 alone;] ~,
56 What] what
56–60] *Ag lines as verse*
58 Come] come

I. iv

5 none.] ~,
7 me,] ~‸
5–8 None...safe?] *Ag lines as verse*
14 you;] ~,
14–18 Not...too.] *Ag lines as verse*
27–8] *Ag lines as verse*
37 money);] ~)‸
43 is—] ~‸
45 for] For
65–6] *Ag lines* Com...emist, | For...farre.
85–6] *Ag lines* What...use | To...dis- covered?
95–8 *gnomic pointing by* " *at the left margin*
105 grace;] ~,

I. v

4 These] these
13 before,] ~;
21 aire;] ~,
51–2] *One line in Ag*
55–7] *Ag lines* Nay...chambers. | Prithee ...good.
58 try;] ~,

I. vi

1] *Ag lines* Undresse mee:— | Is...*Jolina*?
31–2 Goe...enter] *R; One line in Ag*
36] *Ag lines* How now? | Thou...thee,
37–8 Such...messengers] *One line in Ag*
43 ill‸] ~,
45 preparation‸] *R;* ~— *Ag*
47] *Ag lines* A...*Thersames*, | Thou... betray'd
54 out‸] *R;* ~, *Ag*
61–2] *Ag lines* The...why | Thus... speake:
64 ghesse.] ~‸
81–2] *Ag lines* Upon...to | This...dye,
82 Let] let
99–100] *Ag lines* As...nights | To...love:—
105 privation‸] *R;* ~, *Ag*
113 come;] ~,
119–20] Madam...disguise] *One line in Ag*

II. i

1–5] *Ag lines as verse.*
3 it,] ~;
4 doe.] ~,
6 eare,] ~‸
11–12] *Ag lines* No...what | You... taken:
15] *Ag lines* To...yet— | 'Tis...woman.
27 more;] ~,
28–30] *R; Ag lines* 'Tis...lesse | By...ills, | Yet...here?
39] *Ag lines* Ha! | King...indeed,
51–2] *R; Ag lines* Which...make |It...agen.
56 ones‸] ~,
56–7] *R; Ag lines* A...be | Rais'd...circle
64 me,...refuse,] ~‸...~‸
69–70] *Ag lines* Now...Justice, | That... crime
74–5] *Ag lines* None...morrow, | And...I | Must...destinie:

II. ii

1–7] *Ag lines as verse*
10–13] *prose in Ag*
20–1] *Ag lines* I...she | Began...Flames,
26–33] *Ag lines as verse*
27 Mistresse, scurvily;] ~; ~,
41–7] *Ag lines as verse*
41 youth—] ~;
57 Squirrells,] ~‸
62 thee;] ~,

II. iii

2 powers‸] *R*; ~, *Ag*
3 rigour‸] *R*; ~, *Ag*
3 feare‸] *R*; ~, *Ag*
22 thought?] ~,
30 is‸] *R*; ~, *Ag*
36 great‸] *R*; ~, *Ag*
36 ambition,] ~;
59–61] *Ag lines* By...the | Beautie...great | To...prophan'd—
77 (Dearest).] (~)‸
91–2] *Ag lines* And...Ocean | Makes... pay

II. iv

4 unborne‸] ~;
5 so);] ~)‸
4–7] *Ag lines* And...so) | Lookers... croud, | Will...colours | Laid...time,
12 permit‸] ~,
16–20] *Ag lines* Weake, considering | The...number, | And...but | Their... them. | A...what | They...execute.
28–31] *Ag lines* This...say | Has...accompt | Of...Tower | Where... prisoner,
34–6] *Ag lines* And...so, | Hee...command | Till...over.
37–40] *Ag lines* I...more! | I...man; | And...suspect, | Where...dislike: | Th'art...some, | And...night?
42 readinesse;] ~,
42–5] *Ag lines* Get...selfe | Disperse... sure | To...rest.

II. v

1–26] *Ag lines as verse*

III. i

5 ere;] ~,
6 doubt,] ~‸
18 agen. We] ~; we
18 alone;] ~,
26 may, now‸] ~‸ ~,
28 seemes;] ~,
30 'Sdeath] 'sDeath
35–40] *Ag lines as verse*
40 bridge;—] ~;‸
41 you‸] ~,

III. ii

5 false‸—] ~.—
6] *R; Ag lines* It...Prince— | As ...those
8–9] *Ag lines* Welcome above— | Blesse ...death?
33–4] *Ag lines* And...direction, | Thou ...Prisoner;
36 O] ô
38 sight,] ~.
46 posteritie‸] ~,
47–8] *Ag lines* Will...*Aglaura*? | Come... Love!
62 houre;] ~,
65 Harke] harke
65–6] *Ag lines* When...Stakes— | Harke ...hand;
66 hand;] ~,
72–5] *Ag lines* Never...then; | And... glorie: | Enter | Yee...life. | *Zorannes*.—
75 *Zorannes*] *Sorannez*
91 fit?] ~;
92–9] *Ag lines* Such...left | Is...know, | And...now | Than...woman— | And

...Sir? | No...selves: | What...despaire? | Were...safe—
93 worst‸] ~,
96 Sir!] ~?
112 *Zorannes*] *Sorannez*
113 this;] ~,
115–16] *Ag lines* To...thinke | Of...Sir)
124 Storie);] ~)‸
140 Heav'n] *Heav'n*
159 me,] ~‸

IV. i

1–29] *Ag lines as verse*
6 man?] ~.
17 distance,———] ~,
26 now.———] ~.‸
29–30] *Ag lines* Not...thought, | Or...doubt, | Know Sir,
39–40] *Ag lines* The...meanes | To...behinde.
54] *Ag lines* Their...not | Trust them.
69 love;] ~,
69 Sir,] ~‸
74–6] *Ag lines* The...why | You...stealth, | And...disguise— | I...*Ziriff*, | But ... difficultie—
88 As] as

IV. ii

5–13] *Ag lines as verse*
24 move,] ~‸ *Ag*
29 ghest‸] ~,
29–32] *Ag lines as verse*
35–6 As...Innocence] *One line Ag*
39–40 lies, Sir,] ~‸ ~‸
41–3] *Ag lines* Faces...them | Know...still | Much...Reader.

IV. iii

1–3] *Ag lines* Thou...joy. | I...ills | Prov'd...dangerous,
38–40] *Ag lines* How...now, | That...vow—
41 Lord;] ~,
43–4] *Ag lines* 'Tis...impossible. | My...particulars,
56–61] *Ag lines* Shallow...mists, | Or...see, | That...hand | For...himselfe?
71 Prince;] ~,

IV. iv

4–13] *Stanza pattern as in the play text in FA48; Stanza one in Ag indents line 11 and does not indent 12 and 13. Stanza two in Ag indents line 18.*
25 now,] ~;
28 Bees] *Bees*
36–7 Madam...you,] *One line Ag*
52–4] *Ag lines* 'Tis...scales, | Thou...-fortunes, | Be...now.
57 *Thersames*—] *R;* ~. *Ag*
69 *Orithie*;] ~,
77 thing‸ said] thing, said
95 Fortunes;] ~,
99–100] *Ag lines* If . . . punishment | Reach...crimes,
105 mee;] ~,
136–7] *R; Ag lines* Looke...decreed | To ...death.
149 wayes;] ~,
151–2] *One line in Ag*
156 (honour) from mee,] *R;* (honour‸ from mee;) *Ag*
157 *Thersames*,] ~;
158 sure‸] *R;* ~, *Ag*

IV. v

4–5] *R; Ag lines* (And...is | The...issue.—
6 mistake;] ~,
16–17] *Ag lines* In...mine | Worth...greatnesse,
19 O] ô
21 taught;] ~,
33 fate;] ~,
45 place;] ~,

V (t). i

12 womans:] *Ag-c;* ~. *Ag-t*
15 Retreat,] *Ag-c;* ~: *Ag-t*
21–4] *Ag lines as verse*
26 pockets;] ~,
26–8] *Ag lines* So...search | His...will | Discover...Conspiratours.
39 us;] ~,
54 now.] ~‸
65 Crowne‸ too,] *R;* ~, ~‸ *Ag*
66 is lost—] *R;* ~, *Ag*
76 lodging;] ~,
93 thee:] *Ag-c;* ~. *Ag-t*
116 together;] *Ag-c;* ~, *Ag-t*
118–20] *Ag lines as prose*
128] *Ag lines* Must...prepare, | Prepare.—
133 Joyes‸] ~,
141–5] *Ag lines* Upon...lips, | Like ..

Cherrie; | The...ill | That...so, | That ...perswade | Him...againe.—
152 I,] I:
174] *R; Ag lines* Would...severe | Upon ...weaknesses,
177 thou;] ~,
185 O] ô
185–6] *R; Ag lines* Agen...*Aglaura*— | O...Soule.— | Shee's gone.—
190–1] *Ag lines* To...due, | It...too.
193 fist;] ~,

V (t). ii

9 it;] ~,

V (t). iii

1] *R; Ag lines* All...here— | They... night
3] *R; Ag lines* A...quiet. | Oh...you:
5 sweare;] ~,
8 warrant‸ (Madam),] ~, (~)‸
8–10] *R; Ag lines* My...warrant, | (Madam) | And...now, | Had... pleas'd.
10 Prologue;] ~,
13] *R; Ag lines* Yes.— | If...load
32 Lord;] *Ag-c* ~!; *Ag-t*
40–1] *R; Ag lines* If . . . disturbance, | All danger?
45–7] *R; Ag lines* I...one | As...aire: | *Zorannes* lives.
47 aire:] ~,
56 woman;] ~,
62 thoughts,] ~:
73] *R; Ag lines* Ha...too! | Treason— treason—
75 th'art‸—] ~. —
87] *indented in Ag*
87–8] *Ag lines* As...take | The...and | Treasure't...laps,
88 flower‸] *Ag-c;* ~, *Ag-t*
88 laps,] ~.
92] *R; Ag lines* Withers...dies: | So... mee,
95 (Sir);] (~)‸
102 selfe,] ~;
111 heads;] ~,
116 deni'de;] ~,
124 avoyd;] ~,
125 too;] ~,
127 mee.—] *R;* ~. *Ag*
139–41] *Ag lines* Of...be | Of...shall | Come...Oracle.
147 this:] ~,
148–9] *Ag lines* The...just | Such...these.
164–5] *R; Ag lines* What...here? | A... grave?
166 knew:] ~,
180 teares;] ~,
183] *indented in Ag*

EPILOGUE

21 Opinion,] ~;

PROLOGUE

6 here;] ~,

V (c). i

11–12 *Ag-c lines* No...our | Purpose... womans:
21–7] *Ag lines as verse*
33] *Ag lines* The...King— | D'you stare,—
38–9] *Ag lines* Wee...alone, | Follow...be | Master...againe,
41–2] *Ag lines* Thy...cannot | But... conditions:
42 conditions:] ~,
47–8] *Ag lines* If...rule, | I...alone; | Let...man)
48 Alone;] ~,
66 at thee.] ~,
67 thee;] ~,
79 art;] ~,
84 Stay—] *Ag-t;* ~, *Ag-c*
92 then? Is] *Ag-t*; then, is *Ag-c*
104 to] too
105 comes —] *Ag-t;* ~, *Ag-c*
105–7] *Ag lines* Woman...Subject | Of... hereafter,— | —Now...selfe.
109 Goodnesse!] ~?
112 hee!] ~?
114 be!] ~?
116 were;] ~,
118–19] *Ag lines* In...not. | Oh...agen.
122 trouble;] ~,
136–8] *Ag lines* As...besieg'd: | My... know, | Whether't...desperate | Sally ...not!
138 not!] ~?
142 expiation:] ~,
146 greater?] ~.
152 nearer;] ~,
155–6] *Ag lines* My...selfe | You...earnest, | Makes...haste—
183 still;] ~,
188–90] *Ag lines* Some...with | A...not | Breake...selfe?

190 selfe?] ~.
194–5] *Ag lines* And...staring | After't...ship,
218 Sir;] ~,
221 dayes;] ~,
224–7] *Ag lines* Madam...admit | As...will. | 'Twas...bloud,
226 will.] ~,
227–32] *Ag lines* And...Heaven | Will...ease: | Come...bed, | There's...day. | Well...obey, | Though...mee, | But...men,

v (c). ii

All unrevised passages have the same lining as they had in Ag-t, except for lines 42–3 which are lined in Ag-c My...be | Jealous...further. *and lines 66–8 which are lined in Ag-c* That...King | And...fence | That...power | And...change,
1 here—] ~‸
5 sweare;] ~,
8 warrant (Madam),] ~, (~)‸
10 Prologue;] ~,
47 aire:] ~,
54 power!] *Ag-t*; ~: *Ag-c*
56 woman;] ~,
62 thoughts,] ~:
80] *indented in Ag*
81 laps,] ~.
87 (Sir);] (~)‸
95 selfe,] ~;
104 heads;] ~,
109 deni'de;] ~,
110–11] *Ag lines* 'Tis...Sir— | I...her.

v (c). iii

12 her;] ~,
12–13] *Ag lines* See...her, | Sure...destroy | Thy quiet.
14 Lord;] ~,
26–7] *Ag lines* And...shall | Live...night?
34 Sir;] ~,
41 doe?] ~.
46–7] *Ag lines* This...wondrous | Kinde ...runs,
49 *Eccho's*] eccho's
49 return'd;] ~,
54 nothing;] ~,
59 (Sir),] (~)‸
63 kill'd.] ~,
66 Sir;] ~,
67 you;] ~,
74] *Ag lines* In...thought | Upon them.
76 with;] ~,
79 then,] ~‸
92–3] *Ag lines* What...selfe | In...shadowes,
95] *Ag lines* Towards...monstrous | They are.
108] *Ag lines* And...same | Quarrell?
109] *Ag lines* Why...selfe | Have...it.
110 life;] ~,
111–12] *Ag lines* There...have | Redeem'd...reall | Saving...it.
124 them;] ~,
134 agen;] ~,
143–6] *Ag lines* Why...prisoners, | One ...soules, | That...countermine;
148–9] *Ag lines* Lay...instrument: Fond...villany?
155 penitence;] ~,
157 pardon.] ~;
159 selfe;] ~,
160 irrevocable;] ~,
165–7] *Ag lines* I...physick | I...selfe: But...time, | *Diana's* Nunnerie.
179 mee.] ~:
181 desires;] ~,
182 bloud:] ~‸
185 power.] ~,
185 pale;] ~,
204 jollitie;] ~,
206] *not indented in Ag*

THE GOBLINS

A Comedy.

Preſented at the Private Houſe in Black-Fryers, by His *Majeſties* ſervants.

WRITTEN
By Sir JOHN SUCKLING.

LONDON,
Printed for *Humphrey Moſeley*, and are to be ſold at his ſhop, at the Signe of the Princes Armes in S[t] *Pauls* Churchyard.
MDCXLVI.

Title-page of the First Edition, in *Fragmenta Aurea*, 1646.
The Folger Library copy.

TEXTS CONSULTED

FA46	*Fragmenta Aurea*, 1646, the copy text.
FA48	*Fragmenta Aurea*, 1648, a corrected version.
	For 'Some drink, what boy, some drink' (III. ii)
Add.29	British Museum, Additional MS. 29291, *incomplete.*
MuSch	Bodleian Library, Mus. Sch. MS. b. 2, *with music by William Lawes.*
CCC	*Catch that Catch Can*, 1667, with music by William Lawes.
	For 'A round, a round, a round' (III. ii)
Folg.409	Folger Library, MS. V.a.409, with music.
	For 'A health to the nut brown lass' (III. ii)
Add.31	British Museum, Additional MS. 31432, music by William Lawes.
Drexel 40	New York Public Library, Drexel MS. 4041, with music.
WI	*Wits Interpreter*, 1655.
WM	*Wit and Mirth*, 1684.

The Goblins was reprinted in the collected editions of *Fragmenta*, 1658, '1658', 1672, the works of 1694–6, 1709, 1719, 1766, 1770, 1836, Hazlitt's editions 1874 and 1892, Thompson's edition of 1910, and in Dodsley's *Old Plays*, 1744, 1780, and 1825 (the last edited by J. P. Collier). See 'The Collected Editions' for further details.

PROLOGUE.

WIT in a Prologue, Poets justly may
Stile a new imposition on a Play.
When *Shakespeare*, *Beaumont*, *Fletcher* rul'd the Stage,
There scarce were ten good pallats in the age,
More curious Cooks then guests; for men would eat
Most hartily of any kind of meat;
And then what strange variety? each Play,
A Feast for Epicures, and that each day.
But marke how odly it is come about,
And how unluckily it now fals out:
The pallats are growne higher, number increas't,
And there wants that which should make up the Feast;
And yet y'are so unconscionable. You'd have
Forsooth of late, that which they never gave,
Banquets before and after.———
Now pox on him that first good Prologue writ,
He left a kind of rent charge upon wit;
Which if succeeding Poets faile to pay,
They forfeit all their worth, and thats their play:
Y'have Ladies humors, and y'are growne to that,
You will not like the man lesse that his boots and hat
Be right; no play, unlesse the Prologue be,
And Epilogue, writ to curiositie.
Well (Gentiles) 'tis the grievance of the place,
And pray consider't, for here's just the case;
The richnesse of the ground is gone and spent,
Mens braines grow barren, and you raise the Rent.

Prologue. 7 variety?] *FA48*; ~‸ *FA46*   11 growne‸ higher,] *FA48*; ~, ~‸ *FA46*; ~‸ high *Collier*

THE ACTORS

PRINCE, *in love with* Sabrina
ORSABRIN, *Brother to the* Prince, *yet unknowne*
SAMORAT, *belov'd of* Sabrina
PHILATELL, TORCULAR, } *Brothers to* Sabrina
NASHORAT, PELLEGRIN, } *Cavaliers, friends to* Samorat
TAMOREN, *King of the Theeves, disguised in Devils habit*
PERIDOR, *ambitious of* Reginella, *disguised in Devils habit*
STRAMADOR, *a Courtier, servant to the* Prince
ARDELAN, PIRAMONT, } *formerly servants to* Orsabrin's *father*
PHONTRELL, *servant to* Philatell
SABRINA, *belov'd by* Samorat
REGINELLA, *in love with* Orsabrin
PHEMILLIA, Sabrina's *maid*
Captaine and Souldiers
Two Judges
Two Lawyers
Two Sergeants
Gaoler
Constable
Taylor
Two Drawers
Fidlers
Clownes and Wenches
Theeves disguised in Devils habits, living under ground by the Woods
Guard Attendants

The Scene. FRANCELIA

The Actors. 1–30] *FA48*; *om. FA46*; *in FA48 the list of dramatis personae is headed: The Goblins.*

The Goblins

Enter as to a Duell: SAMORAT, PHILATELL, TORCULAR. [I. i]

SAMORAT. But my Lords, may not this harsh businesse
Yet be left undone!
Must you hate me because I love your sister;
And can you hate at no lesse rate then death?
PHILATELL. No, at no lesse:
Thou art the blaster of our fortunes,
The envious cloud that darknest all our day:
While she thus prodigally, and fondly
Throwes away her love on thee,
She has not wherewithall to pay a debt
Unto the Prince.
SAMORAT. Is this all?
TORCULAR. Faith, what if
In short we doe not thinke you worthy of her?
SAMORAT. I sweare that shall not make a quarrell.
I thinke so too;
'Have urg'd it often to my selfe;
Against my selfe have sworn't as oft to her,
Pray let this satisfie.
PHILATELL. Sure (*Torcular*) he thinks we come to talke
Looke you Sir;——— *Drawes.*
And brother since his friend has fail'd him,
Doe you retire.
TORCULAR. Excuse me (*Philatell*)
I have an equall interest in this,
And fortune shall decide it.
PHILATELL. It will not need, hee's come.

Enter ORSABRIN.

ORSABRIN. *Mercury* protect me! what are these?
The brothers of the high-way!
PHILATELL. A stranger by his habit.
TORCULAR. And by his looks a Gentleman.
Sir,—will you make one? We want a fourth.———

The Goblins] Francelia *FA46*, *FA48* I. i. *Headed* ACT I. SCENE I *Other acts headed simply* ACT II., ACT III. *etc. No scene divisions. FA46*, *FA48*

ORSABRIN. I shall be rob'd with a tricke now!
SAMORAT. My Lords excuse me! This is not civill.
In what concernes my selfe,
None but my selfe must suffer.———
ORSABRIN. A duell by this light,———
Now has his modestie,
And t'others forwardnes warm'd me.———*Goes towards them.*
Gentlemen, I weare a sword,
And commonly in readines,
If you want one, speake Sir.——— *To Samorat.*
I doe not feare much suffering.
SAMORAT. Y'are noble Sir,
I know not how t'invite you to it;
Yet, there is Justice on my side,
And since you please to be a witnesse
To our actions, 'tis fit you know our Story.———
ORSABRIN. No Story Sir, I beseech you,———
The cause is good enough as 'tis,
It may be spoil'd i'th telling.
PHILATELL. Come we trifle then.
SAMORAT. It is impossible to preserve, I see,
My honor and respect to her.
And since you know this too my Lord,
It is not handsome in you thus to presse me;
But come.———

TORCULAR *beckens to* ORSABRIN.

ORSABRIN Oh! I understand you Sir. *Exeunt.*

PHILATELL *and* SAMORAT *fight.*

PHILATELL. In posture still?———SAMORAT *receives a slight wound.*
Oh, y'are mortall then it seemes.
SAMORAT. Thou hast undone thy selfe rash man,
For with this bloud thou hast let out a spirit
Will vex thee to thy grave.———

Fight agen, SAMORAT *takes away* PHILATELLS *sword, and takes breath, then gives it him.*

SAMORAT. I'm coole agen,
Here my Lord.———

54 ORSABRIN. Oh] *FA48*; Oh *FA46* 55 still?] *FA48*; ~. *FA46* 55 S.D. SAMORAT...*wound*] *FA48*;—*A slight wound FA46* (*one line below*)

And let this Present bind your friendship.———
PHILATELL. Yes thus.——— *Runs at him.*
SAMORAT. Treacherous, and low.———

Enter ORSABRIN.

ORSABRIN. I have dril'd my gentleman,
I have made as many holes in him
As would sinke a Ship Royall in sight of the Haven:———
How now?——— SAMORAT *upon his knee.*
S'foot, yonder's another going that way too.———
Now have I forgot of which side I'm on,
No matter.
I'le help the weakest; there's some Justice in that.
PHILATELL. The Villaine sure has slaine my brother.
If I have any friends above,
Guide now my hand unto his heart.

ORSABRIN *puts it by, runs at him,* SAMORAT *steps in.*

SAMORAT. Hold noble youth! Destroy me not with kindnesse:
Men will say he could have kil'd me,
And that injustice should not be;
For honours sake, leave us together.
ORSABRIN. 'Tis not my businesse fighting——— *Puts up.*
Th'employment's yours Sir:
If you need me, I am within your call. [*Exit.*]
SAMORAT. The gods reward thee:———
Now *Philatell* thy worst.———

They fight agen, and close, SAMORAT *forces his sword.*

Enter ORSABRIN.

ORSABRIN. Hell and the Furies are broke loose upon us,
Shift for your selfe Sir.———

Flyes into the woods severall wayes pursued by Theeves in Devils habits.

Enter TORCULAR, *weak with bleeding.*

TORCULAR. It will not be,———My body is a Jade:
I feele it tire, and languish under me.
Those thoughts came to my soule
Like Screech-owles to a sick mans window.

Enter THEEVES *back agen.*

THEEVES. Here—here—

They bind him, and carry him away.

76 be;] *FA48*; ~$_\wedge$ *FA46*

TORCULAR. Oh! I am fetcht away alive. *Exeunt.*

Enter ORSABRIN.

ORSABRIN. Now the good gods preserve my senses right,
For they were never in more danger:
'Ith name of doubt, what could this be?
Sure 'twas a Conjurer I dealt withall:
And while I thought him busie at his praiers,
'Twas at his circle, levying this Regiment.
Heere they are agen.

Enter SAMORAT.

SAMORAT. Friend—Stranger—Noble youth—
ORSABRIN. Heere—heere—
SAMORAT. Shift, shift the place, the wood is dangerous,
As you love safety, follow me. *Exeunt.*

Enter PHILATELL.

PHILATELL. Th' have left the place,
And yet I cannot find the body any where———
May be he did not kill him then,
But he recover'd strength, and reacht the Towne———
———It may be not too.———
Oh that this houre could be call'd backe agen.
———But 'tis too late,
And time must cure the wound that's given by fate. *Exit.*

Enter SAMORAT, ORSABRIN.

ORSABRIN. I'th shape of Lions too sometimes, and Beares?
SAMORAT. Often Sir.
ORSABRIN. Pray unriddle.
SAMORAT. The wiser sort doe thinke them Theeves,
Which but assume these formes to rob
More powerfully.
ORSABRIN. Why does not then the State
Set out some forces and suppresse them?
SAMORAT. It often has (Sir) but without successe.
ORSABRIN. How so?
SAMORAT. During the time those leavies are abroad,
Not one of them appeares; there have been
That have attempted under ground;
But of those, as of the dead,
There has been no returne.
ORSABRIN. Strange.

SAMORAT. The common people thinke them a race
Of honest and familiar Devills,
For they do hurt to none, unlesse resisted;
They seldome take away, but with exchange;
And to the poore often give,
Returne the hurt and sicke recover'd,
Reward or punish, as they do find cause.
ORSABRIN. How cause?
SAMORAT. Why Sir, they blind still those they take,
And make them tell the stories of their lives,
Which known, they do accordingly.
ORSABRIN. You make me wonder! Sir,———
How long is't since they thus have troubled you?
SAMORAT. It was immediately upon
The great deciding day, fought
'Twixt the two pretending families,
The *Tamorens* and the *Orsabrins*.
ORSABRIN. Ha! *Orsabrin*?
SAMORAT. But Sir, that storie's sad, and tedious,
W'are entring now the Town,
A place lesse safe then were the Woods,
Since *Torcular* is slaine.
ORSABRIN. How Sir?———
SAMORAT. Yes.———
He was the Brother to the Princes Mistris,
The lov'd one too.
If wee do prize our selves at any rate,
We must embarque, and change the clime,
There is no safety here.
ORSABRIN. Hum.———
SAMORAT. The little stay we make,
Must be in some darke corner of the Towne:
From whence, the day hurried to th'other world,
Wee'le sally out to order for our journey.
That I am forc't to this, it grieves me not;
But (gentle youth) that you should for my sake———
ORSABRIN. Sir, loose not a thought on that.
A storme at Sea threw me on Land,

131 S.P. SAMORA· 'A48; *Sar. FA46* 139 *Tamorens*] *FA48*; *Samorats FA46*
156 that.] ~, *FA48*; ·~‸*FA46*

And now a Storme on Land drives me
To Sea agen.—
SAMORAT. Still noble.

Exeunt.

Enter NASHORAT, PELLEGRIN. [I. ii]

NASHORAT. Why? suppose 'tis to a Wench, you would not goe with me, would you?———

PELLEGRIN. To chuse,—to chuse,—

NASHORAT. Then there's no remedy.———*Flings down his hat, unbuttons himself, drawes.*

PELLEGRIN. What doest meane?———

NASHORAT. Why? since I cannot leave you alive, I will trie to leave you dead.

PELLEGRIN. I thanke you kindly Sir, very kindly. Now the Sedgly curse upon thee, and the great Fiend ride through thee, Booted and Spur'd, with a Sith on his necke; pox on thee, I'le see thee hang'd first; s'foot, you shall make none of your fine Points of honour up at my charge: take your course if you be so hot. Be doing,—be doing. *Exit.*

NASHORAT. I am got free of him at last: there was no other way; h'as been as troublesome as a woman that would be lov'd, whether a man would or not: and h'as watcht me as if he had been my Creditors Sergeant. If they should have dispatcht in the meane time, there would be fine opinions of me.—I must cut his throat in earnest, if it should be so.

Exit.

Enter [TORCULAR,] PERIDOR, TAMOREN, *with other Theeves, A horne sounds.* [I. iii]

THEEVES. A prize—A prize—A prize—

PERIDOR. Some duell (Sir) was faught this morning, this weakned with losse of blood, we tooke; the rest escap't.

TAMOREN. Hee's fitter for our Surgeon, then for us, hereafter wee'le examine him——— [*Two exit with* TORCULAR.]

Agen a shout. [*Enter more Theeves, with Prisoners.*]

THEEVES. A prize—A prize—A prize—

(*They set them down*) ARDELAN, PIRAMONT.

TAMOREN. *Bring them, bring them, bring them in,*
See if they have mortall Sin,

I. ii. 1 Why?] *FA48*; ~; *FA46*
I. iii. 0.1 S.D.] *FA48*; *Enter Theeves, A horne sounds. FA46*

Pinch them, as you dance about,
Pinch them till the truth come out.

PERIDOR. What art?

ARDELAN. Extreamely poore, and miserable.

PERIDOR. 'Tis well, 'tis well, proceed, no body will take that away from thee, feare not,—what Country?

ARDELAN. ———*Francelia.*

PERIDOR. Thy name?

ARDELAN. *Ardelan.*

PERIDOR. And thine.

PIRAMONT. *Piramont.*

PERIDOR. Thy story,—come———

ARDELAN. What story!

PERIDOR. Thy life, thy life.——— *Pinch him.*

ARDELAN. Hold, hold,———You shall have it;———(*He sighs.*) it was upon the great defeat given by the *Tamorens* unto the *Orsabrins*, that the old Prince for safety of the young, committed him unto the trust of *Garradan*, and some few servants more, 'mongst whom I fil'd a place.

TAMOREN. Ha! *Garradan*!

ARDELAN. Yes.

TAMOREN. Speake out, and set me nearer; so; void the place, proceed.——— [PERIDOR *and others withdraw.*]

ARDELAN. We put to Sea, but had scarce lost the sight of Land, ere we were made a prey to Pirates, there *Garradan*, resisting the first Boord, chang'd life with death; with him the servants too, ———all but my selfe and *Piramont.* Under these Pirats ever since was *Orsabrin* brought up, and into severall Countries did they carry him.

TAMOREN. Knew *Orsabrin* himselfe?

ARDELAN. Oh! no, his spirit was too great; we durst not tell him any thing, but waited for some accident might throw us on *Francelia*, 'bout which we hover'd often, and we were neere it now, but Heaven decreed it otherwise.——— *He sighs.*

TAMOREN. Why dost thou sigh?

ARDELAN. Why do I sigh? (indeed,) for teares cannot recall him; last night about the second watch, the winds broke loose, and vext our Ship so long, that it began to reele and totter, and like

24 *Tamorens*] *Samorats FA46* 46 Ship] *FA58*; Ships *FA46*

a drunken man, took in so fast his liquor, that it sunke downe i'th place.

TAMOREN. How did you scape?

ARDELAN. I bound my selfe unto a maste, and did advise my Master to do so, for which he struck me only, and said I did consult too much with feare.

TAMOREN. 'Tis a sad story.———Within there let them have Wine and Fire,———but hearke you,——— *Whispers.*

Enter Theeves with a POET.

THEEVES. A Prize,—A prize,—A prize.—

PERIDOR. Set him downe,———

POET.———*And for the blew,*——— *Sings.*

Give him a Cup of Sacke, 'twill mend his hew.———

PERIDOR. Drunke as I live.———Pinch him, pinch him. What art?

POET. I am a Poet, a poore dabler in Rime.

PERIDOR. Come confesse, confesse.

POET. I do confesse, I do want money.

PERIDOR. By the description hee's a Poet indeed. Well proceed.— *Pinch him.*

POET. What d'you meane?———Pox on you. Prethee let me alone.

Some Candles here,———
And fill us t'other Quart, and fill us
Rogue, Drawer, the t'other Quart,
Some small Beere.———
And for the blew,
Give him a Cup of Sack 'twill mend his hew.

TAMOREN. Set him by till hee's sober, come lett's go see our Duellist drest. *Exeunt.*

Enter Taylor, two Sergeants. [I.

TAYLOR. Hee's something tall, and for his Chin, it has no bush below: marry a little wooll, as much as an unripe Peach doth weare; just enough to speake him drawing towards a man.

SERGEANT. Is he of furie? Will he foine, and give the mortall touch?

TAYLOR. Oh no! He seldome weares his Sword.

53 Within there] *set to right margin as if a* S.D. *FA46* 59 Pinch him, pinch him] *Collier*; *set as* S.D. *FA46* 64.1 S.D. *Pinch him*] *Collier and Hazlitt set as dialogue*

SERGEANT. *Tope* is the word if he do. Thy debt, my little *Mirmidon*?

TAYLOR. A yard and a halfe I assure you without abatement.

SERGEANT. 'Tis well, 'tis wondrous well: is he retired into this house of pleasure?

TAYLOR. One of these hee's entred; 'tis but a little waiting. You shall find me at the next Taverne. *Exit.*

SERGEANT. Stand close, I here one comming.

Enter ORSABRIN.

ORSABRIN. This house is sure no Seminary for *Lucreces*; then the Matron was so over diligent, and when I ask't for meate or drinke, shee look't as if I had mistooke my selfe, and cald for a wrong thing. Well! 'tis but a night, and part of it I'le spend in seeing of this Towne, so famous in our Tales at Sea.

SERGEANT. Looke, looke, mufled, and as melancholy after't as a Gamester upon losse; upon him, upon him.

ORSABRIN. How now my friends, why do you use me thus?

SERGEANT. Quietly; 'twill be your best way.

ORSABRIN. Best way? for what?

SERGEANT. Why, 'tis your best way, because there will be no other; *Tope* is the word, and you must along.

ORSABRIN. Is that the word? Why then, this is my Sword.

SERGEANT. Murder, murder, murder; h'as kil'd the Princes Officer. Murder—Murder—Murder.— *Run away.*

ORSABRIN. I must not stay, I heare them swarme. *Exit.*

Enter Constable, People.

CONSTABLE. Where is he, where is he?

SERGEANT. Here,—here—oh a Manmender, a Manmender, has broacht me in so many places, all the Liquor in my body will run out.

CONSTABLE. In good sooth (neighbour) has tapt you at the wrong end too. He has been busie with you here behind, as one would say; lend a hand, some of you, and the rest follow me. *Exeunt.*

Enter ORSABRIN.

ORSABRIN. Still pursu'd! Which way now? I see no passage; I must attempt this wall,———Oh—a luckie doore. And open. *Exit.*

Enters agen.

Where am I now?
A garden, and a handsome house,

I. iv. 6 *Tope*] *Topo FA46* 24 *Tope*] *Topo FA46* 27 S.D. *Run away*,] *at line* 25 *FA46*

If't be thy will, a Porch too't, and I'm made;
'Twill be the better lodging of the two. *Goes to the Porch.*

Enter PHEMILLIA.

PHEMILLIA. Oh! welcome, welcome Sir,
My Lady hath been in such frights for you.
ORSABRIN. Hum! for me?———
PHEMILLIA. And thought you would not come to night.
ORSABRIN. Troth, I might very well have fail'd her.
PHEMILLIA. Shee's in the Gallery alone i'th darke.
ORSABRIN. Good, very good.
PHEMILLIA. And is so melancholly,——
ORSABRIN. Hum.———
PHEMILLIA. Have you shut the Garden doores?
Come I'le bring you to her, enter, enter.
ORSABRIN. Yes, I will enter:
He who has lost himselfe makes no great venter.
Exeunt.

Enter SABRINA, ORSABRIN. [II.

SABRINA. Oh welcome, welcome, as open aire to prisoners,
I have had such feares for you.
ORSABRIN [*aside*]. Shees warme, and soft as lovers language:
Shee spoke too, pretilie;
Now have I forgot all the danger I was in.
SABRINA. What have you done to day (my better part.)
ORSABRIN [*aside*]. Kind little Rogue!
I could say the finest things to her mee thinks,
But then shee would discover me,
The best way will be to fall too quietly.——— *Kisses her.*
SABRINA. How now my *Samorat*,
What saucy heat hath stolne into thy bloud,
And heightned thee to this?
I feare you are not well.
ORSABRIN [*aside*]. S'foot! 'tis a *Platonique*:
Now cannot I so much as talke that way neither.
SABRINA. Why are you silent, Sir?
Come, I know you have been in the field to day.

41.1 S.D. PHEMILLIA] MAID *FA46* 53.1 *Exeunt.*] *Exit. FA46*

ORSABRIN [*aside*]. How does shee know that?
SABRINA. If you have kill'd my brother, speake:
It is no new thing that true Love
Should be unfortunate.
ORSABRIN [*aside*]. 'Twas her brother I kill'd then,
Would I were with my Devils agen:
I got well of them,
That will be here impossible.

Enter PHEMILLIA.

PHEMILLIA. Oh! Madam, Madam,
Y'are undone; the garden walls are scal'd,
A floud of people are entring th' house.
ORSABRIN. Good—why here's varietie of ruine yet.
SABRINA. 'Tis so,
The Feet of Justice like to those of time,
Move quick, and will destroy I feare as sure:
Oh Sir, what will you do?
There is no ventring forth,
My Closet is the safest, enter there,
While I goe down and meet their furie,
Hinder the search if possible. *Exit.*
ORSABRIN. Her Closet, yea, where's that?
And, if I could find it, what should I do there?
Shee will returne,——— I will venture out.
Exit.

Enter the PRINCE, PHILATELL, PHONTRELL, *Companie, Musique.* [II. ii]

PHILATELL. The lightest aires; 'twill make them more secure,———
Upon my life hee'le visite her to night.——— *Musick plaies and sings.*
PRINCE. Nor shee, nor any lesser light appeares,———
The calme and silence 'bout the place,
Perswardes me shee does sleep.
PHILATELL. It may be not, but hold,
It is enough,—let us retire.
Behind this Pillar, *Phontrell*, is thy place,
As thou didst love thy Master shew thy care;
You to th'other Gate, there's thy Ladder.
Exeunt.

II. ii. 7 retire.] *FA48*; ~^ *FA46*

Enter SABRINA.

SABRINA. Come forth my *Samorat*, come forth,
Our feares were false, it was the Prince with Musicke,
Samorat, *Samorat*. He sleepes,———*Samorat*,
Or else hee's gon to find me out I'th Gallery,
Samorat, *Samorat*, it must be so. *Exit.*

Enter ORSABRIN.

ORSABRIN. This house is full of Thresholds, and Trap-doores,
I have been i'th Cellar, where the Maids lie too,
I laid my hand groping for my way
Upon one of them, and shee began to squeake,
Would I were at Sea agen i'th storme,
Oh! a doore: though the Devill were the Porter,
And kept the Gate, I'de out.

Enter SAMORAT.

ORSABRIN. Ha! guarded? taken in a trap?
Nay, I will out, and there's no other but this.———
Retires and drawes, runs at him.

SAMORAT. *Philatell* in ambush on my life———
Another passe, they close.

Enter SABRINA, *and* PHEMILLIA *with a light.*

SABRINA. Where should he be? Ha!—Good Heavens,
What spectacle is this? my *Samorat*!
Some apparition sure,———
They discover one another by the light, throw away their weapons, and embrace.

SAMORAT. My noble friend,
What angry, and malicious Planet
Govern'd at this point of time!———

SABRINA. (My wonder does grow higher.)

ORSABRIN. That which governes ever:
I seldome knew it better.

SAMORAT. It does amaze me Sir, to find you here.
How entred you this place?

ORSABRIN. Forc't by unruly men i'th street.

SABRINA. Now the mistake is plaine.

ORSABRIN. Are you not hurt?

SAMORAT. No,—but you bleed?

II. iii. 19 Planet‸] *FA48*; ~. *FA46*

ORSABRIN. I do indeed,
But 'tis not here, this is a scratch,
It is within to see this beauty;
For by all circumstance, it was her brother,
Whom my unlucky Sword found out to day.
SABRINA. Oh! my too cruell fancy.——— *Weepes.*
SAMORAT. It was indeed thy Sword, but not thy fault,
I am the cause of all these ills.
Why d'you weep *Sabrina*!
SABRINA. Unkind unto thy selfe, and me,
The tempest this sad newes has rais'd within me,
I would have laid with teares, but thou disturb'st me.
Oh! *Samorat*,
Had'st thou consulted but with love as much
As honour, this had never been.
SAMORAT. I have no love for thee that has not had
So strict an union with honour still,
That in all things they were concern'd alike,
And if there could be a division made,
It would be found
Honour had here the leaner share:
'Twas love that told me 'twas unfit
That you should love a Coward.
SABRINA. These handsome words are now
As if one bound up wounds with silke,
Or with fine knots, which do not helpe the cure,
Or make it heale the sooner:
Oh! *Samorat*, this accident
Lies on our love, like to some foule disease,
Which though it kill it not,
Yet wil't destroy the beauty; disfigur't so,
That 'twill looke ugly to th' world hereafter.
SAMORAT. Must then the Acts of Fate be crimes of men?
And shall a death he pul'd upon himselfe,
Be laid on others? Remember Sweet, how often
You have said it in the face of Heaven,
That 'twas no love,
Which length of time, or cruelty of chance,
Could lessen, or remove.

41 teares] *FA48*; Sheares *FA46* 42 *Samorat*,] *FA48*; ~. *FA46*

Oh kill me not that way *Sabrina*,
This is the nobler;
Take it, and give it entrance any where *Kneeles and presents his Sword*
But here, for you so fill that place,
That you must wound your selfe.

ORSABRIN. Am I so slight a thing? so bankerupt?
So unanswerable in this world?
That being principally i'th debt,
Another must be cal'd upon,
And I not once look't after?
Madam why d'you throw away your Teares
On one that's irrecoverable?

SABRINA. Why? therefore Sir, because hee's irrecoverable.

ORSABRIN. But why on him? He did not make him so.

SABRINA. I do confesse my anger is unjust,
But not my sorow, Sir,
Forgive these teares my *Samorat*,
The debts of nature must be paid,
Though from the stocke of love: should they not Sir?

SAMORAT. Yes.———
But thus the precious minutes passe,
And time, e're I have breath'd the sighs,
Due to our parting, will be calling for me.

SABRINA. Parting?

SAMORAT. Oh yes *Sabrina*, I must part,
As day does from the world,
Not to returne till night be gone,
Till this darke Cloud be over; here to be found,
Were foolishly to make a present
Of my life unto mine enemy,
Retire into thy Chamber faire,
There thou shalt know all.

SABRINA. I know too much already.

Exeunt.

Enter PHONTRELL. [II.

PHONTRELL. Hold rope for me, and then hold rope for him. Why, this is the wisdome of the Law now, a Prince looses a subject, and does not think himselfe paid for the losse, till he looses another:

Well I will do my endeavour to make him a saver; for this was *Samorat.*

Exit.

Enter SAMORAT, ORSABRIN *bleeding.* [II. v]

ORSABRIN. Let it bleed on,—you shall not stirre, I sweare.
SAMORAT. Now by the friendship that I owe thee,
And the Gods beside, I will
Noble youth; were there no danger in thy wound,
Yet would the losse of bloud make thee
Unfit for travell:
My servants waite me for direction,
With them my Surgeon, I'le bring him instantly,
Pray go back.

Exeunt.

Enter PHILATELL, *Guard.* [II. vi]

PHILATELL. There.——— *Places them at the doores.*
You to the other Gate,
The rest follow me.

Exeunt.

Enter ORSABRIN, SABRINA.

SABRINA. Hearke a noise Sir.
This tread's too loud to be my *Samorats.*
SEARCHERS [*within*]. Which way?—which way?
SABRINA. Some villany in hand,
Step in here Sir, quick, quick.——— *Locks him into her Closet.*

Enter PHILATELL, *Guard, and passe ore the Stage.*

PHILATELL. Looke every where.——— PHILATELL *dragging out his Sister.*
Protect thy brothers murderer?
Tell me where thou hast hid him,
Or by my fathers ashes I will search
In every veine thou hast about thee, for him.

ORSABRIN *bounces thrice at the doore, it flies open.*

Enter ORSABRIN.

ORSABRIN. Ere such a villany should be
The Gods would lend unto a single arme

II v. 9.1 *Exeunt.*] *FA48*; *Exit. FA46* II. vi. 1 *doores*] *doore FA46* 1.1 *Exeunt.*] *FA48*; *Ex. FA46* 4 *within*] *to them FA46*; *Enter the Searchers to them FA48* 5 SABRINA. Some] *FA48*; Some *FA46* 6 *into*] *FA46*; *in FA48*

Such strength, it should have power to punish
An Armie, such as thou art.
PHILATELL. Oh! are you here Sir?———
ORSABRIN. Yes I am here Sir.—*Fight.*
PHILATELL. Kill her. *She interposes.*
ORSABRIN. Oh! save thy selfe, faire excellence,
And leave me to my Fate. [*Exit* SABRINA.]
Base. *The Guard comes behind him, catches hold of his Armes.*
PHILATELL. So bring him on,
The other is not far. *Exeunt.*

Enter SABRINA, PHEMILLIA.

SABRINA. Run, run, *Phemillia*, to the Garden walls,
And meet my *Samorat*,
Tell him, oh tell him any thing,
Charge him by all our loves
He instantly take Horse, and put to Sea,
There is more safety in a storme,
Then where my brother is.

Exeunt.

Enter PERIDOR *and the other Theeves.* [II

THEEVES. A Prize—A prize—A prize.
PERIDOR. Bring him forth, bring him forth.

STRAMADOR *led in. They dance about him and sing.*

Welcome, welcome, mortall wight,
To the Mansion of the night:
Good or bad, thy life discover,
Truly all thy deeds declare;
For about thee Spirits hover
That can tell, tell what they are.
———*Pinch him, if he speake not true,*
———*Pinch him, pinch him black and blew.*

PERIDOR. What art thou?
STRAMADOR. I was a man.
PERIDOR. Of whence?
STRAMADOR. The Court.

17 S.D. *interposes*] *FA48*; *interpos'd FA46* 20 S.D. *The Guard*] *FA48*; *om. FA46* III. i. 0.1 S.D. PERIDOR *and the other*] *FA48*; *om. FA46* 2.1 S.D. STRAMADOR *led in.*] *FA48*; *om. FA46* 9 speake] speaks *Collier*

PERIDOR. Whether now bound?

STRAMADOR. To my owne house.

PERIDOR. Thy name?

STRAMADOR. *Stramador.*

PERIDOR. Oh you fill a place about his Grace, and keep out men of parts, d'you not?

STRAMADOR. Yes.———

PERIDOR. A foolish Utensill of State, which like old Plate upon a Gaudy day, 'sbrought forth to make a show, and that is all; for of no use y'are, y'had best deny this.

STRAMADOR. Oh no!———

PERIDOR. Or that you do want wit, and then talke loud to make that passe for it? You thinke there is no wisedom but in forme; nor any knowledge like to that of whispers.———

STRAMADOR. Right, right.

PERIDOR. Then you can hate, and fawn upon a man at the same time, and dare not urge the vices of another, you are so foule your selfe; so the Prince seldome heares truth.

STRAMADOR. Oh! very seldome.

PERIDOR. And did you never give his Grace odde Councels? And when you saw they did not prosper, perswade him take them on himselfe?———

STRAMADOR. Yes, yes, often.

PERIDOR. Get baths of Sulphur quick, and flaming oyles, this crime is new, and will deserve it. He has inverted all the rule of State, confounded policie. There is some reason why a Subject should suffer for the errours of his Prince; but why a Prince should beare the faults of's Ministers, none, none at all.———Cauldrons of Brimstone there.

THEEF. Great Judge of this infernall place allow him yet the mercy of the Court.

STRAMADOR. Kind Devill.———

PERIDOR. Let him be boyl'd in scalding lead a while t'enure, and to prepare him for the other.

STRAMADOR. Oh! heare me, heare me.

PERIDOR. Stay! now I have better thought upon't, he shall to earth agen: for villanie is catching, and will spread: he will enlarge our Empire much, then w'are sure of him at any time, so 'tis enough ———where's our Governour?

Exeunt.

Enter GAOLER, SAMORAT, NASHORAT, PELLEGRIN, *three others in disguise.* [I

GAOLER. His haire curles naturally, a handsome youth.

SAMORAT. The same,——(*Drinkes to him.*) Is there no speaking with him? He owes me a trifling summe.

GAOLER. Sure Sir, the debt is something desperate; there is no hopes he will be brought to cleare with the world, he struck me but for perswading him to make even with Heaven, he is as surly as an old Lion, and as sullen as a Bullfinch, he never eate since he was taken. ——Gentlemen.

SAMORAT. I must needs speake with him, heark in the eare.—— [*Whispers.*]

GAOLER. Not for all the world.

SAMORAT. Nay I do but motion such a thing.

GAOLER. Is this the businesse Gentlemen? Fare you well.——

SAMORAT. There is no choice of waies then.——

Run after him, draw their daggers, set it to his Brest.

Stir not, if thou but think'st a noise,
Or breath'st aloud, thou breath'st thy last.
So bind him now.——
Undoe, quickly, quickly, his Jerkin, his Hat.

NASHORAT. What will you do? None of these Beards will serve,
There's not an eye of white in them.

PELLEGRIN. Pull out the Silver'd ones in his
And sticke them in the other.

NASHORAT. Cut them, cut them out, the bush will sute well enough with a grace still. *They put a false Beard on* SAMORAT.

SAMORAT. Desperate wounds must have desperate Cures,
Extreames must thus be serv'd,——
You know your parts.

NASHORAT. Feare not, let us alone. *Exit.*

Sings a Catch.

Some drinke,—what Boy,—some drinke——
Fill it up, fill it up to the brinke,
When the Pots crie clinke,

III. ii. 23.1 S.D. *They*...SAMORAT.] *They*...*the Goaler. FA48*; *om. FA46* 27 S.D. *Exit.*] *FA48*; *om. FA46* 27 NASHORAT. Feare] *FA48*; Feare *FA46* 28.1 *Sings*] *They sing FA48* 28–34 *See* '*Texts Consulted*' *for a list of variant Mss and a book containing this song.* 28 *what*] *om. Add29, CCC, MuSch* (*the only line of text in this MS. is* 'Some drink boy'.)

And the Pockets chinke,
Then 'tis a merry world.
To the best, to the best, have at her,
And a Pox take the Woman-hater.

The Prince of darknesse is a Gentleman, *Mahu*, *Mohu* is his name. How d'you Sir? You gape as you were sleepy. Good faith he lookes like an———*O yes.*

PELLEGRIN. Or as if he had overstrain'd himselfe at a deep note in a Ballad.

NASHORAT. What think you of an Oyster at a low ebb? Some liquor for him; you will not be a Pimpe for life, you Rogue, nor hold a doore to save a Gentleman, you are———Pox on him, what is he *Pellagrin*? If you love me, let's stifle him, and say 'twas a sudden judgement upon him for swearing; the posture will confirme it.

PELLEGRIN. We're in excellent humour, let's have another bottle, and give out that *Anne* my wife is dead, shall I Gentlemen?———

NASHORAT. Rare Rogue in Buckram, let me bite thee, before me thou shalt go out wit, and upon as good termes, as some of those in the Ballad too.

PELLEGRIN. Shall I so?—Why then foutree for the Guise, Gaines shall accrew, and ours shall be the black ey'd beauties of the time, I'le ticke you for old ends of Plaies.——— *They sing.*

A Round,—A Round,—A Round,—
A Round,—A Round,—A Round— *Knock.*

Some bodie's at doore.

Preethee, preethee, Sirra, Sirra,
Trie thy skill.

NASHORAT. Who's there.

MESSENGER [*within*]. One *Sturgelot* a Jaylor here?———

NASHORAT. Such a one there was my friend, but hee's gone above an houre ago: now did this Rogue whisper in his heart that's a lie, —and for that very reason, I'le cut his throat.———

PELLEGRIN. No prethee now,—for thinking? Thou shalt not take the paines, the Law shall do't———

NASHORAT. How,—how?—

31 *Pockets chink*] *Purse chink, chink Add29, CCC* 32 *Then*] *Ah then Add29, CCC* 34 *take*] *on Add29* 35 *Mahu, Mohu*] *Mahu, Mahu FA48* 37 *O yes*] *set as* S.D. *FA46* 45 in] *FA46*; in an *FA48* 50 Gaines] Saines *FA46*; Saints *Collier* accrew] agree *Collier* 52 ticke] *FA46*; tickle *FA48* 53–7] *See Commentary for readings in Folger MS. 409.* 54 S.D. *Knock.*] *FA46*; *Knocking at the door. FA48* 59] S.D. *Enter a Messenger FA48*

PELLEGRIN. Marry wee'le write it over when wee're gone, he joyn'd in the plot, and put himselfe into this posture, meerely to disguise it to the world.

NASHORAT. Excellent, here's to thee for that conceit. Wee should have made rare Statesmen, we are so witty in our mischiefe. Another song, and so let's go, it will be time.

Sing.

A health to the Nut browne Lasse,
With the hazell eyes, let it passe.
Shee that has good eyes
Has good thighs,
Let it passe,—let it passe.

As much to the lively Grey,
'Tis as good i'th night as day,
Shee that has good eyes,
Has good thighs,
Drinke away,—drinke away.

I pledge, I pledge, what ho, some Wine,
Here's to thine, and to thine,
The colours are Divine.———
But oh the blacke, the black,
Give me as much agen, and let't be Sacke:
Shee that has good Eyes,
Has good Thighs,
And it may be a better knack.

NASHORAT. A reckoning Boy.——— *They knock.*

Enter a Drawer. Paies him the reconing.

There.———Dost heare? Here's a friend of ours 'has forgotten himselfe a little (as they call it.) The Wine has got into his head, as the frost into a hand, he is benum'd, and has no use of himselfe for the present.

BOY. Hum Sir.——— *Smiles.*

72–89] *See 'Texts Consulted' for a list of variant MSS. and books containing this song.* 72 *Nut browne*] *Northerne Add*31 74 *has*] *hath WI, FA*48 75 *Has*] *Hath WI, WM* 77 *As much*] *Add*31, *WI, WM, FA*48; *Amuch FA*46 78 *'Tis*] *They're WM* 78 *i'th*] *by WM* *day*] *WM, Add*31, *Drexel* 40, *WI, FA*48; *the day FA*46 79 *has*] *hath WM* 80 *Has*] *Hath WI* 82 *I pledge, I pledge*] *I'le pledge WM* 83 *thine, and to thine*] *mine and to thine WI, FA*58 85 *the blacke, the black*] *the black WM* 87 *has*] *hath WM* 88 *Has*] *Hath WM* 90.1 S.D. *Enter a Drawer. Paies him the reconing.*] *at line* 89 *FA*48; *paies him FA*46

NASHORAT. Prethee lock the dore, and when he comes t'himselfe, tell him he shall find us at the old place, he knowes where.
BOY. I will Sir.

Exeunt.

Enter ORSABRIN, *in Prison* [III. iii]

ORSABRIN. To die! yea what's that?
For yet I never thought on't seriously;
It may be 'tis.———hum.———It may be 'tis not too.———
Enter SAMORAT, *as Goaler, undoes his Fetters.*
Ha.——— *As amaz'd.*
What happy intercession wrought this change?
To whose kind prayers owe I this, my friend?
SAMORAT. Unto thy vertue—Noble youth,
The Gods delight in that as well as praiers.
I am———
ORSABRIN. Nay, nay,—
Be what thou wilt, I will not question't:
Undoe, undoe.
SAMORAT. Thy friend *Samorat.*
ORSABRIN. Ha?
SAMORAT. Lay by thy wonder, and put on these cloathes,
In this disguise thou'lt passe unto the Prison-gates,
There you shall finde one that is taught to know you;
He will conduct you to the corner
Of the wood, and there my horses waite us.———
I'le throw this Goaler off in some odde place.
ORSABRIN. My better Angell.

Exeunt.

Enter PERIDOR *with the other* THEEVES. [III. iv]

PERIDOR. It is 'een as hard a world for Theeves
As honest men,—nothing to be got—
No prize stirring.
THEEF. None, but one with horses,
Who seem'd to stay for some that were to come,
And that has made us waite thus long.
PERIDOR. A leane dayes worke, but what remedie?

III. iii. 0.1 S.D. *in Prison*] *FA48*; *om. FA46* 1 yea] *FA46*; I *FA48* 3.1 *Goaler, undoes*] ∼‸ ∼ *FA46*; *the Goaler, he undoes FA48*
III. iv. 0.1] *FA48*; *Enter Theeves FA46* 3 S.P. THEEF] 1. *Thee. FA46*

Lawyers, that rob men with their owne consent,
Have had the same: Come, call in our Perdues,
We will away.——— *They whistle.*

Enter ORSABRIN [*with attendants*], *as seeking the horses.*

ORSABRIN. I heare them now, yonder they are.
PERIDOR. Hallow, who are these? Any of ours?
THEEF. No, stand close, they shall be presently.———
Yeeld—yeeld.
ORSABRIN. Agen betraid?
There is no end of my misfortune,
Mischiefe vexes me like a quotidian,
It intermits a little, and returnes
E're I have lost the memory of
My former fit.
PERIDOR. Sentences, sentences,———
Away with him—Away with him. *Exeunt.*

Enter GAOLER, *Drawers, over the Stage.* [II

GAOLER. I am the Goaler, undone, undone,
Conspiracie, a cheat, my prisoner, my prisoner.
Exeunt.

Enter SAMORAT. [II

SAMORAT. No men?—nor horses?—Some strange mistake,—
May it be, th'are sheltred in the wood?
[*Exit.*]

Enter PERIDOR *and other Theeves, examining the young Lord* TORCULAR *that was hurt.* [II

PERIDOR. And if a Lady did but step aside,
To fetch a Masque or so, you follow'd after still,
As if shee had gone proud? Ha; is't not so?
TORCULAR. Yes.
PERIDOR. And if you were us'd but civillie in a place,
You gave out doubtfull words upon't,
To make men thinke you did enjoy.
TORCULAR. Oh! yes, yes.
PERIDOR. Made love to every peece of cried-up beauty,
And swore the same things over to them.
TORCULAR. The very same.

III. vi. 2 May it be] May be *FA48*

PERIDOR. Abominable. Had he but sworne new things,
Yet 't had been tollerable.———

Reades the summe of the Confession.

THEEF. Let me see—let me see. Hum. Court Ladies Eight, of which two great ones.—Country Ladies twelve, Tearmers all.

PERIDOR. Is this right?

TORCULAR. Very right.

THEEF. Citizens wives of severall trades, he cannot count them. ———Chamber maides, and Country wenches, about thirty: ———Of which the greater part, the night before th' were married, or else upon the day.

PERIDOR. A modest reckoning, is this all?

TORCULAR. No.———I will be just t'a scruple.

PERIDOR. Well said,—well said,—out with it.

TORCULAR. Put down two old Ladies more.

PERIDOR. I'th name of wonder, how could he thinke of old, in such variety of young?

TORCULAR. Alas I could never be quiet for them.

PERIDOR. Poore Gentleman. Well what's to be done with him now?

THEEF. Shall he be thrown into the Cauldron with the Cuckolds, Or with the Jealous? That's the hotter place.

PERIDOR. Thou mistakes't, 'tis the same, they go together still: Jealous and Cuckolds differ no otherwise then Sheriffe and Alderman; a little time makes th'one th'other. What thinke you of Gelding him, and sending him to earth agen, amongst his women? 'Twood be like throwing a dead fly into an Ants nest. There would be such tearing, pulling, and getting up upon him, they would worry the poore thing to death,———

THEEF. Excellent, or leave a string as they do sometimes in young Colts: Desire and impotence, would be a rare punishment.

PERIDOR. Fie, fie, the common disease of age, every old man 'has it.

Enter TAMOREN *and more Theeves leading* ORSABRIN.

A prize,—A prize,—A prize. *Hornes blow, Brasse Pots beat on.*

ORSABRIN. This must be Hell by the noise.

TAMOREN. Set him down, set him down;
Bring forth the newest wrack,
And flaming pinching Irons,

III. vii. 17 S.P. THEEF] *Collier*; PERIDOR *FA46* 29 S.P. THEEF] *Collier*; *om. FA46* 40 S.P. PERIDOR] *Collier*; *om. FA46* 40 every] *Collier*; A very *FA46* 41.1 *Enter* ...ORSABRIN.] *FA48*; *Enter The. FA46* 42 S.D. *Pots beat on*] *FA48*; *Plots &c. FA46*

This is a stubborne peece of flesh,
'Twould have broke loose.

ORSABRIN. So, this comes of wishing my selfe with Divels agen.

PERIDOR. What art?

ORSABRIN. The slave of Chaunce, one of Fortunes fooles;
A thing shee kept alive on earth
To make her sport.

PERIDOR. Thy name?

ORSABRIN. *Orsabrin.*

PERIDOR. Ha! he that liv'd with Pirats?
Was lately in a storme?

ORSABRIN. The very same.

TAMOREN (*whispers with* PERIDOR). Such respect as you have paid to me,
Prepare to Revels, all that can be thought on:
But let each man still keep his shape. *Exit.*

They unbind him, all bow to him. Musicke and a Dance.

ORSABRIN. Ha! Another false smile of Fortune?

They bring out severall suite of cloathes, and a banquete.

Is this the place the gowned Clearkes do fright men so on earth with? Would I had been here before. Master Devill; to whose use are these set out?

TAMOREN. To yours Sir.

ORSABRIN. I'le make bold to change a little,———Could you not affoord a good plaine Sword to all this gallantry?

Takes a hat, dresses himself.

PERIDOR. Wee'le see Sir.

ORSABRIN. A thousand times civiller then men, and better natur'd.

Enter TAMOREN, REGINELLA.

TAMOREN. All leave the roome.

PERIDOR. I like not this. *Exit.*

TAMOREN. Cupid, do thou the rest,
A blunter arrow, and but slackly drawne,
———Would perfect what's begun,
When young and handsome meet,
———The work's halfe done. [*Exit.*]

ORSABRIN. She cannot be lesse then a goddesse;
And't must be *Proserpine*:

55 S.D. *with* PERIDOR] *FA48*; *om. FA46* 57.1 *and a Dance*] *FA48*; *om. FA46*
68 S.P. PERIDOR] *FA48*; *om. FA46*

I'le speake to her, though *Pluto's* selfe stood by.———
Thou beauteous Queene of this darke world, that mak'st
A place so like a hell, so like a Heaven,
Instruct me in what forme I must approach thee,
And how adore thee?
REGINELLA. Tell me what thou art first:
For such a creature
Mine eyes did never yet behold.
ORSABRIN. I am that which they name above a man:
I'th watry Elements I much have liv'd,
And there they terme me *Orsabrin.*
Have you a name too?
REGINELLA. Why doe you aske?
ORSABRIN. Because I'de call upon it in a storme,
And save a Ship from perishing sometimes.
REGINELLA. 'Tis *Reginella.*
ORSABRIN. Are you a woman too?
I never was in earnest untill now.
REGINELLA. I know not what I am,
For like my selfe I never yet saw any.
ORSABRIN. Nor ever shall.
Oh! how came you hither?
Sure you were betraied.
Will you leave this place,
And live with such as I am?
REGINELLA. Why may not you live here with me?
ORSABRIN. Yes.———
But I'de carry thee where there is a glorious light,
Where all above is spread a Canopie,
Studded with twinckling Gems,
Beauteous as Lovers eies;
And underneath Carpets of flowry Meads
To tread on.———A thousand thousand pleasures
Which this place can ne're affoord thee.
REGINELLA. Indeed!
ORSABRIN. Yes indeed———
I'le bring thee unto shady walkes,
And Groves fring'd with Silver purling streams,
Where thou shalt heare soft feathered Queristers
Sing sweetly to thee of their own accord.

I'le fill thy lap with early flowers;
And whilst thou bind'st them up mysterious waies,
I'le tell thee pretty tales, and sigh by thee:
Thus presse thy hand and warme it thus with kisses.

REGINELLA. Will you indeed?

Enter King [TAMOREN], PERIDOR *above with others.*

TAMOREN. Fond Girle:
Her rashnesse sullies the glory of her beauty,
'Twil make the conquest cheape,
And weaken my designes,
Go part them instantly.
And bind him as before;
Be you his keeper *Peridore.*

PERIDOR. Yes, I will keep him.

ORSABRIN. Her eyes like lightning shoot into my heart.
They'le melt it into nothing, ere I can
Present it to her, sweet Excellence.———

Enter Theeves and blind him.

Ha! why is this hatefull curtaine
Drawne before my eyes? If I have sinn'd,
Give me some other punishment;
Let me but looke on her still, and double it,
Oh whether, whether doe you hurry me?

PERIDOR. Madam, you must in.——— *Carry him away.*

REGINELLA. Ay me, what's this?———
Must! *Exeunt.*

Enter other Devils.

1. THEEF. We have had such sport; yonder's the rarest Poet without, has made all his confession in blanke verse: not left a God, nor a Goddesse in Heaven, but fetch't them all downe for witnesses; has made such a description of Stix, and the Ferry, and verily thinks has past them. Enquires for the blest shades, and askes much after certaine Brittish blades, one *Shakespeare* and *Fletcher*: and grew so peremptory at last, he would be carried where they were.

2. THEEF. And what did you with him?

1. THEEF. Mounting him upon a Cowle-staffe, which (tossing him something high) he apprehended to be *Pegasus.* So we have left him to tell strange lies, which hee'le turne into verse; and some wise people hereafter into Religion. *Exeunt.*

125.1 S.D. *and blind him*] *FA48*; *om. FA46* 144.1 S.D. *Exeunt*] *FA48*; *om. FA46*

Enter SAMORAT, NASHORAT, PELLEGRIN. [IV. i]

NASHORAT. Good faith 'tis wondrous well, we have ee'n done like eager disputers; and with much adoe are got to be just where we were. This is the corner of the wood.

SAMORAT. Ha! 'tis indeed.

PELLEGRIN. Had we no walking fire, nor sawcer-ey'd Devill of these woods that led us? Now am I as weary as a married man after the first weeke; and have no more desire to move forwards, then a Post-horse that has past his Stage.

NASHORAT. 'Sfoot yonder's the night too, stealing away with her blacke gowne about her, like a kind wench, that had staid out the last minute with a man.

PELLEGRIN. What shall we doe, Gentlemen? I apprehend falling into this Jaylors hands strangely; hee'd use us worse then we did him.

NASHORAT. And that was ill enough, of Conscience: what thinke you of turning Beggars? Many good Gentlemen have don't: or Theeves?

PELLEGRIN. That's the same thing at Court: begging is but a kind of robbing th' Exchequer.

NASHORAT. Looke foure fathome and a halfe Oos———in contemplation of his Mistres: there's a Feast, you and I are out now *Pellegrin*; 'tis a pretty tricke, this enjoyning in absence. What a rare invention 'twood be, if a man could find out a way to make it reall.

PELLEGRIN. Dost thinke there's nothing in't as tis?

NASHORAT. Nothing, nothing.

PELLEGRIN. Did'st never heare of a dead *Alexander*, rais'd to talke with a man? Love's a learned Conjurer, and with the glasse of Fancie will doe as strange things. You thrust out a hand, your Mistresse thrusts out another: you shake that hand, that shakes you agen: you put out a lip; she puts out hers: talke to her, she shall answer you.

NASHORAT. Marrie, when you come to graspe all this, it is but ayer.

SAMORAT. It was unluckie,———(*As out of his Study.*) Gentlemen, the day appeares, this is no place to stay in; let's to some neighbouring Cottage, may be the Searchers will neglect the neerer places, and this will but advance unto our safety.

Enter FIDLERS.

NASHORAT. Who are there?

IV. i. 21 enjoyning] enjoying *FA48* 25 S.P. PELLEGRIN] *om. FA46* 31 S.P. NASHORAT] *om. FA46*

1. FIDLER. Now if the spirit of melancholy should possesse them.

2. FIDLER. Why if it should, an honourable retreate.

NASHORAT. I have the rarest fancie in my head,———Whether are you bound my friends so early?

1. FIDLER. To a Wedding Sir.

NASHORAT. A Wedding?—I told you so.—Whose?

1. FIDLER. A Country wenches here hard by, one *Erblins* daughter.

NASHORAT. Good: *Erblin*: the very place to see how things fall out. Hold, here's money for you. Harke you, you must assist me in a small designe.

1. FIDLER. Any thing.

SAMORAT. What do'st meane?

NASHORAT. Let me alone,—I have a plot upon a wench.

1. FIDLER. Your Worship is merry.

NASHORAT. Yes faith, to see her only. Looke you, some of you shall go back to 'th' Towne, and leave us your Coats, my friend and I am excellent at a little Instrument, and then wee sing catches rarely.

PELLEGRIN. I understand thee not.

NASHORAT. Thou hast no more forecast then a Squirrell, and hast lesse wise consideration about thee. Is there a way safer then this? Dost thinke what we have done will not be spread beyond this place with ev'ry light? Should we now enter any house thus near the Towne, and stay all day, 'twould be suspitious: What pretence have we?

PELLEGRIN. He speaks reason *Samorat*.

SAMORAT. I doe not like it.
Should any thing fall out 'twould not looke well,
I'de not be found so much out of my selfe,
So far from home as this disguise would make me,
Almost for certainty of safety.

NASHORAT. Certainty? Why, this will give it us, pray let me governe once.

SAMORAT. Well, you suffered first with me, now 'tis my turne.

PELLEGRIN. Prethee name not suffering.

NASHORAT. Come, come, your Coats, our Beards will suite rarely to them: there's more money, not a word of any thing as you tender———

41 S.P. 1. FIDLER] *Fid. FA46 makes no distinction between* 1. *Fid. and* 2. *Fid. in* S.P. *from this point to end of scene.* 53 wee...rarely] *FA48*; wee'l sing catches *FA46* 55 S.P. NASHORAT] *FA48*; *om. FA46* 58 ev'ry] ere 'tis *Hazlitt*

2. FIDLER. O Sir.

NASHORAT. And see you carry't gravely too.———Now afore me *Pellagrins* rarely translated. 'Sfoot they'l apprehend the head of the Base Violl as soone as thee; thou art so likely, only I must confesse, that has a little the better face.

PELLEGRIN. Has it so?———Pox on thee, thou look'st like I cannot tell what.

NASHORAT. Why, so I would foole, th'end of my disguise is to have none know what I am:

Enter a Divell.

Looke, looke, a Devill ayring himself. I'le catch him like a Mole ere he can get under ground.

PELLEGRIN. *Nashorat, Nashorat.*

NASHORAT. Pox on that noise, hee's earth't. Prethee let's watch him and see whether hee'le heave agen.

PELLEGRIN. Ar't madde?

NASHORAT. By this light, three or foure of their skins and wee'd robbe. 'Twould be the better way.———Come, come, let's go.

Exeunt.

Enter CAPTAIN *and Souldiers.*

CAPTAIN. Let the Horse skirt about this place, wee'le make a search within. *Exeunt.*

Enter agen.

Now disperse i'th hollow of the wood, wee'le meet agen.

[*Exeunt all but one Souldier.*]

Enter NASHORAT, PELLEGRIN, SAMORAT, *Fidlers.*

SOULDIER. Who goes there? Speake,———Oh! th'are Fidlers. ———Sawe you no Men nor Horse i'th wood to day,—as you came along?

NASHORAT *puls one of the Fidlers by the skirt.*

NASHORAT. Speake, speake Rogue.

1. FIDLER. None Sir,———

SOULDIER. Passe on. *Exit* [*Souldier.*]

NASHORAT. Gentlemen what say you to th'invention now? I'm a Rogue if I do not think I was design'd for the Helme of State: I am so full of nimble Stratagems, that I should have ordered affaires, and carried it against the streame of a Faction, with as much ease as a Skippar would laver against the wind. *Exeunt.*

Enter CAPTAINE *and Soldiers meet agen.*

CAPTAIN. What, no newes of any?

1. SOULDIER. No,—not a man stirring.

Enter other Souldiers.

2. SOULDIER. Sa how, away,—away.

CAPTAIN. What, any discovery?

2. SOULDIER. Yes, the Horse has staid three fellowes, Fidlers they call themselves; there's something in't; they looke suspitiously; one of them has offer'd at confession once or twice, like a weake stomacke at vomiting, but 'twould not out.

CAPTAIN. A little cold Iron thrust downe his throat will fetch it up. ———I am excellent at discoverie, and can draw a secret out of a Knave, with as much dexterity as a Barber-Surgeon woo'd a hollow tooth. Let's joyne forces with them.

Exeunt.

ORSABRIN, *discover'd in* [*a Cave*], *bound.*

ORSABRIN. Sure 'tis eternall night with me;
Would this were all too———
For I begin to thinke the rest is true,
Which I have read in books,
And that there's more to follow.

Enter REGINELLA.

REGINELLA. Sure this is he. *She unbinds him.*

ORSABRIN. The pure and first created Light
Broke through the Chaos thus.———
Keep off, keep off thou brighter Excellence,
Thou faire Divinity: If thou com'st neere,
(So tempting is the shape thou now assum'st)
I shall grow sawcy in desire agen,
And entertaine bold hopes which will but draw
More, and fresh punishment upon me.

REGINELLA. I see y'are angry Sir:
But if you kill me too, I meant no ill:
That which brought me hither,
Was a desire I have to be with you,
Rather then those I live with: This is all,
Beleeve't.

ORSABRIN. With me? Oh thou kind Innocence!

106 S.P. 1 SOULDIER] *Sol. FA46* 107 2. SOULDIER. Sa how] Sa how *FA46*
109 S.P. 2. SOULDIER] 1. *Sol. FA46*
IV. ii. 0.1] S.D. *discover'd in Prison bound FA48*; *om. FA46*

Witnesse all that can punish falshood,
That I could live with thee,
Even in this darke and narrow prison:
And thinke all happinesse confin'd within the wals———
Oh, hadst thou but as much of Love as I.

REGINELLA. Of Love? What's that?

ORSABRIN. Why 'tis a thing that's had before 'tis knowne:
A gentle flame that steales into a heart,
And makes it like one object so, that it scarce cares
For any other delights, when that is present:
And is in paine when't's gone; thinks of that alone,
And quarrels with all other thoughts that would
Intrude and so divert it.

REGINELLA. If this be Love, sure I have some of it;
It is no ill thing, is it Sir?

ORSABRIN. Oh most Divine,
The best of all the gods strangely abound in't,
And Mortals could not live without it:
It is the soule of vertue, and the life of life.

REGINELLA. Sure I should learne it Sir, if you would teach it.

ORSABRIN. Alas, thou taught'st it me;
It came with looking thus.——— *They gaze upon one another.*

Enter PERIDOR.

PERIDOR. I will no longer be conceal'd, but tell
Her what I am, before this smooth fac'd youth
Hath taken all the roome up in her heart,
Ha! unbound! and sure by her! Hell and Furies.
What ho—within there———

Enter other Theeves.

Practice escapes?
Get me new yrons to load him unto death.

ORSABRIN. I am so us'd to this, it takes away
The sense of it: I cannot thinke it strange.

REGINELLA. Alas, he never did intend to goe.
Use him for my sake kindly:
I was not wont to be deny'd.
Ah me! they are hard hearted all.
What shall I doe? I'le to my Governour,
Hee'l not be thus cruell.

Exeunt.

Enter SAMORAT, NASHORAT, PELLEGRIN. [IV. iii]

NASHORAT. 'Tis a rare wench, she 'ith blew stockings: What a complexion she had when she was warme———'Tis a hard question of these Country wenches, which are simpler, their beauties or themselves. There's as much difference betwixt a Towne-Lady, and one of these, as there is betwixt a wilde Pheasant and a tame.

PELLEGRIN. Right:———

There goes such essensing, washing, perfuming, dawbing, to th'other that they are the least part of themselves. Indeed there's so much sauce, a man cannot taste the meat.

NASHORAT. Let me kisse thee for that; by this light I hate a woman drest up to her height, worse then I doe Sugar with Muskadine: It leaves no roome for me to imagine: I could improve her if she were mine: It looks like a Jade with his tayle tyed up with ribbons, going to a Fayre to be sold.

PELLEGRIN. No, no, thou hatest it out of another reason, *Nashorat*.

NASHORAT. Prethee, what's that?

PELLEGRIN. Why th'are so fine, th'are of no use that day.

NASHORAT. *Pellegrin* is in good feeling. Sirra, did'st marke the Lasse 'ith green upon yellow, how she bridled in her head, and danc't a stroake in, and a stroake out, like a young Fillet training to a pace.

PELLEGRIN. And how she kist, as if she had been sealing and delivering her self up to the use of him that came last, parted with her sweet-hearts lips still as unwillingly, and untowardly, as soft Wax from a dry Seale.

NASHORAT. True; and when she kisses a Gentleman, she makes a Curtsey, as who should say, the favour was on his side. What dull fooles are we to besiege a face three moneths for that trifle. Sometimes it holds out longer,———and then this is the sweeter flesh too,———

Enter Fidler.

1. FIDLER. You shall have horses ready at the time, and good ones too (if there be truth in drinke) and for your letters, they are there by this.

SAMORAT. An excellent Officer.

Enter Wedding.

CLOWNE. Tut, tut, tut, that's a good one y'faith, not dance? Come, come, strike up. *Dance.*

IV. iii. 20 training] *FA46*; straining *FA48* 30 S.P. 1. FIDLER] *Fid. FA46* 35 S.D. *Dance*] *om. FA46*; *Dance in that time enter souldiers...cloaks. FA48*

Enter souldiers mufled up in their cloaks.

SAMORAT. Who are those that eye us so severely? Belong they to the wedding?

I. FIDLER. I know 'em not.

CLOWNE. Gentlemen, wil't please you dance.———

Offer their women to them to dance.

I. SOULDIER. No, keep your women, wee'l take out others here. *Samorat*, if I mistake not.

SAMORAT. Ha! betraid?——— *A bussle.*

CLOWNE. How now! what's the matter? abuse our Fidlers?

2. SOULDIER. These are no Fidlers, fools. Obey the Princes officers, unlesse you desire to goe to prison too.

SAMORAT. The thought of what must follow disquiets not at all:
But tamely thus to be surpriz'd
In so unhandsome a disguise?——— *They carry him away.*

PELLEGRIN. I'st ee'n so? Why then,
Farewell the plumed Troops, and the big Wars,
Which made ambition vertue.

NASHORAT. I, I, Let them goe, let them goe.

PELLEGRIN. Have you ever a stratagem *Nashorat*? 'Twood be very seasonable. What thinke you now? Are you design'd for the helme of State? Can you laver against this Tempest?

NASHORAT. Prethee let me alone, I am thinking for life.

PELLEGRIN. Yes, 'tis for life indeed, would 'twere not.

CLOWNE. This is very strange; Let's follow after, and see if we can understand it.

Exeunt.

Enter PERIDOR, ORSABRIN. [IV. iv]

PERIDOR. A meere Phantasme rais'd by Art to trie thee.

ORSABRIN. Good kind Devill, trie me once more.
Help me to the sight of this Phantasme agen.

PERIDOR. Thou art undone,
Wer't thou not amorous in th'other world?
Did'st not love women?

ORSABRIN. Who did hate them?

PERIDOR. Why there's it;
Thou thought'st there was no danger in the sinne,

39.1 S.D. *to them to dance*] *FA48*; *om. FA46* 40 I. SOULDIER.] *Sol. FA46*

Because 'twas common.
Above the halfe of that vast multitude
Which fils this place, Women sent hither:
And they are highliest punisht still,
That love the handsomest.

ORSABRIN [*aside*]. A very lying Devill this, certainly.

PERIDOR. All that had their women with you, suffer with us.

ORSABRIN. By your friendships favour though, there's no justice in that: some of them suffered enough in all conscience by 'em there.

PERIDOR. Oh, this is now your mirth: but when you shall be pinch't into a gellie, or made into a crampe all over, these will be sad truths.

ORSABRIN [*aside*]. He talkes odly now, I doe not like it.———Do'st heare?———Prethee exchange some of thy good counsell for deeds. If thou bee'st an honest Devill, (as thou seem'st to be) put a sword into my hand, and help me to the sight of this Apparition agen.

PERIDOR. Well, some thing I'le doe for thee,———[*aside*] or rather for myself.

Exeunt.

Enter two other Devils. [IV

1. DEVIL. Come, let's goe relieve our Poet.

2. DEVIL. How, relieve him? hee's releas't; is he not?

1. DEVIL. No, no; *Bersat* bethought himselfe at the mouth of the Cave, and found he would be necessary to our Masque too night. We have set him with his feet in a great tub of water, in which he dabbles and beleeves it to be Helicon: there hee's contriving i'th honour of *Mercury*, who I have told him comes this night of a message from *Jupiter* to *Pluto*, and is feasted here by him.

Enter POET *and Theeves.*

2. DEVIL. Oh, they have fetcht him off.

POET. *Carer per so lo carer*, or he that made the Fairie Queene.

1. THEEF. No, none of these: they are by themselves in some other place; but here's he that writ *Tamerlane.*

POET. I beseech you bring me to him, there's something in his Scene betwixt the Empresses a little high and clowdie, I would resolve my selfe.

1. THEEF. You shall Sir. Let me see—the Author of the *bold Beauchams*, and *Englands Joy*

IV. v. 8.1] *FA48*; *one line later FA46* 9 S.P. 2. DEVIL] *De. FA48*; *Th. FA46*

POET. The last was a well writ peice, I assure you, a Brittane I take it; and *Shakespeares* very way: I desire to see the man.

1. THEEF. Excuse me, no seeing here. The gods in complement to *Homer*, doe make all Poets poore above, and we all blind below. But you shall confesse Sir. Follow.

Exeunt.

Enter PERIDOR, ORSABRIN. *Peridor unbinds him and slips away.* [IV. vi]

ORSABRIN. Ha! light and fresh aire agen?
The place I know too.
The very same I fought the Duell in.
The Devill was in the right;
This was a meere Aparition:
But 'twas a handsome one, it left impressions here,
Such as the fairest substance I shall ere behold,
Will scarse deface. Well I must resolve,
But what, or where? I, that's the question.
The Towne's unsafe, there's no returning thither,
And then the Port.———

Enter some [*Clownes*] *to pass over.*

Ha! What means the busie haste of these.—
Honest friend.——— ORSABRIN *cals to one. Passes hastily.*
Do'st heare?—No——— *To another.*
What's the matter pray?

CLOWNE. Gentlemen, gentlemen,——— *Exit.*

ORSABRIN. That's good satisfaction indeed.

Enter another.

Prethee good fellow tell me.
What causes all this hurry?

CLOWNE. One *Samorat* is led to prison Sir,
And other Gentlemen, about Lord *Torcular.* [*Exit.*]

ORSABRIN. Ha! *Samorat*!
There is no meane nor end of fortunes malice:
Oh! 'tis insufferable;
I'm made a boy whipt on anothers backe:
Cruell, I'le not endure't by heaven,

20 S.P. 1. THEEF] *FA46(c)*; om. *FA46(u)*
IV. vi. 11.1 *Enter...over.*] *FA46*; *some passe over hastily. FA48* 13 friend.—*FA48*; friend.—No— *FA46* 13 S.D. ORSABRIN...*one*] *FA48*; *om. FA46* 13 S.D. *Passes hastily.*] *om. FA48* 14 No—] *FA48*; *om. FA46* 15] S.D. *Enter Clowne. FA48* 16 S.D. *Exit*] *FA48*; *om. FA46* 17.1 *Enter another.*] *To another. FA46*; S.D. *to him. Enter another, another. FA48* 22 ORSABRIN. Ha!] *FA48*; Ha! *FA46*

He shall not dye for me: I will not hold
A wretched life upon such wretched termes.
Exit.

Enter TAMOREN, PERIDOR, *and others.* [IV

TAMOREN. Flie; flie abroad, search every place,
And bring him back:
Thou hast undone us all with thy neglect,
Destroi'd the hopes we had to be our selves agen;
I shall run mad with Anger; Fly, be gone.
Exeunt all but TAMOREN.

Enter REGINELLA.

My *Reginella*, what brings you abroad?

REGINELLA. Deare Governour? I have a sute to you.

TAMOREN. To me my pretty sweetnesse, what?

REGINELLA. You will deny me Sir I feare; pray let
Me have the stranger that came last in keeping.

TAMOREN. Stranger? Alas hee's gone, made an escape.

REGINELLA. I fear'd he would not stay, they us'd him so unkindly.
Indeed I would have us'd him better, *Weeps.*
And then he had been here still.

TAMOREN. Come, doe not weep my girle:
Forget him pretty pensivenesse, there will
Come others every day as good as he.

REGINELLA. Oh! never:
I'le close my eyes to all, now hee's gone.

TAMOREN. How catching are the sparkes of love? Still this
Mischance showes more and more unfortunate.
I was too curious.———
Come indeed, you must forget him,
The gallan'st and the godli'st to the eye
Are not the best, such handsome and fine shapes
As those are ever false and foule within.

REGINELLA. Why, Governour, d'you then put
Your finest things still in your finest Cabinets?

TAMOREN. Pretty Innocence: no, I doe not;
You see I place not you there,
Come, no more teares:

IV. vii. 24 godli'st] *FA46*; goodli'st *FA48*

Lets in and have a Mate at Chesse,
Diversion cures a losse, or makes it lesse.

Exeunt.

[V. i]

Enter TAMOREN, PERIDOR, *and other Theeves.*

PERIDOR. Crost all the High-wayes, searcht the Woods,
Beat up and down with as much pain and diligence,
As ever Huntsman did for a lost Deere.

TAMOREN. A race of Criples, are y'all issue of Snayles?
He could not else have scap't us.

[*Enter a Theef.*]

Now? what newes bring you?

THEEF. Sir, we have found him out,
The party is in prison.

TAMOREN. How? in prison?

THEEF. For certaine Sir.
It seemes young *Samorat* and he
Were those that fought the duell t'other day,
And left our *Torcular* so wounded there.
For his supposed death was *Samorat* taken,
Which when this youth had found,
He did attempt to free him (scaling the wall
By night) but finding it impossible,
Next Morning did present himselfe
Into the hands of Justice, imagining
His death that did the fact, an equall sacrifice———

TAMOREN. Brave *Orsabrin.*

THEEF. Not knowing that the greedy Law ask's more,
And doth prescribe the accessarie
As well as principall.

TAMOREN. Just so 'ith nicke? 'ith very nicke of time?———

PERIDOR. Hee's troubled.

TAMOREN. It will be excellent.———
Be all *en chevalier* straight.
Where's *Torcular*?

THEEF. Forth comming Sir.

TAMOREN. How are his wounds? Will they endure the Aire?
Under your gaberdines weare Pistols all.

33 lesse] *FA48*; selfe *FA46*
v. i. 0.1 S.D. *other Theeves*] *FA48*; *others FA46* 19 sacrifice—] ~. *FA46* 23 principall] *FA46(c)*; a principall *FA46(u)* 27 *en chevalier*] en souldier *FA46(u)*; in souldiers *FA46(c)*; in souldiers habits *FA48*

PERIDOR. What does he meane?
TAMOREN. Give me my other habit and my sword.
'Ith' least suspected way hast after me.
THEEF. All?
TAMOREN. All but *Peridor*; I will abroad,
My broken hopes and suff'rings
Shall have now some cure.
Fortune spite of her selfe shall be my friend,
And either shall redresse, or give them end. *Exeunt.*
PERIDOR. I've found it out,
He doe's intend to fetch this stranger backe,
And give him *Reginella*,
Or else—No, no, it must be that;
His anger, and the search declare it;
The secret of the prison-house shall out I sweare.
I'le set all first on fire,
For middle waies to such an end are dull.
Exit.

Enter PRINCE, PHILATELL, *and* PHEMILLIA. [V.

PHEMILLIA. Since she was refus'd to speake with you Sir,
She will not looke on any, she languishes so fast.
Her servants feare she will not live
To know what does become of him.
PHILATELL. Sir 'tis high time you visit her.
PRINCE. I cannot looke upon her, and deny her.
PHILATELL. Nor need you Sir,
All shall appeare to her most gracious:
Tell her the former part o'th' Law
Must passe, but when it comes t'execute,
Promise her that you intend to interpose.
PRINCE. And shall then *Samorat* live?
PHILATELL. Oh!———Nothing lesse! The censure past,
His death shall follow without noise:
'Tis but not owning of the fact,
Disgracing for a time a Secretarie
Or so—the thing's not new———
Put on forgiving looks Sir, we are there———

v. ii. 0.1 S.D. *and* PHEMILLIA] *and Servant FA48*; *om. FA46* 1 S.P. PHEMILLIA] *S. FA46*; *Ser. FA48* 2 She...fast.] *FA48*; Nor looke of any, | Languishes so fast, *FA46*

Enter SABRINA'S *Chamber.*

A mourning silence—
Sister *Sabrina*———
SABRINA. Hence, hence, thou cruell hunter after life:
Thou art a paine unto my eyes as great,
As my deare Mother had when she did bring
Thee forth—And sure that was extreme,
Since she produc't a monster.
PHILATELL. Speake to her your selfe,
Shee's so incenst against me,
She will not welcome happines,
Because I bring it.
PRINCE. Faire ornament of griefe, why are you troubled———
Can you beleeve there's any thing within
My power which you shall mourne for?
If you have any feares, impart them;
Any desires, give them a name,
And I will give thee rest:
You wrong the greatnes of my love,
To doubt the goodnes of it.
SABRINA. Alas, I doe not doubt your love my Lord,
I feare it; 'tis that which does undoe me.
For 'tis not *Samorat* that's prisoner now,
It is the Princes Rivall;
Oh! for your owne sake Sir be mercifull:
How poorely will this sound hereafter,
The Prince did feare another's merit so,
Found so much vertue in his rivall, that
He was forc't to murder it, make it away.
There can be no addition to you, Sir, by his death,
By his life there will; You get the point
Of honour; fortune does offer here
What time perchance cannot agen:
A handsome opportunity to show
The bravery of your minde———
PRINCE. This pretty Rhetorique cannot perswade me (faire)
To let your *Samorat* live for my sake:
It is enough he shall for yours.
SABRINA. Though vertue still rewards it selfe, yet here

2 (faire)] (*faire. FA46 set as if a* S.D.; ‸faire‸ one *FA48*

May it not stay for that; but may the gods
Showre on you suddenly such happines,
That you may say, my mercy brought me this———

PRINCE. The gods no doubt will heare when you doe pray
Right waies: But here you take their names in vaine,
Since you can give your selfe that happines
Which you doe aske of them.

SABRINA. Most gracious Sir, doe not———

PRINCE. Hold, I dare not heare thee speake,
For feare thou now should'st tell me,
What I doe tell my selfe;
That I would poorely bargaine for any favours;
Retire and banish all thy feares,
I will be kind and just to thee *Sabrina*,
What s'ere thou prov'st to me. *Exit* SABRINA [*and* PHEMILLIA].

PHILATELL. Rarely acted Sir.

PRINCE. Ha!———

PHILATELL. Good faith to th' very life.

PRINCE. Acted?—No,—'twas not acted.

PHILATELL. How Sir?

PRINCE. I was in earnest.
I meane to conquer her this way,
The others low and poore.

PHILATELL. Ha?———

PRINCE. I told thee 'twould be so before.

PHILATELL. Why Sir, you doe not meane to save him?

PRINCE. Yes—I doe———
Samorat shall be releas't immediatly.

PHILATELL. Sure you forget I had a brother Sir,
And one that did deserve Justice at least.

PRINCE. He did—And he shall have it:
He that kil'd him shall dye———
And 'tis high satisfaction, that, looke not———
It must be so.

Exeunt.

Enter STRAMADOR, *and* PERIDOR. [IV.

PERIDOR. No Devils *Stramador*, beleeve your eyes—
To which I cannot be so lost,

60 Right] Streight *FA48*

But you may call to minde one *Peridor*.
STRAMADOR. Ha? *Peridor*? thou did'st command that day
In which the Tamorens fell.
PERIDOR. I did———
Yet *Tamoren* lives.
STRAMADOR. Ha?
PERIDOR. Not *Tamoren* the Prince, he fell indeed;
But *Tamoren* his brother, who that day
Led our horse: young *Reginella* too,
Which is the subject of the suit
You have ingag'd your selfe by oath
The Prince shall grant.
STRAMADOR. Oh! 'tis impossible,
Instruct me how I should beleeve thee.
PERIDOR. Why thus———
Necessity upon that great defeat
Forc't us to keep the Woods, and hide our selves
In holes which since we much inlarg'd,
And fortifi'd them in the entrance so,
That 'twas a safe retreate upon pursuite:
Then swore we all allegeance to this *Tamoren*.
These habits better to disguise our selves,
We took at first;
But finding with what ease we rob'd,
We did continue 'em, and tooke an Oath,
Till some new troubles in the State should happen,
Or faire occasion to make knowne our selves
Offer it selfe, we would appeare no other:
But come, let's not loose
What we shall ne're recover,
This opportunitie.

Exeunt.

Enter NASHORAT, *and* PELLEGRIN, *in Prison.* [v. iv]

PELLEGRIN. *Nashorat*, you have not thought of any stratagem yet———
NASHORAT. Yes I have thought———
PELLEGRIN. What?

v. iii. 11 suit‸] *FA48*; ~, — *FA46* 13 Prince] *FA48*; King *FA46*
30.1 *Exeunt.*] *FA48*; *om. FA46*
v. iv. 0.1 S.D. *in Prison*] *FA48*; *om. FA46*

NASHORAT. That if you have any accompts with heaven, they may goe on———This villanous dying's like a strange tune, has run so in my head, no wholsome consideration would enter it. Nothing angers me neither, but that I passe by my Mistresses window to't.

PELLEGRIN. Troth, that's unkinde, I have something troubles me too.

NASHORAT. What's that.

PELLEGRIN. The people will say as we goe along, thou art the properer fellow. Then I breake an appointment with a Merchants Wife, but who can help it?———*Nashorat.*

NASHORAT. Yea who can help it indeed, she's to blame though 'faith, if she does not beare with thee, considering the occasion———

PELLEGRIN. Considering the occasion as you say, a man would thinke he might be borne with. There's a Scrivener I should have paid some money to, upon my word, but———

Enter ORSABRIN, SAMORAT, *Princes servants, with* SAMORAT'*s releasement.*

ORSABRIN. By faire *Sabrina's* name, I conjure you
Not to refuse the mercy of the Prince———

SAMORAT. It is resolv'd Sir, you know my answer.

ORSABRIN. Whether am I falne?
I thinke if I should live a little longer,
I should be made the cause of all the mischiefe
Which should arise to the world———
Hither I came to save a friend,
And by a slight of fortune I destroy him:
My very wayes to good prove ills.
Sure I can looke a man into misfortune:
The Plague's so great within me 'tis infectious.
Oh! I am weary of my selfe:
Sir I beseech you yet accept of it,
For I shall be this way a sufferer,
And an executioner too———

SAMORAT. I'le beg of thee no more,
Thou do'st beget in me desire to live:
For when I finde how much I am behind
In noble acts of friendship,
I cannot chuse but wish for longer time,

8 passe by] pass *Collier*   19.1–2 S.D. *with...releasement*] *FA48*; *om.* *FA46*
34 this] *FA48*; his *FA46*   36 I'le] *FA48*; tI *FA46*

That I might struggle with thee,
For what thou hast too clearly now got from me:
The point of honour———
Oh! it is wisedome and great thrift to dye;
For who with such a debt of friendship and
Of Love, as you and my *Sabrina*
Must expect from me could ere subsist.

NASHORAT. They are complementing; 'sfoot they make no more of it, then if 'twere who should goe in first at a doore———I thinke *Pellegrine*, as you and I have cast it up, it comes to something more———

Enter Messenger.

MESSENGER. Gentlemen, prepare, the Court is setting.

SAMORAT. Friends, this is no time for ceremonie;
But what a racke have I within me,
To see you suffer. And yet I hope the Prince
Will let his anger dye in me,
Not to take the forfeiture of you.

NASHORAT. If he should, *Pellegrin* and I are resolv'd, and are ready, all but our speeches to the people, and those will not trouble us much, for we intend not to trouble them.

Exeunt.

Enter PRINCE, PHILATELL, *and Attendants.* [V v]

PRINCE. Not accept it?
Lose this way too?—What shall I doe?
He makes advantages of mine,
And like a skilfull Tennis-player,
Returnes my very best with excellent designe.
It must not be.
Bring to the Closet here above, the chiefe o'th' Jury:
I'le try another way. *Exeunt.*

Enter Judges, Lawyers, SAMORAT, ORSABRIN, NASHORAT, PELLEGRIN, [*and* GAOLER].

NASHORAT. Of all wayes of destroying mankinde, these Judges have the easiest, they sleep and doe it.

PELLEGRIN. To my thinking now, this is but a solemner kind of

51.1 S.D. *Enter Messenger*] *FA48*; *om. FA46* 56 his] *Collier*; this *FA46*
V. V. 0.1 S.D. PHILLATELL, *and Attendants*] *FA48*; PERODOR *and others FA46* 8.1–2 Enter... PELLEGRIN] *FA48*; *Enter Judges, Prisoners, Lawyers. FA46*

Puppet-play: how the Devill came we to be acters in't? So; it beginnes.

1. JUDGE. The Princes Councell: are they ready?

LAWYER. Here———

1. JUDGE. Begin then———

LAWYER. My Lords, that this so great and strange———

SAMORAT. Most reverend Judges,
To save th'expence of breath and time,
And dull Formalities of Law———
I here pronounce my selfe guilty.

A curtain drawn, PRINCE, PHILATELL, *with others appear above.*

PRINCE. Agen he has prevented me.

SAMORAT. So guilty
That no other can pretend a share———
This noble youth, a stranger to every thing
But Gallantry, ignorant in our Lawes and Customes,
Has made perchance (in strange severity)
A forfeit of himselfe; but should you take it,
The gods when he is gone will sure revenge it.
If from the stalke you pull this bud of vertue,
Before't has spread and shewne it selfe abroad,
You doe an injury to all mankinde;
And publique mischiefe cannot be private Justice.
This man's as much above a common man,
As man's above a beast; And if the Law
Destroyes not man for killing of a beast,
It should not here, for killing of a man.
Oh what mistake 'twould be?
For here you sit to weed the Cankers out
That would doe hurt 'ith' State, to punish vice;
And under that y'oud root out vertue too.

ORSABRIN. If I doe blush, 'tis not (most gracious Judges)
For any thing which I have done, 'tis for that
This much mistaken youth hath here deliver'd.
'Tis true (and I confesse) I ever had
A little stocke of honour (which I still preserv'd)
But that (by leaving me behinde alive)

15] S.D. *in FA48*: PRINCE, PHILATELL *above.* 15 Strange] Strict *Collier* 19.1 S.D. *A...above.*] *FA48*; *om. FA46*; S.P. PRINCE *from above. FA46* 35 what] what a *Collier* 43 preserv'd] preserve *Hazlitt*

He now most cunningly doe's thinke to get from me:
And I beseech your Lordships to assist me;
For 'tis most fraudulent all he desires.
Your Lawes I hope are reasonable, else why
Should reasonable men be subject to them; and then
Upon what grounds is he made guilty now?
How can he be thought accessarie
To th' killing of a man, that did not know
O'th' fighting with him? Witnesse all those pow'rs
Which search mens hearts, that I my selfe,
(Untill he beckned me) knew nothing of it,
If such a thing as sacrifice must be—
Why? Man for mans enough: though elder times
T'appease diviner Justice, did offer up———
(Whither through gallantrie, or ignorance)
Vast multitudes of Beasts in sacrifice,
Yet numbers of men is seldome heard of:
One single *Curtius* purg'd a whole States sin:
You will not say th'offence is now as great,
Or that you ought to be more highly satisfied
Then Heaven.

PRINCE. Brave youths.

NASHORAT. *Pellegrin*, you and I will let our speeches alone.

1. JUDGE. If that the Law were of so fine a web,
As wit and fancie spin it out to, here,
Then these defences would be just, and save:
But that is more substantiall,
Of another make———
And Gentlemen, if this be all,
Sentence must passe———

Enter TAMOREN [*disguised*].

TAMOREN [*whisper*]. *Orsabrin*!

ORSABRIN. Ha! who names me there?

TAMOREN [*whisper*]. A friend: heare me:
I am an Officer in that darke world
From whence thou cam'st, sent thus
Disguis'd by *Reginella* our faire Queene,

62 States] *In all copies of FA46 the final s is mashed almost beyond recognition*; State *FA48*
66 S.P. PRINCE] *P. FA46*; *Pr. FA48* 74.1 S.D. *Enter* TAMOREN.] *FA46*; *Enter* TAMOREN, STRAMADOR. *FA48*

And to redeeme thee.
ORSABRIN. *Reginella*! I'th' midst of all these ills,
How preciously that name doe's sound?
TAMOREN. If thou woult sweare to follow me,
At th'instant th'art releast;
I'le save thee and thy friends, in spite of Law.
ORSABRIN. Doubt not of that;
Bring me where *Reginella* is: and if
I follow not, perpetuall misery follow me:
It cannot be a Hell where she appeares.
TAMOREN. Be confident.———

Goes out and brings TORCULAR.

Behold (grave Lords) the man
Whose death question'd the life of these,
Found and recovered by the Theeves 'ith Woods;
And rescued since by us, to rescue Innocence.
ORSABRIN [*aside*]. Rare Devill,
With what dexteritie h'as raised this Shape up
To delude them.
PRINCE. Ha? *Torcular* alive?
PHILATELL. *Torcular*?
I should as soone beleeve my brother
Ne're in being too.
TORCULAR. You cannot wonder more to finde me here,
Then I doe to finde my selfe.
NASHORAT. Come unbinde, unbinde, this matter's answered.
2. JUDGE. Hold:
They are not free, the Law exacts the same
For breach of prison that it did before.
ORSABRIN. There is no scaping out of fortunes hands.
Doest heare; hast never a trick for this?
TAMOREN. Doubt me not, I have without,
At my command, those which never fail'd me;
And it shall cost many a life yet, Sir,
Ere yours be lost———

Enter PRINCE, PHILATELL *from above.*
STRAMADOR, PERIDOR, REGINELLA *meet them below.*

PRINCE. *Stramador*, you have been a stranger here of late.

99 Ne're] Neere *FA46*; Ne'r *Works 94*; were *Hazlitt* *FA48*; *two lines later FA46*

111.1–2 S.D. *Enter*...*below*.]

STRAMADOR. Peruse this paper, Sir;
You'l find there was good reason for't.
PRINCE. How!
Old *Tamorens* brother, Captaine of the Theeves,
That has infested thus our Countrey?
Reginella too, the heire of that fear'd Familie!
A happy and a strange discovery.
TAMOREN. *Peridor* and *Reginella*, the villaine has betrai'd me.
REGINELLA. 'Tis *Orsabrin*, they have kept their words.
ORSABRIN. *Reginella*? she was a woman then.
O let me goe.
GAOLER. You doe forget sure what you are.
ORSABRIN. I doe indeed: oh, to unriddle now!
STRAMADOR. And to this man you owe it Sir, [*Points to* PERIDOR.]
You find an ingagement to him there;
And I must hope you'l make me just to him.
PRINCE. He does deserve it,———
Seize on him———
[*They seize* TAMOREN.]
TAMOREN. Nay then all truths must out.
That I am lost and forfeit to the Law,
I doe confesse; Yet since to save this Prince———
PRINCE. Prince!
ORSABRIN. (Our *Mephosto-philus* is mad.)
TAMOREN. Yes, Prince, this is the *Orsabrin*———
ORSABRIN. Ha!———
TAMOREN. So long agoe, supposed lost, your Brother, Sir:
Fetch in there *Ardelan* and *Piramont*.
Enter ARDELAN *and* PIRAMONT.
NASHORAT. What mad Planet rules this day! *Ardelan*, and *Piramont*.
ORSABRIN. The Divel's wanton,
And abuses all mankinde to day.
TAMOREN. These faces are well knowne to all Francelians,
Now let them tell the rest.
PIRAMONT. My noble Master living! found in *Francelia*?
ARDELAN. The gods have satisfied our tedious hopes.
PHILATELL. Some Imposture.
ORSABRIN. A new designe of fortune———I dare not trust it.

132 Prince—] ~. *FA46* 134 Yes] *FA48*; Yet *FA46* 134 *Osabrin* —] ~. *FA46*

TAMOREN. Why speake you not?
PIRAMONT. I am so full of joy,
It will not out. Know ye, Francelians,
When Sanborne fatall field was fought,
So desperate were the hopes of *Orsabrin*,
That 'twas thought fit to send away this Prince,
And give him safety in another clime;
That spite of an ill day, an *Orsabrin*
Might be preserv'd alive. Thus you all know,
To *Garradans* chiefe charge he was committed:
Who when our Barke by Pyrats was surpris'd,
(For so it was) was slaine 'ith first encounter;
Since that we have been forc't to wait on Fortunes
Pleasure. And Sir, that all this time we kept
You from the knowledge of your selfe,
Your pardon; It was our zeale that err'd,
Which did conclude it would be prejudiciall.
ARDELAN. My Lords, you looke as if you doubted still:
If *Piramont* and I be lost unto your memory,
Your hands I hope are not———
Here's our Commission:
There's the Diamond Elephant,
That which our Princes Sons are ever knowne by:
Which we, to keep him undiscovered,
Tore from his riband in that fatall day
When we were made prisoners:
And here are those that tooke us,
Which can witnesse all circumstance,
Both how, and when, time and place;
With whom we ever since have liv'd by force:
For on no Kingdome, friend unto *Francelia*,
Did Fortune ever land us, since that houre;
Nor gave us meanes to let our Country know
He liv'd.
TAMOREN. These very truths, when they could have no ends,
(For they beleev'd him lost)
I did receive from them before,
Which gave me now the boldnes to appeare
Here, where I'm lost by Law.

179 He] We *Hazlitt*

Shouts without, { Long live Prince *Orsabrin*.
Long live Prince *Orsabrin*. }

NASHORAT. *Pellegrin*, let's second this: Right or wrong 'tis best for us.

PELLEGRIN. *Orsabrin*, *Orsabrin*.

PRINCE. What shouts are those?

STRAMADOR. Souldiers of *Tamorens*, the first;
The second was the peoples, who
Much presse to see their long lost Prince.

PHILATELL. Sir, 'tis most evident, and all agrees,
This was his colour'd haire,
His Aire, though alter'd much with time.
You weare too strange a face upon this newes;
Sir, you have found a brother;
I, *Torcular*; the Kingdome happines;
For here the plague of Robberies will end.
It is a glorious day.

PRINCE. It is indeed,
I am amaz'd, not sad; Wonder doe's keep
The passage so, nothing will out. Brother
(For so my kinder Stars will have it) I here
Receive you as the bounty of the gods,
A blessing I did not expect,
And in returne to them, this day,
Francelia ever shall keep holy.

ORSABRIN. Fortune by much abusing me, has so
Dul'd my faith, I cannot credit any thing.
I know not how to owne such happines.

PRINCE. Let not your doubts lessen your joyes:
If you have had disasters heretofore,
They were but given to heighten what's to come.

NASHORAT. Here's as strange a turne as if 'twere the fift Act in a Play.

PELLEGRIN. I'm sure 'tis a good turne for us.

ORSABRIN. Sir, why stands that Lady so neglected there,
(That does deserve to be the busines of mankinde)
Oh ye gods: since you'l be kind

189 *Orsabrin*, *Orsabrin*] Observe, Observe *FA46* 191 *Tamorens*,] *Collier*; ~^ *FA46* 196 Aire] *FA46*; Hair *Hazlitt* 199 Kingdome] *FA48*; Kingdomes *FA46* 204 kinder] kindred *Collier*

And bountifull, let it be here.
As fearfully, as jealous husbands aske
After some secrets which they dare not know;
Or as forbidden Lovers meet i'th night,
Come I to thee (and 'tis no ill signe this,
Since flames when they burne highest tremble most.)
Oh, should she now deny me!

REGINELLA. I know not perfectly what all this meanes;
But I doe finde some happinesse is neare,
And I am pleas'd, because I see you are———

ORSABRIN. She understands me not.

PRINCE. He seemes t'have passion for her.

TAMOREN. Sir, in my darke commands these flames broke out
Equally violent, at first sight; and 'twas
The hope I had to reconcile my selfe.

ORSABRIN. It is a holy Magicke that will make
Of you and I but one.

REGINELLA. Any thing that you wou'd aske me, sure I might grant.

ORSABRIN. Harke Gentlemen, she doe's consent,
What wants there else?

PERIDOR. My hopes grow cold, I have undone my selfe.

PRINCE. Nothing, we all will joyne in this;
The long liv'd feud between the Families
Here dyes; this day the Hyminæall
Torches shall burne bright; so bright, that they
Shall dimme the light of all that went before———

Enter SABRINA.

See *Sabrina* too.

TAMOREN. Sir, I must have much of pardon, [*Kneels.*]
Not for my selfe alone, but for all mine———

PRINCE. Rise, had'st thou not deserv'd what now thou su'st for?
This day should know no clouds.

PERIDOR *kneeles to* TAMOREN.

TAMOREN. Taught by the Princes mercy; I forgive too.

SABRINA. ———Frighted hither Sir.
They told me you woo'd not accept the Princes mercy.

SAMORAT. Art thou no further yet in thy intelligence?
See, thy brother lives.

SABRINA. My brother?

TORCULAR. And 'tis the least of wonders has falne out.

248 S.D. *Kneels*] *MS addition in FA46 NjP copy*

ORSABRIN. Yes, such a one as you are, faire,
And you shall be acquainted. REGINELLA *looks at* SABRINA.
SAMORAT [*to* PHILATELL *and* TORCULAR]. Oh could your hate, my Lords, now,
[*to* PRINCE.] Or your love dye.
PHILATELL. Thy merit has prevail'd with me.
TORCULAR. And me.
PRINCE. And has almost with me. *Samorat*,
Thou do'st not doubt thy Mistresse Constancie?
SAMORAT. No Sir.
PRINCE. Then I will beg of her,
That till the Sun returnes to visit us,
She will not give away her selfe for ever.
Although my hopes are faint,
Yet I would have 'em hopes,
And in such jolly houres as now attend us,
I would not be a desperate thing,
One made up wholly of despaire.
SABRINA. You that so freely gave me *Samorats* life,
Which was in danger, most justly, justly, may
Be suffer'd to attempt upon my love,
Which is in none.
PRINCE. What sayes my noble Rivall?
SAMORAT. Sir, y'are kind in this, and wisely doe provide
I should not surfeit: For here is happines
Enough besides to last the Sun's returne.
NASHORAT. You and I are but savers with all this *Pellegrin*. But by the Lord 'tis well we came off as we did, all was at stake.
PRINCE. Come, no more whispers here,
Let's in, and there unriddle to each other———
For I have much to aske.
ORSABRIN. A Life! a Friend! a Brother! and a Mistres!
Oh! what a day was here: Gently my Joyes distill,
Least you should breake the Vessell you should fill.
Exeunt

277 S.P. SAMORAT] *Collier*; *Sab. FA46* 287 fill. | *Exeunt.*] fill. | *FINIS. FA46*

EPILOGUE.

AND how, and how, in faith,—a pretty plot;
And smartly carried through too, was it not?
And the Devils, how, well? and the fighting,
Well too;—a foole, and 't had bin just old writing.
O what a monster-wit must that man have,
That could please all which now their twelve pence gave:
High characters (cries one) and he would see
Things that ne're were, nor are, nor ne're will be.
Romances, cries easie-soules, and then they sweare
The Playe's well writ, though scarce a good line's there.
The Women—Oh if *Stephen* should be kil'd,
Or misse the Lady, how the plot is spil'd?
And into how many pieces a poore Play
Is taken still before the second day?
Like a strange Beauty newly come to Court;
And to say truth, good faith 'tis all the sport:
One will like all the ill things in a Play,
Another, some o'th' good, but the wrong way;
So from one poore Play there comes t'arise
At severall Tables, severall Comedies.
The ill is only here, that 't may fall out
In Plaies as Faces; and who goes about
To take asunder oft destroyes (we know)
What altogether made a pretty shew.

FINIS.

Epilogue 3 how, well?] ∼, ∼; *FA48*; ∼? ∼; *Thompson*   9 cries] crie *FA48*

EMENDATIONS OF ACCIDENTALS

This is a record of the changes that the editor has made in minor punctuation, lining of verse, capitalization, word separation, and the use of italics. After the bracket appears the original reading in *Fragmenta Aurea* 1646. Occasionally an emendation is taken from an early edition, but no attempt has been made to record the alterations of accidentals through all the derivative editions. When *Fragmenta* 1646 has lined prose as verse that fact has been noted, but the exact division not recorded. Many dashes at the ends of speeches have been silently removed.

Prologue

3 *Beaumont*] *FA48; Beamont FA46*
6 meat;] ~,
15 before‸] ~;
23 Epilogue,] ~‸

The Actors (*copy text FA48*)

6 NASHORAT] NASSURAT
11 ARDELAN] ARDELLAN
21 *Gaoler*] *Goaler*

I. i

1] *FA46 lines* But...Lords, | May... businesse
7 day:] ~,
9 thee,] ~;
11–12] *FA46 lines* Faith...thinke | You... her?
18 talke.] ~‸
29 one?] *FA48*; ~! *FA46*
29] *FA46 lines* Sir...one? | We...fourth.—
31] *FA46 lines* My...me! | This...civill.
46 Sir,] ~‸
50 preserve, I see,] ~‸ ~‸
53 me;] ~,
54.1 SAMORAT] SAMORATT *also at* 97.1 *and* 109.1
65] *FA46 lines* As...Royall | In...Haven: —
67 S'foot,] ~,
70] *FA46 lines* I'le...weakest; | There's ...that.
74] *FA46 lines* Hold...youth! | Destroy ...kindnesse:
80] *FA46 lines* If...me, | I...call.
85] *FA46 lines* It...be, — | My...Jade:
100–1] *FA46 lines* Shift...place, | The... dangerous, | As...safety, | Follow me.
105] *FA46 lines* But...strength, | And... Towne—
110] *FA46 lines* I'th...sometimes, | And Bears?
120 appeares;] ~,
120] *FA46 lines* Not...appeares; | There ...been
123 dead,] ~‸
126] *FA46 lines* For...none, | Unlesse resisted;
129 hurt‸] ~,
129 recover'd,] ~‸
130 Reward‸] ~,
144 Sir] S r *all copies*
150–1] *lined as in FA48; FA46 lines* The... be | In...Towne:
155 sake‸ —] ~.—

I. ii

0.1 NASHORAT, PELLEGRIN] NASSURAT, PELLAGRIN
1–19] *FA46 lines as verse*
3 S.P. PELLEGRIN] *Pella. as are the rest of his prefixes in this scene*
9 Fiend‸] ~,
10 thee,] ~‸
12 honour‸] ~,
15 loved,] ~.

I. iii

1–73] *FA46 lines as verse*
2 Sir] *Sir*
3 tooke;] ~,
6.1 PIRAMONT] PIRAMANT
7–10] *roman type as if part of the dialogue*
19 *Piramont*] *Piramant*
33 *Garradan*,] ~‸
35 *Piramont*] *FA48; Piramant FA46*
53 ‸Within there: ‸] (within there‸)
59 Sacke,] *FA48*; ~‸ *FA46*
65 alone.] ~,
66–71] *roman type as if dialogue*

I. iv

1–54] *FA46 lines as verse*
6 do.] ~,
6 *Mirmidon?*] ~.
10 waiting.] ~,
13 *Lucreces;*] *FA48*; ~, *FA46*
15 thing.] ~,
23 other;] ~,
26 Officer.] ~,
34 too.] ~;
34 behind,] *FA48*; ~; *FA46*
34 say;] *FA48*; ~, *FA46*
40 will,] ~‸
40] *FA46 lines* If't...too't | And...made;
42 S.P. PHEMILLIA] PHEMILIA

II. i

18 Come,] ~‸
28] *FA46 lines* Y'are undone; | The... scal'd,
32–3] *FA46 lines* The...Justice | Like... time, | Move quick, | And...sure:
34 do?] *FA48*; ~, *FA46*
35 forth] *FA48*; forrh *FA46*
36] *FA46 lines* My...safest | Enter there,
37 furie,] ~‸
39–41] *FA46 lines* Her Closet, | Yea... that? | And...it, | What...there? | Shee...returne, — | I...out.

II. ii

1] *FA46 lines* The...them | More secure, —
3] *FA46 lines* Nor...light | Appeares,—
9 care;] ~,
10] *FA46 lines* You...Gate, | There's... Ladder.

II. iii

2–7] *FA46 lines* Our...false, | It... Musicke, | *Samorat, Samorat.* | He... *Samorat,* | Or...out | I'th...so. | This... Thresholds, | And...doores, | I... Cellar, | Where...too,
3 *Samorat.*‸] ~.,
9] *FA46 lines* Upon...them, | And... squeake,
11] *FA46 lines* Oh...doore: | Though... Porter,
14] *FA46 lines* Nay...out, | And...other | But this.—
16–17] *FA46 lines* Where ... be? | Ha!— |Good...*Samorat*!
16 Heavens,] ~‸
26 i'th] it'h
31] FA46 *lines* But...here, | This... scratch,
36] *lined as in FA48; FA46 lines* It... Sword, | but...fault,
36 but] bu *ViU, DLC copies; a dim* t *in other copies*
40 tempest‸] ~,
40 me,] ~‸
41 me.] ~,
41] *FA46 lines* I...teares, | But...me.
55] *FA46 lines* Or...knots, | Which... cure,
57 *Samorat,*] ~‸
58] *FA46 lines* Lies...love, | Like... disease,
60] *FA46 lines* Yet...beauty; | Disfigur't so,
64] *FA46 lines* Be...others? | Remember ...often
68 remove.] ~‸
72 place] plaee
72] *FA46 lines* But here, | For...place,
74] *FA46 lines* Am...thing? | So bankerupt?
81–2] *FA46 lines* Why...Sir, | Because... irrecoverable. | But...him? | He...so.
84 sorow,] ~‸
87] *FA46 lines* Though...love: | Should ...Sir?
91] *FA46 lines* Due...parting | Will...me.
95] *FA46 lines* Till...over; | Here... found,
95 over;] ~,

II. iv

1–5] *FA46 lines as verse*

II. v

1] *lined as in FA48; FA46 lines* Let... stirre, | I sweare.—
1 stirre,] ~‸
4 youth;] *FA48*; ~, *FA46*
6 travell:] *FA48*; ~, *FA46*

II. vi

4 ‸Which...way?‸] (~‸)
18 selfe,] ~‸
21 on] one
22.1 PHEMILLIA] PHEMILIA
23 *Phemillia,*] ~‸

23] *FA46 lines* Run...*Phemillia*, | To... walls,
27] *FA46 lines* He...Horse, | And...Sea,

III. i

1 A prize—A prize—] ~—~,
2 forth.] ~;
3–10] *roman type*
5 discover,] ~‸
17–53] *FA46 lines as verse*
34 Councels?] *FA48*; ~. *FA46*
36 himselfe?—] ~.—
39 State,] *FA48*; ~; *FA46*
40 policie.] ~; *FA48*; ~, *FA46*

III. ii

0.1 GAOLER] GOALER *and in* S.P. *at* III. v. 0.1; *his prefixes are Iai., Iay. and Jailer. in this act.*
0.1 NASHORAT] NASSURAT
1–12] *FA46 lines as verse*
4 Sir,] ~‸
4 desperate;] ~,
17–18] *FA46 lines* Undoe, | Quickly, quickly, | His...Hat. | What...do? | None...serve,
22–6] *FA46 lines* The...enough | With... still. | Desperate...desperate | Cures ...serv'd,— | You...parts.
35 The...name.] *italicized as if part of the song FA48; FA46 has roman type for 28–34.*
35 name.] *FA48*; ~, *FA46*
35–72] *FA46 lines as verse*
36 sleepy.] ~,
41 life,] ~‸
51 be‸] ~,
53–4, 56–7] *roman type*
60 one] on
69 conceit.] ~,
72–89] *roman type*
73 *eyes*,] ~‸
78 i'th] it'h
82 *ho*,] ~‸
85 *black*,] ~‸
90–95] *FA46 lines as verse*
91 heare?] *FA48*; ~‸ *FA46*
92 it.)] ~‸)
93 frost] froft

III. iii

3] *FA46 lines* It...hum.— | It...too.—
6 this,] ~‸
7 youth,] ~‸
11] *FA46 lines* Be...wilt, | I...question't:
13–15] *FA46 lines* Lay...wonder, | And ...cloathes, | In...the | Prison...finde | One...you;
17] *FA46 lines* Of...waite | Us.—

III. iv

4] *FA46 lines* Who...some | That...come,
8] *FA46 lines* Have...same: | Come... Perdues,
10–12] *FA46 lines* I...now, | Yonder... are. | Hallow...these? | Any...ours? | No...close, | They...presently.—
12 presently.—] ~,
13–15] *FA46 lines* Agen...misfortune, Mischiefe...me | Like...quotidian,
18 sentences,—] ~, ‸

III. vi

1] *FA46 lines* No...horses?— | Some mistake,—
2 wood?] ~.

III. vii

2–3] *FA46 lines* To...so, | You...still, | As...proud? | Ha...so?
11–12] *FA46 lines* Abominable. | Had... been | Tollerable.—
13–40] *FA46 lines as verse*
13 see‸—] ~.—
14 twelve,] ~.
24 more] *FA46 DLC copy looks more like n.o.e. but 'more' is clear in ViU and others*
41 TAMOREN] TAMERIN
48] *FA46 lines* So...selfe | With...agen.
50] *FA46 lines* The...Chaunce, | One... fooles;
58–66] *FA46 lines as verse*
69 Cupid,] ~‸
70 — Would] ‸~
75 by.—] ~,‸
76–8] *FA46 lines* Thou...world, | That ...hell, | So...me | In...thee,
103] *FA46 lines* To...on.— | A...pleasures
122 heart.] ~‸
123 ere] Eere
123–9] *lined as in FA48; FA46 lines* They'le...nothing, | Ere...her, | Sweet Excellence.— | Ha...eyes? | If... punishment; | Let...still, | And...me?
132–43] *FA46 lines as verse*

IV. i

1 Good] Ggod
1–116] *FA46 lines as verse*
7 weeke;] ~.
10 her,] ~:
10 Like...the] *FA46(c); FA46(u) indents the entire line*
14 enough,] ~‸
19 Oos] OOS
26 things.] ~?
28 hand,] ~‸
42 Wedding?—] ~?‸
42 so.—] ~.‸
44 place‸] ~.
49 alone, —] ~,‸
56 this?] ~!
58 light?] ~.
67–116] *FA46 lines as verse*
96 along?] ~,
100 now] ~,
101 State:] ~,
102 Stratagems,] ~:
104 Skippat‸] ~,

IV. ii

18 all,] ~‸
33 it;] ~,
36 in't] *FA46(c)*; in it *FA46(u)*
42–5] *FA46 lines* I...conceal'd, | But ...am, | Before...youth | Hath... roome | Up...heart, | Ha...her! | Hell ...Furies.
46 What] *P.* What
46 *there*—] *FA46*; IU, ICN, ViU *appear to have a dash alone. Other copies seem to have a period, a colon, or comma before the dash, but the variations are probably due to nicks and bends in the long dash.*
48–9] *FA46 lines* I...this, | It...it: | I... strange.

IV. iii

0.1 PELLEGRIN] PELEGRIN
1–59] *FA46 lines as verse*
44 Obey] obey
53 *Nashorat*] *Nasharot*

IV. iv

1–2] *lined as in FA48; FA46 lines* A... Phantasme | Rais'd...thee. | Good... Devill, | Trie...more.
5] *lined as in FA48; FA46 lines* Wer't... amorous | In...world?
14] *lined as in FA48; FA46 lines* A...this. | Certainly.
14 this,] ~‸
15–26] *FA46 lines as verse*
17 'em] *FA46(c)*; them *FA46(u)*
18 mirth:] *FA46(c); ~; FA46(u)*
21 it.—]it.‸
25 thee, —] ~,‸

IV. v

1–22] *FA46 lines as verse*
10 *Carer per so lo carer*] Carer per so lo carer
10 Fairie] fairie
14–15 I...selfe] *FA46(c); indented FA46(u)*
16 see—] *FA46(c); ~‸ FA46(u)*

IV. vi

8–9] *FA46 lines* Will...deface. | Well... where? | I...question.
14 heare?] *FA58; ~, FA46, FA48*
16 gentlemen,—] ~,‸
21 Gentlemen,] *FA48; ~‸ FA46*
27–8] *FA46 lines* He...me: | I...termes.

IV. vii

1–2] *FA46 lines* Flie...and | Bring... back:
5] *FA46 lines* I...anger; | Fly, be gone.
9–10] *FA46 lines* You...feare; | Pray... keeping.
9 feare;] ~,
12 stay,] ~‸
18–19] *one line in FA46*
19 eyes] ey's *FA46 in a full line*
19 all,] ~‸
24–6] *FA46 lines* The...best, | Such... those | Are...within.
27 Why, Governour,] ~‸ ~‸
33] *Gnomic pointing by " at left margin*

V. i

0.1 TAMOREN] TAMAREN
4 Snayles?] ~,
4–5] *FA46 lines* A...y'all | Issue...us.
24 time?—] ~?‸
26 exellent.—] ~.‸
27 straight.] *FA48; ~, FA46*
29] *FA46 lines* How...wounds? | Will... Aire?
32 sword.] ~‸
43 that;] ~‸

V. ii

13] *FA46 lines* Oh!— | Nothing...past,
16 Secretarie‸] ~,
18–20] *lined as in FA48; FA46 lines* Put... Sir, | We...there— | A...silence— | Sister *Sabrina*— | Hence, hence, | Thou...life:
19 silence—] ~‸
22–4] *FA46 lines* As...did | Bring...was | Extreme...monster.
29] *FA46 lines* Faire...griefe, | Why... troubled—
46 you, Sir,] ~‸ ~‸
47 there] *FA46(c)*; thre *FA46(u)*
48 honour;] *FA48*; ~, *FA46*
49 perchance] *FA46(c)*; percchance *FA46(u)*
86] *FA46 lines* He did— | And...it:
88] *FA46 lines* And...that, | Look not—

V. iii

1–4] *FA46 lines* No...*Stramador*, | Beleeve ...I | Cannot...but | You...minde | One *Peridor*. | Ha . . . did'st | Command...day
10] *FA46 lines* Led...horse: | Young... too,
12 oath‸] ~,
21–2] *One line in FA46*

V. iv

1–19] *FA46 lines as verse*
6 dying's‸] *FA48*; ~, *FA46*
13 *Nashorat*] *FA48*; (*Nashorat FA46*, *set as if a S.D.*
20–1] *lined as in FA48; FA46 lines* By... name, | I...mercy | Of...Prince—
29 My...ills] *indented FA46*
34] *FA46* For...way | A sufferer,
38–43] *FA46 lines* For...am | Behind... friendship, | I...might | Struggle... now | Got...honour—
46–7] *FA46 lines* Of...me | Could...subsist,
48–51] *FA46 lines as verse*
55–7] *FA46 lines* To...suffer. | And...dye | In...you.

V. v

6 be.] ~,
9–12] *FA46 lines as verse*
13] *FA46 lines* The...Councell: | Are... ready?
15 strange‸—] ~.—
20–1] *FA46 lines* So...pretend | A share—
24–5] *FA46 lines* Has...perchance | (In ...himselfe; | But...it,
48–9] *FA46 lines* Your...reasonable, | Else...men | Be...then
52–8] *FA46 lines* To...man, | That... him? | Witnesse...hearts, | That...me) | Knew...thing | As...enough: | Though...Justice, | Did...up—
78–9] *FA46 lines* From...sent | Thus ...Queene,
81] *FA46 lines Reginella*! | I'th'...ills,
85] *FA46 lines* I'le...friends, | In...Law.
87–89] *FA46 lines* Bring...is: | And... me: | It...Hell | Where...appeares—
92] *lined as in FA48; FA46 lines* Found... Theeves | 'ith Woods;
95–6] *FA46 lines* With...this | Shape... them—
95 up‸] ~;
103–5] *FA46 lines* Hold...exacts | The ...before.
108–11] *FA46 lines* Doubt...command, | Those...me; | And...yet, | Sir... lost—
112 *Stramador*,] ~‸
113 paper, Sir;] ~‸ ~,
113–17] *FA46 lines* Peruse...for't. | How ...Captaine | Of...thus | Our Countrey?
120] *FA46 lines* Peridor...villaine; | Has ...me.
120 *Peridor*‸] ~,
124 S.P. GAOLER.] *Jay*.
129 it, —] ~,‸
132] *FA46 lines* I...confesse; | Yet... Prince—
132 confesse;] ~,
136] *FA46 lines* So...agoe, | Supposed lost, | Your...Sir:
136 Brother,] ~‸
138 day!] *FA48*; ~‸ *FA46*
138] *FA46 lines* What...day! | *Ardelan... Piramont*.
146] *FA46 lines* A...fortune— | I...it.
148–9] *FA46 lines* I...out. | Know... Francelians,
149 ye,] ~‸
153–4] *FA46 lines* That...be | Preserv'd alive. | Thus...know,
158–9] *FA46 lines* Since...wait | On... pleasure. | And...kept

169 we,] ~‸
185 *Orsabrin*] *Osabrin*
186 *Pellegrin*,] ~‸
187–8] *FA46 lines Pellegrin*...this: | Right ...us.
191 *Tamorens*,] ~‸
196 time.] ~:
198 brother;] ~‸
199 *Torcular;*] ~,
201–5] *FA46 lines* It...sad; | Wonder...so, | Nothing...out. | Brother...it) | I... gods,
205 gods,] *FA58;* ~; *FA46*
209–10] *FA46 lines* Fortune...has | So ...cannot | Credit...thing.
209 so‸] ~—
215–16] *FA46 lines as verse*
219 (That...mankinde)] *FA48;* ‸~.‸ *FA46*
226 most.)] ~‸)
234 Equally‸ violent,] *FA48;* ~, ~‸ *FA46*
234–5] *FA46 lines* Equally...sight; | And ...selfe.
243 feud] feu'd
244 dyes;] ~,
245–6] *FA46 lines* Torches...bright; | So ...light | Of...before—
250 for?] ~,
253 —Frighted] ‸~
260 hate,] ~‸
262] *FA46 lines* Thy...prevail'd | With me.
263–4] *FA46 lines* And...me. | *Samorat*... Constancie?
263 *Samorat*,] *FA48;* ~‸ *FA46*
264 Constancie?] ~.
270 us,] ~.
274–9] *FA46 lines* Which...danger, | Most...attempt | Upon...none. | What...Rivall? | Sir...doe | Provide... surfeit: | For...returne.
280–1] *FA46 lines as verse*
286] *FA46 lines* Oh...here: | Gently... distill,

Epilogue

9 Romances,] *FA48;* ~‸ *FA46*
9 sweare‸] ~,

BRENNORALT.

A Tragedy.

Presented at the Private House in Black-Fryers, by His *Majesties* servants.

WRITTEN

By Sir JOHN SUCKLING.

LONDON,

Printed for *Humphrey Moseley*, and are to be sold at his shop, at the Signe of the Princes Armes in St *Pauls* Churchyard.

MDCXLVI.

Title-page of the First Edition in *Fragmenta Aurea*, 1646.
The Folger Library Copy.

TEXTS CONSULTED

FA46 *Fragmenta Aurea*, 1646, the copy text.

DC *The Discontented Colonell*, *ca.* 1642, an unauthorized quarto with a debased text.

For 'A hall, a hall' (I. ii)

Add British Museum, Additional MS. 31432, with music by William Lawes.

WI *Wits Interpreter*, 1655.

Brennoralt was reprinted in the collected editions of *Fragmenta*, 1648, 1658, '1658', 1672, the works of 1694–6, 1709, 1719, 1766, 1770, 1836, Hazlitt's editions of 1874 and 1892, and Thompson's edition of 1910. See 'The Collected Editions' for an account of these.

THE ACTORS

SIGISMOND, *King of Poland*
MIESLA
MELIDOR } *Councellors to the King*
A LORD
BRENNORALT, *a Discontent* [*in love with* Francelia]
DORAN, *His Friend*
VILLANOR
GRAINEVERT } *Cavaliers and Officers under* Brennoralt
MARINELL
STRATHEMAN
FRESOLIN, *Brother to* Francelia
IPHIGENE, *young Pallatine of Plocence* [*daughter of* Miesla, *disguised as a man*]
Pallatine of MENSECKE, *Governour, one of the chiefe Rebels*
Pallatine of TROCKE, *a Rebell*
[GENERAL *of the Rebels*]
ALMERIN, *a gallant Rebell* [*betrothed to* Francelia, *friend of* Iphigene]
MORAT, *His Lieutenant Coronell*
FRANCELIA, *the Governours daughter*
ORILLA, *a waiting woman to* Francelia
RAGUELIN, *a servant in the Governors house, but Spie to* Brennoralt
Jaylor
Guard
Souldiers

The Scæne. POLAND

The Actors. 12 *Plocence*] *Florence FA46, DC*

Brennoralt

Enter BRENNORALT, DORAN. [I. i]

BRENNORALT. I say, the Court is but a narrow circuit;
Though somthing elevate above the common;
A kind of Ants nest in the great wilde field,
O're charg'd with multitudes of quick Inhabitants,
Who still are miserably busied to get in,
What the loose foot of prodigality
As fast do's throw abroad.
DORAN. Good:
A most eternall place of low affronts,
And then as low submissions.
BRENNORALT. Right.
High cowards in revenges 'mongst themselves,
And only valiant when they mischiefe others.
DORAN. Stars that would have no names,
But for the ills they threaten in conjunction.
BRENNORALT. A race of shallow, and unskilfull Pilots;
Which doe misguide the Ship even in the calme,
And in great stormes serve but as weight to sinke it.
More, prethee more. *Alarum within.*
'Tis musique to my melancholy.
Enter Souldier.
SOLDIER. My Lord;
A cloud of dust and men the Sentinels
From th'East gate discover; and as they guesse,
The storme bends this way.
BRENNORALT. Let it be.
SOLDIER. My Lord?———
BRENNORALT. Let it be, I will not fight to day:
Bid *Stratheman* draw to the trenches.
On, prethee on.
DORAN. The King imployes a company
Of formall beards, men, who have no other proofes

I. i. I. I] ACT I. SCENE I. *Other acts headed in the same style except* ACT. V. SCEN. I. *No scene divisions FA46*, DC

Of their long life, but that they are old.
BRENNORALT. Right,
And if th'are wise, 'tis for themselves, not others, *Alarum.*
As old men ever are.

Enter second Soldier.

2. SOLDIER. Coronell, Coronell;
Th'enemies at hand, kils all the Centries:
Young *Almerin* leads them on agen.
BRENNORALT. Let him lead them off agen.
2. SOLDIER. Coronell.———
BRENNORALT. Be gone. If th'art afraid, goe hide thy selfe.
2. SOLDIER. What a Divell ayles he? *Exit.*
BRENNORALT. This *Almerin's* the ague of the Camp:
He shakes it once a day.
DORAN. Hee's the ill conscience rather:
He never lets it rest; would I were at home agen.
'Sfoot we lie here i'th' trenches, as if it were
For a winde to carry us into th'other World:
Every houre we expect———
I'le no more on't.
BRENNORALT. Prethee———
DORAN. Not I, by heaven.
BRENNORALT. What man! the worst is but faire death.
DORAN. And what will that amount to? A faire Epitaph.
A fine account.———I'le home I sweare.

Enter STRATHEMAN.

STRATHEMAN. Arme, arme my Lord,
And shew your selfe, all's lost else.
DORAN. Why so?
STRATHEMAN. The Rebels like an unruly floud,
Rowle o're the trenches, and throw downe
All before them.
BRENNORALT. Ha?
STRATHEMAN. We cannot make a stand.
BRENNORALT. He would out-rivall me in honour too,
As well as love; but that he must not doe.
Help me *Stratheman.*——— *Puts on Armour.*
The danger now growes worthy of our swords;

28 others, ‸] *DC*; ~.— *FA46*

And, oh *Doran*, I would to heaven there were
No other stormes then the worst tempest here.

Exeunt.

Enter MARINELL, *throwing downe one he carries.* [I. ii]

MARINELL. There; the Sun's the nearest Surgeon I know,
And the honestest; if thou recoverest, why so:
If not, the cure's paid, they have mauld us.

Enter GRAINEVERT, *with another upon his backe.*

GRAINEVERT. A curse light on this powder: it stayes valour, ere it's halfe way on it's journey: what a disadvantage fight we upon in this age? He that did well heretofore, had the broad faire day to shew it in, witnesses enough; we must beleeve one another—'Tis night when we begin: Eternall smoake and sulpher. Smalke, by this hand I can beare with thee no longer; how now? dead as I live; stolne away just as he us'd to wench. Well, goe thy wayes, for a quiet drinker and dier, I shall never know thy fellow: (*Searches his pockets.*) These trifles too about thee? There was never an honester poore wretch borne I thinke—look i'th' tother pocket too—hum, *Marinell.*

MARINELL. Who's that?

GRAINEVERT. 'Tis I; how goes matters?

MARINELL. Scurvily enough; yet since our Colonell came, th'ave got no ground of us; A weake Sculler against Winde and Tide, would have done as much; harke: this way the torrent beares.

Exeunt.

Enter FRESOLIN, ALMERIN, *Rebels.*

FRESOLIN. The Villaines all have left us.

ALMERIN. Would they had left
Their feares behind them with the enemy.
But come, since we must. *Exeunt.*

Enter BRENNORALT, *Souldiers.*

BRENNORALT. Hoe! *Strathemean*;
Skirt on the left hand with the horse,
And get betwixt these and that Body;
They'r new rallied up for rescue.

I. ii. 8 Smalke,] *DC*; ~; *FA46*; Smalky; *FA48*
2 *Exeunt.*] *DC*; *om. FA46*
21 with the enemy] *DC*; *om. FA46*

DORAN. Th'are ours.

BRENNORALT *charges through.*

BRENNORALT. I doe not see my game yet. *Exeunt.*

A shout within.

Enter BRENNORALT, DORAN, STRATHEMAN, MARINELL.

BRENNORALT. What shout is that?
STRATHEMAN. They've taken *Almerin*, my Lord.
BRENNORALT. *Almerin*? the Divell thanke 'em for't:
When I had hunted hard all day,
And now at length unhearded the proud Deere,
The Currs have snatch't him up; sound a Retreat:
There's nothing now behinde. Who saw, *Doran*?
STRATHEMAN. Shall we bring *Almerin* in my Lord?
BRENNORALT. No; gazing is low Triumph: convey him fairely
To the King, he fought it fairely.
DORAN. What youth was that, whom you bestrid my Lord,
And sav'd from all our swords to day? Was he
Not of the Enemy?
BRENNORALT. It may be so———
STRATHEMAN (*in* DORANS *eare*). The Governors Son, *Fresolin*, his Mistris brother.
BRENNORALT. No matter who. 'Tis pitty, the rough hand
Of warre, should early courages destroy,
Before they bud, and shew themselves i'th'heate
Of Action.
MARINELL. I threw (my Lord) a youth upon a banke,
Which seeking, after the retreate, I found
Dead, and a woman, the pretty daughter
Of the Forrester, *Lucillia*.
BRENNORALT. See, see *Doran*; A sad experiment:
Woman's the cowardly'st and coldest thing
The world brings forth: Yet Love, as fire works water,
Makes it boyle o're, and doe things contrary
To'ts proper nature—I should shed a teare,
Could I tell how—Ah poore *Lucilia*!
Thou didst for me what did as ill become thee.
Pray see her gently bury'd———

28 BRENNORALT. I] I *FA46*; *DC omits the line and makes the S.D. read*: *Bren*. Charge through. *Exeunt.* 30 They've] *DC*; They have *FA46* 35 saw,] ~∧ *DC*, *FA46* 36 my Lord] *DC*; *om. FA46* 37 gazing is] gazing's a *Hazlitt*

Boy, send the Surgeon to the Tent; I bleed:
What lowsie Cottages th'ave given our soules?
Each petty storme shakes them into disorder;
And't costs more paines to patch them up agen,
Then they are worth by much. I'm weary of
The Tenement.
Exeunt.

Enter VILLANOR, GRAINEVERT, MARINELL, *and* STRATHEMAN. [I. iii]

GRAINEVERT. *Villanor*! welcome, welcome, whence camest thou?

VILLANOR. Looke, I weare the Kings high way still on my boots.

GRAINEVERT. A pretty riding phrase, and how? and how? Ladies cheap?

VILLANOR. Faith, reasonable: Those toyes were never deare thou know'st; a little time and industry they'l cost; but in good faith not much: some few there are that set themselves at mighty rates———

GRAINEVERT. Which we o'th' wise passe by, as things o're-valued in the market. Is't not so?

VILLANOR. Y'have said Sir, Harke you, your friend the Rival's married. Has obtain'd the long lov'd Lady, and is such an asse after 't.

GRAINEVERT. Hum. 'Tis ever so. The motions of married people, are as of other naturals; violent, Gentlemen, to the place, and calme in it.

MARINELL. We know this too; and yet we must be fooling.

GRAINEVERT. Faith, women are the baggage of life: They are troublesome, and hinder us in the great march, and yet we cannot be without 'em.

VILLANOR. You speake very well, and Souldier-like.

GRAINEVERT. What? thou art a wit too I warrant, in our absence?

VILLANOR. Hum—no, no, a poore pretender, a Candidate or so, 'gainst the next Sessions: wit enough to laugh at you here.

GRAINEVERT. Like enough, valour's a crime the wise have still reproached unto the valiant, and the fooles too.

VILLANOR. Raillerie *a part*, *Grainevert*, what accommodations shall we finde here?

GRAINEVERT. Cleane straw (sweet-heart) and meat when thou canst get it.

I. iii. 11 Rival's] *DC*; Rivals *FA46* 21 VILLANOR] *Mar. DC*, *FA46* 23 S.P. VILLANOR] *DC*; *Mar. FA46* 25 enough,...crime‸] ~; ~: *FA46*

VILLANOR. Hum? straw?

GRAINEVERT. Yes. That's all will be betwixt Incest: You and your mother earth must lye together.

VILLANOR. Prethee let's be serious; will this last? How goes affaires?

GRAINEVERT. Well.

VILLANOR. But well?

GRAINEVERT. Faith, 'tis now upon the turning of the ballance: A most equall businesse, betwixt Rebellion and Loyaltie.

VILLANOR. What doest meane?

GRAINEVERT. Why; which shall be the vertue, and which the vice.

VILLANOR. How the Divell can that be?

GRAINEVERT. Oh, successe is a rare paint; hides all the uglines.

VILLANOR. Prethee, what's the quarrell?

GRAINEVERT. Nay, for that excuse us; Aske the children of peace. They have the leisure to study it, we know nothing of it; Liberty they say.

VILLANOR. 'Sfoot, let the King make an Act, that any man may be unmarried agen; there's liberty for them. A race of half-witted fellowes quarrell about freedome? And all that while allow the bonds of Matrimony?

GRAINEVERT. You speake very well Sir.

Enter KING, LORDS, [MIESLA, MELIDOR, 3 LORD,] BRENNORALT.

MARINELL. Soft; the King and Councell——

GRAINEVERT. Looke, they follow after like tyred spannels quest sometimes for company, that is, concurre: and that's their busines.

MARINELL. They are as weary of this sport as a young unthrift of's land: any bargaine to be rid on't.

VILLANOR. Can you blame them?——Who's that?

MARINELL. *Brennoralt*, our brave Coronell: a discontent, but what of that? who is not?

VILLANOR. His face speaks him one.

GRAINEVERT. Thou art i'th' right. He looks still as if he were saying to Fortune, Huswife, goe about your busines. Come, let's retire to *Baruthens* Tent. Taste a bottle, and speake bold truths; that's our way now. *Exeunt. Manet* KING *and* LORDS.

MIESLA. ——Thinke not of pardon Sir,
Rigor and mercy us'd in States incertainly,
And in ill times, looke not like th'effects

66 incertainly] *DC*; uncertainly *FA46*

Of vertue, but necessity: Nor will
They thanke your goodnes, but your feares.—

MELIDOR. My Lords;
Revenge in Princes should be still imperfect:
It is then handsom'st, when the King comes to
Reduce, not Ruine———

BRENNORALT. Who puts but on the face of punishing,
And only gently cuts, but prunes rebellion:
He makes that flourish which he would destroy.
Who would not be a Rebell when the hopes
Are vaste, the feares but small?

MELIDOR. Why, I would not.
Nor you my Lord, nor you, nor any here.
Feare keeps low spirits only in, the brave
Doe get above it, when they doe resolve.
Such punishments in infancy of warre,
Make men more desperate, not the more yeelding.
The common people are a kind of flyes;
They're caught with honey, not with wormewood, Sir.
Severity exasp'rates the stirr'd humour;
And State distempers turnes into diseases.

BRENNORALT. The gods forbid, great Polands State should be
Such as it dares not take right Physick. Quarter
To Rebels? Sir! when you give that to them,
Give that to me which they deserve. I would
Not live to see it.

3. LORD. Turne o're your owne, and other Chronicles,
And you shall finde (great Sir)
That nothing makes a Civill warre long liv'd,
But ransome and returning backe the brands
Which unextinct, kindled still fiercer fires.

MIESLA. Mercy bestow'd on those that doe dispute
With swords, do's loose the Angels face it has,
And is not mercy Sir, but policie
With a weake vizard on.

KING. ———Y'have met my thoughts
My Lords; nor will it need larger debate.
To morrow, in the sight of the besiedg'd,
The Rebell dyes: *Miesla*, 'tis your care.
The mercy of Heav'n may be offended so,

That it cannot forgive: Mortals much more,
Which is not infinite, my Lords.

Exeunt.

Enter IPHIGENE [*disguised as a man*], ALMERIN (*as in prison.*) [I.

IPHIGENE. O *Almerin*; would we had never knowne
The ruffle of the world! but were againe
By golden banks, in happy solitude;
When thou and I, Shepheard and Shepheardesse,
So oft by turnes, as often still have wisht,
That we as eas'ly could have chang'd our sex,
As clothes; but (alas!) all those innocent joyes,
Like glorious Mornings, are retir'd into
Darke sullen clouds, before we knew to value
What we had.

ALMERIN (*to himself*). Fame and victory are light
Huswifes, that throw themselves into the armes,
Not of the valiant, but the fortunate.
To be tane, thus!

IPHIGENE. *Almerin.*

ALMERIN. Nipt 'ith' bud
Of honour!

IPHIGENE. My Lord.

ALMERIN. Foil'd! and by the man
That doe's pretend unto *Francelia*!

IPHIGENE. What is't you doe, my *Almerin*? sit still?
And quarrell with the Winds, because there is
A shipwrack tow'rds, and never thinke of saving
The barke?

ALMERIN. The Barke? What should we doe with that
When the rich freight is lost: my name in armes?

IPHIGENE. ———Who knowes
What prizes are behind, if you attend
And waite a second Voyage?

ALMERIN. Never, never:
There are no second Voyages in this,
The wounds of honour doe admit no cure.

IPHIGENE. Those slight ones which misfortune gives, must needs;

I. iv. 3 golden] *DC*; Stolden *FA46*

Else, why should Mortals value it at all?
For who would toyle to treasure up a wealth,
Which weake inconstancy did keep, or might
Dispose of?

Enter MELIDOR.

Oh my Lord, what newes?

MELIDOR. As ill as your owne feares could give you;
The Councell has decreed him sudden death,
And all the wayes to mercy are blockt up. *She weeps and sighs.*

ALMERIN. My *Iphigene*———
This was a misbecomming peece of love:
Women would manage a disaster better.

IPHIGENE *weeps and sighs agen.*

Againe? thou art unkinde———
Thy goodnes is so great, it makes thee faulty:
For while thou think'st to take the trouble from me,
Thou givest me more, by giving me thine too.

IPHIGENE. Alas! I am indeed a uselesse trifle;
A dull, dull thing: For could I now doe any thing
But grieve and pitty, I might help: my thoughts
Labour to finde a way; but like to birds
In cages, though they never rest, they are
But where they did set out at first.

Enter JAYLOR.

JAYLOR. My Lords, your pardon: The prisoner must retire;
I have receiv'd an order from the King,
Denies accesse to any.

IPHIGENE. ———He cannot be
So great a Tyrant.

ALMERIN. I thanke him; nor can
He use me ill enough: I onely grieve
That I must dye in debt; a Bankrupt: Such
Thy love hath made me: My deare *Iphigene*
Farewell: It is no time for Ceremony.
Shew me the way I must——— *Exit.*

IPHIGENE. Griefe strove with such disorder to get out,
It stopt the passage, and sent backe my words
That were already on the place.

MELIDOR. Stay, there
Is yet a way.
IPHIGENE. O speake it.
MELIDOR. But there is
Danger in't *Iphigene*, to thee high danger.
IPHIGENE. Fright children in the darke with that, and let
Me know it: There is no such thing in nature
If *Almerin* be lost.
MELIDOR. Thus then; You must
Be taken pris'ner too, and by exchange
Save *Almerin*.
IPHIGENE. How can that be?
MELIDOR. Why—— *Studies.*
(*To the Jaylor*) Step in, and pray him set his hand, about
This distance; his seale too—— [*Gives him a paper.*]
JAYLOR. My Lord, I know not what this is.
MELIDOR. Setling of money-busines, foole, betwixt us.
JAYLOR. If't be no more.
MELIDOR. Tell him that *Iphigene* and I desire it: *Exit.*
I'le send by *Strathocles* his servant,
A Letter to *Morat* thus sign'd and seal'd,
That shall informe the sudden execution;
Command him as the only meanes
To save his life, to sallie out this night
Upon the quarters, and endeavour prisoners.
Name you as most secure and slightest guarded,
Best pledge of safety; but charge him,
That he kill not any, if it be avoydable;
Least 't should inrage the King yet more,
And make his death more certaine.

Enter JAYLOR *with the writing.*

JAYLOR. He understands you not
He sayes; but he has sent it.
MELIDOR. So——
IPHIGENE. But should *Morat* mistrust now?
Or this miscarry?
MELIDOR. ——Come;
Leave it to me: I'le take the Pilots part;
And reach the Port, or perish in the Art. *Exeunt.*

71 S.D. *Exit*] *DC*; *one line earlier FA46*

Enter ALMERIN (*in prison.*) [II. i]

ALMERIN. Sleep is as nice as woman;
The more I court it, the more it flies me;
Thy elder brother will be kinder yet,
Unsent for death will come.—To morrow—
Well—What can to morrow doe?
'Twill cure the sense of honour lost—
I and my discontents shall rest together;
What hurt is there in this?
But death against the will,
Is but a slovenly kinde of potion;
And though prescrib'd by Heaven,
It goes against mens stomacks:
So does it at fourescore too, when the soule's
Mew'd up in narrow darknes;
Neither sees nor heares,—
Pish, 'tis meer fondnes in our nature;
A certaine clownish cowardise, that still
Would stay at home, and dares not venture
Into forreigne Countries, though better then
It's owne,—ha, what Countries? for we receive
Descriptions of th'other world from our Divines,
As blinde men take relation of this from us:
My thoughts leade me into the darke,
And there they'l leave me, I'le no more on't,
Within there.——— *Knocks.*
Some paper and a light, I'le write to th' King:
Defie him, and provoke a quicke dispatch.
I would not hold this ling'ring doubtfull State
So long againe, for all that hope can give.
Enter three of the Guard (*with paper and Incke.*)
That sword does tempt me strangely——— *Writing.*
Wer't in my hands, 'twere worth th'other two.
But then the Guard,—it sleeps or drinks; may be
To contrive it so that I should not passe,—
Why if I fall in't,
'Tis better yet then Pageantry;

II. i. 7 I‸] *DC*; ~, *FA46* 25 Within there.—*Knocks*] *He knocks* within there *DC*; Within. (*Knocks*)—*Enter*. *FA46* 33 To...passe,—] To contrive it so that if I should not passe,—*FA46*; to contrive. If so, that I could not passe, *DC*

A scaffold and spectators; more souldier-like—

One of the Guard peeps over his shoulder.

Uncivill villaine, read my letter?

1. GUARD. Not I, not I my Lord.

ALMERIN. Deny it too? *Seizes his sword.*

1. GUARD. Murder, murder.

2. GUARD. Arme, arme— *The Guard runs out.*

ALMERIN. I'le follow,
Give the alarum with them.
'Tis least suspitious———Arme, arme, arme. [*Exit.*]

Enter Soldiers running over the Stage, one throwing away his armes.

ALL. —The enemy, the enemy—

SOULDIER. Let them come. Let them come. Let them come. [*Exit.*]

Enter ALMERIN.

ALMERIN. I heare fresh noise,
The camp's in great disorder: where am I now?
'Tis strangely darke—Goddesse without eyes
Be thou my guide, for—blindnes and sight
Are equall sense, of equall use, this night.

Exit.

Enter GRAINEVERT, STRATHEMAN, VILLANOR, MARINELL.

GRAINEVERT. Trouble not thy selfe, childe of discontent: 'twill take no hurt I warrant thee; the State is but a little drunke, and when 'tas spued up that that made it so, 'twill be well agen, there's my opinion in short.

MARINELL. Th'art i'th' right. The State's a pretty forehanded State, and will doe reason hereafter. Let's drinke and talke no more on't.

ALL. ———A good motion, a good motion, let's drinke.

VILLANOR. I, I, let's drinke agen.

STRATHEMAN. Come, to a Mistris.

GRAINEVERT. Agreed. Name, name.

VILLANOR. Any body.—*Vermilia.*

GRAINEVERT. Away with it.

Shee's pretty to walke with:
And witty to talke with:

38 S.D. *Seizes his sword.*] *DC*; *two lines earlier FA46* 38 S.P. 1. GUARD] *DC*; *Guar. FA46* S.P. 2. GUARD] *Guar. FA46*; *om. DC* 41 Arme, arme, arme] *DC*; *italic, as if a stage direction FA46* 48.1 S.D. *Exit*] *DC*; *om. FA46*

And pleasant too to thinke on.
But the best use of all,
Is her health is a stale
And helps us to make us drinke on.

STRATHEMAN. Excellent. Gentlemen, if you say the word, wee'l vant credit, and affect high pleasure. Shall we?

VILLANOR. I, I, let's do that.

STRATHEMAN. What thinke ye of the sacrifice now?

MARINELL. Come wee'le ha't,—for trickling teares are vaine.

VILLANOR. The sacrifice? what's that?

STRATHEMAN. Child of ignorance, 'tis a campe health. An *A-la-mode* one. *Grainevert* begin it.

GRAINEVERT. Come give it me. (*Pins up a Rose.*) Let me see which of them this Rose will serve. Hum, hum, hum.

Bright Star o'th' lower Orbe, twinckeling Inviter,
Which draw'st (as well as eyes) but set'st men righter:
For who at thee begins, comes to the place,
Sooner then he that sets out at the face:
Eyes are seducing lights, that the good women know,
And hang out these a nearer way to show.

MARINELL. Fine, and patheticall: come *Villanor.*

VILLANOR. What's the matter?

MARINELL. Come, your liquor, and your stanzas. Lines, Lines.

VILLANOR. Of what?

MARINELL. Why, of any thing your Mistris has given you.

VILLANOR. Gentlemen, she never gave me any thing, but a boxe oth'eare, for offering to kisse her once.

STRATHEMAN. Of that boxe then.

MARINELL. I, I, that boxe, of that boxe,

VILLANOR. Since it must be, give me the poyson then.

Drinkes and spits.

That boxe, faire Mistris, which thou gavest to me,
In humane guesse, is like to cost me three:
Three cups of Wine, and verses sixe,
The Wine will downe, but verse for rime still sticks.
By which you all may easily Gentiles know,
I am a better drinker then a Po.———

Enter DORAN.

MARINELL. La you there now. *Doran, Doran.*

II. ii. 37 stanzas] stanza's *FA46*; stanzons *DC* 51 La you there now] *DC*; *om. FA46*

GRAINEVERT.
A hall, a hall
To welcome our friend,
For some liquor call,
A new or fresh face,
Must not alter our pace,
But make us still drinke the quicker:
Wine, Wine, oh 'tis divine
Come fill it unto our brother:
What's at the tongues end,
It forth does send,
And will not a syllable smother:
Then,
It unlocks the brest
And throwes out the rest,
And learnes us to know each other.
Wine,—Wine.

DORAN. Mad lads, have you been here ever since?

STRATHEMAN. Yes faith, thou seest the worst of us. We—debauch —in discipline: foure and twenty houres is the time: *Baruthen* had the watch to night, to morrow 'twill be at my Tent.

DORAN. Good, and d'you know what has falne out to night?

STRATHEMAN. Yes: *Grainevert*, and my Lieutenant Coronell: but they are friends againe.

DORAN. Pish, pish—the young Palatine of *Plocence*, and his grave guardian surpris'd too night, carri'd by the enemy out of his quarters.

GRAINEVERT. As a chicken by a Kite out of a back side, was't not so?

DORAN. Is that all?

GRAINEVERT. Yes. My Coronell did not love him: he eats sweet meats upon a march too.

DORAN. Well, harke ye; worse yet; *Almerin's* gone: forc'd the Court of Guard where he was prisoner, and has made an escape.

GRAINEVERT. So pale and spiritlesse a wretch, drew *Priams* curtaine in the dead of night, and told him halfe his Troy was burnt——— He was of my minde. I would have done so my selfe.

52–67] *See 'Texts Consulted' for the variant MS. and book containing this song.* 52 *A hall, a hall*] *A hall, a hall, a hall Add (the bass part)* 53 *friend,*] *FA48*; ~‸ *FA46* 54 *call*] *he DC*; *call hoe Add* 57 *quicker*] *quicker hoe DC, Add* 60–2] *These lines follow* 63–5 *in Add MS.* 60 *the*] *our Add* 61 *does*] *doth DC, Add* 63 *Then,*] *Then, then Add*; *om. WI* 67 *Wine,—Wine.*] *om. Add, DC, WI*

DORAN. Well. There's high suspitions abroad: ye shall see strange discoveries i'th' Councell of Warre.

GRAINEVERT. What Councell?

DORAN. One call'd this morning. Y' are all sent to.

GRAINEVERT. I will put on cleane linnen, and speake wisely.

VILLANOR. 'Sfoot wee'l have a Round first.

GRAINEVERT. By all meanes Sir.

Sings.

Come let the State stay,
And drinke away,
There is no businesse above it:
It warmes the cold braine,
Makes us speake in high straine,
Hee's a foole that doe's not approve it.
The Macedon *youth*
Left behind him this truth,
That nothing is done with much thinking;
He drunke, and he fought,
Till he had what he sought,
The world was his owne by good drinking.

Exeunt.

Enter Generall of the Rebels, Palatine of TROCKE, *Palatine of* MENSECKE, FRANCELIA, ALMERIN, MORAT, IPHIGENE. [II. iii]

GENERAL. As your friend, my Lord, he has the priviledge of ours, and may enjoy a liberty we would deny to enemies.

ALMERIN. I thanke your Excellence———
Oh *Iphigene*, he does not know,
That thou the nobler part of friendship hold'st,
And doe'st oblige, whilst I can but acknowledge.

MENSECKE. Opportunity to States-men is as the just degree
Of heate to Chymists—it perfects all the worke,
And in this pris'ner 'tis offer'd.
We now are there, where men should still begin;
To treate upon advantage.
The Palatine of *Trocke*, and *Mensecke*,
With *Almerin*, shall to the King;
Petitions shall be drawne,
Humble in forme, but such for matter,

As the bold Macedonian youth would send
To men he did despise for luxury.
The first begets opinion of the world,
Which looks not far, but on the outside dwels:
Th'other inforces courage in our owne,
For bold demands must boldly be maintain'd.

TROCKE. Let all goe on still in the publique name,
But keep an eare open to particular offers;
Liberty and publique good are like great *Oleos*,
Must have the uper end still of our tables,
Though they are but for shew.

FRANCELIA [*aside*]. Would I had ne're seen this shape, 't has poyson in't.
Yet where dwells good, if ill inhabits there?

MENSECKE. ———Presse much religion,
For though we dresse the scruples for the multitude,
And for our selves reserve th'advantages,
(It being much pretext) yet is it necessary;
For things of faith are so abstruse, and nice,
They will admit dispute eternally:
So how so e're other demands appeare,
These never can be prov'd unreasonable;
The subject being of so fine a nature,
It not submits it selfe to sense, but scapes
The trials which conclude all common doubts.

FRANCELIA. My Lord, you use me as ill Painters paint,
Who while they labour to make faces faire,
Neglect to make them like.

IPHIGENE. Madam, there is no shipwracke of your
Vertues neare, that you should throw away
Any of all your excellencies
To save the dearest, modesty.

GENERAL. If they proceed with us, we can retreat unto
Our expositions, and the peoples votes.
If they refuse us wholy, then we plead,
The King's besiedged, blockt up so straightly
By some few, reliefe can find no way
To enter to the King, or to get out to us;
Exclaime against it loud,
Till the *Polonians* thinke it high injustice,

II. iii. 22 S.P. TROCKE] *Pal. FA46, DC*

And wish us better yet.
Then easily do we rise unto our ends,
And will become their envy through their pitty.
At worst you may confirme our party there:
Increase it too: there is one *Brennoralt*,
Men call him Gallant, but a discontent:
My Cosen the King hath us'd him ill.
Him a handsome whisper will draw.
The afternoone shall perfect
What we have loosely now resolv'd.

IPHIGENE. If in discourse of beauty,
(So large an Empire) I do wander,
It will become your goodnesse Madam,
To set me right,
And in a country where you your selfe is Queene,
Not suffer strangers loose themselves.

GENERAL. What, making revenges *Palatine*?
And taking prisoners faire Ladies hearts?

IPHIGENE. Yes my Lord.
And have no better fortune in this Warre,
Then in the other; for while I thinke to take,
I am surprized my selfe.

FRANCELIA. Dissembler, would thou wert.

MENSECKE. You are a Courtier my Lord;
The *Palatine* of *Plocence* (*Almerin*)
Will grace the *Hymeneals*;
And that they may be while his stay is here,
I'le court my Lord in absence;
Take off for you the little strangenesses
Virgins weare at first,——— IPHIGENE *sounds*.
Look to the *Palatine*.

ALMERIN. How is't my dearest *Iphegene*?

IPHIGENE. Not well, I would retire.

GENERAL. A qualme.

MORAT. His colour stole away; sanke downe,
As water in a weather-glasse
Prest by a warme hand.

66 wander] *DC*; wonder *FA46* 71 revenges] *FA46*, *DC*; revenge *FA48* 78 S.P. *Mensecke*.] *M. FA46*; *Min. DC* 86 S.P. ALMERIN] *Mer. FA46*; *Min. DC*; *Morat* Thompson 88 S.P. MORAT] *DC*; *Lo. FA46*

Enter a Trumpet blinded.

MENSECKE. A cordiall of kind lookes,———from the King.
MORAT. Let's withdraw, and heare him.

Exeunt.

Enter BRENNORALT, DORAN, RAGUELIN. [II.

DORAN. Yes to be married; what are you mute now?
BRENNORALT. Thou cam'st too hastily upon me, put'st
So close the colours to mine eye, I could
Not see. It is impossible.
DORAN. Impossible?
If't were impossible, it should be otherwise,
What can you imagine there of Constancy?
Where 'tis so much their nature to love change,
That when they say but what they are,
They excuse themselves for what they doe.
BRENNORALT. She hardly knowes him yet, in such an instant.
DORAN. Oh you know not how fire flies,
When it does catch light matter, woman.
BRENNORALT. No more of that; She is
Yet the most precious thing in all my thoughts.
———If it be so *Studies.*
I am a lost thing in the world, *Doran.*
DORAN. How?
BRENNORALT. Thou wilt in vaine perswade me to be other;
Life, which to others is a Good that they enjoy,
To me will be an evill I shall suffer in.
DORAN. Looke on another face, that's present remedy.
BRENNORALT. How ill thou doest conclude!
'Cause there are pestilent ayres, which kill men suddenly
In health, must there be soveraigne as suddenly
To cure in sicknes? 't never was in nature. *Exit, and*
Enters againe hastily.
BRENNORALT. I was a foole to thinke Death only kept
The doores of ill-pay'd love, when or disdaine,
Or spite could let me out as well———
DORAN. Right; were I as you,
It should no more trouble me

92 S.P. MORAT] *Thompson*; *M. FA46*; *om. DC* 92.1 S.D. *Exeunt.*] *DC*; *Exit. FA46*

To free my selfe of love,
Then to spit out that which made me sicke.
BRENNORALT. I'le tell her so; that she may laugh at me,
As at a prisoner threatning his Guard,
He will breake loose, and so is made the faster.
———She hath charmes, *Studies.*
Doran, can fetch in a rebellious heart,
Ev'n while it is conspiring liberty.
———Oh she hath all
The vertues of her sexe, and not the vices,
Chaste and unsullied, as first op'ning Lillies,
Or untouch'd buds———
DORAN. Chaste? why! do you honour me,
Because I throw my selfe not off a precipice?
'Tis her ruine to be otherwise;
Though we blame those that kill themselves (my Lord)
We praise not him that keeps himselfe alive,
And deserves nothing.
BRENNORALT. And 'tis the least.
She doe's triumph, when she doe's but appeare:
I have as many Rivals as beholders.
DORAN. All that encreases but our jealousies;
If you have now such qualmes for that you have not,
What will you have for that you shall possesse?
BRENNORALT. ———Dull hæritique;
Know I have these, because I have not her:
When I have her, I shall have these no more.
Her fancy now, her vertue then will governe:
And as I use to watch with doubtfull eye,
The wavering needle in the best Sun-dyall,
Till it has setled, then the trouble's o're,
Because I know when it is Fixt, it's True:
So here my doubts are all afore me. Sure,
Doran, crown'd Conquerours are but the types
Of Lovers, which enjoy, and really
Possesse, what th'other have in dreames. I'le send
A challenge to him.
DORAN. Do, and be thought a mad-man.
To what purpose?
If shee love him, shee will but hate you more.

Lovers in favour (*Brennoralt*) are Gamesters
In good fortune; the more you set them,
The more they get.
BRENNORALT. I'le see her then this night, by Heaven I will.
DORAN. Where? in the Cittadell?
BRENNORALT. Know what, and why.
DORAN. He raves——*Brennoralt*?
BRENNORALT. Let me alone.——
I conjure thee, by the discretion
Left betwixt us, (that's thine,
For mine's devour'd by injuries of fortune,)
Leave me to my selfe.
DORAN. I have done.
BRENNORALT. Is there such a passage,
As thou hast told me of, into the Castle?
RAGUELIN. There is my Lord.
BRENNORALT. And dar'st thou let me in?
RAGUELIN. If you my Lord will venture.
BRENNORALT. There are no Centrys neare it?
RAGUELIN. None.
BRENNORALT. How to the chamber afterward?
RAGUELIN. Her woman.
BRENNORALT. What's shee?
RAGUELIN. A wicket to my Ladies secrets,
One that stands up to marriage with me.
BRENNORALT. There—upon thy life be secret.—— *Flings a purse.*
RAGUELIN. Else,—All punishment to ingratitude.
BRENNORALT. Enough,
I am a storme within till I am there;
Oh *Doran*!
That that, which is so pleasant to behold,
Should be such paine within!
DORAN. Poore *Brennoralt*!
Thou art the Martyr of a thousand tyrants:
Love, Honour, and Ambition raigne by turnes,
And shew their power upon thee.
BRENNORALT. Why, let them; I'm still *Brennoralt*: Ev'n Kings
Themselves, are by their servants rul'd sometimes;
Let their own slaves govern them at odde houres:
Yet not subject their Persons or their Powers. *Exeunt.*

Enter IPHIGENE (*as in a Garden.*) [III. i]

IPHIGENE. What have I got by changing place?
But as a wretch which ventures to the Wars,
Seeking the misery with paine abroad,
He found, but wisely thought h'had left at home.
Fortune thou hast no tyranny beyond
This usage.——— *Weepes.*
Would I had never hop't
Or had betimes dispair'd, let never in
The gentle theife, or kept him but a guest,
Not made him Lord of all.
Tempests of wind thus (as my stormes of griefe
Carry my teares, which should relieve my heart)
Have hurried to the thankelesse Ocean clouds
And showers, that needed not at all the curtesie,
When the poore plaines have languish't for the want,
And almost burst asunder.———
I'le have this Statues place, and undertake
At my own charge to keepe the water full. *Lies down.*

Enter FRANCELIA.

FRANCELIA. These fond impressions grow too strong upon me,
They were at first without designe or end;
Like the first Elements, that know not what
And why they act, and yet produce strange things;
Poore innocent desires, journeying they know
Not whether: but now they promise to themselves
Strange things, grow insolent, threaten no rest
Till they be satisfied.
What difference was between these Lords?
The one made love, as if he by assault
Would take my heart, so forc't it to defence;
While t'other blew it up with secret mines,
And left no place for it, here he is.———
Teares steale too from his eyes,
As if not daring to be knowne
To passe that way: make it good, cunning griefe,
Thou knowst thou couldst not dresse thy selfe
In any other lookes, to make thee lovely. *Spies* FRANCELIA

IPHIGENE. *Francelia*, if through the ignorance of places,

III. i. 4 found, but] *FA46*, *DC*; found what (*conjecture*) 15 burst] *DC*; burnt *FA46*

I have intruded on your privacies,
Found out forbidden paths; 'tis fit you pardon, Madam:
For 'tis my melancholly, not I, offends.
FRANCELIA. So great a melancholly would well become
Mischances, such as time could not repaire:
Those of the warre, are but the petty cures
Of every comming hower.
IPHIGENE [*aside*]. Why should I not tell her all? since 'tis in her
To save my life; who knowes but she may be
Gallant so far, as to undo her selfe
To make another happy?—Madam,
The accidents of war contribute least
To my sad thoughts, (if any such I have)
—Imprisonment can never be—
Where the place holds what we must love, and yet———
FRANCELIA. My Lord?
IPHIGENE. In this imprisonment———
FRANCELIA. Proceed my Lord.
IPHIGENE. I dare not Madam.
FRANCELIA. I see I do disturbe you, and enter upon secrets—
Which when I know, I cannot serve you in them.
IPHIGENE. Oh most of any, you are the cause of all.
FRANCELIA. I my Lord?
IPHIGENE. You Madam—you alone.
FRANCELIA. Alas! that 'tis too soone to understand.
IPHIGENE. Must not you marry *Almerin*?
FRANCELIA. They tell me 'tis design'd.
IPHIGENE. If he have you, I am for ever lost.
FRANCELIA. ———Lost?
The Heavens forbid they should designe so ill!
Or when they shall, that I should be the cause.
IPHIGENE [*aside*]. Ha! her eyes are strangely kind,
Shee prompts me excellently.
Stars be propitious, and I am safe
———A way I not expected.
FRANCELIA. His passion labours for vent.
IPHIGENE. Is there a hope you will not give your selfe
To *Almerin*?
FRANCELIA. My Lord this ayre is common,

43 comming] *FA46*, *DC*; common *FA48*

The walkes within are pleasanter. *Exit.*
IPHIGENE. ———Invitation!
God of desires, be kind, and fill me now
With language, such thou lend'st thy Favourites,
When thou wouldst give them easie victories:
And I forgive thee, all thy cruelties. *Exit after.*

Enter Pallatine of TROCKE, MENSECKE, ALMERIN, BRENNORALT, *Lords.* [III. ii]

MENSECKE. ———Consider too, that those
Who are necessitated to use violence,
Have first been violent by necessity.
TROCKE. ———But still you judge not right
Of the Prerogative; For oft it stands
With Pow'r and Law, as with our Faith and Reason:
It is not all against, that is above (my Lord.)
2. LORD. You *Lithuanians* had of all least reason;
For would the King be unjust to you, he cannot:
Where there's so little to be had.
ALMERIN. Where there is least, there's liberty (my Lord.)
And 'tis more injurie to pull haires
From the bald, then from the bushy heads.
They go off talking. TROCKE *puls* BRENNORALT.
TROCKE. *Brennoralt*—a word
My Lord, the world hath cast its eye upon you,
And mark'd you out one of the formost men:
Y'have busied fame the eareliest of any,
And send her still on errands.
Much of the bravery of your nation,
Has taken up it's lodging in you.
And gallant men but coppy from you.
BRENNORALT. 'Tis goodly language this, what would it meane?
TROCKE. The *Lithuanians* wish you well, and wonder
So much desert should be so ill rewarded.
BRENNORALT. Good.
TROCKE. While all the guifts the Crown is Mistris of,
Are plac'd upon the empty———
BRENNORALT. Still I take you not.
TROCKE. Then to be plaine; our Army would be proud of you:
Pay the neglected scores of merit double,

All that you hold here of command, and what
Your fortune in this *Sigismund* has suffer'd,
Repaire, and make it fairer then at first.
BRENNORALT. How?
Then nothing, Lord; trifle below ill language:
How came it in thy heart to tempt my honour?
TROCKE. My Lord?
BRENNORALT. Do'st thinke 'cause I am angry
With the King and State sometimes,
I am fallen out with vertue, and my selfe?
Draw, draw, or by goodnesse———
TROCKE. What meanes your Lordship?
BRENNORALT. Draw I say.
———He that would thinke me a villaine, is one:
And I do weare this toy, to purge the world
Of such.

Enter KING *of* POLAND, LORDS, MELIDOR, MIESLA.

Th'have sav'd thee, wert thou good natur'd
Thou wouldst love the King the better during life.
KING. If they be just, they call for gracious answers:
Speedy, (how e're) we promise. *They all kisse the Kings hand.*
ALL. Long live great *Sigismond.*
BRENNORALT. ———The *Lithuanians* Sir,
Are of the wilder sort of creatures, must
Be rid with Cavisons, and with harsh curbs.
And since the war can only make them tride,
What can be used but swords? where men have fal'ne
From not respecting Royalty, unto
A liberty of offending it: what though
Their numbers (possibly) equall yours Sir?
And now forc't by necessity, like Catts
In narrow roomes, they fly up in your face?
Thinke you Rebellion and Loyalty
Are empty names? and that in Subjects hearts
They don't both give and take away the courage?
Shall we beleeve there is no difference
In good and bad? that there's no punishment,
Or no protection? forbid it Heaven!
If when great *Polands* honour, safety too,

III. ii. 52 with Cavisons, and] with Cavilons, and *FA46*; *om. DC*

Hangs in dispute, we should not draw our Swords,
Why were we ever taught to weare 'em Sir?

MIESLA. This late commotion in your Kingdom Sir,
Is like a growing Wen upon the face,
Which as we cannot looke on but with trouble,
So take't away we cannot but with danger.
War there hath foulest face, and I most feare it
Where the pretence is fair'st. Religion
And Liberty, most specious names, they urge,
Which like the Bils of subtle Mountebankes,
Fill'd with great promises of curing all,
——— Though by the wise,
Pass'd by unread as common cosenage,
Yet, By th'unknowing multitude they're still
Admir'd, and flock't unto.

KING. Is there no way
To disabuse them?

MELIDOR. All is now too late.
The vulgar in Religion are like
Unknown Lands; those that first possesse them, have them.
Then, Sir, consider, justnesse of Cause is nothing:
When things are risen to the point they are;
'Tis either not examin'd or beleev'd
Among the World.———
The better cause the *Grecians* had of Yore,
Yet were the Gods themselves divided in't;
And the foule ravisher found as good protection
As the much injur'd husband.———
Nor are you Sir, assur'd of all behinde you:
For though your Person in your Subjects hearts
Stands highly honour'd, and belov'd, yet are
There certaine Acts of State, which men call grievances
Abroad; and though they bare them in the times
Of peace, yet will they now perchance, seeke to
Be free, and throw them off. For know Dread Sir,
The Common People are much like the Sea,
That suffers things to fall and sinke unto
The bottome in a Calme, which in a Storme
Stird and inraged, it lifts, and does keep up

71 on] *DC*, *FA48*; one *FA46* 88 World] *DC*; Warlike *FA46*

Then; Time distempers cures more safely Sir,
Then Physick does, or instant letting-bloud:
Religion now is a young Mistris there,
For which each man will fight, and dye at least;
Let it alone a while, and 'twill become
A kind of marry'd wife: people will be
Content to live with it in quietnesse
(If that at least may be); my voyce is therefore Sir,
For Peace.

MIESLA. Were Sir the question simply War or Peace,
It were no more then shortly to be askt,
Whether we would be well or ill:
Since War the sicknesse of a Kingdome is,
And Peace the health: But here I do conceive
'Twill rather lye, whether we had not better
Endure sharpe sicknesse for a time, to enjoy
A perfect strength, then have it languish on us:
For Peace and War in an incestuous line,
Have still begot each other.———
Those men that highly now have broke all Lawes
(The great one only 'tis 'twixt man and man)———
What safety can they promise, though you give it?
Will they not still suspect (and justly too)
That all those civill bonds (new made) should be
Broken againe to them? so being still
In feares and jealousies themselves, they must
Infect the People: For in such a case
The private safety is the publike trouble.
Nor will they ever want Prætext; Since he
That will maintaine it with his Sword hee's injur'd,
May say't at any time———
Then Sir, as terrible as war appeares,
My vote is for't; nor shall I ever care
How ugly my Physitians face shall be,
So he can doe the cure.

LORD. In entring phisique,
I thinke, Sir, none so much considers
The Doctors face, as his owne body.
To keep on foot the warre with all your wants,

116 a] *DC*; the *FA46* 139 entring] ventring *Hazlitt*

Is to let bloud and take strong potions
In dangerous sicknesse.

KING. I see, and wonder not to finde, my Lords,
This difference in opinion; the subject's large:
Nor can we there too much dispute, where when
We erre, 'tis at a Kingdomes charges; Peace
And warre are in themselves indifferent,
And time doth stamp them either good or bad:
But here the place is much considerable;
Warre in our owne is like to too much heate
Within, it makes the body sicke; when in
Another Countrey, 'tis but exercise;
Conveighs that heat abroad, and gives it health.
To that I bend my thoughts; but leave it to
Our greater Councell, which we now assemble:
Meane time exchange of pris'ners only we
Assent unto.

LORD. Nothing of Truce, Sir?

KING. No: wee'l not take up
Quiet at int'rest: Perfect Peace, or nothing.
Cessations for short times in warre, are like
Small fits of health, in desp'rate maladies:
Which while the instant paine seemes to abate,
Flatters into debauch and worse estate.

Exeunt.

Enter IPHIGENE *as leading to her chamber* FRANCELIA; *Servants with lights*; MORAT, *and another Souldier.* [III. iii]

IPHIGENE. I have not left my selfe a faire retreate,
And must be now either the blest object
Of your love, or subject of your scorne.

FRANCELIA. I feare some treacherie;
And that mine eyes have given intelligence.
Unlesse you knew there would be weak defence,
You durst not thinke of taking in a heart,
As soone as you set downe before it.

IPHIGENE. Condemne my Love not of such fond ambition,
It aymes not at a conquest,

III. iii. 2 either] *DC*; *om. FA46*

But exchange, *Francelia*——— *Whisper.*

MORAT. They're very great in this short time.

SOLDIER. 'Tis ever so: Young and handsome
Have made acquaintances in nature:
So when they meet, they have the lesse to doe.
It is for age or uglines to make approaches,
And keep a distance.

IPHIGENE. When I shall see other perfection,
Which at the best will be but other vanity,
Not more, I shall not love it———

FRANCELIA. 'Tis still one step not to despaire, my Lord.

Exeunt IPHIGENE, FRANCELIA, *servants.*

MORAT. Doest thinke he will fight?

SOLDIER. Troth it may be not:
Nature, in those fine peeces, does as Painters;
Hangs out a pleasant Excellence
That takes the eye, which is indeed,
But a course canvas in the naked truth,
Or some slight stuffe.

MORAT. I have a great minde to taste him.

SOLDIER. Fy! a Prisoner?

MORAT. By this hand if I thought
He courted my Coronels Mistris in earnest.

Enter IPHIGENE: *waiting-woman comming after him.*

ORILLA. My Lord, my Lord, my Lady thinks the Gessimine walks will be the finer, the freshnes of th' morning takes of the strength o'th' heate she sayes.

IPHIGENE. 'Tis well.

MORAT. Mewe—doe it so? I suspect vildly. Wee'l follow him, and see if he be so farre quallified towards a souldier, as to drinke a crash in's chamber. *Exit.*

[*Enter*] RAGUELIN [*who*] *puls* [ORILLA] *the waiting woman backe.*

RAGUELIN. Where are those keyes?

ORILLA. Harke you, I dare not doe it.

RAGUELIN. How?

ORILLA. My Lady will finde———

RAGUELIN. Scruples? Are my hopes become your feares? There was

14 Have] Are *Hazlitt* 33 S.P. ORILLA] *Wom. FA46, DC, and the rest of her speech prefixes in the scene.* 34 of] *DC*; f *FA46, all copies* 40 Where are those] *FA46, DC*; What are these *FA48*

no other way I should be any thing in this lewd world,—and now —'Sfoot, I know she longs to see him too.

ORILLA. Does she?

RAGUELIN. Doe you thinke he would desire it else?

ORILLA. I, but———

RAGUELIN. Why, let me secure it all. I'le say I found the Keyes, or stole them: Come———

ORILLA. Well, if you ruine all now———Here, these enter the garden from the works, that the privy walks, and that the backe staires. Then you know my chamber.

RAGUELIN. Yes I know your chamber.

Exeunt

Enter BRENNORALT. [III. iv]

BRENNORALT. He comes not.
One wise thought more, and I returne:
I cannot in this act seperate the foolish
From the bold so farre, but still it tasts a'th' rash.
Why let it taste, it tasts of love too;
And to all actions 't gives a pretty rellish, that.

Enter RAGUELIN.

RAGUELIN. My Lord?

BRENNORALT. Oh———here.

RAGUELIN. 'Sfoot y'are upon our Centries.
Move on this hand. *Exeunt.*

Enter (agen) BRENNORALT *and* RAGUELIN.

BRENNORALT. Where are we now?

RAGUELIN. Entring part of the Fort,
Your Lordship must be wet a little. *Exeunt.*

Enter (againe [above].)

BRENNORALT. Why are there here no guards?

RAGUELIN. There needs none:
You presently must passe a place,
Where one's an Army in defence,
It is so steep and strait.

BRENNORALT. 'Tis well.

RAGUELIN. These are the steps of danger;
Looke to your way my Lord.

BRENNORALT. I doe not find such difficulty.
Waite me here abouts——— *He drawes the curtaines.*

[*Discover*] FRANCELIA (*as in a bed.*)

So Misers looke upon their gold,
Which while they joy to see, they feare to loose:
The pleasure of the sight scarse equalling
The jealousie of being dispossest by others;
Her face is like the milky way i'th' skie,
A meeting of gentle lights without name.
Heavens! shall this fresh ornament
Of the world; this precious lovelines
Passe with other common things
Amongst the wasts of time, what pity 'twere. *She wakes.*

FRANCELIA. Blesse me! Is it a Vision, or *Brennoralt*?

BRENNORALT. *Brennoralt*, Lady.

FRANCELIA. *Brennoralt*? innocence guard me;
What is't you have done, my Lord?

BRENNORALT. Alas I were but in too good estate,
If I knew what I did.
But why aske you Madam?

FRANCELIA. It much amazes me to thinke
How you came hither.
And what could bring you to indanger thus
My honour, and your owne life?
Nothing but saving of my brother
Could make me now preserve you.

BRENNORALT. Reproach me not the follies you your selfe
Make me commit———
I am reduc'd to such extremity,
That love himselfe (high tyrant as he is)
If he could see would pity me.

FRANCELIA. I understand you not.

BRENNORALT. Would heaven you did, for 'tis a paine to tell you:
I come t'accuse you of injustice (Madam.)
You first begot my passion, and was
Content (at least you seem'd so) it should live;
Yet since would ne're contribute unto it,
Not looke upon't, as if you had desired
Its being for no other end, but for
The pleasure of its ruine.

FRANCELIA. Why doe you labour thus to make me guilty of

III. iv. 18.1 FRANCELIA ... *bed*.] *one line earlier FA46* 32 were but] *DC*; were *FA46*

An injury to you, which when it is one,
All mankinde is alike ingag'd, and must
Have quarrell to me?

BRENNORALT. I have done ill; you chide me justly (Madam.)
I'le lay't not on you, but on my wretched selfe.
For I am taught that heavenly bodies
Are not malicious in their influence,
But by the disposition of the subject.
They tell me you must marry *Almerin*:
Sure such excellencie ought to be
The recompence of vertue,
Not the sacrifice of Parents wisedome,
Should it not Madam?

FRANCELIA. 'Twould injure me, were it thought otherwise.

BRENNORALT. And shall he have you then that knew you yesterday?
Is there in martyrdome no juster way?
But he that holds a finger in the fire
A little time, should have the Crowne from them
That have indur'd the flame with constancy?

FRANCELIA. If the discovery will ease your thoughts,
My Lord, know *Almerin* is as the man
I never saw.

BRENNORALT. You doe not marry then?
Condemned men thus heare, and thus receive
Repreeves. One question more, and I am gone.
Is there to latitude of eternity
A hope for *Brennoralt*?

FRANCELIA. My Lord?

BRENNORALT. Have I
A place at all, when you doe thinke of men?

FRANCELIA. My Lord, a high one, I must be singular
Did I not value you: the world does set
Great rates upon you, and you have first deserv'd them.

BRENNORALT. Is this all?

FRANCELIA. All.

BRENNORALT. Oh be lesse kinde, or kinder:
Give me more pity, or more cruelty, *Francelia*.
I cannot live with this, nor die.

FRANCELIA. I feare my Lord, you must not hope beyond it.

56 one] done *Hazlitt* 65 excellencie] *DC*, *FA48*; excellence *FA46*

BRENNORALT. Not hope? This, sure, is not the body to
This soule; it was mistaken, shufled in *Views himselfe.*
Through haste: Why (else) should that have so much love,
And this want lovelinesse, to make that love
Receiv'd?—I will raise honour to a point,
It never was—do things *Studies.*
Of such a vertuous greatnesse she shall love me.
She shall—I will deserve her, though
I have her not: There's something yet in that.
Madam, wilt please you, pardon my offence?
———(Oh Fates!
That I must call thus my affection!)

FRANCELIA. I will doe any thing, so you will thinke
Of me, and of your selfe (my Lord) and how
Your stay indangers both———

BRENNORALT. Alas!
Your pardon is more necessary to
My selfe, then life to me: but I am gone.
Blessings, such as my wishes for you, in
Their extasies, could never reach, fall on you.
May ev'ry thing contribute to preserve
That exc'lence (my destruction) till't meet joyes
In love, great as the torments I have in't.

Exeunt.

[IV.

Enter BRENNORALT.

BRENNORALT. Why so, 'tis well, Fortune I thanke thee still,
I dare not call thee villaine neither.
'Twas plotted from the first, that's certaine,—
It looks that way? Hum—caught in a trap?
Here's something yet to trust to——— *To his sword.*
This was the entry,
These the staires: But whether afterwards?
He that is sure to perish on the land,
May quit the nicetie of Card and Compasse,
And safe, to his discretion, put to Sea:
He shall have my hand to't. *Exit.*

Enter RAGUELIN, ORILLA, (*the waiting-woman.*)

RAGUELIN. Looke: By this light 'tis day.

107 selfe] *DC*; life *FA46* 111] *Exeunt.*] *DC*; *Exit. FA46*

ORILLA. Not by this, by t'other 'tis indeed.

RAGUELIN. Thou art such another peece of temptation. My Lord raves by this time, a hundred to one the Centinells will discover us too, then I doe pay for night-watch.

ORILLA. Fie upon thee, thou art as fearfull as a young colt; boglest at every thing, foole. As if Lovers had considered houres: I'le peep in— *She peeps.*

RAGUELIN [*aside*]. I am as weary of this wench, as if I were married to her: She hangs upon me like an Ape upon a horse—She's as common too, as a Barbers glasse—Conscienc't too like a Dy-dapper.

ORILLA. *Raguelin*, there's no body within: My Lady sleeps this houre at least.

RAGUELIN. Good, the Divel's even with me—Not be an honest man neither. What course now?

Exeunt.

Enter BRENNORALT *and a guard.* [IV. ii]

1. SOULDIER. Nay Sir, we shall order you now.

BRENNORALT. Dogges.

Enter FRESOLIN.

FRESOLIN. What tumult's this—[*Aside.*] ha! *Brennoralt*! 'tis he in spite of his disguise: what makes he here? Hee's lost for ever if he be discover'd—How now companions, why doe you use my friend thus?

1. SOULDIER. Your friend, my Lord? if he be your friend, h'as us'd us as ill: h'has plaid the Divell amongst us. Six of our men are Surgeons worke this moneth; we found him climbing the walls.

2. SOULDIER. He had no word neither, nor any language but a blow.

FRESOLIN. You will be doing these wilde things (my Lord.) Good faith y'are too blame, if y'had desir'd to view the walls, or Trenches, 'twas but speaking; we are not nice: I would my selfe have waited on you: Th'are the new out-workes you would see perchance. Boy, bring me blacke Tempest round about, and the gray Barbary; a Trumpet come along too; my Lord, wee'l take the neerer way, and privater, here through the Sally-Port.

BRENNORALT [*aside*]. What a Divell is this? sure I dreame. *Exeunt.*

1. SOULDIER. Now, you are so officious. *Manet Soldiers.*

IV. i. 22 *Raguelin*,] *DC*; ———‸ *FA46* (*a long dash instead of the name*) 25 S.D. *Exeunt*] *DC*; *om. FA46*

IV. ii. 0.1 S.D. *Enter*...*guard*] *DC*; *two lines earlier FA46* 12 too] *i.e.* to

2. SOULDIER. Death! could I guesse he was a friend?

1. SOULDIER. 'Twas ever to be thought, how should he come there else?

2. SOULDIER. Friend or no friend, he might have left us something to pay the Surgeon with: grant me that, or I'le beat you to't.

Exeunt.

Enter FRESOLIN, *and* BRENNORALT. [IV

FRESOLIN. *Brennoralt—*
Start not: I pay thee backe a life I owe thee;
And blesse my Starres, they gave me power to do't;
The debt lay heavy on me.
A horse waits you there—a Trumpet too,
(Which you may keep, least he should prate.)
No Ceremony, 'tis dangerous.

BRENNORALT. Thou hast astonish't me:
Thy youth hath triumph'd in one single act,
O're all the age can boast; and I will stay
To tell thee so, were they now firing all
Their Cannons on me; farewell gallant *Fresolin*:
And may reward, great as thy vertue, crowne thee.

Exeunt diverse wayes.

Enter IPHIGENE, FRANCELIA. [IV

FRANCELIA. A peace will come, and then you must be gone;
And whither when you once are got upon the wing,
You will not stoop to what shall rise,
Before ye flye to some lure
With more temptation garnisht, is a sad question.

IPHIGENE. Can you have doubts, and I have not my feares?
By this—the readiest and the sweetest oath, I sweare *Kisses.*
I cannot so secure my selfe of you,
But in my absence I shall be in paine.
I have cast up what it will be to stand
The Governors anger; and which is more hard,
The love of *Almerin.*
I hold thee now but by thy owne free grant,

IV. iv. 6 I have not my] *DC*; I not my *FA46*; I not *Hazlitt* 7 *Kisses.*] *DC*; *om. FA46*

A slight securitie, alas it may fall out,
Giving thy selfe, not knowing thine owne worth,
Or want of mine, thou mayst, like Kings deceiv'd,
Resume the gift on better knowledge backe.

FRANCELIA. If I so eas'ly change, I was not worth your love,
And by the losse you'l gaine.

IPHIGENE. But when y'are irrecoverably gone,
'Twill be slight comfort to perswade my selfe
You had a fault, when all that fault must be
But want of love to me; and that agen
Finde in my much defect, so much excuse,
That it will have no worse name
Then discretion, if I inconcern'd doe
Cast it up—I must have more assurance.

FRANCELIA. You have too much already:
And sure my Lord you wonder, while I blush,
At such a growth in young affections.

IPHIGENE. Why should I wonder (Madam?)
Love that from two breasts sucks,
Must of a child quickly become a Giant.
Dunces in love stay at the Alphabet,
Th'inspir'd know all before;
And doe begin still higher.

Enter waiting woman [ORILLA].

ORILLA. Madam;
Almerin, returned, has sent to kisse
Your hands. I told him you were busie.

FRANCELIA. Must I, my Lord, be busy?
I may be civill though not kind.
Tell him I wait him in the Gallery.

IPHIGENE (*whisper*). May I not kisse your hand this night?

FRANCELIA. The world is full of jealous eyes my Lord:
And were they all lockt up; you are a spye
Once entred in my chamber at strange houres.

IPHIGENE. The vertue of *Francelia* is too safe,
To need those little arts of preservation.
Thus to divide our selves, is to distrust our selves.
A Cherubin dispatches not on earth

23 that] then *Hazlitt* 26 I inconcern'd] *DC*; inconcern'd *FA46*; inconcern'd you *Hazlitt*
37 S.P. ORILLA] *Woman FA46, DC* 49 divide] deny *Hazlitt*

Th'affaires of heaven with greater innocence,
Then I will visit; 'tis but to take a leave,
I begg.

FRANCELIA. When you are going my Lord.

Exeunt.

Enter ALMERIN, MORAT. [IV

ALMERIN. Pish. Thou liest, thou liest.
I know he playes with woman kind, not loves it.
Thou art impertinent.

MORAT. 'Tis the campe talke my Lord though.

ALMERIN. The camp's an asse, let me hear no more on't.

Exeunt (*Talking.*)

Enter GRAINEVERT, VILLANOR, MARINELL. [IV.

GRAINEVERT. And shall we have peace?
I am no sooner sober, but the State is so too:
If't be thy will, a truce for a month only.
I long to refresh my eyes; by this hand
They have been so tyr'd with looking upon faces
Of this country.

VILLANOR. And shall the *Donazella*
To whom we wish so well-a
Look Babies agen in our eyes-a?

GRAINEVERT. Ah—a sprightly girle about fifteen
That melts when a man but takes her by the hand!
Eyes full, and quick; with breath
Sweet as double violets,
And wholesome as dying leaves of Strawberries.
Thick silken eye-browes, high upon the fore-head;
And cheeks mingled with pale streaks of red,
Such as the blushing morning never wore———

VILLANOR. Oh my chops; my chops.

GRAINEVERT. With narrow mouth, small teeth,
And lips swelling, as if she pouted———

VILLANOR. Hold, hold, hold.

GRAINEVERT. Haire curling and cover'd, like buds of *Marjoram*,
Part tyed in negligence, part loosely flowing———

MARINELL. Tyrant! tyrant! tyrant!

GRAINEVERT. In pinck colour taffata petticoate,

IV. vi. 10 about] *DC*; above *FA46*

Lac't smock-sleeves dangling;
This vision stolne from her own bed
And rustling in ones chamber———

VILLANOR. Oh good *Grainevert*, good *Grainevert.*

GRAINEVERT. With a waxe candle in her hand,
Looking as if she had lost her way,
At twelve at night.

MARINELL. Oh any hower, any hower.

GRAINEVERT. Now I thinke on't, by this hand,
Ile marry, and be long liv'd.

VILLANOR. Long liv'd? how?

GRAINEVERT. Oh, he that has a Wife, eats with an appetite,
'Has a very good stomacke to't first:
This living at large is very destructive,
Variety is like rare sawces; provokes too far,
And draws on surfets, more then th'other.

Enter DORAN.

DORAN. So; is this a time to foole in?

GRAINEVERT. What's the matter?

DORAN. Draw out your choise men, and away to your Coronell immediately. There's worke towards, my boyes, there's worke.

GRAINEVERT. Art in earnest?

DORAN. By this light.

GRAINEVERT. There's something in that yet.

This moiety Warre,
Twilight,
Neither night nor day,
Pox upon it:
A storme is worth a thousand
Of your calme;
There's more variety in it.

Exeunt.

Enter ALMERIN, FRANCELIA, *as talking earnestly.* [IV. vii]

ALMERIN. Madam, that shewes the greatnes of my passion.

FRANCELIA. The imperfection rather: Jealousie's
No better signe of love (my Lord) then feavers are
Of Life; they shew there is a Being, though
Impair'd and perishing: and that, affection

48 *Warre*] *FA46*; *were DC*

But sicke and in disorder. I like't not.
Your servant. *Exit.*

ALMERIN. So short and sowre? the change is visible.

Enter IPHIGENE.

IPHIGENE. Deare *Almerin*, welcome, y'have been absent long.
ALMERIN. Not very long.
IPHIGENE. To me it hath appeared so;
What sayes our Camp? am I not blamed there?
ALMERIN. They wonder——
IPHIGENE. While we smile——
How have you found the King inclining?
ALMERIN. Well.
The Treaty is not broken, nor holds it.
Things are where they were;
'T has a kind of face of peace;
You my Lord may when you please returne.
IPHIGENE. I, *Almerin*?
ALMERIN. Yes my Lord, I'le give you an escape.
IPHIGENE. 'Tis least in my desires.
ALMERIN. Hum!
IPHIGENE. Such prisons are beyond all liberty.
ALMERIN. Is't possible?
IPHIGENE. Seemes it strange to you?
ALMERIN. No, not at all.
What? you finde the Ladies kinde?
IPHIGENE. Civill—— *Smiles.*
ALMERIN. You make love well too they say (my Lord.)
IPHIGENE. Passe my time.
ALMERIN. Addresse unto *Francelia*?
IPHIGENE. Visit her.
ALMERIN. D'you know she is my Mistres, Pallatine?
IPHIGENE. Ha?
ALMERIN. D'you know she is my Mistresse?
IPHIGENE. I have been told so.
ALMERIN. And doe you court her then?
IPHIGENE. Why?—— *Smiles.*
If I saw the enemy first, would you not charge?
ALMERIN [*aside*]. He doe's allow it too, by Heaven:
Laughs at me too.—Thou filcher of a heart,
False as thy title to *Francelia*.

Or as thy friendship: which with this I doe *Drawes.*
Throw by—draw.

IPHIGENE. What doe you meane?

ALMERIN. I see the cunning now of all thy love,
And why thou camest so tamely kinde,
Suffering surprise. Draw.

IPHIGENE. I will not draw, kill me;
And I shall have no trouble in my death,
Knowing 'tis your pleasure:
As I shall have no pleasure in my life
Knowing it is your trouble.

ALMERIN. Oh poor—I lookt for this.
I knew th' wouldst find 'twas easier to doe a wrong
Then justifie it—but———

IPHIGENE. I will not fight—heare me:
If I love you not more then I love her;
If I doe love her more then for your sake;
Heaven strangely punish me.

ALMERIN. Take heed how thou dost play with heaven.

IPHIGENE. By all that's just, and faire, and good,
By all that you hold deare, and men hold great;
I never had lascivious thought, or ere
Did action that might call in doubt my love
To *Almerin.*

ALMERIN. That tongue can charme me into any thing;
I doe beleev't, prethee be wiser then.
Give me no further cause of jealousie,
Hurt not mine honour more, and I am well.

IPHIGENE. But well———Of all
Our passions, I wonder nature made
The worst, foule jealousie, her favorite.
And if it be not so, why took she care
That every thing should give the monster Nourishment,
And left us nothing to destroy it with?

ALMERIN. Prethee no more, thou plead'st so cunningly
I feare I shall be made the guilty
And need thy pardon.

IPHIGENE. If you could read my heart you would.
I will be gone to morrow if that will satisfie. Indeed

IV. vii. 48 'tis] *FA46(c)*; is *FA46(u)*

I shall not rest untill my innocence
Be made as plain as objects to the sence.

ALMERIN. ———Come;
You shall not goe, Ile think upon't no more.
Distrusts ruine not friendship,
But build it fairer then it was before.

Exeunt.

Enter BRENNORALT: *Captaines*, STRATHEMAN: DORAN. [IV

BRENNORALT. No more but ten from every company;
For many hands are theeves, and rob the glory,
While they take their share. How goes the night?

STRATHEMAN. Halfe spent my Lord.
We shall have straight the Moones weaker light.

BRENNORALT. 'Tis time then, call in the officers.

[*Enter Officers.*]

Friends, if you were men that must be talkt
Into a courage, I had not chosen you;
Danger with its vizard off before this time
Y'have look'd upon, and out-fac'd it too;
We are to doe the trick agen, that's all.
Here——— *Drawes his sword.*
And yet we will not sweare:
For he that shrinks in such an action
Is damn'd without the help of perjury.
Doran, if from the virgin tow'r thou spiest
A flame, such as the East sends forth about
The time the day should break, goe tell the King
I hold the Castle for him; bid him come on
With all his force, and he shall find a victory
So cheap 'twill loose it's value. If I fall,
The world has lost a thing it us'd not well;
And I, a thing I car'd not for, that world.

STRATHEMAN. Lead us on Coronell;
If we doe not fight like———

BRENNORALT. No like.
Wee'l be our selves similitude,
And time shall say, when it would tell
That men did well, they fought like us.

Exeunt.

IV. viii. 9 vizard‸ off] ~‸of *DC*; ~, oft *FA46* 20 it's] *DC*; the *FA46*
27.1 *Exeunt.*] *DC*; *om. FA46*

Enter Agen. [v. i]

BRENNORALT. What made the stop?
STRATHEMAN. One in's falling sicknesse had a fit
Which choak'd the passage; but all is well:
Softly, we are neere the place.

Exeunt.

Alarum within, and fight, then enter ALMERIN *in his night-gowne.* [v. ii]

ALMERIN. What noise is here to night?
Something on fire—what hoe,
Send to the Virgin-tower, there is disorder
Thereabouts.

Enter Souldier.

SOULDIER. All's lost, all's lost:
The enemie's upon the place of armes:
And is by this time Master of that,
And of the Tower.
ALMERIN. Thou liest. *Strikes him.*

Enter MORAT.

MORAT. Save your selfe, my Lord, and hast unto the camp;
Ruine gets in on every side. *Exit.*
ALMERIN. There's something in it when this fellow flies.
Villaines, my armes, I'le see what Divell raignes.

Exit.

Enter IPHIGENE, FRANCELIA. [v. iii]

IPHIGENE. Looke, the day breakes.
FRANCELIA. You thinke I'le be so kinde as sweare
It does not now. Indeed I will not———
IPHIGENE. Will you not send me neither
Your picture when y'are gone?
That when my eye is famisht for a looke,
It may have where to feed,
And to the painted Feast invite my heart.
FRANCELIA. Here, take this virgin-bracelet of my haire,
And if like other men thou shalt hereafter

v. i. 2. STRATHMAN. One] *Hazlitt*; *FA46*, *DC* v. ii. 11 S.D. *Exit.*] *DC*; *om. FA46*
13.1 S.D. *Exit.*] *DC*; *om. FA46*

Throw it with negligence,
'Mongst the Records of thy weake female conquests,
Laugh at the kinde words, and mysticall contrivement;
If such a time shall come,
Know I am sighing then thy absence *Iphigene*,
And weeping o're thy false but pleasing Image.

ALMERIN [*within*]. *Francelia, Francelia,*
Rise, rise, and save thy selfe, the enemy
That does not know thy worth, may else destroy it.

[*Enter* ALMERIN:] *throwes open the dore.*

Ha! mine eyes grow sick.
A plague has, through them, stolne into my heart;
And I grow dizzie: feet, lead me off agen,
Without the knowledge of my body.
I shall act I know not what else. *Exit.*

FRANCELIA. How came he in?
Deare *Iphigene* we are betrayd;
Lets raise the Castle lest he should return.

IPHIGENE. That were to make all publique.
Feare not, Ile satisfie his anger:
I can doe it.

FRANCELIA. Yes, with some quarrell;
And bring my honour, and my love in danger———

Enter ALMERIN.

Look he returns, and wrecks of fury,
Like hurried clouds over the face of heaven,
Before a tempest, in his looks appeares.

ALMERIN. If they would question what our Rage doth act
And make it sin, they would not thus provoke men.
———I am too tame.
For if they live I shall be pointed at,
Here I denounce a warre to all the world,
And thus begin it.——— *Runs at* IPHIGENE.

IPHIGENE. What hast thou done?——— *Falls.*

FRANCELIA. Ah me, help, help.——— *Wounds* FRANCELIA.

IPHIGENE. Hold.

ALMERIN. 'Tis too late.

v. iii. 16 thy] *DC*; the *FA46* 17 *Francelia, Francelia*] *This speech preceded by* Enter ALMERIN *FA46*, *DC*

IPHIGENE. Rather then she shall suffer,
My fond deceits involve the innocent,
I will discover all.
ALMERIN. Ha!—what will he discover?
IPHIGENE. That which shall make thee curse
The blindnesse of thy rage.—I am a woman.
ALMERIN. Ha, ha, ha, brave and bold!
Because thy perjury deceived me once,
And saved thy life, thou thinkest to escape agen.
Impostor, thus thou shalt. *Runs at her.*
IPHIGENE. Oh hold—I have enough.
Had I hope of life, thou shouldst not have this secret.
FRANCELIA. What will it be now?
IPHIGENE. ———My father having long desir'd
A sonne to heire his great possessions,
And in six births successively deceiv'd,
Made a rash vow; oh how rash vowes are punished!
That if the burthen then my mother went with
Prov'd not a male, he ne're would know her more.
Then was unhappy *Iphigene* brought forth,
And by the womens kindnesse nam'd a boy;
And since so bred: (a cruell pity as
It hath faln out.) If now thou findst that, which
Thou thoughtst a friendship in me, Love, forget it.
It was my joy,—and—death.——— *Faints.*
ALMERIN. ———For curiosity
Ile save thee, if I can, and know the end.
If't be but losse of Blood,—Breasts!
By all that's good, a woman!—*Iphigene.*
IPHIGENE. I thank thee, for I was falne asleep, before
I had dispatcht. Sweetest of all thy sexe,
Francelia, forgive me now; my love
Unto this man, and feare to loose him, taught me
A fatall cunning, made me court you,—and
My owne Destruction.
FRANCELIA. I am amaz'd.
ALMERIN. And can it be? Oh mockery of heaven!

45–7] *Hazlitt rearranged the lines to read*:
My fond deceits involve the innocent;
Rather then she shall suffer,
I will discover all.

54 *her*] *him FA46, DC*

To let me see what my soule often wisht
And mak't my punishment, a punishment,
That were I old in sinnes, were yet too great.

IPHIGENE. Would you have lov'd me then? Pray say you would:
For I like testie sickmen at their death,
Would know no newes but health from the Physitian.

ALMERIN. Canst thou doubt that?
That hast so often seen me extasi'd,
When thou wert drest like woman,
Unwilling ever to beleeve thee man?

IPHIGENE. I have enough.

ALMERIN. Heavens!
What thing shall I appeare unto the world!
Here might my ignorance find some excuse.
———But, there,
I was distract. None but a man enrag'd
With anger to a savadgenesse, would ere
Have drawne a sword upon such gentle sweetnesse.
Be kind, and kill me; kill me one of you:
Kill me if't be but to preserve my wits.
Deare *Iphigene*, take thy revenge, it will
Not misbecome thy sexe at all; for 'tis
An act of pity not of cruelty,
Thus to dispatch a miserable man.

FRANCELIA. And thou wouldst be more miserable yet,
While like a Bird made prisoner by it selfe,
Thou bat'st and beat'st thy self 'gainst every thing,
And vext, passe by that which should let thee out.

ALMERIN. ———Is it my fault?
Or heav'ns? Fortune, when she would play upon me,
Like ill Musitians, wound me up so high,
That I must crack sooner then move in tune.

FRANCELIA. Still you rave,
While we for want of present help may perish.

ALMERIN. Right.
A Surgeon, Ile goe find one instantly.
The enemy too—I had forgot—
Oh what fatality govern'd this night. *Exit.*

96 distract] *DC*; distracted *FA46* 96 a man] *DC*; one *FA46* 108 vext,] *DC*; dost *FA46*

FRANCELIA. How like an unthrifts case will mine be now?
For all the wealth he looses shifts but's place;
And still the world enjoyes it: so will't you,
Sweet *Iphigene*, though I possesse you not.
IPHIGENE. What excellence of Nature's this! have you
So perfectly forgiv'n already, as to
Consider me a losse? I doubt which Sexe
I shall be happier in. Climates of Friendship
Are not lesse pleasant, 'cause they are lesse scortching,
Then those of Love; and under them wee'l live:
Such pretious links of that wee'l tye our souls
Together with, that the chaines of the other
Shall be grosse fetters to it.
FRANCELIA. But I feare
I cannot stay the making. Oh would you
Had never un-deceiv'd me, for I 'had dy'd with
Pleasure, beleeving I had been your Martyr.
Now———
IPHIGENE. Shee looks pale. *Francelia*———
FRANCELIA. ———I cannot stay;
A hasty summons hurries me away:
And—gives—no——— *Dies.*
IPHIGENE. ———Shee's gone:
Shee's gone. Life like a Dials hand hath stolne
From the faire figure e're it was perceiv'd.
What will become of me?———

A noyse within of souldiers. Shee thinkes them ALMERIN.

Too late, too late
Y'are come: you may perswade wild birds, that wing
The aire, into a Cage, as soon as call
Her wandring spirits back.—ha!
Those are strange faces; there's a horrour in them:
And if I stay, I shall be taken for
The murtherer. O in what streights they move
That wander 'twixt death's feares and hopes of love.

[*Draws curtain and hides.*]

Enter BRENNORALT, GRAINEVERT, Souldiers.

141 S.D. *within of souldiers*] *within. Enter souldiers FA46*; *DC places* '*Enter souldiers*' *at lines* 142–3. 148 death's feares] death, feares *FA46*; the feares of death *DC*
148 love.] love. *Exit. FA46*, *DC*

BRENNORALT. Forbeare, upon your lives, the place:
There dwels divinity within it. All else
The Castle holds is lawfull prize,
Your valours wages. This I claime as mine,
Guard you the door———
GRAINEVERT. Coronell shall you use all the women your selfe?
BRENNORALT. Away—'tis unseasonable——— *Drawes the curtaine*
Awake fair Saint and blesse thy poore Idolator.
Ha!—pale?—and cold?—dead.
The sweetest guest fled, murdered by heaven;
The purple streames not drye yet.
Some villaine has broke in before me,
Rob'd all my hopes; but I will find him out,
And kick his soule to hell—Ile doe't—Speak.
Dragging out IPHIGENE.
IPHIGENE. What should I say?
BRENNORALT. Speak or by all———
IPHIGENE. Alas, I doe confesse my selfe the unfortunate cause.
BRENNORALT. Oh d'you so?
Hadst thou been cause of all the plagues
That vexe mankinde, th'adst been an Innocent
To what thou art; thou shalt not think repentance. *Kils her.*
IPHIGENE. Oh, thou wert too suddaine. And——— *Dies.*
BRENNORALT. Was I so?
The lustfull youth would sure have spoil'd her honour;
Which finding highly garded, rage or feare
To be reveal'd, counsell'd this villany.
Is there no more of them? *Exit.*
Enter ALMERIN [*struggling with Souldiers*].
ALMERIN. Not enter?
Yes dogge, through thee—ha! a course laid out
In stead of *Iphigene: Francelia* dead too?
Enter BRENNORALT.
Where shall I begin to curse?
BRENNORALT. Here—If he were thy friend.
ALMERIN. *Brennoralt*;
A gallant sword could ne're have come
In better time.
BRENNORALT. I have a good one for thee,

172 rage‸ or] *DC*; rage, and *FA46*

If that will serve the turne.
ALMERIN. I long to trie it,
That sight doth make me desperate;
Sicke of my selfe and the world.
BRENNORALT. Didst value him?
A greater villaine did I never kill.
ALMERIN. Kill?
BRENNORALT. Yes.
ALMERIN. Art sure of it?
BRENNORALT. May be I doe not wake.
ALMERIN. Th'ast taken then a guilt off from me,
Would have waigh'd downe my sword,
Weakned me to low resistance.
I should have made no sports, hadst thou conceal'd it.
Know *Brennoralt* thy sword is stain'd in excellence,
Great as the world could boast.
BRENNORALT. Ha—ha—how thou art abus'd?
Looke there, there lies the excellence
Thou speak'st of, murdred; by him too;
He did confesse he was the cause.
ALMERIN. Oh Innocence, ill understood, and much worse us'd!
She was alas by accident, but I,
I was the cause indeed.
BRENNORALT. I will beleeve thee too, and kill thee—
Destroy all causes, till I make a stop in nature;
For to what purpose should she worke agen?
ALMERIN. Bravely then,
The title of a Kingdome is a trifle
To our quarrell Sir; know by sad mistake
I kill'd thy Mistres, *Brennoralt*,
And thou kild'st mine.
BRENNORALT. Thine?
ALMERIN. Yes, that *Iphigene*,
Though showne as man unto the world,
Was woman, excellent woman———
BRENNORALT. I understand no riddles, guard thee. *Fight and pause.*
ALMERIN. O could they now looke downe,
And see how wee two strive
Which first should give revenge,
They would forgive us something of the crime.

Hold, prethee give me leave
To satisfie a curiosity—
I never kissed my *Iphigene* as woman.

BRENNORALT. Thou motion'st well, nor have I taken leave. *Rising.*
It keeps a sweetnesse yet—
As stills from Roses, when the flowers are gone.

ALMERIN. Even so have two faint Pilgrims scorch't with heat
Unto some neighbour fountaine stept aside,
Kneel'd first, then laid their warm lips to the Nymph
And from her coldnesse took fresh life againe
As we doe now.

BRENNORALT. Lets on our journy if thou art refresht.

ALMERIN. Come and if there be a place reserved
For heightned spirits better then other,
May that which wearies first of ours have it.

BRENNORALT. If I grow weary, laugh at me, that's all.

Fight a good while. ALMERIN *fals.*

ALMERIN. ———Brave soules above which will
Be (sure) inquisitive for newes from earth
Shall get no other but that thou art Brave.

Enter KING: STRATHEMAN: *Lords*: MENSECKE.

STRATHEMAN. To preserve some Ladies as we guest.

KING. Still gallant, *Brennoralt*, thy sword not sheath'd yet?
Busie still?

BRENNORALT. Revenging Sir
The fowlest murder ever blasted eares,
Committed here by *Almerin* and *Iphigene*.

ALMERIN. False, false; The first created purity
Was not more innocent then *Iphigene*.

BRENNORALT. Lives he agen?

ALMERIN. Stay thou much wearied guest
Till I have thrown a truth amongst them—
We shall look black else to posterity.

KING. What sayes he?

LORD. Some thing concerning this he labours to discover.

ALMERIN. Know it was I that kild *Francelia*!
I alone.

MENSECKE. O barbarous return of my civilities!
Was it thy hand?

230 Come] I come *Hazlitt* 246 black] *DC*, *FA48*; back *FA46*

ALMERIN. Heare and forgive me *Minse*.
Entring this morning hastily
With resolution to preserve
The faire *Francelia*, I found a theefe
Stealing the treasure (as I thought)
Belongd to me. Wild in my mind
As ruin'd in my honour, in much mistaken rage,
I wounded both: then (oh) too late I found
My errour. Found *Iphigene* a woman
Acting stolne love, to make her own love safe
And all my jealousies impossible.
Whilst I ran out to bring them cure,
Francelia dies; and *Iphigene* found here.
I can no more——— *Dies.*

KING. Most strange and intricate.
Iphigene a woman?

MELIDOR. With this story I am guiltily acquainted.
The first concealments, since her love
And all the wayes to it, I have bin trusted with:
But Sir, my greife joyn'd with the instant busines
Begges a deferrement.

KING. I am amaz'd till I doe heare it out.
———But ith' mean time,
Least in these mists merit should loose it selfe,
———Those forfeitures
Of *Trock* and *Menseck Brennoralt* are thine.

BRENNORALT. A Princely gift! But Sir it comes too late.
Like Sun-beames on the blasted blossomes, doe
Your favours fall: you should have giv'n me this
When't might have rais'd me in mens thoughts, and made
Me equall to *Francelia's* love: I have
No end, since shee is not———
Back to my private life I will returne.
Cattell, though weary, can trudge homewards, after.

KING. This melancholy, time must cure: Come take
The bodies up, and lead the prisoners on,
Triumph and funerals must walke together,
Cipresse and Laurell twin'd make up one chaplet.

261 Acting] Acting a *Hazlitt* 276 *Menseck Brennoralt*] *DC*, *FA48*; *Menseck* and *Brennoralt FA46* 277 gift] *DC*, *FA48*; guilt *FA46*

———For we have got
The day; but bought it at so deare a rate,
That victory it selfe's unfortunate.

Exeunt.

FINIS.

SUBSTANTIVE VARIANTS IN THE DISCONTENTED COLONELL, 1642

This is a list of the rejected substantive readings, aside from elisions and many variations in punctuation, found in the quarto of 1642, aside from those already listed at the foot of the pages. Most of these variants are obvious corruptions.

THE ACTORS] *The Actors Names*

I. i

2 above] about
5 to] *om.*
7 do's] doth
13 names] name
26 beards] Leards
26 other] other other
26 proofes] proofe
29 S.D. *second*] *om.*
32 agen] agen then
32 S.P. 2.SOULDIER] *part of dialogue*
34 S.P. 2.SOULDIER] *part of dialogue*
37 Hee's] It is
40 into] in
44 A faire] faire
51 me] us
55 I] *om.*
56 stormes] storme
56 the] this

I. ii

2 honestest;] ~,
4 stayes] spoils
5 on] *om.*
8 Eternall...sulpher] *om.*
9 thee] you
10 wench] a wench
13 thinke] thinks
13 look...too] *om.*
13] S.D. *in DC: she spies Marinell*
16 how] hem how
26 new] *om.*
42–3 *in* DORANS *eare*). The...brother.] The...brother in *Dorancare.*
44 who] whom
44 'Tis] *om.*
46 and] or
57 Ah] *om.*
59 Pray] *om.*
68 And't] And
68 paines] paine

I. iii

1 whence] when
9 o're-] are
11 Harke you,] *om.*
13 after't] after
15 naturals] natural
17 too] so
26 reproached] approach't
27 accommodations] accommodation
38 betwixt] t'wixt
40 the vice] shall be the vice
42 paint] point
51.1] S.D. *one line earlier*
69 Lords] Lord
71 then] the
71 when] *om.*
74 cuts] acts
77 Why] *om.*
78 nor you] *om.*
79 only] *om.*
82 Make] Makes
82 more] the more
84 They're] Are
84 Sir] *om.*

85 stirr'd] stirr'd up
87 forbid] defend
87 Polands] Poland
88 take] to take
88 Quarter] Quarters
95 and] *om.*
97 that doe] *om.*
98 Angels] Angell
100 met] not
101 debate.] debates‸
103 care.] ∼‸
104 Heav'n] high Heav'n
105 forgive: Mortals‸] ∼‸ ∼,

I. iv

3 happy] *om.*
4 When] Where
7 (alas!)] *om.*
8 Mornings] Morning
9 knew] know
10 *To himself*] *om.*
12 fortunate.] ∼,
15 doe's] doth
18 saving] saving of
33 S.D. *She*] *Iphi.*
36 S.D. IPHIGENE] *he*
39 while] whil'st
47 Lords] Lord
53 hath] has
53 deare] dearest
55 the] which
57 and] *om.*
64 by] by that
68 this] that
71 that] *om.*
78 slightest] slightiest
83 you] it
84 has] hath
85 MELIDOR.] *om.*

II. i

4 come.—To] come to
19 though] the
21 Descriptions] Description
21 other] *om.*
22 As] 1 As
22 relation] relations
24 they'l] they
26 paper] papers
29.1 S.D. *three*] *3 or 4*
29.1 S.D. *paper and Incke*] *papers*
30 does] doth
32 or] and
36 and] or
38 S.D. *Seizes*] *Snatches*
40 with them] within
42 S.P. ALL] *om.*
42 S.D. *Enter...armes*] *DC places three lines later after Souldiers speeches*
48 of] and

II. ii

8 agen] *om.*
15 *too*] *om.*
22 ye] you
43 I, of] I,
45 *to*] *om.*
48 *Wine*] *Rime*
49 *may*] *will*
50 *a better drinker*] *better drinke*
54 *For*] *om.*
55 *new or*] *newer*
59 *fill it*] *let us*
68 you] yee
70 *Baruthen*] *Barrutheus*
72 d'you] dee
75 *Plocence*] *Florence*
85 spiritlesse] frightlesse
86 his] *om.*
89 discoveries] discovery
90 Councell] Councell speakes
93 S.P. VILLANOR] DORAN
99 *Makes*] *It makes*
101 *he*] *om.*

II. iii

0.3 S.D. IPHIGENE] *om.*
11 advantage] advantages
14 Petitions] Petition
15 such for] of that
16 youth] youths
17 he] they
18 of] in
23 offers] offer
27 this] that
28 inhabits] inhabit
32 is it] it is
34 eternally] continually
36 unreasonable] unseasonable
38 It] If
38 it selfe] himselfe
39 conclude] concludes
48 Our] *om.*
51 reliefe] that relief
52 to get] yet
55 wish] with

61 hath] has
69 you] *om.*
70 strangers] forrainers to
79 (*Almerin*)] *om.*
81 while] whilst
83 off for] of
83 strangenesses] strangenesse
84 Virgins] Virgins must
88 sanke] sunke *DC*
90.1 S.D. *Enter...blinded.*] *om.*

II. iv

1 Yes] Yet
3 So] Too
3 my] mine
5 If't] It
12 does] doth
14 most precious] preciousest
15 S.D. *Studies*] *om.*
20 in] *om.*
25.1 *againe*] *aper*
30 no more trouble me] trouble me no more
36 & 39 hath] has
43 do you] d'ee
46 my Lord] *om.*
48 And] That
49 doe's triumph] triumphs
49 but] not
58 use to] *om.*
79 devour'd by injuries] divorc't by injury
84 will] dare
86 afterward] afterwards
89 S.D. *Flings*] *Flings him*
90 punishment] punishments due
96 art] art still
101 them] *om.*
102 Persons] Person

III. i

4 thought‸ h'had] ~, and had
6 S.D.] *two lines earlier*
9 of] at
10 Tempests...griefe] Thus as my stormes of griefe
13 that] which
17 S.D. *Lies down.*] *om.*
20 know] knows
33 way:] ~,
34 knowst] knewst
41 could not] cannot
44 not] not now
51 must] more
54 upon] upon your
55 them] *om.*
67 safe] safer
68] Away: I'le not expect it
72 *Exit*] *om.*
73 desires] desire
74 language] languages
74 such] such as
75 victories] victory
76 S.D. *Exit after*] *Exeunt*

III. ii

2 are] are so
7 all] still
8 *Lithuanians*] *om.*
9 to you] *om.*
13.1 *They go off*] *Exe.*
15 hath] has
19 your] the
26 Mistris] master
27 empty] Empire
33 Repaire] Repair'd
33 then] then it was
35 Then] That
43 a] *om.*
46 the King] a King
48 S.D. *They...hand.*] *fused with previous S.D., four lines earlier*
57 (possibly) equall] equalls
58 Catts] cuts
59 up in] upon
62 don't both give] give not both
64 that there's] *om.*
65 Or] Nor
69 Kingdom] Kingdomes
71 but with] without
72 but with] without
73 hath] has
73 most] must
74 pretence] pretext
75 they urge] *om.*
81 unto] to
84 those] and those
86 are risen] is risen
88 Among] Amongst
89 Yore] old
94 in your] in the
97 bare] bore
98 seeke] thinke
99 know Dread] *om.*
101 That] Which
103 does] doth

103–4 up Then;] up. Then
105 does] *om.*
118 lye] be
125 you] they
127 civill] *om.*
127 (new made)] *om.*
131 the publike] a publike
137 face] *om.*
141 your] the
144 and] a
147 charges] charge
151 owne‸] ~.
151 too much] *om.*
156 Councell] Councells
158 unto] to
159 Truce] Truces
162 desp'rate maladies] dangerous sicknesse
164 into] us in

III. iii

0.1 S.D. *her*] *his*
0.2 S.D. *Servants*] *Servant*
5 mine] my
6 knew] know
8 set] sit
11 exchange] *om.*
14 acquaintances] acquaintance
17 And] Or
24 does] doth
33 *waiting-woman comming after him*] *Woman after*
34 the finer] finer
37 doe] does
39 a crash] a ——
39.1 S.D. *the waiting*] *om.*
41 you] ye
44 become] *om.*
45 lewd] lowd
48 Doe you] Dos't
52 these...works] *italic*, *as if* S.D.

III. iv

3 act] art
8 Move] More
9–10 Where...little] *om.*
10.1 *Enter* (*againe*).] *om.*
11 guards] guard
13 Where one's] Whereon's
17 difficulty] difficulties
18 here] there
18 S.D. *curtaines*] *curtain*
28 Amongst] Among
29 Is it] It is
30 innocence] ignorance
37 to indanger thus‸] too in danger thus,
39 brother‸] ~.
41 not‸] ~,
50 seem'd] seem
50 it] that it
51 would ne're] never would
52 Not] Nor
55 thus] that
72 he] this
73 time,] ~?
74 have] *om.*
76 as] *om.*
78 men] man
83 singular‸]~:
84 does] doth
88 with] without
90 sure, is not] is not sure
90.1 S.D. *Views himselfe*.] *om.*
91 mistaken, shufled‸] ~‸ ~,
93 lovelinesse] love lines
96 vertuous] victorious
101 affection] affections
106 life] life's
107 Blessings] Blessing
110 That] Your
110–11 till't meet joyes In love] *om.*

IV. i

1] O? Why so: 'tis wel...thanke *DC*(*u*); Why so 'tis wel:...thinke *DC*(*c*)
6 afterwards] afterward
14 a] an
15 I doe] doe I
16 boglest] boylest
17 had] *om.*
21 too like] like

IV. ii

1 now] *om.*
5 be] *om.*
8 amongst] among
8 are] has
9 the] of the
13 have] had
15–16 Boy...too;] *om.*
18 a Divell is] the Divell's
21 thought] thought so
21 should] could
24 to't] to him

IV. iii

3 do't] doe
9 hath] has
13.1 S.D. *diverse wayes*] *om.*

IV. iv

1 you] thou
2 once are] are once
3 rise,] ~^
4 ye^] ~,
5 is a sad question] *om.*
16 Kings] one
19 the] that
26 discretion] indiscretion
30 affections] perfections
33 quickly become] *om.*
33 a Giant] *as if a* S.D.
35 S.D. *waiting*] *om.*
39 hands] hand
43 hand] hands
43 S.D. *Whisper.*] *om.*
48 those] this
48 arts] art
49 distrust] distract

IV. v

4 though] *om.*
5 S.D. *Talking*] *om.*

IV. vi

2 sober] *om.*
3 be thy will,] be, they will^
4 eyes;] ~^
7 shall] shall not
8 wish so] doe wish
9 eyes-a] eyes
11 a man] man
14 leaves of] *om.*
22 curling and cover'd] colour'd and curling
24 S.P. MARINELL] VILL.
38 very] *om.*
40 more] *om.*

IV. vii

2 imperfection] imperfections
4 they] these
5 that,] ~^
10 hath] has
12 While] Whil'st
14 nor] now
20 in] to
30 D'you] D'ee
32 D'you] Dee
35 S.D. *Smiles.*] *om.*
40 Or as] *om.*
40 friendship: which] friendship
41 draw.] *om.*
43 thy] my
44 And] S.P. *Alm.*
50 trouble] pleasure
54] I will not, first hear me
56 doe] *om.*
60 men] I
66 jealousie] jealousies
67 mine] my
69 I wonder] How came it
74 so] it
76 thy] my
83–4 Distrusts ruine...build] Distrust ruines...builds

IV. viii

2 many] *om.*
3 their] the
6 then] *om.*
7 you] ye
10 out-] have out-
12 Here] *om.*
15 *Doran,*] S.P. *Doran.*
16 East] East wind
17 should] shall
17 goe] *om.*
19 a victory] victory
22 And I, a] And a
22 thing I] thing that
23 us] *om.*

V. i

3 passage] passages

V. ii

0.1 S.D. *and*] *om.*

V. iii

9 this] the
thy] the
12 conquests] conquest
19 does] doth
19.1 S.D. *throwes*] *he throwes*
34 appeares] appeare
38 For...at,] *om.*
42 S.D. FRANCELIA] *her*
54 Impostor] Imposture
61 oh how] and oh
62 then] *om.*

65 nam'd] made
67 hath] has
71 and] *om.*
80 And] *om.*
84 say you] you say
94 might...find] my ignorance might have
98 sweetnesse] softnesse
99 kill me; kill me one] kill me, one
101 Deare] Dearest
102 for] *om.*
103 An] *om.*
104 Thus] *om.*
107 bat'st and] *om.*
110 Fortune, when] For time while
116 goe] *om.*
117 enemy too] enemies at hand too
120 but's] but the
123 excellence] excellency
125 I doubt which] I am in doubt what
126 shall] should
128 Then] With
129 wee'l] shall
130 with] *om.*
131 But] *om.*
134 Martyr.] ~‸
136 pale.] ~,
139 hath stolne] stole
141 Too late, too late] Too too late
145 Those are] These
145 there's a horrour] horrour is
146 And] *om.*
148.2 S.D. *Enter...Souldiers*] *om.*
150 within] in
155 unseasonable] unreasonable
173 villany] villaine
177.1 S.D. *Enter* BRENNORALT] *one line below*
183 the] thy
184 sight] fight
185 the] of the
192 low] love
193 sports] sport
195 could] can
200 worse] swore
205 For...agen?] *om.*
221–2 S.D. *Rising.* | It] — | Rising it
224 Even] *om.*
224 faint] fainting
225 stept] steps
226 Kneel'd] Kneele
233 grow] *om.*
233.1 S.D. *Fight...fals*] *one line earlier*
236 get] yet
243 not‸] ~.
245 a truth] *om.*
249 that] who
256 as] which
258 As] And
259 found‸] ~.
261 her] my
277 A] Tis
278 doe] *om.*
283 life‸] ~.
284 Cattell...after.] *om.*
285 time] Iune
287 funerals] funeral
288 twin'd] turn'd

EMENDATIONS OF ACCIDENTALS

This is a record of the changes that the editor has made in minor punctuation, lining of verse, capitalization, word separation, and the use of italics. After the bracket appears the original reading in *Fragmenta Aurea*, 1646. Occasionally the emendation is taken from an early edition, but no attempt has been made to record the alterations of accidentals through all derivative editions. When *Fragmenta* 1646 has lined prose as verse that fact that has been noted, but the exact division not recorded, for the sake of economy. A number of dashes at the ends of speeches and before stage directions have been silently removed.

THE ACTORS

15 *Trocke*] *Tork*

I. i

1 say] Say
6 prodigality‸] ~,
13 Stars‸] ~,
19–23] *FA46 lines* My...men | The...discover; | And...way. | Let...be. | My Lord?— | Let...be, | I...day:
25–8] *FA46 lines* The...beards, | Men...their | Long...old. | Right...wise, | 'Tis...others,
40–1] *FA46 lines* For...other | World...expect—

53 *Stratheman*] *Strathman*

I. ii

1] *FA46 lines* There; | The...know,
4 powder:] *possibly a damaged semicolon in FA46*
5–19] *FA46 lines as verse*
7 in,] ~:
11 drinker‸] ~,
19 much;] ~,
20–2] *FA46 lines* Would...feares | Behind ...must.
26] *One line in FA46*
34 up;] ~,
37–8] *FA46 lines* No...Triumph: | Convey...King, | He...fairely.
40–1] *FA46 lines* And...day? | Was... Enemy?
48 banke,] ~;
51 Forrester,] ~;

I. iii

15 violent, Gentlemen,] ~‸ ~‸
27 Raillerie] *Raillerie*
27 *Grainevert*,] *Grainvert;*
32 You‸] ~,
42 Oh,] ~:
53 spannels‸] ~:
54 company,] ~;
58 but‸] ~,
62 Fortune,] ~;
63 *Baruthens*] *Barrutheus DC; Barathens FA46*
79 you] yon
90 me‸] ~,
94–5] *gnomic pointing at the left margin indicated by* " *FA46*
99 policie‸] ~;

I. iv

1 *Almerin*] *Almarin*
4 Sheppheardess,] ~;
26 needs;] ~.
28 wealth,] ~;
36 better.] ~—
47] *FA46 lines* My...pardon: | The... retire;
60 *Iphigene*,] *FA46(u), DC;* ~; *FA46(c)*

II. i

7 together;] ~,
13 too,] ~;
15–16] *one line in FA46*
43] *FA46 lines* Let...come. | Let...come.

II. ii

1–106] *FA46 lines as verse*
13–14 *and* 16–17 *not indented FA46*
17 *health*‸] ~,
27 see‸] ~—
33 *good women*] *goodwomen*
36 S.P. VILLANOR] *Vill . FA46 some copies; Villa. other copies*
55–6 *and* 64–5 *not indented FA46*
62 smother:] ~‸
70 *Baruthen*] *Barruthen*
91 call'd] *in all copies a blur in place of an apostrophe*
95 *not indented FA46*

II. iii

1–2] *FA46 lines as verse*
3 Excellence—] ~;
3–4] *FA46 lines* I...*Iphigene*, | He...know,
24 *Oleos*,] ~‸
27 in't.] ~,
52 us;] ~,
56 ends,] ~.
68 right,] ~.
79 *Plocence*‸] ~,
87 well,] ~‸
92–3] *FA46 lines* A...lookes, — | From... King. | Let's withdraw, | And...him.

II. iv

1] *FA46 lines* Yes...married; | What... now?
2 put'st] *the* s *barely prints in some copies*
5–9] *italics FA46*
9 doe.] ~?
12] *italics FA46*
14 ———If] ‸~
16 world,] ~‸
18 other;] ~‸
19 Life,] *comma dimly visible in some copies*
20 evill‸] ~,
19–20] *FA46 lines* Life...they | Enjoy...I | Shall...in—
22 conclude!] ~?
24 suddenly‸] ~,
26 thinke‸] ~,
36 —She] ‸~
36 charmes,] ~.
37 *Doran*,] ~‸

75 what,] *tail of the comma missing in some copies*
76 raves——] ~,
85 Centrys] Centry's
85 it?] ~.
92 there;] ~,
99 Ev'n] "Ev'n
100–2 *gnomic pointing in FA46 by* " *at the left margin.*

III. i

13 curtesie,] ~;
33 griefe,] ~‸
36 *Francelia*,] ~‸
36] *FA46 lines Francelia*, | If...places,
56 any,] ~‸
56] *FA46 lines* Oh...any, | You...all.
66 excellently.] ~,
67 safe‸] ~.
74 language,] ~;

III. ii

5 For] "For
5–7] *gnomic pointing in FA46 by* " *at the left margin*
7 above‸] ~.
7 my Lord] *my Lord*
9 you,] ~‸
11 my Lord] *my Lord*
28 you] yon
30 double,] ~.
39 sometimes,] ~‸
48 *kisse*] *kisle*
62 give‸] ~,
83–4] *gnomic pointing in FA46 by* " *at the left margin*
89 Yore] *Tore*
99 For] "For
100–3] *gnomic pointing in FA46 by* " *at the left margin*
110 quietnesse‸] ~.
111 be);] ~)‸
118 better‸] ~,
123 Lawes‸] ~,
124 man)—] ~)‸
126 suspect‸] ~,
130 For] "For
131 and 133–4] *gnomic pointing in FA46 by* " *at the left margin*
132 Since] "Since
142 bloud‸] ~,
142 potions‸] ~,
151–4 and 161–4] *gnomic pointing in FA46 by* " *at the left margin*

III. iii

5 intelligence.] *FA46(c)*; ~, *FA46(u)*
13] *FA46 lines* 'Tis...so: | Young...handsome
33–60] *FA46 lines as verse*
37 vildly.] ~,

III. iv

4 a'th'] a'th,
21 equalling‸] ~,
29] *FA46 lines* Blesse me! | Is...*Brennoralt?*
31 done,] ~‸
41 follies‸] ~,
48 Madam.] ~‸
52 desired‸] ~,
53 end,] ~;
59 Madam.] ~‸
66 vertue,] ~;
75 thoughts,] ~‸
76 Lord,] ~;
82–6] *FA46 lines* Have...all, | When...men? | My...one, | I...you: | The...you, | And...them.
89] *FA46 lines* I...Lord, | You...it.

IV. i

3–6] *FA46 lines* 'Twas...first, | That's...way? | Hum...trap? | Here's...to— | This...staires: | But...afterwards?
8 Compass,] ~:
11–25] *FA46 lines as verse*
25 neither.] ~—

IV. ii

1 1. SOULDIER] *His prefixes are simply* '*S.*' *in this scene*
1–24] *FA46 lines as verse.*
5 discover'd—] ~;
7 friend,...friend,] ~‸ ~‸
11 Lord.] ~‸

IV. iii

1–2] *FA46 lines Brennoralt*...not: | I...thee;
6 prate.] ~‸

IV. iv

1] *FA46 lines* A...come, | And...gone;
17 gift‸] *the speck visible in some copies is apparently not a mark of punctuation.*
31 Madam?] ~.
40 I, my Lord,] ~‸ ~‸

IV. vi

0.1 GRAINEVERT...MARINELL] GRANIVERT...MARINEL *All Grainevert's prefixes are* '*Grani.*' *in this scene through line 34*; thence *they are* '*Grain.*' *and* '*G.*'
17 wore‸—] ~. —
22 curling‸] ~,
23] *FA46 lines* Part...negligence, | Part ...flowing—
23 negligence,] ~‸
26 Lac't...dangling] *indented in FA46*
29 *Grainevert...Grainevert*] *Granivert... Granivert*
31 way,] ~;
33 MARINELL] *Marm.*
34 hand,] ~‸
43–4] *FA46 lines as verse*
45 towards,] ~‸
48 *Warre*,] ~‸

IV. vii

5 Impair'd‸] ~,
9 *Almerin*,] ~‸
16 peace;] ~,
18 I,] ~‸
36] *FA46 lines* If...first, | Would... charge?
38 too.—Thou] too; thou
40 doe‸] ~—
49 have] *FA46(u)*; ha ve *FA46(c)*
55 more‸] ~,
83–4] *gnomic pointing in FA46 by* " *at the left margin*

IV. viii

3 How] how
5] *FA46 lines* We...straight | The...light.
5 straight‸] ~,
15 *Doran*,] ~;
22 for,] ~;
25 similitude,] ~‸

V. ii

3 disorder‸] ~—
10 selfe,] ~‸
13 Villaines,] ~‸

V. iii

2 kinde‸] ~,
4 neither‸] ~,
13 contrivement;] ~.
18 selfe,] ~,
40 it.—] ~‸—
41 done?—] ~‸—
46 innocent,] ~;
50 I am a woman] *italics FA46*
59 possessions,] ~.
68 Love,] ~;
71 end.] ~‸
73 good,] ~‸
77 me‸] ~,
89 woman,] ~‸
103 cruelty,] ~:
108 by‸] ~,
130 other‸] ~.
148.1 GRAINEVERT] GRANIVERT
151 holds‸] ~,
151 prize,] ~;
154 S.P. GRAINEVERT] *Grani.*
156 Idolator.] ~‸
162] *FA46 lines* And...doe't— | Speak.
169] *FA46 lines* Oh...suddaine. | And—
204–5] *FA46 lines* Destroy...stop | In... she | Worke agen?
209 Mistres,] ~‸
210 *Iphigene*,] ~‸
213 riddles,] ~‸
218 Hold,] ~‸
221 leave.] ~‸
225 aside,] ~‸
233.1 *a*] *a-*
236.1 S.D. MENSECKE] MINSE
240 eares,] ~‸
248] *FA46 lines* Some...to | Discover.
249 *Francelia*!] ~?
251 S.P. MENSECKE] *Mins.*
251 civilities!] ~‸
252 *Mince*.] ~‸
255 *Francelia*,] ~.
258 rage,] ~‸
262 impossible.] ~‸
263 cure,] ~;
264 here.] ~‸
267 acquainted.] ~‸
269 it,] ~‸
270 Sir,] ~‸
283 Back‸] ~,
284] *gnomic pointing in FA46 by* " *at the left margin*

COMMENTARY

The Sad One

(i) *Date*. This sketch of a revenge tragedy was written sometime before 1637, the date of Suckling's first completed play, *Aglaura*. The notes have called attention to the extensive passages in *The Sad One* that were reworked for the dialogue of *Aglaura*. The plot also served as the framework of *Aglaura*, and it seems clear that the unfinished work preceded rather than followed the finished play. As G. E. Bentley remarked, 'the great success of *Aglaura* makes it unlikely that Suckling should have started in *The Sad One* to rework part of it' (v. 1213). The preoccupation with removal of 'great Favorites' (III. iv. 69) and 'lustful Peers . . . smooth-fac'd Favorites' (IV. iv. 5–6), the latter an adaptation of an allusion to the Duke of Buckingham in an early Suckling poem, suggests composition early in the reign of Charles I, though not necessarily before the death of Buckingham. The parallels between the fate of Old Clarimont in the play and Lionel Cranfield's mistreatment at the hands of Buckingham must have been prominent in Suckling's mind. But, of course, at any later date he could remember these family wounds. Nevertheless, among Suckling's letters the allusions to Cranfield's disgrace are most persistent between 1629 and 1631. So he may have worked on *The Sad One* shortly after his return from his travels on the continent—that is, after April 1632.

(ii) *Sources and analogues*. The story has no counterpart in Sicilian history, as far as I can discover; Suckling may have invented the plot by analogy with popular old plays such as *Hamlet* and *The Revenger's Tragedy*. The character Multecarni, however, can be identified with Ben Jonson. He is called the poet laureate, he drinks at the Mermaid, and he writes elaborate masks for the court. A. H. Thompson (p. 400) is not altogether justified in saying that this means that the play had to be written before Jonson's death, but it would seem less pointed to refer to Jonson's masking days as late as 1637 or 1638. After Jonson died, Suckling portrayed a drunken court poet in the underworld (see *The Goblins*, IV. v).

(iii) *Transmission of the Text*. Humphrey Moseley's remark 'that this Copy [the printed play, 1659] was a faithful Transcript from [Suckling's] own handwriting . . . in the same state I found it, without the least addition' may be accepted without much question, for the text shows Suckling's preferences for long dashes and parentheses, and it contains few signs of editing. No other text besides the one in *The Last Remains of Sir John Suckling* (1659) has any authority. However, the act and scene divisions in 1659 probably were inserted by an editor, because the play is not near its conclusion in what is called 'Act. 5 Scæn. 2'. A big scene with a mask and a bedroom scene in which the favourite, Bellamino, is killed would have had to follow. Perhaps the king too was destined to die. None of the other plays by Suckling is divided into scenes, and the act divisions in the other plays do not follow Moseley's style with a period after 'Act' and the abbreviation 'Scæn'. The most improbable feature of the divisions is their symmetry. Acts II, III, and IV each are made into five scenes, and two scenes are left for Act V to balance two scenes in Act I. One would not expect a mixture of drafts of an unfinished play by an inexperienced dramatist to be so neat and orderly. Nevertheless, I have retained the divisions for convenience of reference and have noted their style in the apparatus. In two instances I have added divisions, to conform to the conventions of printing English plays.

Since the play never had a final form, the best editorial procedure is to emend with extreme caution. Only printer's errors have been corrected. Inconsistencies in names, uncertainties about stage business, and irregularities of lining are allowed to stand. Silent alterations of speech prefixes and other accidentals conform to the practices of the rest of this edition.

The Folger Library copy (DFo) of *The Last Remains*, 1659, on which this edition is based, has been collated against thirteen others: copies in the Bodleian Library (Bodl), the British Museum 643. c. 70 (BM^2), E 1768/2 (BM^2), the University of Chicago Library (ICU), the Cornell University Library (NIC), Indiana University Library (InU), the Newberry Library (ICN), the Carl H. Pforzheimer Library (Pforz), the Library Company of Philadelphia (PPL^1 and PPL^2), the University of Virginia Library (ViU), the Yale University Library (CtY), two copies owned by Mr. Clayton, and my copy. Press correction was found in only one forme, in two stages:

SHEET E (inner forme)

First stage corrected: CtY, ICU, Pforz, PPL^2, ViU, Beaurline
Uncorrected: ICN

Sig. E7ᵛ.
II. i. 17 *Clarimont*] *Claremont*
35 *Clarimonts*] *Claremonts*
36 discontent's] discontent's,

Second stage corrected: Bodl, BM^{1-2}, $Clayton^{1-2}$, DFo, InU, NIC, PPL^1

Sig. E5ᵛ.

I. i. 71 uncertain] incertain

Sig. E7ᵛ.
II. i. 41 let's lose] let' slose

TO THE READER

In some copies of *The Last Remains* 1659, this preface is bound with the other introductory matter at the beginning of the volume, but in others (such as the Folger copy) it follows the title page of *The Sad One*, where it was meant to be placed. See W. W. Greg, *Bibliography*, iii. 1133–4.

6. *my former Epistle*. 'The Stationer to the Reader' reprinted in volume i of the present edition, p. 6.

9. *Venus Picture*. Pliny says that the picture was finished, but later damaged, and no artist dared try to repair it. Moseley changed the tale to fit Suckling's case. *Historie of the World*, P. Holland, trans. (1601), XXXV. x. 2Z6^{v}.

14. *his Third Volume*. See W. W. Greg, *Bibliography*, iii. 1079–80, for problems concerning these fragments in Jonson's 1640–1 folio.

16–17. *Sir Kenelme Digby*. This is the principal evidence that Digby was associated with the publication of the second folio of Jonson's works. It should be noted that Moseley does not say Digby edited the folio, as is usually assumed.

25–6. *A hand or eye By Hilliard*. Donne's 'The Storme', 3–5. Moseley quotes from the 1635 or 1639 edition of Donne's poems.

THE ARGUMENT

Moseley or an editor apparently wrote this summary of antecedent events from Suckling's notes. Some of the details do not correspond with the play. The Floretties do not appear at all, but Old Clarimont and Clarimont Junior fill their parts. Lorenzo is probably a later name given to young Cleonax. These uncertainties of names suggest that Suckling left behind various drafts or one draft in various states of revision.

5. *Floretties*. The name 'Florellies' occurs in IV. ii. 24.3, and the one spelling could be an error for the other, but the brothers, Florelio senior and Florelio junior, have nothing to do with an execution or banishment, as the argument's Floretties do.

I. i

11. *Fraught*. freight.

24. *Great men*. Suckling's uncle, Lionel Cranfield, first Earl of Middlesex, Lord Treasurer under James I, was impeached by Parliament and (briefly) imprisoned at the instigation of the Duke of Buckingham, in 1624. On his release he retired to the country in bitterness, and refused to take part in public life until 1640. See Suckling's letters, especially no. 15, in volume i of this edition, and Menna Prestwich, *Cranfield: Politics and Profits under the Early Stuarts* (1966).

32–7. Cf. *Aglaura*, I. ii. 13–17, for the same speech rewritten.

50. Tilley L391, 'He that lives well shall die well'.

59. *looks asquint*. Cf. Letter No. 19. 5, in volume i.

71. *incertain*. The uncorrected form of the press variant, *incertain*, was acceptable but less-common seventeenth-century English, and since proof-readers seldom consulted manuscript copy, *incertain* probably stood in the original. In Letter No. 40, in volume i of this edition, Suckling wrote *inconcernd*.

72–3. Cf. Letter No. 23. 49–50 in volume i, and *Brennoralt*, I. iii. 86.

I. ii

0.1. Thompson observes that the dumb-show here recalls its use in earlier revenge plays, such as *The White Devil*, II. ii, and *The Duchess of Malfi*, III. iv.

6. *dotage of the King*. The aged King James had favoured Middlesex to the very end. See the note to I. i. 24.

17. A variation on two proverbs: Tilley N148 'Ill news has wings' and P489 'The lame post brings the truest news'.

28. *great mens death*. It is unnecessary to emend to 'a great man's death' or 'great men's deaths', as Hazlitt and Thompson did, because such inconsistencies of number were common. See 'By childrens birth and death', John Donne, 'Niobe' (ed. Milgate, 1967), and 'That God hath given to venge our Christians' death', *Tamburlaine*, Second Part, II. i. 52–3 (ed. U. M. Ellis-Fermor, 1930).

29. *set you safe*. A peculiar expression, possibly related to setting the mark in a game of bowls, *OED*, *set v.* 54e. *Safe* is used in the sense of 'certain', beyond the power of doing harm, or being harmed. There is also the meaning of *set* as to fix upon a victim (*OED* 125). A bowl knocked into the ditch is said to be 'dead'.

35–6. Cf. *Aglaura*, III. i. 6–7.

II. i

11–12. Cf. *Aglaura*, V(t).i. 122–3.

13–15. Cf. *Aglaura*, II. iii. 30.

17. *Claremont*. On earlier pages it is spelled *Clarimont*. The uncorrected state of the press variant here and at line 35 probably represent the form in Suckling's manuscript; the proof-reader corrected the inconsistency.

II. ii

7–8. Cf. *Aglaura*, IV. i. 86.

II. iii

1–5. Fidelio probably speaks 'Though . . . oft' aside, which explains *LR*'s assignment of consecutive speeches to the same character.

II. iv

5–9. Cf. *Aglaura*, I. iii. 19–21.

11–18. This is Suckling's earliest treatment of one of his favourite debates, between violent love and an intellectually controlled passion.

34–5. A similar interview between the lecherous king, Thersames, and Aglaura ends with the king's command that the court join him in a hunt (*Agaura*, I. iii. 48–50).

II. v.

17–18. Cf. *Hamlet*, III. ii. 91–2.

22. *Cockatrices eye.* Tilley C495, *Aglaura*, V (t). i. 61–3.

III. i

23–32. Cf. *Aglaura*, II. iv. 1–9, 12–15.

III. ii

6. *hug.* 'Hugging' in bowls is accompanying the jack, the 'mistress', closely.

10. *Six hours ago.* There is an unresolved conflict in the time scheme here, because the conception of Lorenzo's plot occurred only four hours earlier (II. i. 44), assuming that this scene is the promised meeting 'in the gallery'.

14. *one while.* At some future occasion, *OED*, *while sb.* 6b.

23. Since one would not normally go to battle 'Rockt in a douny coach', a semicolon belongs after *battel*.

26. *Looking alow. OED*, *look v.* 29, to humble oneself. *Along*, which makes little sense, is an easy misreading.

29–33. Another glance at the Duke of Buckingham, Ganymede to King James. See the note to I. i. 24.

III. iii

1–4. Cf. *Aglaura*, II. v. 9–11.

8–9. Cf. *Aglaura*, II. v. 5–8.

13–14 and 41. Cf. *Aglaura*, IV. ii. 39–40, 52.

23–6. One wonders if Suckling is recalling Gertrude's description of Ophelia's death (*Hamlet*, IV. vii. 165–82) and offering an explanation of Gertrude's failure to rescue Ophelia. Ophelia is just too pretty a picture to disturb.

36. *waste.* Cf. Suckling's poem 'A Pedler of Small wares' and *2 Henry IV*, I. ii. 138–9, for the same pun.

43. *Where there were any.* Hazlitt's emendation seems unnecessary if we construe the meaning to be 'In faces where there were a few perfections, your wit could make all features perfect'.

III. iv

1. *God night.* The variant spelling *god* for *good* survived longer in this expression because of the old formula 'God give you good night' and the parallel with 'god b'w'y'. See Suckling's 'A Ballade Upon a Wedding)' line 120 in volume i.

51–2. Cf. *Aglaura*, I. vi. 69–70.

57–9. Cf. *Aglaura*, II. i. 8–10.

IV. i

4–10. Cf. Suckling's poems 'His Dream', lines 15–18, and 'Upon my Lady Carliles walking', lines 7–9 in volume i. Ambergris was rubbed on the lips to sweeten breath.

54. *Mine in respect of hers, are no respects at all.* The speech is ambiguous, but since he is a villain, he probably means 'With regard to her, I have no consideration' (*OED*, *respect sb.* 3 and 13d).

IV. ii

0.1. The list of dramatis personae uses the form *Doco Discopio.*

19–20. Hazlitt saw a reference to Prynne here, and Thompson, noting that William Prynne's ears were cut off in 1634 and 1637 and Henry Burton's in 1636 (actually 1637) suggests that 'These dates may point . . . to the earliest date at which this fragment may have been written.' Their opinion notwithstanding, Docodisapio is a sympathetic character here, and he echoes Fidelio's remarks in II. iii. 15–20. Therefore, he seems to speak for the author, and I doubt if Suckling would be coming to the defence of Prynne. Enough others lost their ears to make the reference general.

24.3. *Florellies.* See the note on the 'Argument of the Scenes'.

IV. iv

1–18. Cf. Suckling's poem 'Love and Debt alike troublesom', in volume i of this edition.

5–6. Adapted from Suckling's poem, 'A Dream', lines 18–19, in volume i of this edition. 'Smooth-fac'd Favorites' was 'Smooth fac'd Buckingham' in the poem.

21.1. *all along.* During the whole course of the song, *OED*, *along adv.* 5.

22–31. This charming parody of Ben Jonson's 'Have you seen but a bright lily grow', in *The Devil is an Ass*, II. vi (1631) and *The Underwood* (1641), may have been meant for the original music by Robert Johnson, printed in John P. Cutts, *Musique de scène de la Troupe de Shakespeare* (1959), pp. 54–5. Cutts cites other parodies by James Shirley and the Duke of Newcastle, but he is mistaken when he says that *The Sad One* was 'joué par les King's Men à Blackfriars, 1637–40' (p. 151). Since the words of Suckling's song also appear among the poems in 1659, the song probably circulated separately from the play.

A source for the thought of Suckling's poem is the Latin proverb

> *Quid pluma levius? Pulvis. Quid pulvere? Ventus.*
> *Quid vento? Mulier. Quid muliere? Nihil.*

found in this form in Francis Davison's *A Poetical Rhapsody*, 1601 (ed. Hyder Rollins), i. 123, with this translation:

> Dust is lighter than a Feather,
> And the Winde more light than eather.
> But a Womans fickle minde,
> More than Feather, Dust, or Winde.
> W[alter] D[avison]

Another version, less like Suckling's, is in *The First Part of the Return from Parnassus* (*The Three Parnassus Plays*, ed. J. B. Leishman) line 1391. Rollins cites other versions from Greene and Robert Hayman's *Certaine Epigrams*.

25. *winds.* R. G. Howarth, *Minor Poets of the Seventeenth Century*, and Thompson prefer *waves*, but *winds* are notoriously fickle, like women, and the idiom is 'rude winds cross' i.e. go counter to the prevailing winds (Tilley W412, W698); moreover 'ruder winds' contrast with 'wanton blasts'.

31. The fickle, vain, and false world is the Iron Age in contrast with the Golden Age recalled in Florelio's previous speech; Ovid, *Metamorphoses*, i. 141–8, Golding's trans. (1567).

41. *head-ach.* From the horns of a cuckhold.

45. The conventional expression is 'True as a turtle to her mate' (Tilley T 624).

68–9. Cf. *Aglaura*, III. ii. 130–1.

IV. V

1. *one must act two parts.* For the practice of doubling parts in small companies, see W. J. Lawrence, 'The Practice of Doubling and its Influence on Early Dramaturgy', *Pre-Restoration Stage Studies* (1927), and David Bevington's *From Mankind to Marlowe* (1962), pp. 104–14.

10. *admired.* Wondered.

11. *against your own rules.* Cf. the Prologue to *Every Man in His Humour* (1616 version), in *Jonson*, iii. 303. Thompson observes that Ben Jonson's great size

is referred to in the name Multecarni. The Mermaid Tavern (line 27) was the reputed scene of Jonson's drinking bouts (*Jonson*, i. 49–50).

15. *Lord Treasurer*. Thompson observed that Suckling had dealings with Lord Treasurer Weston (see volume i, Letter No. 19) and may be making a satirical allusion to him.

20–1. *old Cook . . . will please all palates*. A commonplace which Ben Jonson liked to repeat. Cf. *Neptune's Triumph* (*Jonson*, vii. 683), the conversation between the Cook and the Poet.

24. *If it does not take*. Cf. *Sad One*, v. i. 2, and *Cynthia's Revels*, Epilogue (*Jonson*, iv. 183), 'By (—) 'tis good, and, if you lik't, you may.' Although Jonson probably meant the remark as a joke, a self parody, he was never allowed to forget it.

28. *Aristippus*. A cant name for canary wine.

31. *Come, come away*. The song books' version first printed in *A Musicall Banquet* (1651), with music by John Hilton, preserves two additional lines (see Textual Notes). J. W. Ebsworth, *Choyce Drollery* (1876), pp. 323–4, says that the version in *The Sad One* lacks 'the final couplet, which recalls to memory Francis' rejoinder in *Henry IV, pt. i*. Suckling was accustomed to introduce Shakespearian phrases into his plays, and we believe these two lines are genuine.' The setting by Hilton is a three-part round, which requires three couplets. There may be more than a coincidence that three characters, here, sing the song. I am inclined to agree with Ebsworth, but since the four line song fits the context of the play, where there is no drawer, it must be allowed to stand as in *Last Remains*, 1659.

IV. vi

1. *tears of Crocodiles*. Tilley C831. Cf. *Aglaura*, II. iii. 83, and 'the Crocodiles weeping'—'so false is she' in the parody of Jonson's song, in IV. iv above.

10. *Brother*. Brother-in-law.

10. *clear up*. *OED* gives no examples of this phrase used outside a context of clouds. *Cheer up* was the usual expression. But Suckling used *clear'd up* in the last stanza of 'A Sessions of the Poets' where some manuscripts have the variant *cheer'd up*.

33. *with our*. Thompson allowed the senseless reading *without* to stand. Hazlitt is right because Florelio has just been disputing the question, with reasons, i.e. arguments.

V. i

2. *'tis good*. See the note on line iv. v. 24.

4. *the Poet Laureat*. Ben Jonson, who received regular royal grants after 1616, never styled himself 'Poet Laureat' in print, but others apparently did. John

Selden added a chapter to *Titles of Honour* (1631) in which, at Jonson's request, he discussed the custom of giving laurel to poets (see *Jonson*, xi. 384). Sir William Davenant was the first to receive the title officially. Percy and Evelyn Simpson accept this passage as a 'glance' at Jonson. See E. K. Broadus, *The Laureateship* (1921), pp. 47–50.

7–8. Masks during the early 1630s, designed by Inigo Jones, made much of seascapes and movable clouds by which persons entered and left the stage. Jonson's *Chloridia* (1630) and Carew's *Coelum Britannicum* (1634) are prominent examples.

V. ii

12. *thick.* Fast.

Aglaura

(i) *Date.* In July 1637 George Garrard wrote from Hatfield to Viscount Conway that Sir John Suckling had 'Pen'd' a play 'which my lady she . . . its every line . . . My lady of N[orthum]berland hath also a Play which Sir J . . . when he was at Constantinople; A Rare Peece he holds . . .' (S.P. Domestic, 16/364. 110). Suckling's name is no longer discernible on the page much destroyed by damp, but other facts in the letter were remarked upon by Conway in his reply, on 24 July; 'pray send hither Sir Jhon Sucklings Play and I begin with this request that you may the better remember, and least I should forget it' (Portland MSS., Harley Papers 1630–40, ii, ff. 151–2). Garrard complained in his next letter, 26 July, 'How doe you thinke I should gett Sir John Sutlins Playbooke; tis none of mine. He is going to marry young Mrs. Whymen a hansome wench, You have more Use of her then of Playbookes, or bookes, aske Ned Brough else. I wish I cold send her unto you' (S.P. Domestic, 16/329. 45). On 31 July Conway replied, 'if you would have gone any farther then wishes the Play booke would have endured cariadge, and allthough it be none of yours, you might have stollen it, . . . but if it be not a second Play we neede it not' (Portland MSS., op. cit., ff. 153–4).

Garrard's side of the correspondence does not imply that he had seen the manuscript, but had heard of its existence. Since the manuscript is only Suckling's first ('not a second Play'), and since *Aglaura* was performed the following Christmas, we may assume that they are talking about it (Bentley, v. 1206).

(ii) *Sources.* After abandoning *The Sad One*, Suckling found a more exotic subject in Plutarch's *Life of Artaxerxes* (or possibly some undiscovered intermediary). It was the story of the love between Prince Darius and Aspasia, mistress of the old king Artaxerxes (North translation, 1579, pp. 1026–9).

When the king discovered their mutual affection, he took Aspasia from Darius, his eldest son, and threatened to put her in a 'Nunrie of Diana'. Darius took the blow patiently until he was stirred up by the Court trouble-maker, Tiribazus.

> For he dayly blewe into his eares, that it was to no purpose for him to weare his hat right up, if his affaires also went not rightly forward: and that he deceived him selfe much, if he did not know that his brother (by meanes of women he kept) secretlie aspired to the crowne: and that his father being so unconstant as he was, he must not trust in any sorte to suceede his father in the kingedome, what proclamation soever he hath made in his behalfe to the contrarie . . . But whatsoever the cause was, thus was it that handled: that *Darius* flatly conspired against his father *Artaxerxes*, together with *Tiribazus*. Now, they having gotten many conspirators to joyne with them, one of the kings Euenukes perceiving it, ranne and told the king of it, and howe they had sodainly determined to assaile him, knowing certainly that it was agreed among them selves, that they should kill him in his bedde in the night. *Artaxerxes*. . . thought . . . that it were too great lightnes in him so sodainly to beleve his Euenuke, without better proofe or knowledge. So he tooke this way with him selfe. He commaunded the Euenuke that had geven him this informacion, to keepe companie still with the conspirators, and to follow them wheresoever they went, to see their doings: and in the meane time . . . [he cut a hole in the wall behind his bed, as a means of escape, saw the attackers, captured them and had them executed.] Now *Darius* being dead, *Ochus* his brother stoode in good hope to be next heire to the crowne, and the rather, through the meanes and frendshippe of his sister *Atossa*: [he frightened Ariaspes into committing suicide and induced Tiribazus to kill the other brother, Arsames.]

The same story attracted the French dramatists Jean Desmarets de Saint Sorlin (*Aspasie*, 1636) and François le Métel de Boisrobert (*Le Couronnement de Darie*, 1642). Neither adaptation seems really to have influenced Suckling, especially since *Aglaura* and Plutarch agree in one peculiar detail not found in the French plays—the 'Nunnrie of Diana' as the place of confinement. Nevertheless, important features in Boisrobert are in Suckling and not in Plutarch: the important change that makes Ariaspes the major villain; the use of Arsames (named 'Arsame' in Boisrobert) as not only the brother of Darius but also his close friend, just as Orsames is the close friend of Thersames; the use of Tiribase combining the intriguer and the ex-lover of the queen (similar to Zorannes); and the use of a peculiar name *Zoare* for the captain (i.e. Zorannes). In any case the date of Boisrobert's play makes it difficult for it to have influenced Suckling; possibly the influence went from England to France instead. More likely the two had a common source—an Italian play listed by Leone Allacci in his *Drammaturgia* (1666) under the title *Dario Coronato*, a tragi-comedy by Pietro Cioffi, '*in Ronciglione appresso Domenico Dominici.* 1611', which has eluded my search.[1]

Suckling's problem with *The Sad One*, a lack of an interesting complication between the inception of the revenge and its execution, was solved in *Aglaura*

[1] For further details of the long tradition of the story of Darius, see Max Goldstein, *Darius, Xerxes und Artaxerxes im Drama der Neuren Literaturen*, Beitrage zur Romanischen und Englishen Philologie, number 54, 1912.

by a romantic and political love story of sufficient variety, so he pushed the revenge into the background. The play opens and closes with material taken from *The Sad One*, but the love, courtship, and marriage of Thersames and Aglaura which fill the middle were taken from Plutarch. The icing on the cake, the elegant talk of courtiers and their ladies, came from Suckling's own lyric poetry, popularizing on the stage the standard situations between libertine gentlemen and coquettish ladies. Richard Flecknoe recognized that the pretty speeches were important in dramatic history, when he said, 'For Playes, *Shakespear* was one of the first who inverted the Dramatick Stile from dull History to quick Comedy, upon whom *Johnson* refin'd; as *Beaumont* and *Fletcher* first writ in the Heroick way, upon whom *Suckling* and others endeavoured to refine agen; one saying wittily of his *Aglaura* that 'twas full of fine flowers, but they seem'd rather stuck then growing there' (Spingarn, *Critical Essays of the Seventeenth Century*, 1908, ii. 92). The notes below record the numerous borrowings from his verse.

The whole effect is one of variety and novelty, awkwardness and lyrical grace, wit and insipidity, that Suckling himself seems to have understood in the epilogue to the tragi-comic version, when he said

> Playes are like Feasts, and everie Act should bee
> Another Course, and still varietie:
> . . . . may bee
> 'Twas here, as in the Coach-man's trade, and hee
> That turnes in the least compasse, shewes most Art:

Consequently I think that the scholars and critics have misunderstood the play when they tried to force it into one familiar mould. The very variety of interpretations suggests the play's true form. Kathleen Lynch calls it 'Platonic drama' and sees it as a precursor of the heroic play and of Restoration comedy (*The Social Mode of Restoration Comedy*, 1926, and 'Conventions of Platonic Drama in the Heroic Plays of Orrery and Dryden', *PMLA*, xliv [1929], 456–71). Fletcher Henderson opposes her theory, saying that Suckling did not mean us to interpret this as a platonic play; the author advocated the side of the libertines ('Traditions of *Précieux* and *Libertin* in Suckling's Poetry', *ELH*, iv [1937], 274–98). Alfred Harbage disagrees with both views: the platonic affectations of the women and scoffing of the men are subsidiary and do not affect the major characters one bit. He thinks that it is more of a 'Fletcherian tragedy of court intrigue', a decadent and overripe form, not the green and fresh, experimental form of the 'Cavalier mode'. *Cavalier Drama* (1936), pp. 111–12. Fredson Bowers, in his *Elizabethan Revenge Tragedy* (1940), pp. 242–4, sees *Aglaura* as a revenge tragedy in its last gasps. These conflicting interpretations need not puzzle us once we see how Suckling put the play together.

If all the disparate elements form a semblance of a whole, they are unified only in the theme. The theme is announced in the main plot by Thersames

(I. vi): the consummation of love in virtuous marriage is the suitable end of the love-game; the marriage bed lies at the end of the journey, within the besieged fort. Aglaura accepts this view too, but she rightly warns against their excessive gratification, for fear of satiety. The rest of the play concerns their difficulties in coming together, and in the tragi-comic version, copulation is the highest triumph of their happiness—enacted almost on the stage itself, when the bed is thrust out showing the satisfied lovers asleep. Aglaura and Thersames are in the temperate zone of love, to borrow a metaphor from 'No, no, faire Heretique' 'Thersames' song' in Act IV. Other characters love in the torrid or frigid zones, too passionately or too intellectually, except for Zorannes, whose revenge drives out his feelings of love (II. iii. 82–100).

The play's notable technical feature that Dryden admired became Suckling's signature in *Brennoralt* and *The Goblins*: almost every scene begins in the midst of discourse, as if talk had been going on for some time before the actors walked on stage. A character answers a question, 'Married? and in Diana's Grove!', refuses a request, 'I say they shall not live', or disputes a position that has not been stated to the audience, 'Thinke you it is not then the little jealousies (my Lord).'

(iii) *Transmission of the text.* Two good independent authorities survive for the tragedy: the printed edition, a small folio (1638), contains the complete play, carefully set forth; and a manuscript (B.M. Royal 18 C xxv) has the full play except for the alternate fifth act.[1] Both the folio and the manuscript appear to have come from non-theatrical sources; both contain a few of the same errors; neither has overwhelming signs of autograph papers as copy, but a slightly greater authority resides in the printed text.

The common ancestry of both texts is easily seen in their common errors, at IV. ii. 41, V(t). i. 100, 104 & 110 (the notations V(t) and V(c) distinguish the tragic and the tragi-comic fifth acts). Both texts have the 'literary' kind of stage directions, often imprecise about the number of characters who should be on stage; for instance, the directions at II. ii. 0.1, II. v. 0.1, III. i. 0.1, III. i. 14.1, IV. i. 0.1, IV. i. 19.1, IV. ii. 0.2, and V(t). iii. 141. Only the revised fifth act (in the folio alone) has stage directions that are unquestionably from theatrical copy. A comparison of the corresponding directions is instructive, showing the sharp difference here between the non-theatrical and playhouse copy. '*Goes to the mouth of the Cave*' becomes 'ZIRIFF *goes to the Doore*'. '*They goe out and enter agen*' becomes '*Exeunt. And enter both agen*'. The tragi-comic act shows a concern for props and offstage noises that are not mentioned in the tragic version, even though appropriate: '*A Taper, Table out*', '*A little noyse below*', '*A State set out*', '*A bed put out*', '*Draw in the bed*'. Most obvious

[1] A fragment of the play is found in B.M. Harleian MS. 3889, ff. 28–31^v^, containing the personae, the first prologue, and I. i. 1–I. ii. 16, followed by 76 blank leaves and a list of books, mostly of the mid seventeenth century. Its substantive readings are similar to those in *R*.

of all is the warning twenty-five lines ahead of an entrance, '*Be ready Courtiers, and Guard, with their swords drawne, at the brests of the Prisoners.*'

John Haviland printed the 1638 folio for Thomas Walkley, just after the second extravagant performance at Court. It was an extravagant piece of printing too: extra large paper, conspicuously wasted by wide margins, unused spaces at the top and bottom of certain pages, and duplicate title-pages, collating A–L^2 (L1+χ1) M–O^2 (–O2), 28 leaves. The format was pretentious for a single play, as if it were a poem or a literary 'work'. Thus the book appears to be a specially printed piece for the amusement of an amateur, comparable to the folios containing Sir William Alexander's *Recreations with the Muses* (1637), William Habington's *The Queene of Arragon* (1640), Sir William Berkeley's *The Lost Lady* (1638), and Sir John Denham's *The Sophy* (1642). And tradition confirms this impression, for Elijah Fenton said, 'A small number of *Suckling*'s Plays were printed for himself, to present to the Quality when they were acted at Court.'[1] The date of the licence, 18 April, falls after the Easter performance at Court that year (3 April), but that should not cause us to doubt Fenton's story, because licences were often procured some time after printing (as in the case of the *Last Remains*).

The Royal manuscript also appears to have had some intimate connection with the author. It is a pretty piece of professional calligraphy in fancy contemporary binding, in twenty-six leaves (numbered 2–26+*27*).[2] The old wrapper supplies an outside limit for its date, 25 December 1638, because it contains weather predictions for 26 January, 27 February, 28 March, and so forth, throughout 1639. Either the body of the manuscript went without a wrapper until after 1638 or the manuscript was not finished until that date. Internal evidence points to the former, because the manuscript contains only the tragic version, first performed in the Christmas season of 1637. The tragic-comic ending was written some time between Christmas and the following Easter. We also know from the book list in Bodleian MS. Smith 34, ff. 105–12, that the manuscript was in the King's collection at Whitehall about 1641. The very presence of such a pretty manuscript in the Royal Library has led Greg to say that it was 'almost certainly' a presentation copy for the first performance at Court, Christmas 1637 (*Dramatic Documents from the Elizabethan Playhouses* (1931), ii. 332–3).

Textual evidence tells more about the Royal manuscript, for it lacks as well as the alternate fifth act a few scattered lines of verse, especially the rhapsodic speech at I. vi. 1–12, and has thirty-odd changes or corrections that do not always bring the manuscript into agreement with the printed text.

[1] *The Works of Edmund Waller Esqr.* (1729), p. xix. Thomas Nabbes's dedication to *Covent Garden* (1638) implies Suckling's personal role in the publication: 'your selfe by your selfe in making the world . . . happy in the publication of your late worthy labour, have prevented the intentions of many to dignifie that in you which is so farr above them.'

[2] These leaves bear the 'I CLOVVET' watermark. In front of f. 2 are two leaves having a 'LONDON' watermark and grapes. These were obviously the old wrapper. The text of the play begins on f. 2.

The puzzling changes at III. i. 36 and the revisions at III. ii. 121 suggest that the corrector of the Royal manuscript must have consulted a second manuscript that contained authorial revisions. (All substantive corrections that depart from *Aglaura*, 1638, are recorded in the textual notes. Further description of the manuscript can be found in W. W. Greg, *Dramatic Documents*, ii. 332.)

The accidentals of the printed text show a slight favour toward Suckling's habits, not of spelling so much as of punctuation: dashes, semicolons, and parentheses abound. A. H. Thompson thought that many dashes 'indicative of high tragic feeling' disfigured early copies of the plays, but since three different printers set his plays from good manuscript copy, and all used an unusual number of long dashes, I doubt that compositors alone put in the dashes. The only substantive text of his plays without the usual dashes is the obviously corrupt *Discontented Colonell* (1642). The Royal manuscript is lightly punctuated: it has fewer dashes than the folio, scanty end punctuation, and few parentheses. For a time, however, I was impressed by the similarites of spelling between Suckling's holograph letters and the Royal manuscript. But any two manuscripts of the time would normally look more alike than a manuscript and a printed text, since manuscript spellings are generally more archaic. The other example of the scribe's writing, the Folger manuscript of John Fletcher's *Beggar's Bush*, displays the same habits as the manuscript of *Aglaura*. The only words that I can detect in the Royal manuscript spelled differently from those in *Beggar's Bush* but identical with Suckling's spellings are *leadd*, *gaurd*, and *whether* (for *whither*). Does this mean that the scribe was influenced by his copy of Suckling's hand or by his copy of Fletcher's? There is not enough evidence to answer.

Since the manuscript of *Aglaura* has only those possibly authorial spellings to argue in its favour, whereas the folio shows definite signs of authorial punctuation (and it is complete and the author may have seen it through the press), I have chosen the folio as copy-text. Ultimately this was a decision based on convenience rather than any overriding arguments either way: the folio text requires fewer changes in accidentals than the manuscript in order to make a readable critical text. At any rate, I have felt the need to reline some of the verse and to clarify the punctuation rather more frequently than most editors of seventeenth-century plays.

(iv) *The text of the alternate fifth act.* As noted above, the manuscript behind the printed text of the tragi-comic fifth act must have been a playhouse copy, with its great concern for warnings and props. But close examination shows that the folio has been contaminated by passages in the tragic fifth act. About 200 lines remained unchanged when Suckling rewrote the last act, and the printer saved a little time by printing most of these lines from standing type, left from the tragic version. At least 100 lines—V(c). i. 1–4, and iii. 7–111—were not distributed from formes I and K, and then were used in the duplicated speeches in formes L, M, and N. Someone in the printing house compared the standing type with the corresponding lines in the copy for V(c) and changed a few words and some punctuation. Where the differences were too great for simple substitution of a word or phrase, he reset whole lines or large numbers of lines. The consequence is a mixed text, part identical with V(t) and part of independent authority.

These strange circumstances create unusual textual problems, especially when there are variants with the Royal manuscript as well. Ultimately, the agreements between the manuscript on the one hand and one of the two versions in the folio, on the other hand, lend a certain weight to the value of the manuscript. For they suggest that the folio is sometimes more corrupt than we might suspect in Acts I–IV and that an editor should take all the manuscript readings fairly seriously. For these reasons I have adopted several manuscript passages, in all acts of the play, even when the folio makes reasonable sense, if I thought the manuscript makes better sense.

In Act V, when the tragic version agrees with the comic version, V(c) is of limited importance. It may be a confirmation of a reading in V(t), but it may also mean that the compositor failed to see any difference in the copies before him. However, when V(c) differs from V(t), the difference carries greater weight. And occasionally a correction in V(c) agrees with a reading in *R* (tragic version), against a reading in *Ag* V(t). When this happened—at V(t). iii. 28, 64, 111, with standing type in V(c), and at V(t). i. 17, 51, and V(t). iii. 1, with new type in V(c)—I had to emend the reading in V(t). At least once, the variant word in V(c) rectifies corruptions in both the manuscript and the printed text at V(t). I. 115. The other revisions in V(c) are discussed in the notes below.

(v) *The manuscript corrections in the Selden copy of Aglaura, 1638.* Written in a seventeenth-century hand, an important group of corrections in speech headings or additional stage directions in the tragi-comic fifth act are preserved in the Bodleian Library, Selden copy of *Aglaura*, 1638. All the changes help the understanding of the action, all clear up obscurities, and all are quite sensible. Clearly the annotator knew a great deal about the play, and he knew things that could not be inferred from reading just the printed text, such as his additions at V(c). i. 120, 142, V(c). iii. 170, 178, and 179. Either he consulted a manuscript with fuller and more accurate stage directions, or else he saw a performance from which he remembered the actions. The hand is not John Selden's, nor is it Suckling's. Possibly Suckling gave away copies to his friends and got a scribe to correct the errors made in printing. The result is like the corrected copies of the second edition of Sir William Berkeley's *The Lost Lady* (see R. C. Bald, 'Sir William Berkeley's *The Lost Lady*', *The Library*, 4th ser. xvii [1937], 395–426).

(vi) *Handling of the copy-text.* In addition to the usual silent alterations mentioned in 'The Treatment of the Text', I have silently capitalized the first letter of every line of verse. I have not made wholesale changes in the lining, as Thompson did so disastrously, because I think Suckling had a flexible notion of the dramatic verse he used. More formal speeches fall into pentameter lines, but witty speeches and workaday dialogue fall into three- or four-foot lines. His other three plays contain much of this irregular verse, as does the manuscript of *Aglaura*, so we cannot attribute it to careless printers. From time to time, however, the printer was puzzled by some short lines or by some lined prose, and since there were no capitalized beginnings of verse lines, the easy distinction between verse and prose was difficult. Consequently prose was sometimes set as verse, and verse was occasionally pieced out in six and seven stress lines. The apparatus lists, at the end of the play, the relining of verse, but not the absurd lining of prose in the copy-text nor the variations in lining in the manuscript.

All known copies of the 1638 folio were collated against the Harvard copy (MH): British Museum C. 71 ff. 2 (BM^1), British Museum, Ashley 5058 (BM^2), Bodleian Library, Mal 25 (3) ($Bodl^1$), Bodleian Library, H1.g. Art. Seld. ($Bodl^2$), Christ Church, Oxford, Evelyn copy (Ch^1), Christ Church, Oxford, c. 13 (Ch^2) an imperfect copy lacking sigs. A1–2 and O1, and a copy in the Huntington Library (CSmH). Variants appear in four formes:

SHEET C (inner forme)

Corrected: BM^1, $Bodl^1$, MH
Uncorrected: CSmH, BM^2, $Bodl^2$, Ch^{1-2}

Sig. $C1^v$.
I. v. 39 Lord?] Lord ¿

SHEET D (outer forme)

Corrected: Σ
Uncorrected: BM^2

Sig. D1.
I. vi. 122 concerne] concenre

SHEET F (outer forme)

Corrected: Σ
Uncorrected: Ch^2

Sig. $F2^v$.
III. ii. 136 your] yours
III. ii. 144 age;] ~,

INSERTED LEAF L+1 (probably part of sheet O)

Corrected: Σ
Uncorrected: BM^2

Sig. L+1^v.

Prologue (T–C) 11 lik'd] like'd
16 lik'd] like'd

Prologue to Court (T–C) 5 asleepe‸] asleepe,
11 deifie] defie

The original reading *defie*, found only in the Ashley copy, is surely what Suckling wrote, and the press corrector made a bad guess. I take the sense to be in line 11 of the Prologue to the Court, that poets contradict reason and philosophy by reversing fate and by creating out of nothing—against the principle that nothing can come from nothing.

(vii) *Stage history*. Bentley lists the performances at Court and Blackfriars in 1637–8 (two before 7 February and one 3 April), and the seven recorded Restoration performances (v. 1202–5). An account of the sumptuous costumes and scenery and the furore that they caused are recounted in Bentley (see Clayton, xliv–v). Richard Brome's repeated attacks on Suckling and this play have been discussed fully by R. J. Kaufmann, *Richard Brome: Caroline Playwright* (1961), pp. 151–68. However, there is some additional evidence among the original stage designs by Inigo Jones, now in the Devonshire collection at Chatsworth. I am inclined to believe that the large unidentified drawing, number 400 in *Designs by Inigo Jones for Masques & Plays at Court*, eds. Percy Simpson and C. F. Bell (1924), of a forest scene was made for Suckling's play. 'In the middle at the bottom are two steps, and, on either side, huge boulders, with bushes amongst them, masking the flights of stairs ascending to the stage. On these rocks are erected the side pilasters of the border which show alternative designs. At the base of that on the left is a group of four figures, one a man stooping forward to raise a falling companion, the pair behind supporting a cornice' (Simpson and Bell, pp. 140–1). This group is reminiscent of the hunting scene in the first act of *Aglaura*, when Orsames has been thrown from his horse and is helped to his feet by several others. On the right side of the drawing is 'a group of three figures, a kneeling woman and two others bearing a cornice which supports what appear to be more figures or a trophy'. This tableau is less particularized than the left side, but it could have been meant to suggest the scene in Act IV when Aglaura pleads with the King and Zorannes. 'The scene shows undulating ridges ending in low hills, planted with trees, on each side. In the middle distance a row of four trees crosses the stage. Just in front of it are horsemen and dogs pursuing a stag towards the right. Behind are the hills rising towards the horizon.' This suggests the hunting scene in Act I. The trees in the middle distance may be Diana's Grove or the place where Jolas and Ariaspes hide to observe the movements of Thersames and Aglaura. (In *Festival Designs by Inigo Jones* (1967), item 105, Roy Strong mentions this identification as a 'possibility', but he neglects to acknowledge his informant.)

If we accept drawing number 400 as a design for the production of *Aglaura*, we must accept 394 and 395, which are alternate drawings of the background of the same set. Especially interesting is the diagram on the back of 395, which shows the plan of the stage presumably for the hunting scene, with the steps in front, wings, and back-shutter.[1] Also in the Devonshire collection, a drawing of a Persian costume by Inigo Jones gives some idea of the styles that may have been used for *Aglaura* when 'She that in Persian habits, made great brags' ('Upon Aglaura in Folio' in *Musarum Deliciae*, 1655). The figure has 'Long mustaches. Large round turban with aigrette in front. Long tunic reaching to the knees, with short sleeves edged with fringe above elbows. Loose trousers and high boots' (Simpson and Bell, p. 150, drawing no. 445). Suckling spent £300 or £400 on this kind of thing.

Possibly some of these sets were adapted for use at Blackfriars or at the Globe, because allusions (Bentley, v. 1202–5) imply public performances with gaudy scenes too.[2] Samuel Harding's *Sicily and Naples*, an unacted play, is praised for,

Scorning all glory that is not her owne,
Nor needing a *Blacke Fryers* shaven crowne,
(As some,) to wispe her temples, though put forth
So poore, that *six-pence* charge buyes all she's worth;
She'le out-blaze bright *Aglaura*'s shining robe:
Her scene shall never change, the world's her *Globe*.[3]

Knowledge of the first performances is further extended by the survival of musical settings for the songs, one by William Lawes and one by Henry Lawes, listed in the notes to IV. ii and iv.

A prompt copy for use at the Theatre Royal in the 1670s (see p. 293 below) survives in the Bodleian copy of *Fragmenta Aurea*, 1658 (Vet. A3. F 824). There were no cuts from the dialogue, and Michael Mohun was Zorannes; Edward Kynaston, Aglaura; Theophilus Bird, possibly Philan.[4] Four changes of scene sufficed: a court, wood, chamber, and garden. At the beginning of IV. iii there is a warning to 'Fitz', probably meaning Theophilus Fitz, violinist to the King, who should have played for the song 'Why so pale and wan', in the following scene.

Title-page. The second edition, 1646, has a note on the title-page to the tragic version, 'Presented At the Private House in *Black-Fryers*, by his Majesties Servants', which does not agree with George Garrard's statement that the

[1] The use of shutters that slid back on grooves at the sides and back of the scene is explained by Richard Southern in *Changeable Scenery* (1952), pp. 44–56.

[2] Mr. John Freehafer (*J.E.G.P.* lxvii. 249–65) carries the possibility farther by conjecturing that the public performance of *Aglaura*, with scenery, was 'The Italian Night Piece' attributed to Massinger and alluded to by Sir Henry Wotton (see Bentley, iv. 792–3). I do not see that there is anything especially Italian about Suckling's play.

[3] S. Hall's verses commending the first edition, 1640.

[4] Only Mohun is mentioned by name in the prompter's notes. The other names come from John Downes, *Roscius Anglicanus*, ed. Summers [n.d.], p. 19, and from Pepys, *Diary*, ed. Wheatley, 1893, 24 September 1662.

play was acted at both Court and the Blackfriars (Bentley, v. 1202). The two prologues confirm that the tragic version was intended to be acted at both places. The title-page to the alternate fifth act says 'Represented At the Court, by his Majesties Servants'. The various prologues suggest that Suckling intended it to be acted in public too. However, it is curious that the note would be associated with the tragi-comic version unless there were some tradition that it was performed only at Court. Possibly the alternative version never was acted elsewhere, for the recorded performances never mention the tragi-comic version. The Restoration prompt copy has no marks on the alternative ending, and Sir Henry Herbert (*Dramatic Records*, J. Q. Adams, ed., p. 118) notes a production on 27 February 1661/2 'the tragicall way'.

PROLOGUE

15. *London measure*. The habit of drapers' giving something beyond the standard yard.

PROLOGUE TO THE COURT

1. *still*. instill.

16. 1. *To the King*. Placing this on the right margin, as if it is a stage direction, the manuscript is clearly correct to signal a change of address from the Court at large to the King himself.

DRAMATIS PERSONAE

The names *Ariaspes*, *Orsames*, and *Zorannes* come from the tradition begun by Plutarch's *Life of Artaxerxes* (see section (ii), above). The name *Aglaura* may have come from *Aglaia*, one of the graces, 'which is interpreted brightnesse, cleernesse, beautie, pleasure, or majestie' (Thomas Cooper's *Thesaurus*, 1578). *Aglauros* appears in Ovid's *Metamorphoses*, bk. ii, but she has nothing to do with Aglaura.

12. *platonique*. A believer in the 'new religion in love' (II. ii. 24). The fashionable Court platonism encouraged by Queen Henrietta Maria is best described in the early chapters of Alfred Harbage's *Cavalier Drama* (1936).

I. i

1–5. Dryden paraphrases these lines admiringly in the *Wild Gallant*, v. v. 60–3, ed. Dearing (1962):

> Married!
> And in *Diana*'s Grove boy.
> Why 'tis fine by heaven; 'tis wondrous fine; as the Poet goes on sweetly.

8. *steale as 'twere ones owne*. Beaufort, in *The New Inn*, IV. iii. 76–7, states the principle in lower terms when he remarks on the masquerade of Stuffe and his wife: 'A fine species of fornicating with a mans owne wife.' *Jonson*, vi. 467.

11. *pursuite*. The folio's *sport* appears to be a misreading.

I. ii

3. *Carbonadoes.* 'Carbonadoe, a rasher on the coales; also, a flash over the face, which fetcheth the flesh with it', Cotgrave, *Dictionary* (1611).

13–17. Cf. *The Sad One*, I. i. 31–8.

16. The Harleian manuscript, which breaks off the text at this point, has many blank pages following, to suggest that the copier meant to finish his task eventually.

I. iii

1–6. 'A Tyrant is to all men hatefull; hee builds the whole bodie of his State upon the colums of feare; his ruines arise from either not fearing, or not being feared: confidence destroyes him, feare secures him not', Malvezzi's *Romulus and Tarquin*, trans. H. Carey (1637). Suckling wrote commendatory verses to the second edition (1638). Also see Tilley C866.

19–21. Cf. *The Sad One*, II. iv. 5–9.

50. *uncouple.* To set the dogs free for the chase.

56. *neere, and onely neere a crowne.* Cf. Sir John Denham's *The Sophy* (1667 ed., p. 79).

> Will you be the scorn of fortune,
> To come near a Crown, and only near it?

I. iv

21–51. Similitude debates such as this and the one in II. ii became Suckling's speciality. Earlier examples occur in the speeches at barriers such as that following Jonson's *Hymenaei* and in Lyly's courtly comedies.

54–9. Cf. Suckling's poem 'Against Absence', lines 33–6.

76. *false opticke.* Cf. volume i, letter no. 23 and *Aglaura*, V(t). i. 93. He seems to be talking about lenses with multiple refraction which Burton called multiplying glasses (*Anatomy of Melancholy*, Pt. 2, sec. 2, mem. 4). 'There be glasses also wherein one man may see another man's image, and not his owne; others to make manie similitudes; . . . that make great things seeme little, things farre off to be at hand': Reginald Scot, *The Discoverie of Witchcraft* (1584), p. 316. A painting which presents one image when viewed from the front, another image from the side was called a false optic too.

104. *that tale.* Giving myself the 'name of vertue'.

106. *double key.* A key which fits two different doors, perhaps with a bit at either end. *OED* has no example of this phrase, but Denham uses it in *The Sophy* (1667 ed.), p. 45.

> They with their double key of conscience bind
> The Subjects souls, and leave the Kings unconfin'd.

113. *high-flowne and selfe-less'ning bird.* A high flying hawk is the best kind. Tilley H229, 'High-flying hawks are fit for princes.'

115. *imp and binde.* 'to ympe . . . take another quill that is lesser, that it may go into the broken or bruised quill . . . force the end of the feather into the new quill that is cut. . . . For to bind in a feather that were slipped out of the pynion [make a paste on a linen cloth] the which you shall binde on both sides of the place where the feather slipped.' George Turberville, *The Booke of Falconrie* (1611), sig. G1–G1ᵛ.

116. *this.* The folio reading *thus* fails to carry the sense over to the sententious conclusion that follows.

I. v

1–59. Cf. volume i, Suckling's poem, 'Against Fruition [II]'.

7. *rare.* The folio's *some new strange* may be an unmetrical elaboration by a copyist, whereas *rare* and *true* at least satisfy the rhythm.

15. *Flesh't in the chase.* 'they rewarde the houndes with that and the braynes all hote and bleeding . . . those rewardes will much better flesh and encourage the hounds.' [George Gascoigne], *The Noble Arte of Venerie* (1908, Tudor and Stuart Library ed.), p. 131.

21. Tilley M226: 'A man cannot live on air like a cameleon.'

23–42. Two other treatments of 'love's diet' are in Ben Jonson's *The Alchemist*, II. ii. 72–88 and Robert Herrick's 'Oberon's Feast'.

27. *curiositie.* Ingenuity or fastidiousness, one of Suckling's favourite words: curious Heraldrie (II. iii. 7), curious posteritie (III. ii. 46–7), and curious studiers (IV. i. 92), as Thompson observed.

36. *Je-ne-scays-quas.* The emendation is confirmed by the passages in volume i, Suckling's letter no. 48. 21 and in his 'Sonnet II', line 4, showing Suckling's interest in *je ne sais quas. Jene strayes* is not recorded in *OED* or contemporary dictionaries.

37. *beanes first blossomes.* Cf. Suckling's poem 'Upon my Lady Carliles walking', lines 7–8.

I. vi

17. *sacietie.* Satiety.

20–1. Cf. Suckling's poem, 'Upon my Lord Brohalls Wedding', line 32.

29. *tinder.* Probably the correct reading (rather than *cinder*), for Abraham Cowley uses it in about the same way in 'The Inconstant', *Poems* (1656), sig. 2H4ᵛ.

> But my consum'd and wasted Heart
> Once burnt to *Tinder* with a strong Desire,
> Since that by every *Spark* is set on Fire.

38. *messengers.* The manuscript's *messengers* is a slightly harder reading than *messages*.

54. *stocke thee out.* Supply you until the day of judgement. In IV. iv. 83–4 the word *stock* appears as a noun in the same sense.

70. *besiege, not force affection.* Cf. *The Sad One*, III. iv. 52–3. This must have been a common idea concerning the actions of a ruler; see Chapman's *Bussy D'Ambois*, II. ii. 124–5 (ed. Brooke, 1964).

75. *lost their light.* An enormous lantern hoisted at the highest part in the stern of a lead ship was used by following ships to steer at night.

II. i

9–10. Cf. *The Sad One*, III. iv. 60–1.

11. *quarrie.* 'The Quarry is the fowl which is flown at, and slain at any time, especially when young Hawks are flown thereto.' *The Ornithology of Francis Willughby*, by John Ray (1678), p. 399.

66–7. *string of a watch.* The string was not used to wind old watches, but a key was. However, a string wound on a fusee connected with the mainspring. If the watch was wound too tight, this string broke (F. J. Britten, *Old Clocks and Watches and their Makers*, 1911, pp. 78–81). Other clock metaphors are in Suckling's poems 'That none beguiled be' and 'Sonnet II'.

II. ii

3. *too heartifye.* There is nothing wrong with *too* (*R*, *FA46*), as a dative infinitive common in seventeenth-century English (see *OED* blame: too blame). Manuscript's *heartifye* is not recorded in contemporary use, but possibly Suckling meant to write that as a comic coinage, i.e. to emblazon in my heart.

10–15. Cf. Suckling's poem ''Tis now since I sate down'.

19. The best cure for love-melancholy is to be allowed to have one's will (Burton, *Anatomy of Melancholy*, Pt. 3, sec. 2, mem. 5, subs. 5).

21. A parody of William Cartwright's *The Royal Slave*, acted in 1636 at Oxford, in 1637 at Hampton Court (*Plays and Poems*, ed. Evans, 1951), lines 939–51.

> I can distinguish betwixt Love, and Love,
> 'Tweene Flames and good Intents, nay between Flames
> And Flames themselves . . . consuming, and consum'd.
> But the pure clearer Flames, that shoot up alwayes
> In one continued Pyramid of lustre,
> Know no commerce with Earth, but unmixt still,
> . . . neither devouring,
> Nor yet devour'd.

31. *ignorant Conjurers.* Cf. Suckling's letter no. 23. 66–7 and Tilley D319; also *Romeo and Juliet*, II. i. 23–6.

37. *chargeable.* Weighty, expensive.

II. iii

1–18. 'Such an argument was supposed to indicate the corruption of reason by passion': Lawrence Babb, *The Elizabethan Malady* (1951), p. 153. Massinger in *The Unnatural Combat* (*Plays*, ed. Gifford, 1813), I. 216, has a character make a similar case for incest.

8–11. Cf. Suckling's 'An Account of Religion', lines 346–51.

18. *individuall.* 'Not to bee parted, as man and wife', Henry Cockeram, *The English Dictionarie* (1623). Cf. 'An Account of Religion', lines 353–5. Robert Greville, Lord Brooke, in *The Nature of Truth* (1640), pp. 40–1, says, 'I conceive all the senses are but one, and that is *Tactus*. For their Energie is nothing till the ray from the object to the organ, and from the organ to the object touch in one. It is most happily expressed by Sir *Iohn Suckling;* [*Who having drawn the brests of wit and fancie drie, May justly now write* Man, *must not a* Suckling *die.*] When he saith, The circumambient aire doth make us all | To be but one bare Individuall. [Sir *Iohn Suckling* in his Play, Act 2, Scene 1.]' Greville may be quoting from memory or a lost manuscript source.

21. *beddred.* Bedridden.

27–8. Cf. Denham, *The Sophy* (1667), p. 48: 'as a wild Bull [in] the net: There let him struggle, and toyl himself to death'.

30. Cf. *The Sad One*, II. i. 15–18, and *The Sophy*, p. 88: 'my brother's ghost, whose birth-right stood 'Twixt me and Empire, like a spreading Cedar That grows to hinder some delightful prospect, Him I cut down.'

42. *addition.* Something annexed to a man's name to show his rank, as in *Othello*, IV. i. 103–5.

70. *truch-man.* 'an interpreter', Blount's *Glossographia* (1656).

83. *False as a falling Star.* Cf. Suckling's poem 'Farewel to Love', line 13, and Donne's 'Ecclogue 1613', lines 204–5 (*Poems*, ed. Grierson, 1933).

91–4. Zorannes's metaphor comes from the belief in the movement of water underground, back to the sources of rivers from the sea. 'Great rivers Rob smaller brookes; and them the Ocean . . . I thought these parts had lent and borrowed mutuall . . . Say they doe so: 'tis done with full intention Nere to restore, and that's flat robbery.' Thomas Tomkis's *Albumanzor*, lines 59–74 (ed. Dick, Calif. Publ. Eng. 13). A similar idea is in Robert Herrick's 'Proof to no Purpose' (ed. Martin, 1956), pp. 244–5, and in Henry Vaughan's 'The Water-fall' (ed. Martin, 1957), lines 15–16. The point of Zorannes's complaint is that she had no right to take his heart; therefore she is less just than the ocean, which, after all, pays back what it steals. See textual note.

96–7. *Chalking.* Thompson thought this made no sense and had to be *caulking*, but the metaphor concerns harbingers who went in advance of a royal progress to secure lodgings by chalking the doors. George Herbert's 'The

Forerunners' (ed. Hutchinson, 1941), p. 177, uses the metaphor. A close parallel is in Thomas Tomkis's *Albumanzor* (ed. Dick, Calif. Publ. Eng. 13), 153–6:

> I have no reason, nor spare roome for any,
> Love's herbinger hath chalk't upon my heart,
> And with a coale writ on my braine, for *Flavia*;
> This house is wholy taken up for *Flavia*.

II. iv

1–15. Cf. *The Sad One*, III. i. 25–34.

7. *water colours*. Cosmetics. See M. P. Tilley, 'I have Heard of Your Paintings too', *RES*, v (1929), 312–17.

II. v

5–6. Cf. *2 Henry VI*, I. ii. 1–3.

6–8. Cf. *The Sad One*, III. iii. 8–9.

9–11. Cf. *The Sad One*, III. iii. 1–4.

22.–3 *dreames halfe solid pleasures*. This nice phrase exactly typifies the 'Cavalier mode'—hovering between ideal dreams of love and actual gratification, as in some of Suckling's poems.

III. i

6–7. Cf. *The Sad One*, I. ii. 35–6.

13–14. Tilley S714, especially *3 Henry VI*, IV. viii. 7.

36. *Sunke*. He apparently means that they have 'earthed', as a fox is run to earth. The layers of revision that survive for this passage are difficult to interpret. The earliest version in the manuscript shows the author mixing his metaphors—foxes and didapers (see the note below), which he clarifies in the revised version of the manuscript. The folio reading 'Two of them are certainly here abouts' is his final colloquial turn of phrase. I presume that 'Sunke I thinke' was overlooked by the compositor, possibly because deletions were confusing in his copy.

36. (*textual variant*) *didapers*. A kind of loon which 'so soon as it is risen above the water it holds up its Head, looks about it, and with wonderful celerity plunges it self under water again'. *The Ornithology of Francis Willughby*, by John Ray (1678), p. 341. The notion of a person's sinking into the earth like an animal is found in *The Goblins*, IV. i. 86–7.

III. ii

43–5. Tilley S473. The proverb is especially close to that form in Fletcher and Massinger's *The False One*, V. ii: 'If we prosper 'Twill be stil'd lawful, and we shall give laws To those that now command us.' Cf. *Brennoralt*, I. iii. 42.

49–51. Cf. Tourneur's *The Atheist's Tragedy* (ed. Nicoll, 1929), pp. 175–6.

62–5. Cf. Andrew Marvell's 'Daphnis and Cloe', lines 85–9 (ed. Macdonald, 1952):

> Gentler times for love are ment:
> Who for parting pleasure strain
> Gather Roses in the rain,
> Wet themselves and spoil their Scent.

101–3. Cf. Suckling's poem 'Against Absence', lines 20–1.

106. *pleasures . . . dreams.* See II. v. 22, note.

108. *monster, Expectation.* Cf. Suckling's poem 'Against Fruition [II]', line 15.

121. (*textual variant*) *businesse.* Work. Again, as at III. i. 36, the compositor of the folio has misunderstood deletions and revision in his copy, or the final revision 'journey' did not get into his copy.

124. *big in Storie.* Worthy of heroic legend, as William Habington used the phrase in *The Queen of Aragon* (1640), sig. C2–C2ᵛ:

> Thou hast done wonders, wonders big with story,
> Fit to be sung in loftie Epick straine.

130–1. Cf. *The Sad One*, IV. iv. 68–9. The ultimate source may be a proverb; but it is significant that Jean P. Camus uses the same metaphor in *Iphigene* (p. 255 of the English translation, 1652), from which Suckling derived the plot of *Brennoralt.*

158. 1. *up out of the vault.* The vault, or cave, was surely a part of the scenery made for court performance. See the frontispiece of the present volume, which seems to allow for a cave below the stage.

161. *but advance.* Serve to give increased benefits, beyond the normal.

IV. i

5–6. *as good Pictures.* Hazlitt says this alludes 'to the peculiarity of the portraits by Titian and other old masters, that, at whatever point you place yourself, they seem to be fixing their eyes on you'. It appears to have been a commonplace, the earliest mention of which I find in Pliny's *Historie of the World*, trans. Holland (1601), ii, 545; also in Lomazzo's *A Tracte Containing the Artes of Painting*, trans. Haydocke (Oxford, 1598), p. 186.

11–12. *upon the place.* The presence, the crucial place.

13–15. A young hawk should be generously rewarded with the quarry 'which will so encourage her that she will have not fancy' to go after other birds. *The Ornithology of Francis Willughby*, by John Ray (1678), p. 404.

18–19. Cf. volume i, Suckling's letter no. 39. 12–15. Lions were kept on view in the Tower.

53–4. *sicklied ore Their resolutions.* One of the few genuine recollections of

Hamlet (III. i. 84–5) in the play. D. J. McGinn, cites other alleged parallels, in *Shakespeare's Influence on the Drama of His Age* (1938), pp. 48–51.

86. Cf. *The Sad One*, II. ii. 7–8.

IV. ii

1–32. W. R. Bowden, *The English Dramatic Lyric 1603–1642* (Yale Studies in English, vol. 118, 1951), p. 29, says that a song was conventionally used, as it may be here, to symbolize sexual intercourse, taking place off stage.

7. *Bittorne whooping in a reed.* 'That a Bittor maketh that mugient noise, or as we term it Bumping, by putting its bill into a reed as most believe . . . is not so easily made out. For my own part, though after diligent enquiry, I could never behold them in this motion', Sir Thomas Browne, *Vulgar Errors* (ed. Keynes, 1964), II. 256–7.

10. *put's not to't.* To 'put to' means to set a male animal to a female for breeding. With regard to women, Shakespeare makes the meaning clear: she 'deserves a name As rank as any flax-wench that puts to Before her troth-plight', *The Winter's Tale*, I. ii. 276–8.

11. *Musicians of the woods.* The birds.

14–28. The earliest musical setting, by William Lawes, was probably for the first performance (MS. Drexel 4041 printed in Murray Lefkowitz's *William Lawes*, 1960, pp. 201–2). Lewis Ramondon's was for a revival of Dryden's *An Evening's Love* (1705). He changed the words considerably, adding many repetitions of words (*Songs Compleat*, 1709, v. 194–5). Thomas Arne's setting (in *Clio and Euterpe or British Harmony* [1759], i. 86) involved more drastic changes. The last stanza reads:

> Quit for Shame this will not gain her,
> This will never, never do;
> If thy whining can't attain her;
> Then no more no more persue.
> Fly from her, as she flys from you.

Grove's Dictionary lists six recent settings. 'Why so pale and wan: An Essay in Critical Method', *Texas Studies in Literature and Language*, iv (1963), 553–63, discusses the poem in its dramatic context. See Suckling's *Poems*, Appendix A.i. for an answer to the song.

41. The error in speech prefix ORI. for ORS. may have been in the archetype, for surely this cynical speech is not in character of Orithie, a platonic lady.

IV. iii

49. Again the folio lacks part of the revised reading of the manuscript.

54. *Planet strooke.* 'how am I planet struck, how suddenly Depriv'd of strength?' Sir William Davenant, *The Platonic Lovers* (*Dramatic Works*, 1872), p. 100. Johnstone Parr, *Tamburlaine's Malady* (1953), pp. 58–9, lists the many refer-

ences to the power of the planets to strike felling blows, and he cites mortality certificates from 1632, in which thirteen persons were said to have died because they were 'Planet struck'.

IV. iv

4–23. The earliest musical setting of this song was by Henry Lawes (Lawes MS., Drexel 4041, and Drexel 4257). The view-point of 'Thersames song' is focal for the play, distinct from both the libertine and platonic views of love expressed in scene ii.

20–1. *flame would die, Held downe.* The emblem of a burning torch held down is in Whitney's *A Choice of Emblems* (1586), p. 183, with the following verses:

> Even as the waxe dothe feede, and quenche the flame,
> So, love gives life; and love, dispaire doth give:
> The godlie love, doth lovers croune with fame:
> The wicked love, in shame dothe make them live.
> Then leave to love, or love as reason will,
> For, lovers lewde doe vainlie languishe still.

24–5. Aglaura's remarks after the song are quite the contrary of the usual curative effects of music, like Richard II: 'How sour sweet music is | When time is broke and no proportion kept' (V. v. 41–2). She is so out of sorts that even music cannot help her.

26. *maine-spring, Hope.* Cf. Suckling's poem 'That none beguiled be', line 7.

28–9. *Bees When they have lost their King.* Pliny, *Historie of the World*, trans. Holland (1601), i. 319, explains the old lore concerning the King of the Bees, making the appropriate analogies with politics.

62–3. Tilley H219: 'To shipwreck in the haven.'

64. *odds in it.* Difference in the way of benefit.

71–85. Cf. Suckling's poem 'My Dearest Rival'.

111–15. Cf. Suckling's poem 'Purjury disdain'd'.

116–19. Tilley L499: 'Love cannot be compelled (forced).'

IV. v

24–33. Cf. 'The Miracle' in Suckling's *Poems* and Durfée, *Astrée*, I. iii. 160 (1646–7 ed.): 'A la verité, respondit Ligdamon, me faire brûler & geler en mesme temps n'est pas une des moindres merueilles qui procedent de vous: mais celee-cy est bien plus grande, que c'est de vostre glace qui procede ma chaleur, & de ma chaleur vostre glace'; cited by Kathleen Lynch, p. 76.

34–8. *honest Swaine etc.* Thompson thought this came from *The Winter's Tale*, III. iii. 86–98, but it was a commonplace in romance literature from Heliodorus, Sidney, and Camus. The passage in *Iphigene* (p. 28 of the 1652 trans.) is characteristic. 'As secure Shepherds standing to feed their flocks upon some eminent Hill neer the Sea-side, behold from those firm and solid heights the tossing agitation of ships beaten with stormy weather: So did Hee contemplate, in the weakness of those spirits . . . the imbecillity of a Sex, which bred in him rather Pity than Envy, and Compassion rather than Love.' The *locus classicus* is Lucretius, *De Rerum Natura*, ii. 1–6, ed. H. A. J. Munro (1914), p. 41.

51. *roare.* The emendation had already been made before a similar passage in Beaumont and Fletcher's *The Maid's Tragedy* came to my attention. 'Rather believe the sea Weeps for the ruin'd merchant, when he roars', II. ii. 17–18 (ed. McIlwraith, 1953). Cf. *The Winter's Tale*, III. iii. 96–8. I assume 'heare' was an error in the archetype.

61–7. Cf. Suckling's poem 'The Invocation'.

V(t). i

6–10. Since Suckling revised the passage at least twice, the manuscript seems to have the most primitive reading; the tragic version in the folio is the first revision, and the touching up for the tragic-comic version, only in the folio, is the second revision. I import the author's last intention here, from the tragi-comic version. Similar last minute revisions in passages that survive in both tragic and tragi-comic acts may be observed in lines 21, 45, 95, etc.

17. *Is hee.* This is the first of a series of variants where the manuscript agrees with the tragi-comic fifth act, against the reading in the tragic version. Since the manuscript dates from the first court performance and it lacks the tragi-comic ending, the folio, in the tragic version, must be corrupt here. Also see lines 23, 55, V(t). iii. 1, 3, 28, 64, and 111.

62–3. *look'd my selfe into revenge.* Cf. *The Sad One*, II. v. 22–3.

82. *Dog-star.* Said to be a hot star with malignant influence, its rising causes storms, madness, and hot brains (Johnstone Parr, *Tamburlaine's Malady*, 1953, p. x).

93. *false Opticks.* See note to I. iv. 76.

111. *in.* Burning, lighted, the opposite of *out*, especially used in the expression *to blow in.*

115. *disrouted.* Put to rout, scattered. *Distracted* means drawn apart, rent asunder, or incapable of judgment (as in *Hamlet*, IV. iii. 4). This case of divergent errors again shows how a reading from the tragi-comic version can be used to restore the tragic version. *Disrouted* preserved the military metaphor and is the less common expression.

163. *Unriddle.* Apparently a common expression, for it appears in *The Goblins*, I. i. 112 and in Henry Peacham's *The Compleat Gentleman* (1634), p. 111: 'I will give you two or three examples [of shorthand inscriptions], with which and some practice you may easily unriddle the rest.'

173–5. The reading in the Royal manuscript, giving the speech to Aglaura, is probably correct because v(c). i. 180–2 assigns a similar speech to her.

176–7. *widowes doo't.* Widows' false tears, a commonplace (Tilley W340), were made into a clever and bitter play by Chapman, *The Widow's Tears* (*c.* 1604).

190. *Bankrupt heart.* Cf. *Romeo and Juliet*, III. ii. 57.

193. *well metled Hauke.* 'it is the manner of such great metteld and selfe wild hawkes, not to abide nor tarry at the first no longer, then they be where they may command their pray.' Simon Latham, *Latham's Falconry* (1615), p. 21.

194. *baiting to be gone.* 'And as the hooded hauke which heares the partrich spring, Who though she feele hir selfe fast tied, yet beats hir baiting wing', *The Whole Woorkes of George Gascoigne* (1587), sig. M8ᵛ.

v(t). ii

7. *great Prince, in prison.* Thompson thought this was an allusion to Donne's 'Ecstasy', but the same metaphor is elaborately worked out in Sir John Davies's *Nosce Teipsum* (*Poems*, ed. Howard, 1941), pp. 126–7.

v(t). iii

16–25. This trick of repetitive dialogue can also be seen in Beaumont and Fletcher's *The Maid's Tragedy*, II. i. 155–9 (ed. McIlwraith, 1953).

68. *fence.* Defences.

69. *on a change.* One hunts change when one takes after another scent, picked up by chance having crossed the first scent. The words do not appear to have any direct connection with the salmon metaphor that follows.

70–2. Salmons 'will force themselves over the tops of *Weirs*, or *Hedges*, or *stops* in the water, by taking their tails into their mouthes. . . . young *Salmons* . . . have been taken in *Weirs*, as they swimm'd towards the salt water', Isaac Walton, *The Compleat Angler* (1653), sig. K4.

139–40. *mysterious Number.* Five, combining the male number 2 with the female number 3, symbolizing union, as Ben Jonson suggested (*Hymenaei*, lines 198 ff., *Jonson*, vii. 216). See Alastair Fowler's *Triumphal Forms* (1970).

v(c). i

0. 3. *A State set out.* The state, usually a raised throne under a canopy, is not used until v(c). iii. 40.

200. *bow.* 'I have heard, if there be any life, but bow The body thus, and it will shew itself.' Beaumont and Fletcher, *The Maid's Tragedy*, V. iv. 233–4 (ed. McIlwraith, 1953).

v(c). ii

79. (*textual note*). *Prompt*. This is probably a carry-over from the printer's manuscript, which was theatrical copy, in the form of a warning for the entry of Pasithas and the Guard at line 111. *Prompt* was a synonym for *ready*, the word which frequently appears in warnings in Restoration prompt books.

v(c). iii

37. *pitcht my nets*. 'The dextrous Huntsman . . . pitches Toyls to stop their [deer's] flight.' Dryden's translation of Virgil's *Georgics*, iii, 572–3.

162. *Tyara*. A sign that the wearer is of royal blood.

191. *Mathematick point*. 'A *Point*, is a thing Mathematicall, indivisible, which may have a certayne determined situation', Dr. John Dee, Preface to Euclid's *Elements of Geometrie*, trans. H. Billingsley (1570), sig. *j.

The Goblins

(i) *Date*. The allusion to 'The Ballad' of the Wits means *The Goblins* was not written before September 1637 (see note on III. ii. 49). The assumption that Antonio de Mendoza, author of *Querer por solo Querer*, died in 1639 led Thompson to place the play later (IV. v. 10), but, as G. E. Bentley observed (v. 1211), authorities all agree that Mendoza died in 1644; therefore the passage concerning *Querer por solo Querer* is no evidence for dating the play. The allusion to Stephen Hammerton in the Epilogue is echoed in the epilogue to Thomas Killigrew's *The Parson's Wedding*, which was first written about 1639–40, but the complex problem of the date of Killigrew's play and its text makes it an uncertain guide for our purposes (see Bentley, iv. 702–4). However, on 7 August 1641, *The Goblins* was in a list of King's Men plays protected from unauthorized publication (*Malone Society Collections*, ii. 398–9).

(ii) *Sources*. Dryden commented on Suckling's indebtedness to Shakespeare, in the Preface to *The Tempest, or the Enchanted Island* (1670):

> our excellent *Fletcher* had so great a value for it [*Tempest*], that he thought fit to make use of the same Design, not much varied, a second time. Those who have seen his *Sea-Voyage*, may easily discern that it was a Copy of *Shakespear*'s *Tempest*: the Storm, the desart Island, and the Woman who had never seen a Man, are all sufficient testimonies of it. But *Fletcher* was not the only Poet who made use of *Shakespear*'s Plot: Sir *John Suckling*, a profess'd admirer of our Author, has follow'd his footsteps in his *Goblins*; his *Regmella* [*sic*] being an open imitation of *Shakespear*'s *Miranda*; and his Spirits, though counterfeit, yet are copied from *Ariel*.

Miss Ruth Wallerstein said that Suckling wrote *The Goblins* 'with Shakespeare's *Tempest* in mind', but most of the analogues she cites are from *Hamlet*, *The Winter's Tale*, *Twelfth Night*, and *Much Ado about Nothing* (*RES*, xix [1943], 290–5). Her general point is well taken, however: that although the main design of the play is not Shakespearian, the various elements suggest the way a mid seventeenth-century man experienced Shakespeare. The play is especially important as a door to the Restoration view of Shakespeare, for Suckling began adapting Shakespeare's methods to the prevailing sentimental and heroic forms of drama.

A thorough investigation of the question should include more analogies with works in the romance tradition, beginning with Heliodorus' *Ethiopica. The Goblins* is surely more romance than comedy, for here is the typical long separation of children from their relatives, the outlaws in the forest, the tokens, idyllic love in a cave, sudden reversals, and spectacular recognition scenes. Suckling's most characteristic addition to a conventional story is the description of a country wedding through the eyes of cynical courtiers (as Miss Wallerstein observed). He is best at this kind of oblique representation of the simple, reflected by a sophisticated mirror; or the sophisticated, reflected by the naïve, as in the 'Ballad Upon a Wedding'. I see little in the play to justify its classification as a 'platonic drama' (cf. Lynch, *The Social Mode of Restoration Comedy*, 1926).

A number of details in III. ii suggest that Suckling has represented some popular drinking games from tavern life of the time, and details in IV. i may have come from popular lore concerning Robin Goodfellow (see the commentary below).

(iii) *Transmission of the text.* The first edition in *Fragmenta Aurea*, 1646, was printed from non-theatrical copy, according to the evidence of the stage directions. Every act bears the stamp of either authorial papers or a private transcript: vagueness about the number of characters who enter (I. iii, III. vii), omission of many entrances and exits, and clearly literary stage directions (III. ii, III. vii, IV. ii). The characteristic use of long dashes and frequent parentheses suggests that the copy may have been prepared by the same hand that lies behind *Aglaura* (1638) and *The Sad One* (1659). I assume that this hand is Suckling's or that of his amanuensis.

The text probably harbours more errors than I have detected, if the corruptions in *Aglaura* and *Brennoralt* are a basis of comparison; but in general *Fragmenta*, 1646, presents an orderly and accurate play. Three errors appear to be authorial and probably stood in the copy: *Samorats* for *Tamorens* (I. i. 139), corrected in *Fragmenta*, 1648; the same error again (I. iii. 24), not corrected in 1648; and *King* for *Prince* (V. iii. 13). The speech headings *Per.* for *Theef.* (III. vii. 17) and *Sab.* for *Sam.* (V. v. 277) as well as the ten omitted speech headings may be a copyist's or compositor's errors.

The printer's ornaments identify the printing house as Susan Islip's, which was also engaged in other work for Moseley. One compositor (possibly two) cast off the copy and set by formes. One case of type and one set of running titles sufficed. Shortages in roman capital I's occurred at the ends of A(o), B(o), C(i), C(o), D(i), D(o). A(i) and B(i) began with shortages. Specific pieces of broken type and distinctive nicks on the long dashes recur in alternating formes, suggesting that the inner forme of, say, A was distributed before setting inner B, the outer forme of A before setting outer B.

The Library of Congress copy (DLC) of *Fragmenta Aurea*, 1646, has been collated against copies in the following libraries: British Museum G. 13439 (BM[1]), British Museum 1076.h.20 (BM[2]), British Museum, Ashley (BM[3]), Bodleian Library (Bodl), Boston Public Library (MB), Clark Library, 1646 (CLU-C[1]), Clark Library, 1646a copy 1 (CLU-C[2]), Clark Library, 1646a copy 2 (CLU-C[3]), Folger Library (DFo), Harvard Library, Widener copy (MH[1]), Harvard Library, Houghton copy B (MH[2]), Harvard Library, Houghton copy A (MH[3]), University of Illinois (IU), University of Michigan (MiU), Newberry Library (ICN), University of North Carolina (NcU), Pforzheimer Library, No. 995 (Pforz[1]), Pforzheimer Library, No. 996 (Pforz[2]), Princeton University (NjP), University of Texas, Wh. copy 1 (TxU[1]), University of Texas, Wh. copy 2 (TxU[2]), University of Texas, Hanley (TxU[3]), University of Texas, Ah (TxU[4]), Wellesley College (MW), and the University of Virginia (ViU). Variants were found in sheets C and D at the following places:

SHEET [3]C (outer forme)

Corrected: Σ
Uncorrected: MiU

Sig. [3]C2[v].
IV. i. 10. Like . . . the] *indented three spaces*

Sig. [3]C5.
IV. ii. 36 in't] in it

Sig. [3]C6[v].
IV. iv. 17 'em] them
18 mirth:] ~;

Sig. [3]C7.
IV. v. 14–15 I . . . selfe] *indented two spaces*
16 see—] ~‸
20 1. *Th.* Excuse] Excuse *even with the left margin*

Sig. [3]C8[v].
V. i. 23 principall] a principall
27 in souldiers] en souldier

SHEET [3]D (inner forme)

Corrected: Σ
Uncorrected: MH[3], NjP, TxU[1]

Sig. D1[v].
V. ii. 47 there] thre
49 perchance] pecchance
49 agen‸:] ~:

The outer forme of C has the most numerous changes, and since the uncorrected state appears in only one copy of twenty-six collated, the corrections probably were made very early in the printing of this sheet. Perhaps other sheets were similarly corrected, but few of the uncorrected states survive. The variant *in souldiers*/*en souldier* (v. i. 27) is especially peculiar. The uncorrected state suggests the French expression *en chevalier*, which I believe is what Suckling wrote. *Chevalier* was a normal English word since the thirteenth century, and Dryden, for one, used *en chevalier* in his prose; whereas *en souldier* is not recorded in seventeenth-century French or English dictionaries. The corrector who prepared the text for *Fragmenta Aurea*, 1648, changed *in souldiers* to *in souldiers habits*. If Suckling wrote *en chevalier* but a scribe misread it as *en souldier*, we assume that the press corrector of *Fragmenta*, 1646, changed it to *in souldiers* because he did not consult the printer's copy: a simple interpretation. Evidence suggests that the corrector in *Fragmenta*, 1648, had access to another manuscript—one that was especially clear about stage directions—which contained words that were not in the first edition. (See the note below on the corrections in *Fragmenta*, 1648.) If we presume that *in souldiers habits* is the original, the printer's manuscript omitted *habits* or it was written in the margin and overlooked by the compositor and *in* was misread *en*: a rather complex interpretation. I favour the simpler, and assume 1648's reading is a sophistication.

(iv) *The corrections in Fragmenta, 1648.* About eighty alterations in *The Goblins* were made for the second edition of *Fragmenta* in stage directions, wording, and significant punctuation. The corrector or the manuscript source he consulted provided appropriate exits at many places and added or clarified the stage directions, such as the following:

1646	1648
A slight wound.	SAMORAT *receives a sleight wound.* (I. i. 55)
Enter Theeves.	*Enter* PERIDOR, TAMOREN, *with other Theeves,* (I. iii. 0. 1)
to them.	*Enter the Searchers to them.* (II. vi. 4)
Enter Theeves.	*Enter* PERIDOR *and other Theeves.* (III. i. 0. 1)
[no direction]	STRAMADOR *led in.* (III. i. 2. 1)
[no direction]	*They put a false Beard on the Goaler.* (III. ii. 23)
[no direction]	*Enter a Messenger.* (III. ii. 59. 1)
[no direction]	*Enter a Drawer.* (III. ii. 91)
Enter ORSABRIN.	*Enter* ORSABRIN, *in Prison.* (III. iii. 0. 1)
Hornes blow, Brasse Plots &c.	*Hornes blow, Brasse Pots beat on,* (III. vii. 42)
Enter Theeves.	*Enter Theeves and blind him.* (III. vii. 124. 1)
Offer their women.	*Offer their women to them to dance.* (IV. iii. 39)
[no direction]	ORSABRIN *cals to one.* (IV. vi. 13)
Enter ORSABRIN . . . *servants.*	*Enter* ORSABRIN . . . *Servants, with* SAMORAT's *releasement.* (V. iv. 19. 1–2)

Pri. from above.	*A curtain drawn*, PRINCE, PHILATELL, *with others appear above.* (V. v. 19. 1)

Several speech prefixes are corrected, at II. vi. 5, III. ii. 27, III. vii. 68, and IV. i. 55. Words have been added to the dialogue at some places:

1646	1648
then wee'l sing catches.	then wee sing catches rarely. (IV. i. 53)
Nor looke of any, Languishes so fast,	She will not look on any, she languishes so fast. (V. ii. 2)

A number of plausible emendations are helpful, such as the straightening out of a confusion of names at I. i. 139, the change of *Sheares* to *tears* (II. iii. 41), *interpos'd* changed to *interposes* (II. vi. 17), reordering of Orsabrin's words to the clowns (IV. vi. 13–22), the change from *selfe* to *lesse* (IV. vii. 33), and the clarification of Philatell's speech at V. v. 199.

Occasionally the change in *FA48* seems unnecessary, sophisticated, or sometimes mistaken, as *tickle* for *ticke* (III. ii. 52), *May be* for *May it be* (III. vi. 2), *enjoying* for *enjoyning* (IV. i. 21), and *straining* for *training* (IV. iii. 20), but these errors may be the compositor's work. Altogether, the number of changes is so great and their character so inherently plausible that it is hard to deny that the corrector consulted an independent manuscript, different from the printer's copy for *Fragmenta*, 1646. The corrected speech prefixes, the emendations in dialogue, and the added words are the strongest evidence. Knowing that important substantive corrections were made in the poems, for the same 1648 edition, we may attribute these to the same hand. Whether or not his supposed manuscript source was authorial, scribal, or theatrical cannot be determined, but the stage directions are rather more full than in the usual theatrical manuscripts of the time. In one of the songs in *The Goblins* (III. ii. 72–89) the corrected version of 1648 agrees with plausible readings in independent manuscripts, which the corrector could have found in a private transcript of contemporary music. Even if the supposed manuscript of *The Goblins* behind the corrections in 1648 were a scribal copy prepared for some private person, it must ultimately have been derived from an author's manuscript. I am inclined, therefore, to believe that many of the alterations in *FA48* represent an independent manuscript tradition, and at certain places they restore the text to its original purity. In the present edition, I follow most of *FA48*'s substantive changes, although I preserve the texture of accidentals in *FA46*.

(v) *The verse.* It is not possible to make the verse of this play resemble iambic pentameter, as an inspection of Thompson's relining will show. As in *Aglaura*, most lines are three, four, or five feet; therefore I have allowed many short lines to stand as in the first edition, except where a two- and a three-foot line be contiguous. Many speeches by Nashorat and Pellegrin were mistakenly printed as verse in *Fragmenta*, 1646.

(vi) *Stage history and adaptations.* The title-page says *The Goblins* was 'Presented at the Private House in Black-Fryers, by His *Majesties* servants' but no record survives of its court performance; it was among the plays protected for the King's Men, August 1641. Samuel Sheppard borrowed heavily from III. ii and III. vii for his playlet *The Committee-Man Curried* (1647), described by Hyder E. Rollins, *SP*, xxiv (1927), 509–55. The King's Men at the Theatre Royal performed it at least three times in 1666–7 (Bentley, v. 1211), but the copy of *Fragmenta*, 1658, used for prompting *Aglaura* and *Brennoralt* has no marks on *The Goblins*.

Richard Brinsley Sheridan at his death left behind manuscripts of several unfinished plays, among them three acts of an adaptation of *The Goblins* and a further revision of the same materials entitled 'The Foresters'. The samples printed in Tom Moore's *Memoirs of Sheridan* (4th ed., 1826), i. 307–23, show numerous borrowings from *The Goblins*, *Aglaura*, and *Brennoralt*, but the most come from *The Goblins*.

PROLOGUE

11. *higher*. Richer, more luxurious. Collier says that his copy of *Fragmenta*, 1646, reads *high* and other editions *higher*, but I have not seen this.

21. *boots and hat*. High boots and broad-brimmed hats in fashion.

Head-title. 'Francelia', the head-title in all early editions, was possibly Suckling's own title and the King's Men may have suggested 'The Goblins', under which the play appears in the Lord Chamberlain's Office Book. The heroines of *The Sad One* and of *Brennoralt* are Francelia and there was a fashion for naming plays after their heroines, but in that case he would have called *The Goblins* 'Reginella'. Perhaps a scribe mistook the location of the scene for the head-title. The corrector for the 1648 edition placed '*The Goblins*' above the dramatis personae which he supplied, but he left 'Francelia' as the head-title.

I. i

26. *brothers of the high-way*. In the fellowship of highwaymen.

29. *make one*. Be a part of our company.

55. *In posture still*. A particular position of a weapon in duelling.

96. *at his circle*. Conjuring; a humorous reference to the French style of duelling within a circle, moving in prescribed geometric patterns.

100. *shift the place*. Quit the scene.

109. Tilley T325: 'Time cures every disease.'

110. *I'th shape*. Ruth Wallerstein cites this exposition, opening in mid-dialogue, using a slight detail to set atmosphere as similar to Shakespeare's method (*RES*, xix. 291).

121. *attempted under ground.* An expression invented here by analogy with 'attempted port', endeavoured to find haven underground, as devils will do.

139. *Tamorens.* Since the same error, *Samorats* for *Tamorens*, is found at I. iii. 24, it is unlikely to be a compositor's, and it probably stood in the manuscript copy.

I. ii

1–19. Miss Lynch observes that Nashorat and Pellegrin are prototypes of the affected wits of Restoration comedy, *Social Mode of Restoration Comedy* (1926), p. 92.

1. Apparently Nashorat was to have been the duelling opponent of Torcular, and he was unable to rid himself of Pellegrin.

3. *To chuse.* By preference.

8–9. *Sedgly curse.* Tilley D264. Thompson says *back* (rather than *neck*) is the right reading, but Suckling frequently varies a proverb, as he does in *Brennoralt*, IV. i. 20, for the sake of piquancy.

11–12. *Points of honour.* As in the previous scene Samorat observed points of honour in the duel.

12. *take your course.* Go your way.

I. iii

24. *Tamorens.* See I. i. 139 note.

46. *reele and totter.* Psalm 107: 23–9 and Beaumont and Fletcher's *The Sea Voyage*, I. i. 13. The same well-known description of a storm at sea lies behind the opening scenes of *The Tempest*.

54. 1. *a Poet.* The drunken poet here may have been intended to refer to Ben Jonson, the only drunken poet in 'The Wits' ('A Sessions of the Poets'). Suckling may be imagining what the recently dead Jonson (d. August 1637) would find in hell. See the commentary on *The Sad One*.

57. *for the blew.* A health for the blue, the sky? In *The Eighth Liberal Science: or a new-found Art and Order of Drinking* (1650) there is the expression 'drink 'till the ground looks blew' that may be closer in meaning, similar to the last line of a catch, 'Old Sack . . . can charm away cares when the Ground looks blew', in Hilton's *Catch that Catch Can* (1667), p. 78, and to the drinking song in Lyly's *Sapho and Phao*, II. iii (1632 edition) that ends 'And part not till the ground looke blew'.

I. iv

1–35. The image of a creditor's sergeant (I. ii. 17) is now worked out in a scene.

4. *of furie.* Of furiosity, quick to anger.

4. *foine*. Thrust, as in fencing, with a pun on sexual play, since Orsabrin has unwittingly gone into a brothel (*2 Henry IV*, II. iv. 230, 'fighting o' days and foining o' nights').

6. *Tope*. A French term in gambling, from *toper* to cover a bet, accept the challenge; *tope, je tope*. Thompson tried to justify *Topo*, the reading in all early editions, as the Italian word for *rat*, and some connection with *Hamlet*, III. iv. 23. *Tajo*, another possibility, was a technical term in fencing among Italians, meaning *a cut, a stroke*. Orsabrin (line 25) takes the word as a challenge. Another possibility is *Tol is the word*, by analogy with 'Bilbo's the Word', Congreve's *Old Bachelor*, III. i. 259 (ed. Davis, 1967). *Tol* was short for 'Toledo', a fine Spanish sword.

6–7. Apparently the tailor is asking the sergeants to arrest a man for debt and he says the man must pay for a yard and a half of cloth.

6. *Mirmidon*. Usually applied to soldiers, or in slang, to constables' attendants. The application to a tailor suggests the folk-tale of the brave little tailor who killed seven flies and advertised himself as 'seven at one blow'. Our little Mirmidon, a little merry Greek, retires to a tavern to await the results of the encounter.

8. *'Tis well, 'tis wondrous well*. See the note on *Aglaura*, I. i. 5.

30. *Manmender*. A surgeon.

II. i

10 *fall too*. i.e. fall to.

15 *Platonique*. Cf. *Aglaura*, II. ii. 1–46, where platonic ladies are spoofed.

25 *got well of them*. *OED* has no example of this use of *well*, but it cites 'come well on' and 'send well'. Perhaps he means 'I got free of them.'

II. ii

10 *thy Ladder*. Guard it well and you have the means to climb the ladder in court.

II. iv

1 *Hold rope*. Hold tack, stand to a bargain. See Tilley T7: 'To stand to one's tackling.' *Hold rope* is not recorded in *OED*.

4. *make him a saver*. Compensate for loss, a gambling term.

II. vi

20. *comes behind*. Again Philatell is 'uncivil' in the management of his quarrel.

III. i

23. *Gaudy day*. When double commons is served in colleges at the annual dinner honouring founders or benefactors.

34–6. *odde Councels.* There is a significant point for Suckling here that the criticism of courtiers and statesmen seems to be directed at the inner circle of the king's advisors, as in *The Sad One*, *Aglaura*, and *Brennoralt*. Suckling's sympathy is with cavaliers who are out of favour.

III. ii

7. *sullen as a Bullfinch.* A bullfinch has a plaintive whistle and is anti-social.

19. *an eye of white.* A slight shade or tinge of white.

24. Tilley D357. 'A desperate disease must have a desperate cure.'

28–34. A musical setting of this song, by William Lawes, is found in *Catch that Catch Can* (1667), B.M. Add. MS. 29,291, but there is no music, only words, in Bodl. MS. Mus. Sch. B. 2.

35–6. *The Prince . . . name.* A quotation from *King Lear*, III. iv. 144 Isaac Reed thought that Suckling and Shakespeare were referring to a popular catch, but these words are not part of the song. Samuel Harsnet's *A Declaration of Egregious Popish Impostures* (1603), pp. 45–50, confessions of people who pretended demonic possession, in which Shakespeare found the devils' names, spells them *Maho* and *Modu*, and Harsnet's informant emphasizes that these are strange *new* names. *Lear* contains *Modo* and *Mahu* in the quartos and folios, and Suckling's *Mahu* and *Mohu* (the reading in *FA48 Mahu* and *Mahu*) is closer to *Lear* than to Harsnet. I assume that Suckling misquoted as he often did. Confusion compounds when Reed and Staunton, cited in the Variorum *Lear*, misquote both Harsnet and Suckling. Shakespeare could have got the idea for the line 'The Prince of Darkness is a gentleman' from Harsnet, p. 189. Sara Williams confessed 'of a pretended vision of a Ladie, accompanied with Gentlemen all booted, that should offer her to be a Lady, if she would go with them'. Sara's devil was named *Maho*. Richard Mainy (Harsnet, pp. 268, 281) confessed that his pretended devil, *Modu*, was 'Prince of all the devils'. Therefore it is not necessary to assume existence of a lost ballad or catch.

37. *O yes.* Miss Lynch noticed that Brisk in Congreve's *Double-Dealer*, III. i. 576 (ed. Davis, 1967), repeats the simile; when Lady Toothless laughs, it is 'Like an Oyster at Low Ebb, I' gad—ha, ha, ha.' Nashorat puns on *Oyez*. The gaoler has been gagged.

42. Since Nashorat runs out of similitudes, he bears the sign of a false wit, as Miss Lynch observed. Pellegrin has the same difficulty at IV. i. 79–80. Ben Jonson was one of the first comic writers to use the device. See *Every Man in His Humour*, IV. ii. 25 and Simpson's note (ix. 380).

46. *Give out that Anne my wife is dead.* Cf. *Richard III*, IV. ii. 54–5.

47. *Rare Rogue in Buckram.* Cf. *I Henry IV*, II. iv. 189–90.

47. *let me bite thee.* '*Mordre l'oreille à*, as much as, *flatter*, *ou caresser mignonne-*

ment; wherin the biting of th' eare is, with some, an usuall Action.' Cotgrave's *Dictionary* (1611).

47–8. *before me . . . go out*. Excel me.

49. *the Ballad*. 'A Ballad made of the Wits', Garrard's title of 'A Sessions of the Poets'. From a note on the Cranfield manuscript of the poem we know that Lionel Cranfield thought it was 'about London' in September 1637. According to a letter by George Garrard it was sung before the King at New Forest in August of the same year, presumably a new composition. Therefore *The Goblins* could not have been written before the autumn of 1637, or at least this passage was written later than the poem. See vol. i., p. xliv.

50. *foutree for the Guise*. I don't care a *foutre* for fashion. Pistol said 'A foutra for the world' (*2 Henry IV*, v. iii. 101). Steevens thought Pellegrin's remark was 'A proverbial expression during the League', but I have not found it. *Guise* was short for disguise or manners of fashion, and the French word *foutre* was often accompanied by an indecent gesture.

50. *Gaines shall accrew*. Mr. John Crow suggested this apt emendation and pointed out to me the parallel with Pistol's remark in *Henry V*, II. i. 112, 'profits will accrue' (F1), 'profit will occrue' (Q1600). Dodsley thought it should be 'Saints shall agree'.

51. *the black ey'd beauties of the time*. This must be another tag from a play.

52. *ticke you for old ends of Plaies*. A certain kind of drinker was 'He that rimes *extempore*, or speaks Play speeches', according to *The Eighth Liberal Science* (1650). *Tick* means to go on tick, incur a debt, so Pellegrin says 'Let's have a contest, gamble for credit not cash'. Dryden speaks of 'playing on tick' (*An Evening's Love*, III. i). Therefore the alteration in *FA48*, *tickle*, is probably a sophistication.

53–7. *A Round*. The complete song, with music, is found in Folger MS. V.a.409, f. 3; and printed in Playford's *Catch that Catch Can* (1667), p. 73:

> Round a Round a Round a Round
> Round a Round a Round a
> Prethee prethee sirra sirra shew thy skill
> And againe let the mill goe round a

After a repeat sign, one says 'Soe goe Cant sing soe fast Tom' (manuscript version), or 'Pew Maw cant sing so fast Tom' (printed version).

66. *write it over*. Send a notice.

76. *Let it passe*. Let the bottle pass on to the next drinker.

89. *knack*. *Knick-knack* is slang for pudendum (Farmer and Henley, *Slang and its Analogues*), but the bawdy meaning of *knack* may be present in the signification of *trick*. Music for this song, by William Lawes, has been printed in Playford's *Treasury of Music* (1669), where it appears erroneously under

Henry Lawes's name. The correct attribution of the music is in B.M. Add. MS. 31432. No author, aside from Suckling, has been suggested.

III. iv

8. *Perdues.* Concealed sentinels. Cf. 'A Supplement of an imperfect Copy of Verses', line 11, in Suckling's *Poems.*

III. vi

2. *May it be.* 'How far may it be?' *OED*, *v.* B.II. 7a.

III. vii

3. *gone proud.* Sexually excited, in heat.

14. *Tearmers.* Women 'who resorted to London in term . . . for amusements, intrigues, or dishonest practices', *OED.*

22. *t'a scruple.* A very small quantity, exactly.

38. *leave a string.* 'Instead of cutting off the stern [of a young Spaniel], it is better to twist it off . . . And if thus pulled off, there is a string that comes out with it which doth hinder their madness', *OED* (quoting Richard Blome, *The Gentleman's Recreation*, ii. 61, 1686).

50. *Fortunes fools.* Cf. *Romeo and Juliet*, III. i. 135 and *Timon of Athens*, III. vi. 95.

91. *like my selfe I never yet saw any.* Cf. *The Tempest*, III. i. 48.

107. *feathered Queristers.* Cf. 'To a Lady that forbidd to love before Company', line 12, Suckling's *Poems.*

135–6. *description of Styx . . . Fletcher.* See the note on IV. v. 1–30.

140. *Cowl-staffe.* 'To be set astride a pole and be carried in derision about the streets; a rough form of popular punishment', *OED.*

IV. i

5. *walking fire. Ignis fatuus,* Will o' the Wisp. A 'Company of young men having beene making merry with their sweet hearts, were at their comming home, to come over a Heath: *Robin Good-fellow* knowing of it, met them; and to make some pastime, hee led them up and downe the Heath the whole night, so that they could not get out of it, for hee went before them in the shape of a walking fire, which they all saw and followed till the day did appeare', *Robin Good-fellow, his Mad Prankes*, Second Part (1628), sig. C3. From the same book, Suckling could have got the idea of a disguise as a fiddler at the country wedding, sig. D1^{v}–D3.

12–13. *apprehend . . . strangely.* Fear extremely.

19. *foure fathome and a halfe Oos.* Deep oh's or sighs, as in meditation. St. Bridget composed her *Fifteen O's*, meditations on the passion of Christ, each beginning with *O Jesu.* 'Thys be the xv. oos the whych the holy virgyn

saint brigitta was wonte to say daily.' (*Hore beate marie virginis*, 1510, cited by *OED*). Nashorat refers to the Samorat's meditation on his absent mistress. The nautical measurement in fathoms may recall the root meaning of fathom, an embrace; that meaning was still in use in the seventeenth century in the verb *to fathom*, to clasp, and since 'enjoyning' and 'graspe' occur in the next ten lines, the suggestion must be taken seriously.

21. *enjoyning*. Taking part in, attaching oneself; 'Enjoyning the company of Euclide, Archimedes', Leonard Digges, *Pantometria* (1571). The idiom of *enjoying* (*FA48*) is *the enjoying of*; therefore *FA46* has the better reading.

25. *dead Alexander*. Cf. Lyly, *Campaspe*, prologue (World's Classics): 'Appion, raising Homer from Hell, demanded only who was his father and we calling Alexander from his grave, seek only who was his love.'

58. *ev'ry light*. Every will-o'-the-wisp; see Thomas Wright's *Dialect Dictionary*. Collier thought it should be 'this place ere 'tis light'.

76–7. *head of the Base Violl*. Some seventeenth-century viols had a man's head carved on the pegbox; see plate 17 in Francis W. Galpin's *Old English Instruments of Music* (1911). Nashorat means that the officers will recognize the head on the viol as soon as they penetrate Pellegrin's disguise. Thompson's citation of Shakespeare's *Comedy of Errors*, IV. iii. 23 is irrelevant.

104. *laver*. Laveer, to tack.

107. *Sa how*. Soho. '*Sa how* sayeth one, as soone as he me spies', [Gascoigne] *Venerie* (1575), p. 177. *away*. Away there, pull away.

IV. ii

36. *strangely*. To an exceptional degree.

IV. iii

10. *Let me kisse thee for that*. Cf. III. ii. 47. Miss Lynch thinks these are the 'companion fops' similar to Witwood and Petulant in *The Way of the World*, but Suckling here presents them as if they are at the top of their class. The sophistocates' description of a country wedding is the obverse of 'A Ballad Upon a Wedding' where a country fellow reduces a city wedding to his understanding.

20. *stroake*. A single movement of the legs.

20. *training to a pace*. *FA46* is probably correct. See book ii of G. Markham's *Cavelarice* (1607), sig. 3I4, where he explains how to teach a horse the amble, the broken amble, a train or rack. *Straining* (*FA48*) meaning *restraining* makes almost as good sense.

31. *if there be truth in drinke*. *In vino veritas*, Tilley W465.

50. *Farewell the plumed Troops*. Cf. *Othello*, III. iii. 351. The reading *plumped* in

the *Works* of 1694 caused P. A. Daniel (*Athenaeum*, 14 January 1871) to wonder if it was a misquotation or misprint. But all earlier editions read *plumed.*

IV. iv

16–17. Suckling expressed similar sentiments in his Sonnet III.

18–20. Cf. *The Tempest*, IV. i. 261. Robin Goodfellow also pinched his victims, bad people he wanted to reform.

IV. v

1. Scene iv was probably played in the back of the stage or curtained area; then Peridor closed the curtain for scene v, and re-opened it for scene vi.

1–23. The association between the drunken poet and Ben Jonson is reinforced here because of the plans for a mask in which Mercury is prominent. In *The Fortunate Isles* (1624) Jonson called up dead writers; characters asked for Plato, Aesop, Pythagoras, and Archimedes, but they had to settle for Scogan and Skelton. Jonson criticized *Tamburlaine* for 'scenicall strutting', but these remarks were not printed until 1640 (*Jonson*, viii. 587). Thomas Carew, at whom Suckling frequently poked fun, could also have been identified with the poet. His *Coelum Britanicum* used Mercury and Plutus; and Carew, like Jonson, was noted for his drunkenness and he regularly invoked classical mythology. Suckling carefully avoided conventional references to the gods in his poems. My inclination is to interpret the poet as Suckling's answer to *Jonsonus Virbius*, published in 1638.

10. *Carer per so lo carer.* See the discussion of dating above. The English translation of Antonio Mendoza's *Love for Love's Sake* was not published until 1670.

13–14. *Scene betwixt the Empresses.* See Marlowe's *Tamburlaine* Part I, III. iii.

16. *bold Beauchams.* A notorious play, now lost. See Arthur Clark's *Thomas Heywood, Playwright and Micellanist* (1931), pp. 13–15, and Tilley B162.

17. *England's Joy.* See E. K. Chambers, *Elizabethan Stage*, iii. 500–3 for an account of the hoax. The point of the passage lies in the Poet's inability to distinguish Shakespeare's work from the crudest plays.

V. i

22. *prescribe.* Proscribe, condemn.

24. *'ith nicke.* At the critical moment.

27. *en chevalier* and the variants *en souldier*, *in souldiers*, and *in souldiers habits.* See the discussion of press variants above. A distant possibility in the uncorrected state is the French phrase *en souillure*, in strained or spotted garments. But *en chevalier* is the plainest and most satisfactory reading. The printers and scribes seem to have had much trouble with Suckling's common use of French phrases, as with *je ne sais quas* in *Aglaura* I. v. 36.

30. *gaberdines.* A long coat or mantle worn by soldiers, gentlemen, beggars, and almost all other classes when they travelled.

45. *secret of the prison-house.* Apparently a genuine borrowing from *Hamlet*, I. v. 14, unlike other alleged parallels that Thompson cites.

V. ii

13. *Nothing lesse.* Nothing of the sort, anything rather than that.

13. *censure.* Sentence.

60. *Right waies.* In the correct ways (*OED*, *right adv.* 9b). Since the Prince goes on to say she has not prayed correctly, the reading in *FA46* must be original. The corrector of *Fragmenta*, 1648, seems to be guessing here with *Steight waies*, although he usually seems right.

V. iv

30–1. The plague was commonly thought to be communicated by air and looks. Sir Thomas Browne uses this as a premise from which to affirm the power of the basilisk (*Vulgar Errors*, iii, ch. 7).

V. v

8–19. The changes in stage directions in *FA48* suggest that the corrector had reference to some manuscript with more elaborate directions.

15. *strange.* Extreme.

30. *publique mischiefe cannot be private Justice.* Tilley P600. Cf. *Brennoralt*, III. ii. 131.

35. *what mistake.* What a mistake (*OED*, *what* BII. 4).

36. *Cankers.* An inferior kind of wild rose, a dog rose.

38. *under that.* By that rule.

55. *he beckned.* At I. i. 54 where Torcular 'becens to *Orsabrin*'.

91. *question'd.* Challenged, accused.

99. *Ne're in being.* Never existed. Besides the emendations in 1694 and in Hazlitt, *Here in being* is a possibility.

133. *Mephosto-philus is mad.* Cf. 'Thou art not lunatike, art thou? and thou bee'st, avoide Mephistophiles'; Jonson, *The Case is Alter'd*, II. vii. 134–5.

149. *Sanborne fatall field.* Abbott's *Shakespearian Grammar*, sec. 22, 430, has a long list of such genitives, such as 'Here in *Philippi* fields', *Julius Caesar*, V. v. 19; hence we should not emend.

204. *kinder Stars.* 'But happy they . . . Whom gentler stars unite', James Thomson, *Spring*, 1113–14.

212–14. Cf. *Aglaura*, V(c). iii. 199–200, and Tilley R73 'Remembrance of past sorrow is joyful'.

233. *darke commands.* The secret regions under my commands.

242. *Nothing.* The Prince answers Orsabrin's rhetorical question.

280. *savers.* Gamblers who escape loss, 'though without gain' (Samuel Johnson). In the game of bowls, 'You'd need have a clear way, because y'are a bad pricker. *Mrs. Low.* Yet if my Bowl take bank, I shall go nigh To make my self a saver', Middleton, *No Wit like a Womans*, II. iii (1657), sig. D5^{v}. Cf. Prologue to *Aglaura*, line 18.

286–7. See Bentley, iv. 840, for the relation of this passage to Thomas May's *Old Couple*.

EPILOGUE

4. *old writing.* The playwriting of older days, presumably Elizabethan or Jacobean, the kind of comedy that only Richard Brome still wrote. See R. J. Kaufmann's *Richard Brome: Caroline Playwright* (1961). Thompson thought that *old* was purely intensive as in 'At this feast there was old drinking'. *OED* cites *old bell ringing* but not *old writing*.

6. *twelve pence.* The price of admission to the private theatres.

8. *ne're were, nor are, nor ne're will be.* Cf. Pope's *Essay on Criticism*, ii. 54, and Suckling's 'Against Fruition [II]', line 26. Pope is slightly closer to the poem than the play.

11. *Stephen.* 'Stephen Hammerton evidently played Orsabrin', Bentley, ii. 461. Exactly the same sentiment appears in the Epilogue to Killegrew's *The Parson's Wedding* (acted 1641) and in Henry Harrington's verses in the Beaumont and Fletcher folio (1647).

19–20. *Play . . . Tables.* Possibly a pun on playing backgammon at 'Tables'.

Brennoralt

(i) *Date.* In *The Court Beggar* (by Richard Brome, *c.* 1640) a caricature of Suckling, Sir Ferdinando, imagines he has been captured by the Scottish Covenanters, and he challenges them to a game of cribbage, gleek, or hazard. Then he confesses

> And though I lose all, I have yet a project
> That at the end o' th' war, and the great sitting
> Shall fetch all in agen. But O my Muse!
> How dare I so neglect thy inspirations?
> Give me Pen, Inke and Paper.
>
> *Five New Playes* (1653), sig. P6.

We cannot be sure exactly what new project Brome refers to, but the allusion implies that Suckling had returned to writing after a period of inactivity. *Brennoralt* was the chief production at the time, and the political theme suggests that he wrote the play shortly after his return from the disastrous First Bishops' War. He was in London on 30 September 1639 (letter no. 43), and the play was in the King's Men's repertory by 7 August 1641 (*Malone Society Collections*, ii. 398–9) among plays protected from unauthorized publication. The title was listed as 'The discontented Colonell'.

(ii) *Sources.* Suckling probably saw the dramatic possibilities of Jean Pierre Camus's romance *L'Iphigene* (Paris, 1625)[1] because of the similarity of the Polish-Lithuanian background of the tale with the struggle between England and Scotland during the late 1630s. Poland and Lithuania were ruled by the same king, Sigismund, and the larger country attempted to dominate the smaller. In the last books of *Iphigene*, the Lithuanians, under the Palatines of Troc and Minsce, rose against the king. Besieged by the king's forces, in the city of Minsce, the rebels eventually sent letters to the king, asking that their grievances be put before him, seeking their ancient liberties and prerogatives. Such episodes gave Suckling a chance to remind the audience of King Charles and his advisors, conferring at York or on the Banks of the Tweed in the First Bishops' War, June and July 1639, and to make satiric remarks about the petitions of the Covenanters, as well as to give advice about the foolishness of the Pacification of Berwick.

The figure of Brennoralt, not in Camus, comes out of the heroic tradition of the soldier-lover—Melantius, Bussy d'Ambois, Mark Antony, and Tamburlaine. (See Eugene Waith, *The Herculean Hero* [1962].) Malcontent, impetuous, high-minded, he wears his sword 'to purge the world of villains', but his mistress is the daughter of his enemy. So he must slip across the lines at night. From this point on, the play resembles Restoration heroic plays. (See Kathleen Lynch, 'Conventions of Platonic Drama in the Heroic Plays of Orrery and Dryden', *PMLA*, xliv [1929], 456–71.)

It is curious, however, that Suckling insisted on making Brennoralt a colonel and more curious that the title was changed from *Brennoralt* to 'The Discontented Colonell', or the other way around whichever was the original title. The prototype is usually much higher in rank. I suspect that the reason lies in Brennoralt's scorn of the weak councillors and disapproval of the king's excessive mercy. Brennoralt probably was intended to represent one or more of the disaffected young noblemen who openly criticized the Pacification of Berwick. Suckling himself wrote cynically about the truce in letters nos. 41 and 42.[2] Lord Goring, his friend at this time and also a colonel of a troop of horse, was notorious for his dashing manner and high living. The Earl of Essex, general of the infantry, received inducements like Brennoralt from the enemy, General Leslie, to stop the war, but he loyally turned the

[1] An English version published in 1652 under the title *Natures Paradox*, is somewhat abbreviated, in twelve books, the French version being in eighteen books.

[2] Mr. Herbert Berry, who is preparing a biography of Suckling, communicated to me privately that he thinks Brennoralt was supposed to be Suckling himself.

correspondence over to the king. There was 'unrestrained intercourse between the king's camp and Edinburgh' (Clarendon, *History of the Great Rebellion*, ii. 42, 1849 ed.). 'A raid on the Postmaster's office, carried out on Secretary Windebank's instructions, proved only what was already suspected, that the Scots were in friendly correspondence with some of the most influential men in England' (C. V. Wedgwood, *The King's Peace*, 1955, p. 255). The episode in which Trocke attempts to lure Brennoralt into defection (III. ii. 14–46) glances at such popular events. Therefore it seems probable that some contemporary persons stand behind Brennoralt, no matter how conventional he is.

For complications of the plot, Suckling borrowed from Camus the love story of Iphigene and Liante (once disguised as 'Almeria', hence Suckling's source for the name Almerin). Born a woman, Iphigene concealed her sex from her father and her beloved Liante. She learned to fight like a man and numerous women fell deeply in love with her. During the war Liante joined the rebels and Iphigene the King's side, but trouble started when Liante fell in love with Amiclea (Suckling's Francelia), daughter of the Palatine of Minsce, for Iphigene became jealous and allowed herself to be captured by the rebels. Scorning Liante, Amiclea fell in love with Iphigene, and so on through amazing reversals and discoveries and endless dialogues.

Not satisfied with this rich mixture, Suckling doubled the plot, making Brennoralt also in love with Francelia–Amiclea. This supplied an opportunity for more genuine rivalry and high-flown generosity. Then Suckling turned the conclusion into a blood bath rather than the typical happy ending in Camus. To his credit, Suckling suppressed all of Camus's leering tone and he made very little of the transvestism that roars through the romance. Specific borrowings have been cited in the notes on relevant passages.[1]

(iii) *Transmission of the text*. Apparently the protection of the Lord Chamberlain did not restrain Francis Eglesfield on 5 April 1642 from entering the play in the Stationers' Register, under the title 'The Discontented Colonell' by 'Sr Iohn Sucklyn kn^{t}.' Greg observes that the quarto 'bears no evidence of being authorized'; 'Suckling was already beyond the sea at the time of entrance' (*Bibliography*, no. 621). Riddled with errors but no signs of memorial corruption, the first edition, *The Discontented Colonell* (*c*. 1642), ought to be classed as a 'bad quarto', that was rushed into print to capitalize on the political situation. New rebellion in Ireland and new trouble between parliament and king offered adequate parallels with the play. Therefore Eglesfield probably on his own initiative, secured whatever copy he could find.

The printing appears to have been normal, collating A^{2} B–G^{4} H^{2}, 28 leaves. Two skeleton formes alternated (inner and outer formes, B–F), one

[1] See Bradford Field, 'The Use of Prose Fiction in English Drama 1616–1642', an unpublished dissertation, University of Maryland, 1963; Fletcher Henderson, 'Camus' Iphigene', *TLS*, 4 February 1939, pp. 73–4; Julius Krzyzanowski, 'Source of Suckling's Brennoralt', ibid., 9 April 1938, p. 252.

skeleton for both formes of sheet D, and two headlines from each skeleton used for the half-sheet H. On this basis, we can presume that half-sheet H was printed with half-sheet A, the preliminaries, and later the sheet was cut. In a comparison of the University of Chicago copy (ICU), Newberry (ICN), Library of Congress (DLC), Folger (DFo), and Huntington Library copies (CSmH), minor press correction has been detected in sheets B(o), D(i), F(i), and H(i). The only substantial correction appears on F1^{v} (IV. i. 1), where the uncorrected state seems right in the second half of the line 'fortune I thanke thee still', but wrong in the first half 'O? Why so: 'tis wel:' but the 'corrector' introduced an error in the second half 'fortune I thinke thee still'. This does not suggest that an author or trusted friend read the proofs. (See the long list of variants in *The Discontented Colonell*, 1642.)

The other substantive text, in *Fragmenta Aurea*, 1646, is wholly independent of the quarto—with over 600 substantive differences and innumerable accidental variations. *Fragmenta*, 1646, is not a new version of the play, as some bibliographies suggest, but it supplies the most reliable witness for Suckling's text, apparently printed from the author's manuscript or from a generally accurate transcript of his manuscript. Since Moseley omits his usual claim from the title-page 'printed by his owne copies', I presume that the manuscript was a transcript, but we cannot take the title-page as much evidence, since it was made up from standing type of *The Goblins*'s title.

If we supposed that the text in *Fragmenta*, 1646, were really set from marked copy of the quarto, we should expect to find some signs of trivial agreement between the witnesses, such as Philip Williams found between the quarto and folio of *Troilus and Cressida* (*SB*, iii [1950–1], 131–43). But the random variations in the quarto have not influenced the random variations in *Fragmenta*, 1646. Abbreviations of speech prefixes offer the most convenient evidence, because compositors usually normalized these; for instance, Brennoralt is usually *Bren.* in both editions. But occasionally, by presumed influence of copy, the quarto has *Bre.* where *Fragmenta* reads *Bren.*; occasionally *Fragmenta* has *Bre.* where the quarto has *Bren*; the same lack of congruence occurs with *Iph.*/*Iphi.* and *Gra.*/*Grain.*/*Grani.*/*Gran.* Other plays from the same shop as *Fragmenta* show a consistent preference for the spelling *Colonell* and the compositor of the quarto has the same preference. Suckling wrote *Coronell* in his letters. Therefore the large number of *Coronell*'s in *Fragmenta* probably show the influence of manuscript rather than printed copy. *Fragmenta* contains a great deal of gnomic pointing and hundreds of long dashes, both absent from the quarto; one would not expect an annotator to insert such minutiae. The only coincidence of accidentals that has been observed is the use of italics for all words in entrances, throughout the quarto and frequently in 1646, sheets C–H, but this is of little consequence and may be attributed to a change of compositors rather than the influence of the quarto.

Among the substantive differences, *Fragmenta* contains the manifestly correct reading most of the time, and more than fifty additional words and phrases and lines. Nevertheless the quarto clearly supplies the superior reading at least twenty times. We would not expect an annotator of the quarto to turn clarity into nonsense quite as often as it happens in *Fragmenta* (see *guilt*, V. iii. 277; *if inconcern'd*, IV. iv. 26; and *Stolden*, I. iv. 3). Most significantly, the two texts have few common errors (*Plocence* in the personae, and at III. i. 2–4); although several times they are both wrong at the same place, the errors are divergent, suggesting a faulty archetype. Examples are *Barutheus*/*Barathens* (I. iii. 63), *Mer.*/*Mim.* (II. iii. 86), and *'twixt death, feares and hopes of love*/*the fears of death and hopes of love* (V. iii. 148).

Brennoralt, like *The Goblins*, in *Fragmenta Aurea*, 1646, was printed in Susan Islip's shop, from cast-off copy set by formes, the work of possibly two compositors. Two sets of running-titles were used, except for one used in sheet D, printed with half-sheet imposition. Again, the nicks and bends on the long dashes and the broken letters suggest that only one type-case served, but the slight change in spelling habits and the sudden use of italics in entrances may indicate that a second compositor took over the work on sheets C and D.

Evidence of press correction survives only in sheet A and sheet C, from collation of the same twenty-six copies as were compared for *The Goblins*.

SHEET [4]A (inner forme)

Corrected: Σ
Uncorrected: DFo, NjP, MiU

Sig. [4]A8.
I. iv. 60 *Iphigene*,] ~;

SHEET [4]C (inner forme)

Corrected: Σ
Uncorrected: ICN, TxU[3]

Sig. [4]C1[v].
III. iii. 5 intelligence.] ~,
Sig. [4]C7[v].
IV. vii. 48 'tis] is
49 ha ve] have

Such meagre variation between copies seems hardly the result of stop-press alteration, and I am inclined to believe that at least the change in sheet A is from pulled type, as are several irregularities in catchwords in sheets A and B.

The notes at the foot of the pages record substantive departures from *Fragmenta*, 1646, along with some few corrections in *Fragmenta*, 1648. I have occasionally noted emendations from later editions, but the recent editions are of little use because neither Hazlitt nor Thompson consulted the quarto.

Since there are a great many obvious corruptions in the quarto, I have listed the rejected readings from it in a separate tabulation at the end of the play.

(iv) *Stage History.* Since the words on the title-page in *Fragmenta*, 1646, 'Presented at the Private House in Black-Fryers, by His *Majesties* servants', were printed from standing type of the title-page of *The Goblins* (set and printed before *Brennoralt*), we should not interpret them narrowly. The play may have been performed at Court as well, but Bentley observes that it lacks the usual prologues and epilogues for private performances. 'Perhaps the King's men were not ready for a court performance before the Army Plot was revealed in May 1641, and therefore it was thought indiscreet to produce Suckling at court' (v. 1209). Strangely, there are few allusions to *Brennoralt* before the Restoration, but the play may have come too late to achieve notoriety before the closing of the theatres. Six performances are recorded between 1661 and 1669, but at least one additional production belongs to the early 1670s.

The Bodleian copy (Vet. A3. F 824) of *Fragmenta Aurea*, 1658 (the genuine edition of that date), served as a prompt book for the King's company, probably at the Theatre Royal in Drury Lane, some time about 1673–5. Unlike the prompt book of *Aglaura* in the same volume, this one has almost all the actors' names noted at each entrance, possibly suggesting that the play was revived after some years of neglect. We can be fairly certain that the following cast is correct.

[Michael] Moone	Brennoralt
[Charles] Hart	Almerin
Mrs. [Margaret] Rutter	Iphigene
Mrs. [Rebecca] Marshall	Francelia
[John] Lacy	Grainevert
[Robert] Shottrell	Villanor
[William] Wintersell	Melidor
[John Coysh?] Cosh	Goaler, Soldier, Morat
[William] Cartrite	Miesla (or the King)
[Marmaduke] Watson	King (or Miesla)
[Martin] Powell	Fresolin
[George] Morris	Soldier, Guard, Servant
[Nathaniel] Cue	Soldier
Abram	Soldier
Mrs. [Anne] Reeves	Orilla
[Theophilus?] Bird [Jr.?]	Raguelin
Vener	Trocke or Mensecke
[George?] Beeston	Mensecke or Trocke
[Edward] Lydall	General
[Edward] Kinaston	Doran
[Thomas] Hancock	Stratheman
[Joseph] Harris	Marinell

Cue and Venner are first recorded in *The Empress of Morocco*, c. 1673, and young Bird last recorded in the same cast. Mrs. Reeves, according to J. H. Wilson (*All the King's Ladies*, 1958, p. 183), was active between 1670 and 1672, but William Van Lennep (*The London Stage*, part i, 1964, p. 220) lists her in casts of 1674–5. Hancock, a very minor actor, appears in none of the printed casts of the time, according to Mr. John Freehafer of Temple University, who has generously helped me to date the prompt book; and Mrs. Rutter is absent from the usual lists in 1672–3, but she evidently acted in *Othello*, late in 1674 or early 1675, and in two other roles in 1674–5. Abram has hitherto not been found in a cast of the time. All things considered, Mr. Freehafer seems right in placing the prompt book in the seasons of 1673–5.

THE ACTORS

2. *Miesla.* The form in Camus's *L'Iphigene* (1625) is 'Mieslas'. A speck between the uprights of the *sl* ligature in *Fragmenta*, 1646, caused the compositor of the 1658 edition to adopt the form 'Miefla', which Thompson and Hazlitt misread as 'Miesta'.

16. *General of the Rebels.* See II. iii. 0.1 (note).

I. i

15–17. A witty version of the proverb 'In a calm sea every man may be a pilot', Tilley S174.

20. *A cloud of dust.* Cf. volume i, letter no. 40. 24.

26. *formall beards.* Cf. *As You Like It*, II. vii. 155. The reading in *DC Leards*, may have entered because of the play's association with the 'Scottish business', but the lines that follow support *beards*.

34. *What a Divell.* A common expression, as in *1 Henry IV*, I. ii. 6–7.

35. *ague of the Camp.* In Camus, Iphigene's good appearance caused a 'Coqueluche de la Cour' (ii. 127 and xvii. 619).

45. *A fine account.* Cf. *1 Henry IV*, V. i. 135.

51. *me. FA46* is correct and *DC*'s reading *us* is mistaken because Almerin is Brennoralt's rival in love, no one else's.

56. *worst tempest here.* He wishes that the only storms in the world were external; the tempest in his breast worries him more.

I. ii

4. *stayes. FA46* supports the metaphor of a journey; *DC*'s *spoils* is merely literal.

21. *with the enemy. DC* is more precise. Almerin means that he wishes that the cowards in his army had left their fears with the enemy. *FA46* omitted the phrase possibly because a copyist thought that 'they' referred to the enemy; hence 'with the enemy' made no sense to him.

28. *my game.* Almerin.

35. *Who saw, Doran*? Without the comma the speech suggests that Brennoralt has not seen Doran and did not see him in battle. Both *DC* and *FA46* indicate Doran's entrance with Brennoralt at the beginning of the scene.

61. *lowsie Cottages.* The sentiment is conventional. 'We . . . may be turned out of these clay cottages at any hours warning', Joseph Hall, *Remaining Works* (1660), p. 205.

I. iii

3. *and how*? How is it? *OED*, *adv.* 4.

15. *place.* Place of battle.

21. Since Villanor just arrived, this speech belongs to him; Marinell has been in camp.

24. *Sessions.* 'Sessions of Wit' or 'Sessions of the Poets'; cf. *Goblins*, III. ii. 49, alluding to Suckling's poem which bore various titles.

25. *Like enough.* Probably.

42. *successe is a rare paint; hides all uglines.* Tilley S473: 'Successful sin passes for virtue.'

48. *unmarried agen.* Suckling and Milton agree on one thing, but 'License they mean when they cry libertie', Sonnet XII, *Poems* (1673).

52. The conference of Lords and King begins the series of allusions to the First Bishops' War against the Scottish Covenanters, in the summer of 1639. C. V. Wedgwood, *The King's Peace*, 274–5, tells of the protracted conferences that Charles had with the Privy Council while the army advanced north and after it encamped on the banks of the Tweed. The young blades were in favour of aggressive action to punish the rebels, but there was much hesitation from other counsellors. Suckling's letter to the man in Norfolk (no. 38) shows that he was on the side of the daring young men.

53. *spannels.* Spaniels.

54. *concurre.* To run together in hostility, *OED*, *v* 1b. There may be a pun on 'cur'.

63. A French proverb, 'Apres bon vin bon cheval', Cotgrave, *Dictionary* (1611), s.v. *cheval*, related to *parler à cheval*: to talk big.

65 ff. See volume i, letters nos. 41 and 42.

71. 'la clemence est toujours plus convenable à ceux qui gouvernent, qu'une rigoureuse Justice' (Camus, xiii, 87–8).

74–7. 'la gresle qui donne sur le saffran, au lieu de le perdre comme elle fait les autres plantes, le fait profiter: & le fer qui tranche la vigne la fait fleurir, & est cause qu'elle jette de nouveaux pampres, dont la grandeur & la beauté efface le lustre de l'ancien bois' (Camus, iii. 136, 1625 edition).

83-4. *flyes . . . wormewood.* Tilley F403: 'More flies are taken with a drop of honey than a tun of vinegar.'

95–6. *brandes . . . unextinct, kindled still fiercer fires.* Tilley S714: 'Of a little Spark a great fire.'

97–100. *Mercy . . . on those that doe dispute With swords.* Tilley P153: 'To make peace with a sword in his hand.'

105–6. *Mortals . . . not infinite.* Since mortals are not infinite, their capacity for mercy is smaller than Heaven's, and even God sometimes is too offended to forgive.

I. iv

2. *ruffle of the world.* Ostentatious bustle or display; cf. Shakespeare, 'Lover's Complaint', line 58.

3. *golden banks. DC*'s reading is probably correct; *Stolden* (*FA46*) is not an English word. In the pastoral adventures of Iphigene and Liante, they dally in 'un ruisseau voisin . . . un argent liquide sur un sable tout d'or'. This occurs in the clothes-changing scene that is alluded to below in lines 4–8 (Camus, viii. 498, 1625 edition).

4–8. 'Piside . . . disoit . . . peut-estre Iphis devenant Serife estoit devenue fille en quittant les habits du masle' (Camus, x. 631). Calliante to Serife: 'sous les ornemens qui maintenant vous parent, vous m'esbloüissez de telle façon que je puis bien oublier si vous etes homme' (Camus, xii. 706).

8. *glorious Mornings.* The sexual context is also similar to Shakespeare's Sonnet 33.

10–12. 'comme les supplices ne sont pas tousiours pour les plus meschans, mais pour les insfortunez, aussi la gloire estoit une [infa]me Courtisane, qui ne se rendoit pas tousiours entre les bras des plus vaillans, mais de plus heureux' (Camus, xiv. 261).

22. *behind.* Still to come.

25. *wounds of honour doe admit no cure.* Tilley W928: 'An ill wound is cured, not an ill name.'

52. *Bankrupt.* Cf. *Aglaura*, v(t). i. 189.

74. *informe.* Bid, direct.

II. i

3. *elder brother.* Tilley S526: 'Sleep is the brother of death.'

10. *slovenly.* Nasty, disgusting.

33. *so that I.* In *FA46* the compositor's eye picked up *if* from the line below, and in *DC if so* seems a simple misreading; but it is strange that the same word should be involved in both errors.

46–8. Cf. *Aglaura*, v(t). i. 97–9.

II. ii

5. *forehanded.* Prudent.

6. *doe reason.* Give satisfaction; in drinking, do the honours; 'First I'll drink to you, Sir. Upon my faith I'll do you reason Sir', Dryden, *The Wild Gallant* (Dearing ed., 1962), I. iii. 3–4.

17. *stale.* 'A wife thats more then faire is like a stale, Or chanting whistle which brings birds to thrall', Ariosto's *Satires*, trans. Toft (1608), p. 56.

19–20. *vant credit.* Cast out all thought of honour and reputation. This is possible if *vant* is a spelling of *vent.* Perhaps *vant* is an error for *vamp*, i.e. to renew credit, as to vamp a score.

20. *affect.* Practice.

22–50. *the sacrifice.* A drinking 'method' as in William Cartwright's *Royal Slave*, III. i, in G. B. Evans's edition. Thompson thought it had something to do with the custom of pinning up a rose to symbolize the secrecy of a conversation, but the obvious meaning is in the text: a man must pin up or display an object given to him by his mistress and compose a poem on it. In *The Eighth Liberal Science: or a new-found-art and order of Drinking* (1650), a man who professes 'poetry' as he drinks is 'he that rimes *ex tempore*, or speaks Play-speeches', sig. A6v.

23. *for trickling teares are vaine.* Cf. *1 Henry IV*, II. iv. 385.

31–2. *to the place . . . at the face.* '*Face of a place* is the front, that is comprehended between the flanked Angles of two neighbouring bastions', Nathan Bailey, *Dictionarium Britannicum* (1727), a term in fortification.

52. *A hall, a hall.* Make way; a cry for room to be made for a dance or masque and to call company together for entertainment. See *Romeo and Juliet* I. v. 27.

70. *in discipline.* In order or by method.

78. *back side.* Back yard.

85–6. An extensive borrowing from *2 Henry IV*, I. i. 70–3.

87. *done so my selfe.* Done as Almerin did.

II. iii

0.1. *Generall of the Rebels.* Suckling's narrative source does not contain a General of the Rebels. He was evidently inserted in the story to represent the Scottish general, Alexander Leslie. It is curious that he is not in the *dramatis personae* in *Fragmenta*, 1646, but both *DC* and *FA46* consistently assign speeches to him, and the prompt book assigns an actor to his small part.

14–15. *Petitions . . . Humble in forme.* The Scots' 'Humble Supplications' to the King. See State Papers Domestic, 6 June 1639, and Suckling's letter no. 38, in volume i of this edition.

24–6. *great Oleos.* See volume i, letter no. 15.

50. *The King's besiedged.* The standard complaint against Charles's advisers.

62. *handsome whisper.* The Covenanters made personal appeals to English soldiers, including the Earl of Essex (Wedgwood, *King's Peace*, 264–5).

82. *court my Lord in absence.* This puzzling remark may be a fossil from the source, where Liante (Almerin) has been dispossessed by Mieslas, and before he can marry Olavius, her father tried to make Mieslas revoke the confiscation. He even thought of making the revocation one of the Articles of Capitulation; hence he was courting 'my Lord' Mieslas, in absence. A less-complicated interpretation is 'while I am away on this embassy, I'll hasten this marriage, and thus do honour to Iphigene, the Palatine of Plocence'.

86. *Almerin.* The speech heading *Mer.* probably stood in the manuscript as an abbreviation of *Almerin. Morat* is the wrong prefix because he is consistently hostile to Iphigene and would not call her 'dearest'.

88. *Morat.* The prompt book for performance at the Theatre Royal gives the speech to *General.*

89. *weather-glasse.* A thermometer.

91. *cordiall of kind lookes.* Intended to create a good impression on the trumpet who has just entered.

II. iv

5–9. Tilley W674: 'A woman's mind is always mutable.'

11–12. 'A woman is flax, man is fire, the devil comes and blows the bellows', *Oxford Dictionary of English Proverbs*, and see Tilley F262.

52. *qualmes.* Fits of depression, faintness of heart.

59. *needle in the best Sun-dyall.* Certain portable sundials had a means of adjustment by use of a compass. See Margaret Gatty, *Book of Sundials* (enlarged, 1900), plate vii.

71. *set.* Wager against.

87. *wicket to my Ladies secrets.* Cf. Congreve, *The Old Bachelour* (1693), III. i. 195 (ed. Davis): 'Thou art the Wicket to thy Mistresses Gate, to be opened for all Comers.'

88. *stands up to.* Is inclined to, hankers after, *OED*, *vb.* 76d.

94–5. Tilley L505a: 'Love is sweet torment.'

99–103. Cf. The central situation of *The Royal Slave* (1639), by William Cartwright.

III. i

2–4. An anecdote in Camus clarifies the intent of this passage. 'An antient *Historian* makes mention of a *Souldier*, who despairing of his Life by reason of an intestine *Pain*, which tormented him, casting himself into the hottest of the *Battle* to purchase an honourable *Death*, received a thrust with a *Sword* through the Body, which broke an *Impostume* within, and was so favourable to him, that hee found *health* where hee expected *Death*' (1652 trans., p. 287). Suckling changes the story to fit Iphigene's case; the wretch sought to alleviate his misery by seeking pain abroad, and he found abroad the same misery he thought he had left at home. The passage may not be corrupt, just elliptical. Another reading of line 4 may be: 'He found, but wisely thought h' had left it home.'

12. *thanklesse Ocean.* Cf. *Aglaura*, II. iii. 91–4 (note).

16. *Statues place.* A baroque commonplace. Cf. Donne, 'Twickenham Garden', line 16; Jonson, 'Slow, slow, fresh fount', *Cynthia's Revels*, I. ii. 65–75; and the closing lines of Marvell's 'Nymph Complaining for the Death of Her Faun'.

20. *first Elements.* Simple substances of which a complex substance is made.

43. *comming.* The reading *common* in *FA48* creates a pun for 'common whore' that seems gratuitous.

III. ii

7. *not all against, that is above.* 'Estre au dessus du vent encontre', Cotgrave, *Dictionary* (1611), s.v. *dessus.* Trocke contradicts the saying.

53. *tride.* A full gallop can be slightly controlled or tride to make short and swift movements.

58–9. *Catts in narrow roomes.* Tilley C132: 'If a cat shut into a roome, much baited and straightened, turne to be a Lyon'.

93–9. *Nor are you . . . assur'd of all behinde you.* An allusion to King Charles's personal popularity but lack of support from his people during the Scottish campaign.

100–3. 'Multitudo omnis, sicut natura maris, per se inmobilis est, ventis et aurae cient', Livy, *Histories*, xxviii. 27.

121–2. *Peace and War in an incestuous line.* An improvement on the proverb, 'La guerre nourrit la guerre'. 'What can Warr, but endless warr still breed', Milton, Sonnet XV, to Lord Fairfax (1648).

124. *'twixt man and man.* The law of self preservation, or one man's word given to another?

131. *The private safety is the publike trouble.* Tilley P600: 'Preferre not a private grudge before a common griefe.'

132–3. *Maintaine it with his Sword.* A variation on 'Arma tenenti Omnia dat, qui justa negat', Lucan, *Pharsalia*, i. 348.

138. *entring.* Beginning, *OED* 13.

149. *time doth stamp them.* Tilley T336: 'Time tries all things.'

III. iii

20. *Not more.* Not more perfect.

38–9. *a crash.* A bout of revelry.

III. iv

8. The stage business illustrates the versatility of the old theatres. Brennoralt met Raguelin on the main stage, they went out of one door and entered by another, exited, and entered on the upper stage and ascended by a ladder or steps directly to the main stage, where Brennoralt discovered Francelia within the curtained area.

19–22. Cf. volume i, letter no. 23, 68–72.

61–3. A view shared by some opponents to judicial astrology, such as John Calvin and Gervase Marstaller, cited by Don Cameron Allen, *The Star-Crossed Renaissance* (1941), pp. 62, 72.

76. *as.* This peculiar construction is illustrated in *OED*, *adv.* 11.

86. *lesse kinde, or kinder.* This idea is the reverse of 'No, no, faire heretic' and similar to Thomas Carew's 'Give me more Love, or more Disdain'.

94. *raise honour to a point.* The spurned lover now has typically heroic motives.

106. *My selfe.* This reading, from *DC*, seems to fit Francelia's previous remark better: 'Think of yourself'.

IV. i

1. The sense and grammar of *FA46* are clearer. Since neither the corrected nor uncorrected states of *DC* agree with *FA46*, in this line, we have additional evidence of the independence of *DC* and *FA46*. See pp. 239, 291 above.

21. *common too, as a Barbers glasse.* Tilley B73: 'As common as a barber's chair.' Suckling improves the proverb.

21. *like a Dy-dapper.* Changeable, as the didapper is known for diving deep and reappearing in surprising places.

IV. ii

10. *no word.* Pass-word or watchword.

24. *beat you to 't.* Force you to do it. *OED*, *beat vb*[1] 16.

IV. iv

3–5. *stoop . . . flye to some here . . . garnisht.* Tilley T298: 'In time all haggard hawks will stoop to lure.'

16–17. *Resume the gift.* 'If the king make any graunt which is not sufficient in the law or is deceived in the making of the same by reason it was made upon a false suggestion, [this] case if [his] highnes doth [resume] this grant and adnull it *jure regis* as he may . . .', Sir William Stanford, *Exposition of the Kings Prerogative* (1567), fol. 84.

23–7. *that agen finde in my much defect . . . I inconcern'd.* This awkward piece of preciosity appears to mean 'and that [fault] in turn must find in my great deficiency so great an excuse that it [your 'fault'] will have no worse name than discretion [i.e. discrimination, good judgment], if I as an impartial judge were to cast it up.' The reading, *indiscretion*, in *DC*, line 26, seems easier but pointless.

24. *much*. Great.

38–9. *kisse your hands*. Hand or hands seem to have been interchangeable in this expression. In letter no. 43.24 (in volume i of this edition) Suckling wrote *hands*.

IV. vi

7–9. These lines may be from a contemporary song.

9. *Babies*. To see small images of oneself in the pupils of another's eyes. Tilley B8.

10–32. The vision of a girl stealing into a man's chamber derives from Ovid's *Amores*, I. v. See Helen Gardner's note on Donne's 'To His Mistress Going to Bed' for a list of other imitations.

10. *about fifteen*. Without having seen *DC*, Hazlitt emended thus, and Thompson justified *above* as meaning 'upwards of, getting on for fifteen'. I cannot find that meaning in the *OED*. The passage implies that the girl is young and innocent, and *above* fifteen seems too indefinite.

13. *double violets*. When transplanted, a violet 'redoubles still and multiplies', gets more than twice as many petals. The violet had erotic associations in classical poetry but invariably suggested modesty, purity, and virginity to Elizabethans. See Helen Gardner, *Elizabethan and Jacobean Studies Presented to F. P. Wilson* (1959), pp. 296–300.

14. *dying leaves of Strawberries*. The leaves boiled and applied 'as pultis taketh away the burning heate in wounds', John Gerarde, *The Herball* (1633), p. 998; hence the leaves are wholesome, because they take the poison away. The berry was good for the breath, according to *The Profitable Arte of Gardening* (1574), pp. 89–90. Although the reading in *DC*, 'wholesome as dying Strawberries', is quite plausible, I cannot see how *leaves* could have come into *FA46* unless Suckling wrote it.

15–16. *Thick silken eye-browes*. The thick, dark eyebrows, large eyes, and pale cheeks are like portraits of Queen Henrietta Maria, and they were imitated by court ladies of the time. Before the influence of the Queen most British women were shown with blonde hair. See David Piper, *The English Face* (1957), p. 96.

16. *pale streaks of red*. Cf. Suckling's 'Ballad upon a Wedding', lines 58–9, in volume i of this edition.

18. *my chops*. They begin to water.

22. *Haire curling and cover'd, like buds of Marjoram*. See John Parkinson, *Theatricum Britanicum* (1640), pp. 11–12, for a description of the hood on marjoram. *DC*'s reading *color'd* does not fit the buds of marjoram as precisely as *cover'd*;

the buds have little caps on them and the petals curl around the edge. Van Dyke's portraits illustrate this hair style: the portraits of Dorothy Sidney, Countess of Sunderland (Devonshire Collection) and of Marie Ruthven (M. J. C. Harford Collection, London) show the hair smooth on top, dishevelled ringlets on the brow and sides. See Pierre Imborg's *Van Dyke* (1949) nos. 77–8. Nymphs' garlands were often made of sweet marjoram. The analogy, however, is older, as in Shakespeare's Sonnet 99: 'buds of marjoram had stol'n thy hair'.

25. *pinck colour taffata.* As distinct from 'a fair hot wench in flame-coloured taffeta', *1 Henry IV*, I. ii. 10–11.

44. *towards.* In prospect.

48. *Warre.* Since neither the *OED* nor the concordances of the period note an adjectival use of *moiety*, and since the syntax of *FA46* is awkward, I am tempted to accept the reading of *DC.* Doran just said 'By this light', so Grainevert's song picks up the remark and says in effect 'there is not much light, only a twilight'. Nevertheless, if we understand the first four lines of the song as an exclamation not a declarative sentence, it makes satisfactory sense.

IV. vii

2–6. 'La Jalousie, qui est un Amour malade' (Camus, xiii, 237). In Sir Charles Sedley's *The Mulberry Garden* (1668), III. i. 59–63 (*Works*, ed. V. de Sola Pinto, 1928), Miss Lynch noted an imitation of Suckling. The pointing of *FA46* emphasizes the parallel between *they* (feavers) and *that* (Jealousie).

70–2. *jealousie . . . monster.* A conventional image, with little relation to *Othello*, III. iii. 167–8, Thompson notwithstanding. The closest analogue is Spenser's 'An Hymn in Honour of Love', lines 267–72.

IV. viii

9. *vizard off.* Either *DC* or *FA46* makes sense. The face of danger, however, would be seen with the vizard off; therefore I prefer *DC*'s reading *of*, a common spelling doublet of *off.* 'This vizzor of holy and zealous revenge falling off, discovered the face of covetousnesse so much the more uglie', Ralegh, *History of the World* (1614), III. 65.

V. i

0.1. This is a strange place for an act division. But both *DC* and *FA46* place it here; the prompt book contains the usual warning 'Act Ready', and 'Ring' appears after Brennoralt's last speech of IV. viii, i.e. a signal for the musicians to play or, as some have thought, 'ring the curtain down'.

2. *had a fit.* A curious detail, that may represent some actual occurrence during a recent campaign; however, it is the kind of detail that Suckling liked to use at the beginning of a scene to set the tone.

v. ii

3. *Virgin-tower.* Not in Camus. Thompson wondered if the 'Maiden's Tower' at Windsor was the reference.

v. iii

6–8. See Shakespeare's Sonnet 47, lines 3–6 for a close parallel:

When that mine eye is famished for a look,
Or heart in love with sighs himself doth smother,
With my love's picture then my eye doth feast
And to the painted banquet bids my heart.

32. *wrecks of.* *OED*, *reck v* 1, inclines toward.

39. *denounce a warre to all the world.* Almerin proclaims himself an outcast, an enemy of society (see *OED*, *denounce v* 4), typical of the Herculean hero (see discussion of sources above).

45–7. The order of clauses in *FA46* and *DC* makes good sense and must be allowed to stand, contrary to Hazlitt and Thompson. 'Rather than she shall suffer [and] my fond deceits [shall] involve', etc.

88. *seen me extasied.* An episode elaborately developed in Suckling's source (Camus, viii. 495–6, 1625 edition).

96. *distract.* Suckling's favourite past participial form. The further error in the line occurred because of the expansion to *distracted*, which overloaded the line, so the compositor shortened *a man* to *one*.

108. *vext, passe by.* The harder reading from *DC* is chosen, rather than *dost passe by* from *FA46*.

111–12. *wound me up so high that I must crack sooner than move in tune.* Tilley L201: 'Where strings are high set, they breake or grow out of tune.'

128. *under them.* A metaphor from geography, 'under climate of that part . . . Affrike is comprehended', *OED*, *climate sb* 1b.

139. *Dials hand.* The hand on a clock or sundial. See Shakespeare's Sonnet 104, lines 9–10: 'yet doth beauty, like a dial hand Steal from his figure, and no pace perceived'.

141–65. Francelia has died in bed; soldiers enter the main stage; Iphigene withdraws to the alcove and pulls the curtain. Later Brennoralt moves into the enclosed area to find Francelia's body and to pull out Iphigene.

193. *sports.* Duel or fight.

204. *in nature.* Arrive at the basis of things.

223. *stills.* Distillations, minute drops discharged.

232. *of ours.* Of our spirits.

237–8. Hazlitt arbitrarily reverses the order of the King's and Stratheman's speeches, putting the King's question first. The order in *FA46* and *DC* is more characteristic of Suckling, to give the impression of our hearing only the end of a conversation.

244. *wearied guest.* Almerin is addressing his soul.

252. *Minse.* The preferred form of his name in Camus is *Minsce.* The usual form in other passages in *FA46* is *Minsecke. Minse* is most common in *DC.*

277. *comes too late.* Again, the theme of rewards too late from the crown, as in *Aglaura*, IV. i. 44–9. The Earl of Strafford had complained of the same fault in King Charles, and belatedly Charles began creating peers and currying popular favour. Suckling's 'To Mr. Henry German' urged substantially the same course for the king, to gain popular support. See Wedgwood, *King's Peace*, 263–5, for some amusing anecdotes about this sudden change in royal behaviour.

284. 'One can go a long way after one is weary', a French proverb cited by Dean Trench, *Lessons in Proverbs* (1853), p. 75, no source given. The idea that the weariest horse is able to run when the stable door is in sight is noted by Tilley O108. Cotgrave, *Dictionary* (1611), s.v. *boeuf*: 'The wearie Oxe goes slowly; men that are beaten to the practise of the world are calme, and moderate in their proceedings.' Cotgrave is perhaps closest to *Brennoralt.*